Springer
Tokyo
Berlin
Heidelberg
New York
Barcelona
Hong Kong
London
Milan
Paris
Singapore

Matsuba Masafumi

The Contemporary Japanese Economy

Between Civil Society and Corporation-Centered Society

With 21 Figures
and 107 Tables

Springer

INSTITUTE OF SOUTHEAST ASIAN STUDEIS

Matsuba Masafumi
Professor
Faculty of Social Sciences
Ritsumeikan University
Kyoto 603-8577, Japan

Soft cover edition (ISBN 981-230-126-7) first published in Singapore in 2001 by the Institute of Southeast Asian Studies, 30 Heng Mui Keng Terrace, Pasir Panjang, Singapore 119614 (http://www.iseas.edu.sg/pub.html) for exclusive distribution in the ASEAN countries, India, Korea, Taiwan, China, and Australia/New Zealand.

Printed on acid-free paper

Typesetting: Best-set Typesetter Ltd., Hong Kong
Printing and binding: Hirakawa, Japan
SPIN: 10780775

Preface

This book examines the diverse development of the Japanese economy since the 1980s. Part 1 considers the position of the Japanese economy in the world; Part 2 analyzes the internal structure of the large corporation system; and Part 3 looks at the large corporation system and the life of the people. I have focused on an investigation of the content and significance of the historical and structural changes in the Japanese economy before and after the so-called bubble economy of the latter half of the 1980s, and on an investigation of the concrete economic basis of the living conditions of the social strata in Japanese society. Taking account of the diversity of the objects of discussion, I would like to emphasize their interrelationship in a framework, rather than focusing on a minute description of each economic factor or phenomenon.

The introduction includes a detailed discussion of the methodology employed in this book. Here I want to emphasize the following three points, each of which has methodological significance. (1) I categorize the structure of the contemporary economy in advanced countries as a large corporation system. Here "large corporation system" means an economic and social system centered on large corporations. There are two main types of large corporation system: the European type, which involves democracy within the system; and the Japanese type, where the hegemony of capital is overwhelmingly superior. In addition, there is a third type, that of the US, which lies, as discussed later, in the middle between the other two types. Thus, the Japanese large corporation system alone is characterized by the exclusive ruling hegemony of capital without the social regulation of counterprinciples and counterpowers in either the internal structure of the enterprise or the social system as a whole. (2) This large corporation system formed a corporation-centered society owing to high economic growth in Japan. Here the "corporation-centered society" is a society where economic value is overwhelmingly superior to other social values, and where large, i.e. huge, corporations form the nucleus of social relations, influence political society, and put pressure on civil society. In Japan, the corporation-centered society, of which the corporation (i.e. enterprise) was originally only a part of civil society, reorganizes the whole of civil society to fit its interests. In Japan a pricing system controlled by corporations coexists with the general pricing system, which reflects the relationship between corporation-centered society and civil society. The stock prices and land prices that rose rapidly in the bubble period represent typically the movement of the corporate pricing system. The collapse of the bubble economy reflects the self-destroying process of the corporate pricing system. (3) I have attempted to pay attention to the corresponding relations between economic phenomena in Japan and Japanese cultural attitudes, the most noteworthy feature here being the indifference to a system of absolute and universal values. Examples include the relentless development of corporate ownership and the phenomena of corporate capitalism (a malfunction of individual responsibility), and the formation and development of a widespread and minutely differentiated structure of wages and labor conditions (the weakness of universal values in Japanese society).

The changes in international politics and economy affecting Japan in the 1990s were very large and important. Prior to the fall of the Berlin Wall in 1989, the US regarded Japan as its special ally in East Asia, crucial to its anti-Soviet, anti-communist strategy. Thus it was US policy at this time to protect and assist the economic growth of Japan. This changed in the 1990s and the US began to deal with Japan as an equal competitor with no need for special treatment. This change has had little visible impact on daily life in Japan. In practice, however, it has had a profound influence on the Japanese economy since the 1990s. In addition, a number of countries and peoples have emerged as powerful competitors in the world market, for example, the former socialist countries and the East Asian countries including China. Japan's position in the world economy and the conditions facing it have become more severe in comparison with the situation in 1980s.

The largest problems facing the Japanese economy today are above all the fiscal crisis and the bad loan problem. As part of the government budget for FY 2000, government bonds totaling ¥32.6 trillion will be issued in order to cover the revenue loss, and the degree of dependence on government bonds will reach 38.9%. Because government bonds worth between ¥20 trillion and ¥30 trillion were issued annually after 1995, their outstanding value will grow from ¥225 trillion in 1995 to ¥364 trillion at the end of FY 2000. Adding the government guaranteed bonds and borrowing to the government bonds, the outstanding value of government long-term liabilities will reach ¥485 trillion, and adding further the outstanding value of the local government bonds, the total amount will reach ¥645 trillion. The ratio of these government long-term liabilities, including the local government bonds, to GDP is 129%, the worst among the advanced countries. On the pretext of giving priority to measures to stimulate business, fiscal reconstruction or fiscal reform has been entirely shelved in recent years. However, the increase in public bond issues and their huge outstanding value has reached the point where it can no longer be sustained. A delay in tackling this problem and transferring the burden to future generations will not improve the present situation and will destroy the possibility for the sound development of the national economy. If the current situation continues, the economic confusion and crisis will intensify in the following way: a sudden fall in government bond prices will lead to heavy latent losses in the financial institutions which hold a great quantity of government bonds, and that in turn will lead to a recurrence of the financial crisis.

On the bad loan problem, I have presented in the main text a detailed discussion of the trend up to recent years. Therefore, here I will refer only to the following point. In every important field of advanced technology in the 21st century—the information technology industry, the biotechnology industry, the aerospace industry, and the financial sector—the Japanese economy cannot afford to take the initiative or assume hegemony in international competition in the world market. When we recall the existence and scale of the bad loans/bad debts in the financial sector, the construction industry, and real estate business, we can understand the deep causal relationship these have with the long stagnation of the Japanese economy since 1990. In the meantime, an enormous amount of money has been used in vain for writing off the bad loans and a vast amount of public funds has been spent inefficiently on old-type public utilities on the pretext of business recovery. Japan cannot create its own future without a decisive change in politics and economic policy, based on wise and sound political will. Along with the process of coping with the bad loan problem, a chain of reorganization has occurred among large banks, namely, the birth of the "Mizuho" financial group formed by Fuji Bank, Dai-Ichi Kangyo Bank, and the Industrial Bank of Japan; the fusion of Sumitomo Bank and Sakura Bank; and the integration of Sanwa Bank and Tokai Bank. It is difficult now to give an accurate forecast of these trends and their influence on the whole economic process. However, it is obvious that these reorganizations do not in themselves contribute essentially to a positive solution of the bad loan problem.

The chapters that comprise this book originated as papers that were written and published between 1992 and 1997. In the process of reorganizing those papers for this book, I reconsidered the method and the whole composition, added some materials and data, and finished writing the text in November 1999. When I began putting my papers together into a book, I originally intended not only to reorganize the composition, but also to supplement and update all statistical figures. Before long, unfortunately, it became clear that this was an impossible task. To revise one point leads immediately and consecutively to a need to modify others and sometimes requires changes to whole sections of the book. It was impossible for me, not a native English speaker, to make all these revisions within the limited time available. As a result, the description of this book relates mainly to the economic process from 1985 to 1995. However, I am convinced that it can offer the data and criteria needed to assess the significance of events for the Japanese economy today.

The composition of this book is as follows. In Part 1, The Position of the Japanese Economy in the World, I survey, in Chapter 1, the results of the rapid economic growth in the 1960s, '70s, and '80s; how each indicator of Japanese production, income, labor, agriculture, and national life has changed; and how the international position of the Japanese economy has changed. In Chapter 2, the development of foreign trade is investigated through the following factors: the position of Japanese foreign trade in the world, the significance of foreign trade for the Japanese economy, the historical trends of the trade balance and its main characteristics, and the features of trade by commodity group and by region in an international comparison. In Chapter 3, I examine the development of Japanese capital export—focusing on the activities of Japan's multinational corporations—and clarify the large increase of Japanese foreign net assets and investment income.

Part 2, The Internal Structure of the Large Corporation System, examines the structure of the six large corporation groups that are at the heart of the Japanese large corporation system. The special significance of corporate ownership, interlocking stockholdings, financing by financial institutions of the same group and delegations of directors, as well as the characteristics and significance of Japanese-style management that has attracted so much attention both inside and outside Japan, are investigated in Chapter 4. In Chapter 5, I examine the earning capacity of Japanese large corporations and the problems of their latent assets, and discuss in concrete terms the formation and collapse process of the bubble economy up to the end of the 1990s. In Chapter 6, taking account of its special importance, I examine the trends in central government finance in Japan.

In Part 3, The Large Corporation System and the Life of the People, in Chapter 7, I present a detailed investigation of the wages and labor conditions of workers and employees in Japan and point out that there is a wide and minutely differentiated structure, in which foreign workers occupy the lowest strata. In Chapter 8, I consider a part of the economic basis of farmers' lives and the socioeconomic position of small enterprises in Japan. In Chapter 9, I explain the fundamental characteristics of income and assets composition of the Japanese and refer to the problems of the Japanese social security system and its differential structure. Finally, I investigate the housing and land problems which are deeply related to the problems of bad loans and financial insecurity. These have became the most difficult and pressing issues in the Japanese economy today.

In the preparation of this book, I have been assisted and supported directly and indirectly by many people. Prof. Sasaki Ken, who was my respected teacher in my doctoral program in graduate school, has always presented important and enlightening views that have helped my research. I owe a huge debt of academic gratitude to the three professors, Watanabe Hisashi, Ozaki Yoshiharu, and Sugimoto Shoshichi, who were the members of my committee when I received the degree of Doctor of Economics. I would like to thank an honorary professor Fujiwara Sosuke, once a colleague at my faculty, for his kind assistance. In addition, I must also express my gratitude towards the late Prof. Yamaguchi Masayuki, who was a great benefactor in my life; the late Prof. Hirata Kiyoaki, whose research I deeply respect and who was once a visiting professor at my faculty; the late Prof. Yagi Hiroshi, who was my respected teacher when I was an undergraduate student; and the late Ueno Tadashi, who was a respected teacher at my junior high school.

I studied abroad for one year in Bonn from 1988 to 1989. Since then, I have become acquainted with Manfred J. M. Neumann, who is a professor at the Faculty of Law and Economics at the University of Bonn and is the director of the Institute for International Economics. In regard to the theme and the method of research, there are some differences between him and me, but we continue our exchange of ideas in a cordial atmosphere. Since the fall of the Berlin Wall, I have participated in a joint research project on the economies of Germany and Japan after World War II with Lothar Baar, who was a professor (now, emeritus) at the Faculty of Economics at the Humboldt-University of Berlin and the director of the Institute for Economic History. His consideration and friendship towards me have been immeasurable. Since 1988 I have been on friendly terms with Prof. Michael Schneider and Dr. Patrik von zur Mühlen, who work at the research section in the Friedrich Ebert Foundation/Bonn. Since 1983 when I first visited the Kiel Institute of World Economics to collect materials, I have been supported by Dr. Hans-Georg Glaeßer, who works in the library there.

Although I started my research primarily in the field of German economic history, in recent years I have also focused on the contemporary Japanese economy and the theory of civil society. As a result, I have had increased opportunities for exchange with British researchers. Particularly, the research exchanges with three professors, Bob Jessop, Andrew Sayer, and John Urry, in the Department of Sociology at Lancaster

University, have been very useful for me and given me a better understanding of the concept of civil society.

In addition, I want to note the names of three people—Okamura Takao, Wada Takao, and Toyoshima Norio—who, despite not being researchers, have been a great support to me in life.

I thank Peter Gobel, a lecturer in English at my faculty, and David Peaty, a professor at my university, for proofreading the manuscripts of my primary papers. I am also very grateful to my colleague Ian Hosack, an associate professor at my faculty, for his kind and useful suggestions on the final manuscript for this book. Ms. Hata Mariko assisted me in making the tables and Dr. Sakurai Junri helped me to draw up the bibliography. Here I express my sincere gratitude.

From December 1994 to March 1995 I was in Germany for research financed by the German Academic Exchange Service (Deutscher Akademischer Austauschdienst, DAAD) and on that occasion visited the universities of Berlin, Halle, Bonn, and Kiel to meet researchers and to exchange views on the problems of the German and Japanese economies. The results of these exchanges show themselves in this book. I would like to thank the DAAD for giving me that opportunity.

The publication of this book was made possible by a subsidy from my university, Ritsumeikan University in Kyoto, Japan, and I am very grateful for this assistance. In addition, my university provided financial support to the international research project Changes in Industrial Society and Reconstruction of Civil Society, in which I participated in 1996, 1998, and 1999. I worked as chief secretary in this project and now remember with gratitude the cooperation with many colleagues, friends, and graduate students, both inside and outside Japan. I would like to note here only the names of five colleagues at my faculty, professors Sato Yoshikazu (representative of the project), Shinoda Takeshi, Kida Akio, Akai Shoji, and Kunihiro Toshifumi. The publication of this book would not have been possible without the academic results of this research project. I want to thank all participants for their cooperation.

It was at the beginning of September 2000 that I submitted the final manuscript to the editorial department of Springer-Verlag, Tokyo. After that, much consideration and assistance was given me by the staff of the department and I would like to express my gratitude to them. In particular, I want to extend my sincere thanks to the anonymous copy editors for their careful reading of the manuscript and the numerous improvements they made to the English. To publish a book is, first of all, to make one's views open to society. If my book succeeds in doing this, it is largely thanks to the help of these copy editors and my three native English-speaking colleagues mentioned above.

In the final proofreading before the printing of this book, I also received invaluable assistance from Dr. Takashima Masaharu. I sincerely thank him for it.

Lastly, this book is dedicated to my mentor, my academic supervisor in graduate school, Prof. Sasaki Ken.

Matsuba Masafumi
Kyoto, November 2000

Contents

Part 2 The Internal Structure of the Large Corporation System

Part 3 The Large Corporation System and the Life of the People

Explanatory Notes and Abbreviations

Japanese names throughout this book have been written in the Japanese order, that is, family names first.

[J] indicates that the book or the article was written and published in Japanese.

AM	Asahi Shinbun (Newspaper) [J], morning edition
AE	*op. cit.*, evening edition
NM	Nihon Keizai Shinbun (Newspaper) [J], morning edition
NE	*op. cit.*, evening edition
FY	fiscal year
s.y.	selected years

AFI	Agricultural Financial Institutions
ASEAN	Association of Southeast Asian Nations
CAD/CAM	Computer-aided design/manufacturing
CEFS	Comparative Economic and Financial Statistics, Japan and Other Major Countries, Bank of Japan
CIM	Computer-integrated manufacturing
DAC	Development Assistance Committee
DIC	Deposit Insurance Corporation
EC	European Community
EOS	Electronic ordering system
ESA	Economic Statistics Annual, Bank of Japan
FA	Factory automation
FMS	Flexible manufacturing system
FRC	Financial Reconstruction Commission
FSA	Financial Supervisory Agency
GATT	General Agreement on Tariffs and Trade
GDP	Gross domestic product
GNE	Gross national expenditure
GNP	Gross national product
IBRD	International Bank for Reconstruction and Development

IMF	International Monetary Fund
JETRO	Japan External Trade Organization
Jusen	Japanese private housing finance companies
LAN	Local area networks
MAFF	Ministry of Agriculture, Forestry and Fisheries
MCA	Multichannel access
MOF	Ministry of Finance
NC	Numerical control
NIEs	Newly industrializing economies
OA	Office automation
ODA	Official Development Assistance
OECD	Organization of Economic Cooperation and Development
POS	Point of sales
RSSR	Ritsumeikan Sangyo Shakai Ronsyu (Ritsumeikan Social Sciences Review), Kyoto
VAN	Value-added network
WPIT	White Paper on International Trade Japan [J], Ministry of International Trade and Industry
WPJE	White Paper on Japanese Economy [J], Economic Planning Agency
WPL	White Paper on Labour in Japan [J], Ministry of Labour
WP-Land	White Paper on Land in Japan [J], National Land Agency
WPSE	White Paper on Small Enterprises in Japan [J], Small and Medium Enterprise Agency

Introduction

High Economic Growth and the Formation of the Corporation-Centered Society

In order to clarify the problems associated with the present stage of the contemporary Japanese economy, it is essential to explicate the content and significance of the high economic growth period from 1955 to 1973. This period of high economic growth drastically changed the socioeconomic structure of postwar Japan as much as, and maybe more, than postwar reform. Here, at the beginning of this book, I want to refer to the characteristics, historic background and socioeconomic substance of this high economic growth.

High economic growth was, in short, the rapid development of the Japanese economy led by large corporations. During this period, Japan's GNP was increasing at an annual rate of 11% (real) and its share in the world's GNP increased from 2.4% to 9.5%. Based on this economic development, the national income and living expenditure per capita of the Japanese people increased remarkably. Looking at this process from the viewpoint of industrial structure, high economic growth was a dynamic development process for the heavy and chemical industries, proceeding with changes in the distribution of labor, with dramatic falls in primary industries and increases in secondary and tertiary industries. Due to this high economic growth, rural districts were changed into areas in which capitalistic commodities circulated and residents enjoyed almost the same style of living as in urban districts. With regard to foreign economic relations, the above-mentioned sophistication of the industrial structure projected its characteristics onto the trade (export) structure. Japanese capital exports entered a stage of rapid development at the beginning of the 1970s. Furthermore, during this period, Japan's gold and foreign exchange reserves changed from a state of chronic shortage to vast holdings. In addition, this high economic growth was accompanied by a retreat and decline of the radical labor union movement, a rise of the labor–capital collaborative labor union movement within the internal structure of the large corporation system and also by frequent incidents of environmental pollution and a deterioration of urban problems (especially housing and land).

I will now consider the historic background of the high economic growth period. With regard to domestic conditions, above all, we must make note of a series of measures, introduced due to the pressure of the American Occupation Army, which brought about economic democratization as part of the postwar reform. The *zaibatsu* dissolution broke down the cliquish form of capital possession that had prevailed before World War II and led to the appearance after the war of modern corporation groups centered on banks. The labor reform legislated in the Trade Union Law, the Labor Standard Law and the Labor Relations Adjustment Law brought about basic democratic legal rights for the workforce and formed a framework for social reform of industrial relations. In addition, land reform fundamentally dissolved the landowner–tenancy relationships that existed before the war, produced a large number of new landed farmers and abolished the pre-modern relationships in farming villages and a great part of their material foundation. One can say that, as a result of these three major reforms, the basic structure of the military and semifeudalistic Japanese capitalism was destroyed.[1]

As an internationally favorable condition of high economic growth, it can be pointed out that the capitalist world was unified through the formation of the IMF, IBRD, GATT etc., and that this led to economic recovery soon after Japan was incorporated into the Western world, centered on the US, by the San Francisco Peace Treaty and the US–Japan Security Treaty in 1951. The restoration of the postwar Japanese economy was enhanced by special procurements of the Korean War, and the basis for continuous development was then set and thus the conditions for high economic growth were formed. Incidentally, with regard to international conditions, I want to refer to the later Vietnam War. It is clear today that Japanese capitalism, which was already at the stage of developing high economic growth, made rapid economic progress and strengthened its position as an economic great power because of its dependence on the spending of the US government during the Vietnam War. Thus, the fact that the development of the postwar Japanese economy was deeply related to wars and to the sacrifices of other nations in Asia, even if this did not involve direct Japanese military invasions as in the prewar period, should not be ignored.[2]

Next, I want to examine the socioeconomic substance of high economic growth. The economic substance was the modernizing and strengthening process of the large corporation system[3] with regard to both its internal structure and its sphere of economic influence. Here "large corporation system" refers to an economic and social system centered on large corporations, and the "modernization of the internal structure" refers to the development of technical innovations and the improvement of production facilities in the heavy and chemical industries as well as in advanced technology industries, and also refers to the continuous supply of good quality labor to these industries. The "modernization of the sphere of economic influence" refers to the rapid development of farmer differentiation, which was propelled by the Structural Improvement Policy, namely a conspicuous decrease in the rural population and its transition to a workforce of urban laborers, and the reorganization of medium and small enterprises as elements of the large corporation system. Of course, the above-mentioned processes assisted each other.[4]

Through these processes, the large corporation system, which evolved to gain excess profit and was based on stable industrial relations, was enlarged and strengthened, and also the system to share and redistribute excess profit was further developed in both civil society and the state. Simultaneously, the organizing ability of the large corporation system was becoming more sophisticated. Here "organizing ability" refers to

(a) the organizational system of huge scale production and labor in the large corporations themselves, (b) the organizing ability of oligopolies formed in the main economic sectors, (c) the organic, economic and financial relevance and personnel connections (including economic and employers' organizations) between industry and banking, (d) the relationships with labor unions and other social organizations, and (e) the inclination to organize the national economy with bureaucracy and state mechanisms.

Thus, as a result of high economic growth, the large corporation system was formed in Japan on a large scale and the social forces opposed to this development were hampered. Historically speaking, we can say that because of this high economic growth, the long-cherished desire of Japan since the Meiji Revolution (Restoration) of "escape from Asia and admission to Europe" (Fukuzawa Yukichi), was accomplished economically. Of course, with regard to politics, culture and ideology, the problem must be evaluated in a different way. However, with regard to productive power, Japan took up the second position, next to the US, in the Western world during this period.

Furthermore, the corporation-centered society was formed through high economic growth in Japan. Here "corporation-centered society" is a society where economic values are overwhelmingly superior to other social values,[5] and where large (huge) corporations are the nucleus of social relationships and regulate the tendency of political society and put pressure on civil society. Conversely, in this corporation-centered society, the structure and energy of the civil society is eroded not only by the political society, but also, and to a greater degree, by the corporation-centered society. Here, civil society, namely a society where self-reliant individuals communicate equally with each other with regard to social and cultural values without the power of state and enterprise, has shrunk to informal and meager social relationships in frugal leisure hours.

Notes

1. Regarding the postwar reforms, refer to: Ohishi K. "The Historical Position of Postwar Japanese Capitalism and the Postwar Reforms." In: *Contemporary Japanese Capitalism*, Vol. 2 [J]. Tokyo: Ohtsuki Shoten, 1981, pp. 38–40.
2. This applies not only to the postwar period, but also to all Japanese modern history after the Meiji Revolution. From the Taiwan Expedition (1874), the Unequal Treaty with Korea (1876), the Sino–Japanese War (1894/95) and the formation of the gold standard by its reparations (1897), and the Annexation of Korea (1910) to aggression on China and East Asia, economic advances made by Japan were almost always connected with sacrifices made by other Asian nations.
3. With regard to the large corporation system, refer to: Galbraith J.K. *The New Industrial State*, 2nd edn. Boston: Houghton Mifflin Co., 1972.
4. It is more important that the modernizing process of the large corporation system progressed in a similar way in each advanced country during the period of high economic growth after World War II and, as a result, the "homogenizing" process of the reproduction structure in advanced countries progressed remarkably (Sasaki K. *Contemporary European Capitalism. Its Structure Centered Around the Economic Integration Policy* [J]. Tokyo: Yuhikaku. 1975, pp. 10f). This also contributed to facilitating the progress of reproduction on an international scale in world capitalism.

   The above-mentioned is a relative characteristic in comparing pre- and post-war world capitalism. I do not deny, of course, that important structural differences and peculiarities exist today among the capitalist countries. It is an essential theoretical subject for economics, especially economic history, to investigate their details (for example, see: Albert M. *Capitalisme Contre Capitalisme*. Paris: Editions du Seuil, 1991.)

5. Certainly, in Japanese society, economic interests take priority and economic value is superior. However, one cannot say that genuine capitalism exists in Japan, because it is obvious that the fundamental elements of capitalism (i.e. self-responsibility, openness of information, individualism, and priority of stockholders, on which market economies develop), work typically better in anglo–saxon countries than in Japan.

Corporation-Centered Society and Two Types of the Large Corporation System

In a structural consideration of the substance of the corporation-centered society in its economic process, I define it as a large corporation system. This means, as mentioned in the first section, an economic and social system centered on large corporations. Both concepts are closely related and resemble each other, but the former definition emphasizes the social aspect, while the latter emphasizes economics.

"Large" corporation is, of course, a relative term and it is clear that a "huge" corporation is more dominant than a large corporation. In this sense, one can define the contemporary Japanese economy as a system of huge corporations. However, we had better not restrict the ruling elements of the real economy to too small a number, because we want to express more precisely the structure and movement of the real system. Because, in addition, small enterprises are subcontracted by large corporations, as well as huge corporations, and they gain benefit according to the mechanisms of the parent company to acquire and distribute excess profit, it is appropriate that we allow the scale of corporations some latitude in defining the ruling elements of economic process. However, this does not mean that we avoid defining the ruling elements of the contemporary Japanese economy. We can definitively identify a core part of the large corporation system in Japan as the president club members of the six large corporation groups and other huge and large corporations that coexist with them.

Of course, it is not only in Japan that large corporations are the center of the economic process as ruling elements, this is a common feature of advanced capitalistic countries. However, on the international scene, there are in my opinion, two main types of large corporation system, namely the European type, which involves democracy within the system, and the Japanese type, where the hegemony of capital is overwhelmingly strong (a third type, that of the US, lies midway between these two types, and is discussed below).

In Europe, after World War II (although the roots of the system lie in the period immediately after World War I), the large corporation system was systematically democratized by the struggle of the workers and mainly under the leadership of social democratic governments. This democratization included the acknowledgment and development of basic labor rights and fundamental social rights, the improvement of labor conditions, especially a large reduction in labor hours and the introduction of long vacations, the development of an economic democracy (e.g. the labor–management joint decision law in Germany, the management participation law and labor fund conception in Sweden and the results of collective agreements on the ground of the labor charter in Italy etc.). There we can also find even a partial realization of classic socialist ideas, namely the large reduction in annual working hours (e.g. around 1,600 hours in Germany and France), the maintenance of a social security system and the size of the ratio of social security costs to the GNP, a respect for fundamental human rights, the coexistence of various values and the social development of pluralism, the existence of an active civil society, high development of social relations of labor etc.

In contrast, in Japan, although the democratization of society progressed greatly due to the postwar reforms, corporate centricism also developed during the high economic growth period, and democracy then all but disappeared from the internal structure of the large corporation system and the subordination of labor to capital was seriously strengthened. Therefore, the working conditions in Japan are considerably inferior to those in Europe, for example with regard to the length of working hours, the situation of the social security system, and the development of economic democracy. Furthermore, looking at the whole social system, the hegemony of capital is very strong and solid. So, Japanese capitalism appears almost to be a form of capitalism without counterprinciples. (Compare this with European capitalism, where labor unions, christianity, individualism[1] within workers and the concept of fundamental human rights work well as real counterprinciples to capitalism.)

With regard to US capitalism, it is similar to Japanese capitalism as far as the overwhelming predominance of capital over labor in the internal structure of the large corporation system goes, but it is similar to European capitalism in that it is confronted in the wider society with real pluralistic principles and social forces, such as christianity, individualism in workers and various social movements. Thus, only Japanese capitalism has an exclusive ruling capitalist hegemony without any social regulation by counterprinciples and counterpowers in both the internal structure of the enterprise and the social system as a whole.

In this Japanese-style large corporation system, management control derived from corporate ownership is superior,[2] the social distinction between labor and staff is almost abolished and the mobility of employees within an enterprise is high. Managers regard their communications with employees as important and, consequently, the company (corporate business) has a strong cohesive force for employees.[3] Thus, the corporation-centered society, which is very efficient for the building up of capital, was formed, accompanied by the exclusive ruling power of capital without counterprinciples. It is obvious that this corporate centricism heightened the economic power of and material living conditions within Japan. Japan is an "affluent society" in the sense that a great majority of its people have stable and secure material living conditions.

However, in the historical tradition in which the Japanese people tend to be united in their commitment to conformity in different spheres, many problems and contradictions have arisen in Japanese society, including the intensity of work, a neglect or ignorance of fundamental human rights within the enterprise, extensive and detailed differentials among individuals in all social spheres where universal principles scarcely develop, and the lack of the coexistence and interchange of pluralistic values and ideas. These problems and the general inadequacy of a common social philosophy become serious impediments for Japanese society to make sound development, either inside or outside the country.[4,5] Japan, which has single-mindedly sustained economic development in the half century since World War II, is now facing a turning point in the 1990s after the collapse of the unprecedented boom bubble.

Incidentally, looking back at the development of industrial relations in postwar Japan, we can summarize the factors that have contributed to the development of the Japanese-style large corporation system as follows:[6]

a. Within several years of the end of World War II, enterprise labor unions had become established and the formation of industrial unions had failed. This was a strong factor in determining the essential weakness of social democratic parties and held back the development of a welfare state in Japan.

b. The successive defeat of the big strikes in large private manufacturing enterprises from the 1950s to the first half of the 1960s related reciprocally to the development of innovation and new ways of labor management, the estrangement of staff from labor unions, the split of labor unions and the retreat of the left wing in enterprises.

c. The integration of workers under the leadership of capital within huge manufacturing enterprises, which was established in the mid-1960s, extended later to large enterprises, small enterprises, and the public sector.

d. The campaign against the Japan–US Security Treaty in 1960, the anti-pollution movements and the appearance of many progressive local governments from the latter half of the 1960s to the first half of the 1970s all showed, to a greater or lesser extent, a protest against the existing order and the will for reform. However, the criticism at the heart of these movements did not reach the core of the socioeconomic system centered around corporations and the consciousness of workers dependent on enterprise was almost unaffected by them.

e. We can find no evidence of workers actually resisting the hegemony of capital in the economic process after the first oil price shock in 1973/74, particularly after the defeat of the large civil servant strike, who demanded the right to strike in 1975. We should see this clear stagnation of the labor movements after 1975 as the actualization of the substance in industrial relations formed in the high economic growth period beginning with the oil shock, rather than as a change in industrial relations after the end of the high economic growth period.

f. Incidentally, the formation of the Japanese-style large corporation system is not the inevitable product of Japanese culture or the mental structure of the Japanese people, but these have contributed, in no small part, to its development, in particular, the indifference to transcendent and absolute values, the strong subordination of the individual to the group, the this-worldly character of the culture, and the overwhelming superiority of economic values over other social values.

Notes

1. Certainly individualism is one of the major sources behind the development of capitalism, but it is not limited only to this respect. Looking at it historically, individualism preceded capitalism by many centuries. In addition, we can see examples every day that individualism works as an element to restrain uncontrolled capitalism. Furthermore, modern capitalism is mainly corporate capitalism, not only private capitalism.
2. Okumura H. *Corporate Capitalism. A System for Company* [J]. Tokyo: Asahi Bunko, 1991, p. 68.

3. Institute of Social Science, University of Tokyo (eds). *Contemporary Japanese Society*, Vol. 1 [J]. Tokyo: University of Tokyo Press, 1991, p. 13.
4. In Japan, when we reflect on the fair formation of public intentions, there is a serious social problem that relates to the Japanese concept of "*kou*" (public). Although in western Europe the word "public" denotes private interests accompanied by a degree of openness, in Japan the concept refers solely to bureaucracy or government and is completely distinct from the private sector. In Japan, even if the concept of "public" is taken to mean "common", its subject or carrier is the bureaucracy or the government, not the groups of private individuals that make up civil society. We can say that the immaturity of civil society and the predominance of the state in Japan is starkly epitomized by this concept of "public" (Hoshino E. *A Recommendation to Civil Law* [J]. Tokyo: Iwanami Shinsho, 1998, pp. 81–99.)
5. The argument that Japan comprises not so much "society" as "*seken*" (the world close to the individual) cannot be ignored (see: Abe K. *What is the "Seken"?* [J]. Tokyo: Kodansha Gendai Shinsho, 1995). Logically speaking, it is impossible to form a civil society in a place where there is no society. On the one hand, society consists of contract relations among self-reliant individuals under the paradigm of universal values (law, justice etc.). On the other, peoples' lives are restrained by "*tatemae*" (stated principles) and "*giri*" (obligations) in the narrow groups or organizations to which they belong. In the latter world, *seken*, people's ideas and actions are seldom regulated by the paradigm of universal values. In the *seken*, there is usually an unhappy severance and tension between "*honne*" (real intentions) and *tatemae* and it is rare that people argue openly and discuss their *honne*, grounding them in universal values as in the Western world. (In this context, we can see why K. van Wolferen characterizes Japan as a stateless nation (the subtitle of his book *The Enigma of Japanese Power* is *People and Politics in a Stateless Nation*).) Therefore, in this *seken*, the fair formation of public intentions encounters considerable difficulties.

   For example, in Kato Shuichi's "*A History of Japanese Literature*" (Kato S. *His Collected Works*, Vol. 5 [J]. Tokyo: Heibonsha, 1980, p. 523; here, translated and annotated by Matsuba) we find the following passage:

   > What is there deep at the bottom of their [the Japanese people's] hearts? Sympathy and cunning dwell together in their hearts, but do not produce critical minds. Though obedience and antipathy to authority live side by side, they do not amount to resistance. Although bound by absurd superstitions and habits, they are good at calculations of practical loss and gain, and are ingenious at contriving devices for daily life. They have an unlimited ability to resign themselves to miserable situations. They know nothing about the world outside of the village but know everything about its internal structures and functions. Their manners and customs, values and behavior patterns, their whole cultural system . . .

   We can say that the human image depicted here is, in a sense, the typical figure of the Japanese who lives in the *seken*. Of course, there are some characteristics that Japanese people have in common with westerners. However, it seems to me that there are more differences than similarities.

   We cannot say that Japan has never had social systems based on law or social paradigms of law. The historical periods both before and after the Meiji Revolution (1868) witnessed such systems. We cannot deny that the prevailing Japanese system, which, since World War II, has been based on Constitution and law, resembles elements of the systems in modern Western countries. (The Japanese people, however, have rarely been conscious of these laws or social paradigms of law as being of universal application, having, as they do, tense relations with transcendent and absolute values.) Of course, we should not forget that there have been many cases of the arbitrary use of law and the legal system by rulers, administrators and bureaucrats. Moreover, struggles against these rulers and their attempts by the citizenry to regulate them have been very weak in Japan.

Acknowledging the fact that the traditional Japanese mentality and the social dynamics of Japan are apt to work to preserve the framework of the *seken*, we should strive to strengthen civil society and the rule of law.

6. Goto M. "From Non-Civil Society to Japanese-Style Mass Society." In: Watanabe O. *Contemporary Japanese Society* [J]. Tokyo: Rodo Junposha, 1996, pp. 343–357; Matsuba M. *An Essay on Contemporary Japanese Capitalism. A Survey Based on Statistics* [J]. Kyoto: Minerva Shobo, 1987, final Ch.

Civil Society and Its Immaturity in Japan

We can define civil society for the present as the diverse and intermediate sphere between state and individual. However, in order for this concept to be a more effective tool for the analysis of real processes, in a general sense, the definition of civil society must be connected to the problems of state and individual. Namely, the contemporary concept of civil society has to take into account the problems relating to the internal structure and the function of state power and to the ideas, consciousness, and feelings of individuals. Furthermore, it is desirable that the following definitions are also taken into account: "modern and democratic society, where free, equal, and independent individuals interact together";[1] and "voluntary connective relations of free, equal and reasonable individuals"[2] as a historically and logically necessary aspect of civil society which will, therefore, also be required in future.

Keeping this in mind, the concept of civil society can be provisionally defined as "the place where self-reliant individuals communicate equally with each other with regard to the social and cultural values of human beings without the intervention of state and enterprise. This place signifies a social and cultural common space and the space where economic activity develops. In the legal system formed by this space, human rights must be superior to civil rights. In addition, relations of social organizations, especially the articulation and connection of these organizations, rational formation of public will and intention, and the form of hegemonic projects in this space, regulate strongly and seriously the trend and character of political society and state power." Using this definition, it is then very difficult for us to consider theoretically the factor "enterprise". On the one hand, it is an economic unit and, therefore, originally situated in civil society with regard to the state. On the other, there exists a power relationship of order and rule subordination in the concept of "enterprise": in this sense, it is also a political system. It is quite possible for enterprise rather than state power to control humans and to rule them. Indeed, Japan is a place where such a possibility has developed to the fullest extent.[3]

It is not appropriate to examine the history of the theory of civil society here. However, it is necessary to comment briefly on the fundamental features or factors of civil society. They are as follows: free and self-reliant individuals, peaceful and reasonable government, competition in the marketplace, voluntary cooperation and association, non-existence of excessive social inequality and of an authoritarian state, the guarantee of fundamental human rights, an arena for public debate, the social development of pluralism, due processes of law, constitutional government and parliamentary representation, open publication of all official information and surveillance of official administrative processes by citizens.[4] In civil society, ". . . work, achievement and success, not birth and privilege, should determine the distribution of wealth, status and power. Education should be of utmost importance. The public use of reason should replace legitimation by tradition. Private and public life should be clearly distinguished."[5]

With regard to this concept of civil society, we must also note the following elements that will strongly affect civil society in the future: corporatization, state expansion, congestion, technoculture,[6] and problems in resource procurement and environment (the idea of sustainable development). As new elements that strengthen civil society, we can make note of voluntary associations, autonomous social movements and the growth of a non-profit, altruistic sector in the economy.[7]

However, we cannot blindly idealize civil society. Equality (i.e. competition) among equivalent individuals (i.e. commodity owners) would lead socially to substantial inequality between capital and labor and the unequal distribution of wealth if there was no regulation from the welfare state and social movements. We must make note of this fact. In addition, in contemporary civil society, not only must the civil rights of native citizens be guaranteed, but those of other inhabitants and refugees must also be guaranteed. In this sense, the regulations of the Charter of the United Nations (1945), the Universal Declaration of Human Rights (1948) and the International Covenant on Civil and Political Rights (1966) are very important.

According to the above-mentioned general features of civil society, how can we evaluate present Japanese society? Certainly, we can find some features (or their signs) of a civil society in Japan after the development of Japanese capitalism for more than 100 years (in particular, we must note the Liberal Democratic Movement in the former half of the Meiji period, Taisho Democracy, postwar reforms, and the deepening and augmentation of the national market in the high economic growth period).

However, Japanese civil society is immature and fragile because of the existence of the corporation-centered society (although there are concerns about civil self-government instead of the existing party system, attempts to reduce price differences in consumer goods between domestic and foreign markets, efforts to overcome the Japanese system for company, which aim for a state that has a high standard of living corresponding to the economic power of Japan, increasing concern about non-government and non-profit organizations, demands for a reduction in the number of US army bases in Okinawa prefecture, and calls for direct compensation by the Japanese government for the so-called "comfort women" during World War II[8]).

Although Japan has caught up with Western countries in terms of productivity, because of the immaturity of Japanese civil society, it is now difficult for Japan to creatively adapt to the era of post-fordism and to an information society. This is because, while hitherto the important factors have been the existing technical application and organizational cooperation of workers in the heavy and chemical industries and in the assembling and processing industries, in the postindustrial period the decisive factor is the intellectual and creative activity of each individual. Modern west European-type civil society is a good training ground for such talent.[9] (I have no wish to glorify one-sidedly or overstate the achievements of West European modernity. If there were concretely another more attractive and balanced human type and social life style, I might refer to that instead. As a Japanese, I would hope this might include the land of Japan) Now, for Japan, civil society is not only the object of intellectual aspirations but also one of the fundamental conditions for the country's future survival. The reorganization of corporation-centered society and the restoration (creation) of civil society is actually a necessary condition for the future of Japan.

Notes

1. Koga E. Civil Society. In: *Encyclopedia Nipponica 2001*, Vol. 11 [J]. Tokyo: Shogakukan, 1989 (1986), p. 217.
2. Matsushita K. Civil Society. In: *Lexicon of Economics*, 3rd edn [J]. Tokyo: Iwanami Shoten, 1992, p. 621.
3. Matsuba M. A Note on the Concept of "Civil Society". Centered on the Perspective of Professor Hirata Kiyoaki [J]. In: *RSSR*, Vol. 31, No. 4. Kyoto: 1996, pp. 69f.
4. Kocka J. "The Difficult Rise of a Civil Society. Societal History of Modern Germany." In: Mary Fulbrook. *German History Since 1800*. London et al.: Arnold, 1997, pp. 498f.
5. *Ibid.*, p. 499.
6. Giner S. "Civil Society and its Future." In: Hall J.A. (ed.). *Civil Society: Theory, History, Comparison*. Cambridge: Polity Press, 1995, pp. 310–315.
7. *Ibid.*, pp. 319f.
8. Kim Y-H. A Proposal to the 21st Century [J]. In: *Asahi Newspaper* (International Edition), December 1, 1996.
9. There is, of course, a separation between the normative and descriptive significance of the concept of civil society in every country and in each era. However, the degree of separation is narrower in Western countries, larger in Japan or East Asia, larger in the 19th century, and smaller in the latter half of the 20th century.

Part 1 The Position of the Japanese Economy in the World

Chapter 1 The Present Stage of the Japanese Economy: An International Comparison

1.1 Main Indices of the Economy and Production

It is clear that the Japanese economy is one of the top economies in the world. For example, its GNP reached US$2,890 billion in 1989 (GDP US$4,687 billion in 1994), being second only to the next to the GNP of the US of US$5,201 billion in 1989 ($6,931 billion in 1994). The GNP per capita in Japan in 1989 reached US$23,472 (US$37,509 in 1994; first in the world), second among advanced countries only to Switzerland with a GNP per capita of US$28,055 ($36,809 in 1994).[1] Moreover, although problems with such assessments because of exchange rates and purchasing power parity remain, the Japanese GNP per capita practically became the first in the world among advanced countries that have populations of more than several tens of millions. Considering the defeat of Japan in World War II and the postwar ruins of the country, we can safely say that no one could have forecast the achievements of the Japanese economy. Table 1.1 shows the GNP statistics of selected countries in 1989.

Comparing steel and motor vehicle production by Japan with that by the US, UK, Federal Republic (F.R.) of Germany, France and Italy, in 1989 steel production was 108, 88, 19, 41, 19, and 25 million metric tons, respectively, while there were 12.4, 10.9, 1.6, 4.8, 3.9, and 2.2 million vehicles produced, respectively. In both cases, Japanese production of steel and motor vehicles was greater than that of the US, and far exceeded that of the advanced European countries.[2] In addition, the gold and foreign exchange reserves of Japan amounted to US$77.1 billion in 1990 (third largest in the world next to those of the US and Taiwan), and 184.5 billion in 1995 (the largest in the world).[3]

With regard to business enterprise, there were 111 Japanese companies within the list of the largest 500 industrial corporations in the world as ranked by sales in 1989. This compares with 167 US companies, 43 UK companies 32 companies in the F.R. Germany and 29 in France. Of the 50 highest-ranking companies among these 500 companies, there were 17 US companies, ten in Japan (13 in 1993; 6th was Toyota Motor, 9th was Hitachi, 12th was Matsushita Electric Industrial, 17th was Nissan Motor, 24th was Toshiba, 30th was Honda Motor, 32nd was NEC, 42nd was Mitsubishi Electric, 44th was Nippon Steel, and 49th was Fujitsu); six in the F.R. Germany, five in the UK and four in France. Thus, one can say that Japanese

TABLE 1.1 GNP at Current Prices (1989)

	1989	Per capita		1989	Per capita		1989	Per capita
	US$ million	US$		US$ million	US$		US$ million	US$
Japan	2,889,920	23,472	Brazil	315,490	2,184[1]	Saudi Arabia	78,819	5,462
US	5,200,800	20,907	Mexico	133,611	1,645[2]	China, P.R.	376,534	341[1]
UK	840,681	14,697	India	279,183	350[1]	USSR	1,011,601	3,566[1]
F.R. Germany	1,194,255	19,265	Thailand	68,765	1,240	Poland	72,925	1,927
France	956,270	17,028	Malaysia	35,605	2,099	Hungary	27,239	2,575
Italy	861,622	14,980	Indonesia	89,359	499	Yugoslavia	62,829	2,666[1]
Canada	528,868	20,170	Philippines	44,253	736	Reference		
Switzerland	186,564	28,055	Korea	210,088	4,957	OECD	11,797,830	14,161
Belgium	155,365	15,646	Taiwan	150,300	7,479	EC	3,425,800	10,510
Netherlands	223,044	15,040	Hong Kong	62,891	10,919	Asian NIEs	452,171	6,376
Spain	376,727	9,707	Singapore	28,891	10,780			
Sweden	185,590	21,834	Australia	294,612	17,526			

[1] Data for 1988; [2] data for 1987.

Source: *CEFS*, 1991, p. 31.

corporations have a consolidated position within the both world's biggest 50 and 500 firms.

Japan's economic position is stronger in world banking. There were 22 Japanese banks (21 in 1993) among the world's 50 largest commercial banks as ranked by assets in 1989, and, in particular, 14 Japanese banks among the world's 20 biggest banks, eight banks among the world's ten biggest banks, and, among monopolies, all five Japanese banks (Dai-Ichi Kangyo Bank, Sumitomo Bank, Fuji Bank, Mitsubishi Bank, Sanwa Bank) were included in the world's five biggest banks.[4] Japan's ratio of international banks' external assets balance increased from 26.1% (US$707 billion) in 1985 (US second at 21.9%; US$593 billion) to 37.4% (US$2,120 billion) in 1990 (US second at 12.6%; US$712 billion); thus, the position of Japan's banks was prominent in the world economy.[5]

In this situation, the ratio of the Japanese GNP in the world increased from 2.4% in 1955 to 9.5% in 1973, 14.3% in 1988 (US GNP in 1988 24.4%) and 18.2% in 1994 (US gross domestic product (GDP) 25.7%).[6]

As one of the main causes of Japanese economic growth, one can first point out the high ratio of gross fixed capital formation and the relatively low ratio of consumption expenditure in the GNE. For example, the total ratio of private and government final consumption and the ratio of gross fixed capital formation in 1989 in selected countries were as follows: Japan 66.4%–32.3%, US 83.9%–16.5%, UK 83.0%–19.4%, F.R. Germany 72.5%–20.0%, France 78.4%–21.2%, and Italy 79.5%–20.4%.[7] Furthermore, the ratio of fixed capital formation, except for residential building, in the GNP of selected countries for the past 30 years is shown in Table 1.2. Obviously, in Japan, in contrast with other major countries, the amount of newly produced wealth used for expanded reproduction is large. This vividly shows the tendency for rapid economic growth in Japan.

Moreover, labor productivity in Japan, the US and the F.R. Germany changed, as shown in Figure 1.1. We can see that the economic growth rate of Japan is greater than that of the other two countries. However, with regard to labor productivity, for international comparisons, not only growth rates but also absolute levels of growth must be compared. Table 1.3 gives the statistics announced by the Japanese Ministry of Labor in February 1992. As shown, Japanese labor productivity based simply on the foreign exchange rate is more than that of other countries. However, with regard to real labor productivity based on purchasing power parity, Japan is ranked lowest. In addition, conditioned by long work hours, Japan's labor productivity per hour is lower,

TABLE 1.2 Investment Ratio of Each Country (Fixed Capital Formation except Dwellings/GNP) Over the Period 1960–87

(Unit: %)

	US	Japan	UK	France	F.R. Germany	Italy	Canada
Average 1960–87	13.25	25.15	14.29	15.52	16.07	16.33	16.89
1960s	13.30	26.14	14.24	16.05	17.55	16.67	17.51
1970s	13.50	25.58	15.13	15.94	15.91	16.67	16.90
1980s	13.22	23.39	13.31	14.34	14.41	15.47	16.10

Source: *WPJE*, 1990, p. 499.

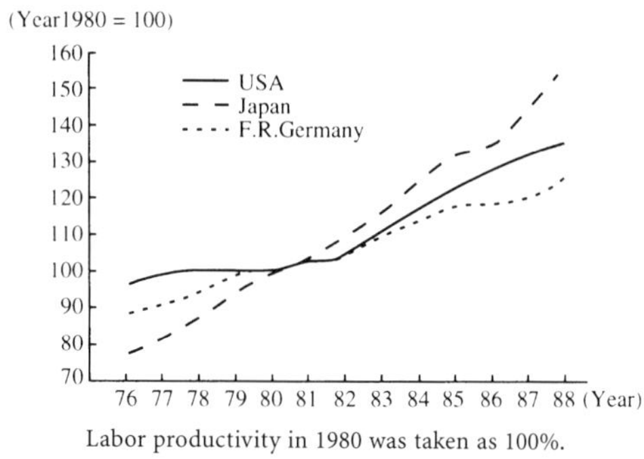

FIG. 1.1 Trends in Labor Productivity
Source: *WPIT*, 1990 p. 81.

TABLE 1.3 International Comparison of Labor Productivity over the period 1987–89

		US (1989)		F.R. Germany (1988)		France (1989)		UK (1987)	
	Japan	Ex.R.	P.P.P.	Ex.R.	P.P.P.	Ex.R.	P.P.P.	Ex.R.	P.P.P.
Labor Productivity	100	95	141	93	108	95	120	68	105
(per hour)	100	109	162	119	139	116	146	—	—
Manufacturing	100	80	118	77	90	80	101	52	81
(per hour)	100	88	130	103	120	105	132	58	90
Agriculture, forestry and fisheries	100	212	313	95	111	153	194	123	189
Commerce	100	129	190	107	125	153	193	71	109
Exchange rates	¥	137.96	204	72.98	85.25	21.62	27.31	236.34	364.57

Data are the tentative calculations of the Japanese Ministry of Labor.
Ex.R., exchange rate; P.P.P., purchasing power parity.
Source: *NM*, February 8, 1992.

even when converted using an exchange rate, than that of other countries. In manufacturing, the labor productivity of Japan, although higher in terms of the exchange rate than that in other countries, does not necessarily coincide with a strength in international competitive ability of the manufactured products in terms of purchasing power parity and is lower than that of the US and France. Naturally, Japan's labor productivity per hour is considerably lower than that of the other countries, except for the UK.

Furthermore, that Japan's agriculture, forestry, fisheries and commerce are characterized by the kind of low labor productivity illustrated in Table 1.3 is a fact well known both inside and outside of the country. These statistical figures of international comparisons of labor productivity suggest a cause of imbalance between the powerful international competitive ability of Japan and the lack of scope in the life style of its people.

Here I would like to make mention of the high savings rate with respect to the causes of Japanese economic development and the high rate of economic growth. As shown in Table 1.4, the savings rate of Japan (i.e. both the household savings rate and the gross savings rate) is higher than that of other major countries. It is clear

TABLE 1.4 Savings Rates in Selected Countries for 1976–92 (s.y.)

(Unit: %)

Year	Gross Savings Rate				
Year	Japan	US	UK	F.R. Germany	France
1976	32.6	15.9	15.8	22.5	22.9
1978	32.3	18.2	18.5	22.5	22.5
1980	31.1	16.2	17.4	21.7	23.5
1982	30.4	14.1	17.0	20.3	19.7
1984	30.7	15.1	17.5	21.7	19.1
1986	31.9	12.4	17.0	23.9	20.0
1988	33.3	13.2	17.1	24.5	20.5
1990	34.3	13.0	15.8	24.8	21.5
1992	33.6	11.9	13.6	22.7	19.9
	Household savings rate				
Year	Japan	US	UK	F.R. Germany	France
1976	23.2	9.1	7.6	13.3	12.9
1978	20.8	9.0	7.7	12.0	14.2
1980	17.9	9.0	10.0	12.8	17.6
1982	16.5	8.8	8.1	12.8	17.3
1984	16.0	8.6	6.6	11.4	14.5
1986	16.4	6.7	3.1	12.2	13.2
1988	14.8	6.6	−0.5	12.6	12.2
1990	14.1	4.3	4.2	13.9	7.2
1992	14.3	5.5	8.8	12.8	7.9

Source: *Opinion Research on Savings*, 1990 [J], Tokyo, p. 164; *op. cit.*, 1994, p. 173.

that this is an important factor for the expanded reproduction of the Japanese economy.

And yet, when we think about Japanese economic development, we must make note of the ratio of military spending to the GNP. This ratio hovered at a level of approximately 1% in the 1970s and 1980s, and there is no doubt that the relatively "small" ratio of military spending that depletes outside growth has contributed advantageously to the growth of the Japanese economy in comparison with other countries. However, it should not be forgotten that Japanese military spending is at an absolute level close to that of the UK, the F.R. Germany and France, and that its growth rate in Japan from 1981 to 1989 was the highest among the major advanced countries (indices in 1989 taking 1981 as 100%: Japan 146.1%, US 129.7%, UK 113.5%, France 110.1%, and F.R. Germany 102.4%).[8]

In addition to these general points, I would like to direct attention towards the supplementary factors or characteristics that have seemed to be important for Japanese social and economic development in the 1980s.

First, there is the tendency of energy/oil conservation of the Japanese economy after two oil crises (1973/74 and 1979/80). As shown in Table 1.5, in Japan, throughout the oil crises and further into the 1080s, energy consumption per fixed GDP unit decreased more than in any other major country and remarkable energy saving results

TABLE 1.5 Trends in Energy Consumption per Fixed GDP Unit in Advanced Countries for 1972–88 (s.y.)

Year	72	73	74	76	78
France	98.1	100	95.0	90.8	91.2
F.R. Germany	98.0	100	96.8	95.0	92.7
Japan	97.3	100	102.4	95.9	89.1
UK	103.3	100	97.7	91.9	89.0
US	101.2	100	98.8	99.4	95.7
Year	**80**	**82**	**84**	**86**	**88**
France	90.3	82.3	84.1	84.2	81.8
F.R. Germany	88.6	81.8	81.5	80.5	77.4
Japan	83.0	73.8	73.6	69.5	68.2
UK	85.2	81.4	76.6	76.6	71.2
US	90.3	84.7	79.4	74.8	74.2

Data from 1973 were taken as 100%.
Source: *WRJE*, 1991, p. 480.

TABLE 1.6 International Comparison of Research and Development Expenditures in Selected Countries

R&D expenditure (including military research cost)/GNP (1970–88, s.y.) (Unit: %)

Year	70~74	75~79	80~84	85	86	87	88
Japan	1.662	1.731	2.159	2.526	2.515	2.566	2.620
US	2.367	2.175	2.461	2.683	2.653	2.624	2.593
UK	2.097	2.110	2.237	2.221	2.295	—	—
France	1.815	1.749	2.034	2.268	2.257	2.300	—
F.R. Germany	2.281	2.382	2.574	2.798	2.751	2.815	—

R&D expenditure (excluding military research cost)/GNP (Unit: %)

Year	70~74	75~79	80~84	85	86	87	88
Japan	1.648	1.719	2.145	2.508	2.495	2.545	—
US	1.693	1.657	1.888	1.980	1.861	1.855	1.856
UK	1.590	1.594	1.571	1.564	1.703	—	—
France	1.415	1.403	1.560	1.789	1.805	1.807	—
F.R. Germany	2.133	2.248	2.466	2.662	2.618	2.676	—

R&D, research and development.
Source: *WPJE*, 1990, p. 495.

were observed during this period. In particular, oil consumption was reduced by 9.8%, from 321 million liters in 1973 to 289 million liters in 1989, as a result of energy saving and the diversification of energy sources, while the Japanese real GNP increased 1.9-fold from 1973 to 1989. Consequently, oil consumption per fixed GDP unit was reduced by 48.2% from 1973 to 1989.[9] It seems clear that the development of energy saving strategies has played a large role in the growth of the Japanese economy and the strength of its international competitive ability.

Second, I will refer to research and development costs. Table 1.6 shows an international comparison of GNP ratios. Evidently, the Japanese ratio increased in the 1980s.

TABLE 1.7 Trends in the Ratio of Technological Balance of Payments in Selected Countries (1972–89, s.y.)

Year	1972	1974	1976	1978	1980
Japan	0.128	0.151	0.219	0.24	0.267
US	9.42	11.04	9.03	8.77	9.79
F.R. Germany	0.464	0.45	0.417	0.446	0.486
France	0.299	0.384	0.351	0.511	0.483
UK	1.1	1.12	1.26	1.19	1.16
Year	1982	1984	1986	1988	1989
Japan	0.319	0.306	0.28	0.326	0.379
US	8.39	5.89	6.83	5.24	—
F.R. Germany	0.542	0.569	0.5	0.494	0.535
France	0.417	0.488	0.555	0.512	—
UK	1.21	1.09	1.08	—	—

Source: *WPJE*, 1991, p. 487.

Although recently (2.57% in 1987) it still did not equal that of the ratio of the F.R. Germany (2.82%), it nearly reached the level of the US (2.62%). Except for military expenditure on research and development, Japan's ratio (2.55% in 1987), along with that of the F.R. Germany (2.68%), is considerably higher than that of other countries. In addition, the ratio of research and development costs of the private sector in Japan's GNP was 2.1% in 1987, which was higher than that of the F.R. Germany (1.7%) and of the US (1.3%).[10] Thus, it can be said that the research and development expenditure in Japan helped not only the technical but also the economic development of Japan.

Next, I will consider the Japanese technological balance of payments, which has a strong connection with the power of technological development mentioned above. Because this is an important issue that relates strongly with the characteristics of the Japanese modernization process since the Meiji revolution and to Japanese economic development after World War II, this theme will be examined in some detail. Let us look at the ratio of the technological balance of payments (receipts/payments). As shown in Table 1.7, although the ratio of receipts/payments in the 1980s in Japan became better than in the 1970s, it is still the lowest among the group of major countries. There we can see the weakness in Japan's power of creative and independent technological development. However, the figures for Japan in Table 1.7 are based on the "Balance of Payments Monthly" of the Bank of Japan, and there are other statistics in Japan that show the trends in Japan's technological balance of payments. These include data from the Statistics Bureau, Management and Coordination Agency, Japan. There are many differences between these two sets of statistics.

Comparing the data from the bank of Japan and the Statistics Bureau of the Management and Coordination Agency, it can be seen that the former has only the royalty in the narrow sense as its object and surveys all enterprises and institutions, while the latter has not only royalties, but also know-how and technological rental fees, as its object, but excludes the commercial and financial sectors. I dare say that the latter shows the situation in the industrial sectors more clearly than the former. Both sets of statistics since the 1970s are shown in Table 1.8 (although there are some gaps in

TABLE 1.8 Japan's Technological Balance of Payments (1970–94, s.y.)

Item	Statistics from the Bank of Japan			Statistics from the Statistics Bureau, Management and Coordination Agency			New contract section		
	Receipts (A)	Payments (B)	Ratio	Receipts (C)	Payments (D)	Ratio	Receipts (E)	Payments (F)	Ratio
FY	million ¥	(million $)	(A)/(B)	million ¥	(million $)	(C)/(D)	million ¥	(million $)	(E)/(F)
1970	21,128 (59)	155,057 (433)	0.136	—	—	—	—	—	—
1972	22,740 (75)	173,430 (572)	0.131	42,172 (139)	173,916 (574)	0.242	18,206 (60)	14,462 (48)	1.259
1974	33,007 (113)	209,728 (718)	0.157	57,102 (195)	159,832 (547)	0.357	20,101 (69)	14,635 (50)	1.373
1976	51,312 (173)	250,924 (846)	0.204	83,404 (281)	177,302 (598)	0.470	27,030 (91)	17,860 (60)	1.513
1978	57,650 (274)	261,106 (1,241)	0.221	122,049 (580)	192,058 (913)	0.635	47,110 (224)	38,183 (181)	1.234
1980	85,693 (378)	326,221 (1,439)	0.263	159,612 (704)	239,529 (1,057)	0.666	74,263 (328)	27,675 (122)	2.683
1982	131,276 (527)	447,384 (1,796)	0.293	184,921 (742)	282,613 (1,135)	0.654	63,336 (254)	44,439 (178)	1.425
1984	164,588 (693)	550,288 (2,317)	0.299	277,512 (1,168)	281,447 (1,185)	0.986	90,906 (383)	31,841 (134)	2.855
1986	170,017 (1,009)	568,688 (3,375)	0.299	224,078 (1,330)	260,577 (1,546)	0.860	51,849 (308)	33,636 (200)	1.541
1988	215,504 (1,681)	650,743 (5,076)	0.331	246,255 (1,921)	312,195 (2,435)	0.789	47,362 (369)	54,572 (426)	0.868
1990	373,874 (2,582)	869,379 (6,004)	0.430	339,352 (2,344)	371,907 (2,568)	0.912	58,584 (405)	73,388 (507)	0.798
1992	408,481 (3,224)	903,118 (7,128)	0.452	377,691 (2,981)	413,908 (3,267)	0.912	57,689 (455)	94,396 (745)	0.611
1994	560,056 (5,480)	880,358 (8,614)	0.636	462,128 (4,521)	370,693 (3,627)	1.246	56,488 (553)	52,422 (513)	1.078

FY, fiscal year.

Source: *Indicators of Science and Technology*, 1991, pp. 88f.; *op. cit.*, 1996, pp. 84f.

the figures from the Bank of Japan in Tables 1.7 and 1.8). Apparently, while the technological balance of payments has started to balance in recent years in the statistics from the Statistics Bureau, according to the statistics of the Bank of Japan, the payments are still considerably more than the receipts. This is mainly because recently the balance of know-how and technological rental fees, which are not included in the statistics from the Bank of Japan but are included in those from the Statistics Bureau, were relatively improved. In addition, payments in the sectors of commerce, finance and real estate are included in the statistics from the Bank of Japan but are not included in those from the Statistics Bureau.[11] In any case, looking at the sustained improvement in the balance of the statistics from the Bank of Japan, the equilibrium of receipts and payments in the statistics from the Statistics Bureau, which strongly show the situation in the industrial sector, and the continuity of the trend towards excess receipts related to newly contracted data in the same series, we can say that the self-reliance of technological development in industrial fields is increasing rapidly in Japan.

Furthermore, I will now refer to the development process for information system equipment and microelectronics machinery that is an important feature of the recent Japanese economy. For a start, comparing the number of industrial robot installations that were actively performed in the 1980s, the Japanese installed 219.7 thousand in 1989 (67.0 thousand in 1984; 377.0 thousand in 1994) respectively, which far exceeded that installed in the US (37.0, 13.0, and 55.0 thousand in 1989, 1984 and 1994, respectively), the UK (5.9, 2.6, and 9.3 thousand in 1989, 1984 and 1994, respectively), the F.R. Germany (22.4, 6.6, and 48.8 thousand in 1989, 1984 and 1994, respectively), France (7.1, 2.8, and 13.0 thousand in 1989, 1984 and 1994, respectively), and Italy (10.0, 2.6, and 22.0 thousand in 1989, 1984 and 1994, respectively).[12] Moreover, with regard to the efficiency of Japanese industrial robots, their high degree of development is remarkable. For example, comparing the capacity of industrial robots in 1980 and 1987, the ratio of manual manipulators and fixed-sequence robots with simple functions was reduced from 86% to 30%, while variable-sequence robots, playback robots, numerically-controlled (NC) robots and intelligent robots with higher and more complex functions increased from 14% to 70%.[13] It is clear that these factors brought about diversification of commodities and the reduction of cost and, still more, contributed to the strengthening of the international competitive ability of the Japanese economy.

Moreover, we must make note of the following: recent (particularly in the latter half of the 1980s) development of information system equipment and microelectronics machinery in Japan has been performed as part of the production process and also as part of the fields of research and development, distribution, service and commerce (i.e. in almost every field of social production and life). Namely, the automation of individual offices and factories (OA, FA) that also existed in the past, the formation of a flexible manufacturing system (FMS) with advanced NC machines and industrial robots with computer-aided design/manufacturing (CAD/CAM) systems, and the appearance of local area networks (LAN) combined to create a computer-integrated manufacturing (CIM) system that unifies research and development, the ordering of spare parts and materials, manufacturing, inspection and marketing.

The information network on the manufacturing level represented by this CIM is linked to foreign countries by an international value-added network (VAN) and to

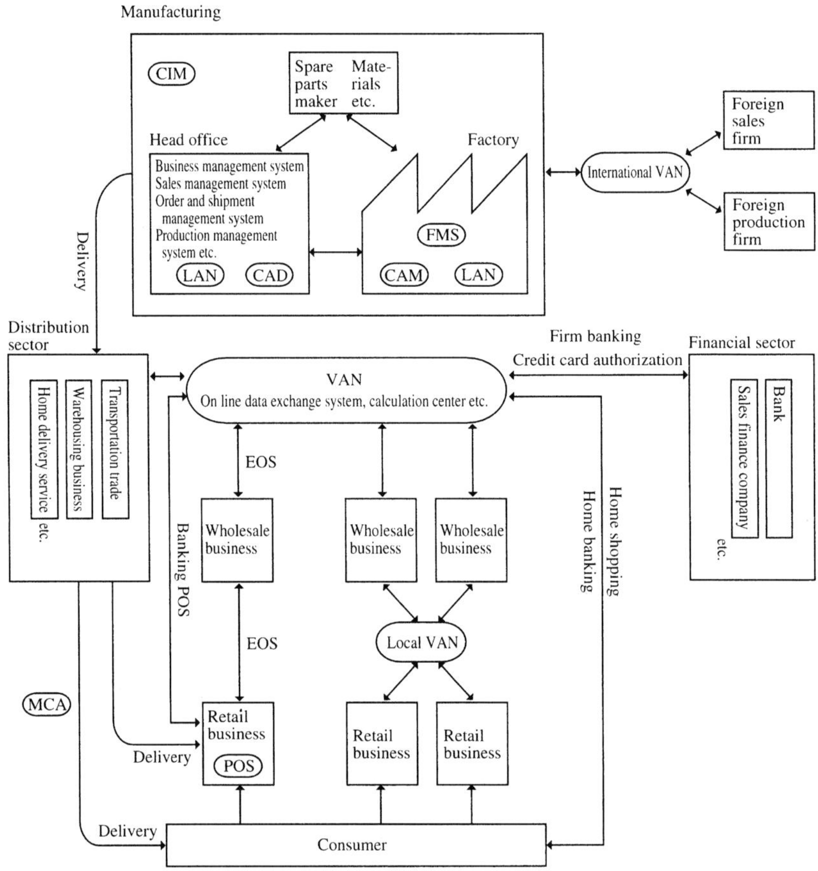

CIM, Computer-integrated manufacturing; LAN, local area network; CAD, CAM, computer-aided design/manufacturing; FMS, flexible manufacturing system; VAN, value-added network; EOS, electronic ordering system; POS, point of sales.

FIG. 1.2 A Conceptual Plan of the Information Network
Source: *WPJE*, 1990, p. 220.

international distribution processes by a point of sales (POS) system and an electronic ordering system (EOS), which concentrate the information on a retail and wholesale level, and VAN and multichannel access (MCA) systems, which integrate the information on an area level. Furthermore, these systems are connected with on-line, home banking, bank POS of financial institutions and, consequently, the information network of production and life on a society scale is developing.[14] Figure 1.2 illustrates the above-mentioned process.

We cannot rashly decide on the significance that the development of this information system equipment and microelectronics machinery has for the development of the Japanese economy. It is too optimistic if we conclude immediately that it directly enables the production process to satisfy various demands and the interests of people and that it simplifies demand control and makes stable growth possible. However, we cannot deny that it is useful in strengthening the international competitive ability of the Japanese economy and that it may be a material basis of a new rational production system in the future.

Notes

1. *CEFS*, 1996, p. 29.
2. *CEFS*, 1991, pp. 3f.
3. *Ibid.*, p. 157; *op. cit.*,1996, p. 167.
4. the above-mentioned regarding corporation rank; *Fortune*, July 30, 1990, pp. 43–105; *op. cit.*, July 25, 1994, pp. 49, 152.
5. *White Paper of JETRO* [J], *Investment Part*, 1992, p. 19.
6. *The Weekly Toyo Keizai*, [J] June 8, 1991, p. 17; Matsuba M. *An Essay on Contemporary Japanese Capitalism. A Survey Based on Statistics* [J]. Kyoto: Minerva Shobo, 1987, p. 13; *Annual Report on World Economy* [J]. Tokyo: Economic Planning Agency, 1996, p. 41.
7. *CEFS*, 1991, pp. 33–36.
8. *Defence of Japan* [J]. Tokyo: Defence Agency, 1991, pp. 262–264; *AM*, December 30, 1990.
9. *WPJE*, 1991, p. 268.
10. *op. cit.*, 1990, p. 149.
11. *Ibid.*, pp. 152f; Iinuma K. and Nagata M. Japan Is Now a Technological Power [J]. In: *The Weekly Toyo Keizai*, April 13, 1991, pp. 142–149.
12. *CEFS*, 1991, pp. 193f; *op. cit.*, 1996, pp. 207f.
13. *WPJE*, 1989, pp. 112–114.
14. Above mentioned, *WPJE*, 1990, pp. 214–224.

1.2 Indices of Agriculture, Labor, and Life

Table 1.9 shows the fundamental indices of Japanese agriculture. From Table 1.9 we can see the reduction of farm households and agricultural workers during the period 1960–94. We can also see an increase in the proportion of households combining farming with other forms of work and particularly in the proportion of farming households relying on other work as the main source of income. What we find, then, is an increase in the ratio of non-agricultural income. In connection with this trend, although the output price of agricultural products increased absolutely, the ratio of primary industry in the Japanese national income decreased from 14.9% in 1960, to 7.8% in 1970, 3.6% in 1980, and 2.4% in 1989.[1]

Another important problem from the point of view of the national economy is the big fall in self-sufficiency rates for agricultural foodstuffs in Japan. Refering to Table 1.10, it can be seen that the self-sufficiency rates for vegetables and eggs are high, and the tendency for a decline in the self-sufficiency rates for stock farm products and fruits is comparatively mild. However, except for rice, where production cost and income compensation is given to farmers by the state, the self-sufficiency rate for cereals declined markedly. In addition, from 1960 to 1970 and from 1980 to 1989, the self-sufficiency rates of all foodstuffs were reduced from 91% to 81% and 75% to 68%, respectively, while those of cereals were similarly reduced from 82% to 46% and 33% to 30%, respectively.[2] Considering that most EC countries, in addition to the US and

TABLE 1.9 Fundamental Indices of Japanese Agriculture (1960–94, s.y.)

	Units	1960	1970	1980	1985	1989	1994
Farm households	1,000	6,057	5,342	4,661	4,376	4,194	3,644
Ratio of Part-time farm households	%	65.7	84.4	86.6	—	—	—
(Ratio of mainly other job)	(%)	(32.0)	(50.7)	(65.1)	(67.5)	(70.7)	—
Ratio of non-agricultural receipts (FY)	%	49.8	68.1	78.8	—	—	—
Population engaged in agriculture (FY)	million	11.96	8.11	5.06	4.36	4.07	3.35
(Percent of total)	(%)	(26.8)	(15.9)	(9.1)	(7.6)	(6.5)	(5.2)
Cultivated land	1,000 ha	6,071	5,796	5,461	5,379	5,279	5,083
(Utilization rate)	(%)	(133.9)	(108.9)	(103.2)	(103.7)	(102.8)	(99.3)
Agricultural products	billion ¥	1,914.8	4,664.3	10,196.2	11,629.5	11,051.3	11,327.5

Sources: Onodera Y. Agricultural Cooperative at the Turning Point. *Economic Review* [J], August, 1982, Tokyo, p. 79; *Statiscal Appendix of White Paper on Agriculture Japan* [J], 1990, Tokyo, pp. 8–11, 26, 42; *op. cit.*, 1995, pp. 14–17.

TABLE 1.10 Self-Sufficiency Rates for Essential Agricultural Products (1960–95, s.y.)

(Unit: %)

	FY 1960	1970	1980	1985	1989	1995
Rice	102	106	100	107	100	103
Wheat	39	9	10	14	16	7
Barley/rye	107	34	15	15	15	—
Pulses	44	13	7	8	9	5
Soybean	28	4	4	5	6	—
Vegetables	100	99	97	95	92	85
Fruit	100	84	81	77	67	49
Eggs	101	97	98	98	98	96
Milk and dairy products	89	89	82	85	80	72
Meat	91	89	81	81	72	57
Beef	96	90	72	72	54	—
Pork	96	98	87	86	77	—
Sugar	18	22	27	33	35	35

Source: *White Paper on Agriculture Japan* [J], 1990, Tokyo, p. 28; *op. cit.*, 1996, p. 75.

Australia as traditional foodstuff-exporting countries, attain fundamental self-sufficiency of foodstuffs today and export surplus foodstuffs, it must be said that the self-sufficiency rates for agricultural foodstuffs in Japan are particularly low compared with other advanced countires.[3]

With regard to employment distribution by industry, which is relevant to both agriculture and industry; as shown in Table 1.11, in Japan, through the period of high economic growth (from 1955 to 1973), the ratio people employed in primary industries declined dramatically, while that for people employed in secondary industries

TABLE 1.11 Employment Distribution by Industry (1950–95, s.y.)

(Unit: %)

Year	Primary industry	Secondary industry	Tertiary industry
Japan			
1950	48.3	21.9	29.8
1960	32.6	29.2	38.2
1970	19.3	33.9	46.8
1980	10.4	34.8	54.8
1990	7.2	33.6	59.2
1995	5.7	33.6	60.7
US (1990)	2.8	26.4	70.8
F.R. Germany (1987)	5.1	40.5	54.4
France (1990)	5.6	29.6	64.8
Italy (1989)	9.2	31.9	58.9
UK (1989)	2.1	29.1	68.8

Sources: *Japan* 1983. *An International Comparison*, Tokyo p. 14; *CEFS*, 1985, p. 142; *op. cit*, 1991, p. 107; *op. cit.*, 1996, pp. 117 f.

increased at first and thereafter remained steady and for people employed in tertiary industries the ratio increased markedly. The employment distribution ratio changed slowly in the 1980s in comparison with the former period. Furthermore, making international comparisons, of employment distribution by industry at present, we notice that there is a similarity in the distribution pattern among countries after a period of high economic growth and following economic development, and that each country's peculiarities cannot be ignored. For example, there is a conspicuously low ratio of primary industries and a high ratio of tertiary industries in the UK and the US, and a high ratio of secondary industries in the F.R. Germany. The pattern of employment distribution in Japan is positioned in the middle ground among the advanced countries.

The labor force rates for the population aged above 15 years of selected countries for 1970, 1980 and 1988 are as follows: Japan, 65.4%, 63.3%, and 62.6%, respectively; US, 61.0%, 64.1%, and 66.2%, respectively; UK, 60.2%, 59.7%, and 61.0%, respectively; F.R. Germany, 56.2%, 56.0%, and 56.5%, respectively; and France, 55.8%, 56.4%, and 55.3%, respectively. In recent years, the Japanese labor force rate is second only to that of the US.[4]

With regard to the unemployment ratio of selected countries over the past several decades, as shown in Table 1.12, the Japanese unemployment ratio has remained extremely low among the advanced countries, despite the oil shocks, into the 1980s. Of course, it is well known that the calculation of the unemployment rate in Japan is based on basic data obtained from sample surveys of approximately 40,000 households; lay-offs and those engaged in paid work for one hour or more during the survey period (the last 7 days of every month) are excluded from the definition of "unemployed"; members of the armed forces are included in the labor force for which the unemployment rate is calculated. These methods of calculation bring the Japanese unemployment rate down in comparison with that of other countries.[5] Nevertheless, it can be said that the unemployment rates, in Japan after the latter half of 1970s have

TABLE 1.12 Unemployment Rates in Selected Countries (1960–95, s.y.)

(Unit: 1,000 persons, %)

Year	Japan		US		UK		F.R. Germany		France	
	Unemployment	Ratio	Unemployment	Ratio	Unemployment	Ratio	Unemployment	Ratio	Unemployment	Ratio
1960	750	1.7	3,850	5.4	360	1.6	270	1.3	130	—
1965	570	1.2	3,370	4.4	340	1.5	150	0.7	140	—
1970	590	1.1	4,090	4.8	600	2.6	150	0.7	260	—
1975	1,000	1.9	7,930	8.3	900	3.9	1,070	4.7	840	—
1980	1,140	2.0	7,637	7.1	1,665	6.8	889	3.8	1,451	6.7
1982	1,360	2.4	10,678	9.7	2,917	10.9	1,833	7.5	2,008	8.2
1984	1,610	2.7	8,539	7.5	3,160	11.7	2,266	9.1	2,310	10.2
1986	1,670	2.8	8,237	7.0	3,289	11.8	2,228	9.0	2,517	10.4
1988	1,550	2.5	6,701	5.5	2,370	8.4	2,242	8.7	2,563	9.9
1990	1,340	2.1	6,874	5.5	1,665	5.8	1,883	7.2	2,505	8.9
1992	1,420	2.2	9,613	7.5	2,779	9.8	2,979	7.8	2,910	10.4
1995	2,100	3.2	7,404	5.6	2,326	8.3	3,612	9.4	2,979	11.6

The units of unemployment before 1980 and for all Japanese data were originally per 10,000 persons.
Sources: *Handbook of Labor Statistics in Japan* [J]. 1984, Tokyo, p. 208; *CEFS*, 1990, pp. 145–147; *op. cit.*, 1991, 109–111; *op. cit.*, 1996, pp. 123–125.

TABLE 1.13 International Comparison of Compensation of Employee Rates (1975–88, s.y.)

(Unit: %)

Year	1975	1976	1978	1980	1982	1984	1986	1987	1988
Japan	80.9	80.4	78.5	76.9	77.9	77.8	77.2	77.9	77.6
US	81.5	81.1	80.0	81.0	81.4	79.2	79.6	79.7	79.7
UK	86.3	82.9	81.2	85.2	83.8	79.6	80.0	77.1	—
F.R. Germany	91.3	90.8	90.2	90.0	88.8	87.4	88.2	—	—
France	88.4	89.4	88.2	88.3	89.9	88.8	85.0	84.8	—

Source: *WPJE*, 1990, p. 534.

been comparatively good. Actually, not only is the unemployment rate in Japan low but, in additions the ratio of available jobs to the number of applicants was over 1 from the third quarter of 1988 until the spring of 1992 and the demand for labor was continuously high. However, this ratio has dropped below 1 since 1993 (0.76 in 1993; 0.64 in 1994; 0.63 in 1995; 0.70 in 1996).[6]

Next, labor's relative share in macroeconomics will be compared internationally. Viewed along with the rate of compensation for employees (compensation of employees/(national income—private unincorporated entrepreneurial income)), as shown in Table 1.13, for example, in 1986 the relative share in the US, UK, F.R. Germany, France and Japan was 79.6%, 80.0%, 88.2%, 85.0%, and 77.2%, respectively. In recent years labor's relative share in Japan has still been low.

Moreover, I want to examine the problem of a differential between commodity prices at home and abroad. Table 1.14 shows a recent comparison of prices in Japan/Tokyo with those in New York and Hamburg. If prices in Tokyo are set at 100, those in New York are 76 and those in Hamburg are 80. Foodstuff prices in foreign cities are three-quarters of the prices in Tokyo. Other daily necessities (e.g. clothing and footwear, energy and water charges, and services concerned with real estate) are more expensive in Japan. (Another investigation of retail prices of foodstuffs in 1991 by the Ministry of Agriculture, Forestry and Fisheries Japan shows that, in the case of prices in Tokyo being set at 100, New York prices are at 82, London prices are 88, Paris prices are 84, Hamburg prices are 87, and Toronto prices are 79. In addition, according to results of another investigation in November, 1990, if the prices of electricity, gas and rice in Japan are set at 100, these prices are, respectively, 81, 46, and 51 in the US, 87, 48, and 67 in the UK, 109, 57, and 60 in the F.R. Germany, and 92, 68, and 49 in France.[7] These differentials between commodity prices at home and abroad, even though they are caused by the complicated Japanese distribution network and the special feelings of Japanese consumers for high-priced foreign luxury goods, symbolize the internal weak buying power of the Yen in comparison with its external strong exchange rate and must be corrected in the interests of social justice and the progress of national life.

At any rate, as shown in Table 1.15, among major countries the internal commodity prices of Japan in the 1980s have been the most stable along with prices in the F.R. Germany. As the main causes of this stability, we can point to the higher Yen exchange rate, low and stable oil prices (both factors coming into play especially in the latter half of the 1980s), the rise of labor productivity and few demands for pay rises by the moderate and conciliatory labor movement in Japan.

TABLE 1.14 Cost of Living, an International Comparison of Prices (surveyed 1988, estimated 1990)

Item	Tokyo prices = 100	
	New York prices (US$1 = ¥129.08)	Hamburg prices (DM1 = ¥86.81)
All items	76	80
Food	74	75
Cereals	56	79
Meat	56	70
Perishables	87	69
Milk and eggs	65	69
Liquor	66	71
Durable goods	82	113
Clothing and footwear	65	79
Miscellaneous goods	83	107
Cosmetics/accessories	89	77
Energy/water charges	50	89
Transport and communication	74	111
Transport	103	105
Communication	66	123
Health/medical care	118	28
Education	117	61
Land leasing service	55	63
Rent	57	60
Miscellaneous services	121	86
Dining out	102	106

Source: *Prices Report* [J]. 1991, Tokyo: Economic Planning Agency, p. 80.

Under these conditions and in the boom of the latter half of the 1980s, the existing style of durable consumer goods was still increasing.[8] However, new features began to appear in Japanese consumer life. For example, labor-saving durable consumer goods for housework, in addition to the electric washing machine, refrigerator and vacuum cleaner, which were already becoming more common, electric cooking ranges and drying machines for clothes, *futon* (i.e. Japanese bedding) and tableware started to become available and are still gaining market share. With regard to air conditioning, there was a shift from existing electric fans and oil stove heaters to more comfortable room air conditioners and warm-air heaters. In terms of leisure, there was a spread in ownership of cassette recorders, stereo players, compact disk (CD) players, video tape recorders (VTR) and cars. For communication and information, sales of push-button telephones, word processors and facsimile machines etc. increased rapidly. Moreover, in the latter half of the 1980s the spread of the above-mentioned commodities was occurring along with characteristics of high classification and diversification, for example, multisound television (TV), big-type TV (over 21 inches), large refrigerators (over 300 liters), Hi-Fi VTR, home electronic products with fuzzy controls, air conditioners for both summer and winter, high-grade cars with over 2000 cc displacement etc.[9] As shown in Figure 1.3, households that have a number of the same durable consumer goods are increasing.

TABLE 1.15 Trends in Consumer and Wholesale Prices in Selected Countries
(Indices, 1985 = 100) (1980–89, s.y.)

Year	Japan		US		UK		F.R. Germany		France		Italy	
	CP	WP	CP	WP	CP	WP	CP	WP	CP	WP	CP	WP
1980	87.2	99.5	76.6	87.1	70.7	72.2	82.8	81.9	63.3	65.0	52.4	57.5
1983	95.8	100.7	92.6	98.2	89.8	89.8	95.7	94.9	88.0	87.7	83.2	84.4
1984	98.0	100.8	96.6	100.5	94.3	95.0	98.0	97.6	94.5	95.8	92.0	93.2
1985	100	100	100	100	100	100	100	100	100	100	100	100
1986	100.6	95.3	101.9	97.1	103.4	104.3	99.9	97.5	102.7	97.2	106.2	99.1
1987	100.7	92.3	105.6	99.7	107.7	108.3	100.1	95.1	105.9	97.8	111.1	101.7
1988	101.4	91.9	109.9	103.7	113.0	113.2	101.4	96.3	108.7	102.9	116.5	106.5
1989	103.7	93.6	115.2	108.8	121.8	119.0	104.2	99.3	112.7	108.6	124.2	113.3

CP, consumer prices; WP, wholesale prices.
Source: *Statistics on Japanese Standard of Living* [J]. 1991, Tokyo, p. 211.

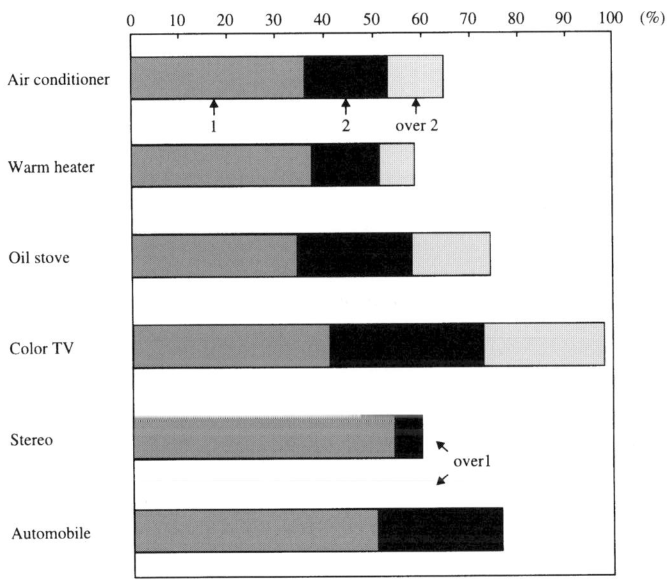

FIG. 1.3 Plural Possession of Durable Consumer Goods
Source: *Annual Report on the National Life* for Fiscal 1990 [J]. Tokyo, p. 159.

Furthermore, the rapid increase in the number of Japanese traveling abroad in recent years must be mentioned. This number steadily increased from 2.47 million in 1975, to 3.91 million in 1980, to 4.95 million in 1985 and exceeded 10 million in 1990. The total amount spent by Japanese tourists in 1990 must have reached approximately US$30 billion.[10] This increase in the number of Japanese traveling abroad depended mainly on the higher exchange rate for the Yen and the boom in the latter half of the 1980s and, consequently, overseas travel became not uncommon for the general public in Japan.

TABLE 1.16 Indicators of Social Capital and Living in Selected Countries

(Figures in parentheses: data year)

Items/Unit	Japan	UK	F.R. Germany	France	Italy	US
Waterworks ratio (%)	93.1 (1984)	99 (1984)	98 (1984)	98 (1984)	90 (1980)	99.3 (1977)
Sewerage ratio (%)	40 (1989)	95 (1982)	91 (1983)	64 (1983)	55 (1980)	73 (1986)
	Tokyo 23 Wards	London	Bonn	Paris	Rome	Washington
Per capita park area (m^2)	2.5 (1988)	30.4 (1976)	37.4 (1984)	12.2 (1984)	11.7 (1973)	45.7 (1976)
Ratio of superhighway extension km/1,000 Cars	85 (1988)	153 (1981)	306 (1981)	263 (1981)	309 (1981)	557 (1979)
Population per hospital bed, persons	79 (1986)	119 (1977)	89 (1982)	170 (1982)	103 (1979)	171 (1980)
	Tokyo	London	Bonn	Paris		New York
Ratio of under ground electric cables (%)	22.1 (1982)	100 (1982)	100 (1982)	100 (1982)	—	72.1 (1977)
Number of TV sets in use per 1,000 persons	587 (1987)	434 (1987)	385 (1987)	333 (1987)	257 (1987)	811 (1987)
Number of telephones in use per 1,000 persons	555 (1985)	524 (1984)	640 (1986)	608 (1985)	469 (1986)	760 (1982)
Number of passenger cars in use per 1,000 persons	251 (1988)	323 (1988)	475 (1988)	403 (1988)	424 (1987)	555 (1987)
Social security benefit, per capita, US$	2,275.6 (1989)	754.7 (1987)	2,273.7 (1988)	2,948.2 (1988)	2,491.3 (1988)	1,343.4 (1988)
Area of housing per capita, (m^2)	25.2 (1988)	35.2 (1988)	32 (1982)	30.7 (1984)	—	60.9 (1985)

Sources: *WPIT*, 1990, p. 261; *CEFS*, 1991, pp. 195–198.

Finally, the figures for social capital and national living of Japan will be compared international. As shown in Table 1.16, the population per hospital bed is better in Japan than in other selected countries. The waterworks ratio and social security benefits per capita are at relatively good levels. However, the sewage ratio, paved road ratio, park area per capita and the area of housing per capita are far lower than those of other countries. In this sense, we cannot say that economic development has resulted in a sufficient improvement of the fundamental living conditions in Japan.

However, with regard to crime, in 1989 the number of murders per 100,000 persons were (incidence number and arrest rate, respectively), 8.7 and 68.3% in the US, 9.1 and 78.0% in the UK, 3.9 and 94.4% in the F.R. Germany, 4.6 and 83.3% in France, and 1.1 and 95.9% in Japan. The number of thefts are, similarly, 5078 and 18.0% in the US, 5544 and 29.0% in the UK, 4148 and 28.8% in the F.R. Germany, 3716 and 16.3% in France, and 1204 and 41.7% in Japan. Apparently, the incidence rate in Japan is the lowest of all; conversely, the arrest rate in Japan is the highest. We can say that public peace and social life is very good in Japan.[11] Life expectancy at birth in 1989 in Japan was 75.91 and 81.77 years for males and females, respectively, with people in Japan having the longest life expectancy in the world.[12]

Notes

1. *CEFS*, 1972, p. 16; *op. cit.*, 1982, p. 5; *op. cit.*, 1991, p. 3.
2. *White Paper on Agriculture Japan* [J], 1990. Tokyo: Association of Agriculture and Forestry Statistics, p. 28.
3. *Ibid.*, p. 34; Okumura S. et al. (eds). *Data World Economy* [J]. Tokyo: Tokyo University Press, 1990, pp. 90f.
4. *Handbook of Labor Statistics in Japan* [J], 1984. Tokyo: Ministry of Labor, p. 207; *op. cit.*, 1991, p. 213.
5, *CEFS*, 1991, pp. 263f.
6. *WPJE*, 1991, p. 466; *ESA*, 1996, p. 361.
7. *Prices Report 1991* [J]. Tokyo: Economic Planning Agency, pp. 85, 98.
8. See: *Statistics on Japanese Standard of Living* [J], 1991. Tokyo: Center of National Life, pp. 90f.
9. *WPIT*, 1991, pp. 126f; *WPJE*, 1989, pp. 68–70.
10. *WPJE*, 1989, p. 66; *AM*, November 30, 1990.
11. *White Paper on Crime Japan* [J], 1991. Tokyo: Ministry of Justice, pp. 24f.
12. *Statistics on Japanese Standard of Living* [J]. 1991, p. 202.

Chapter 2
The Development of Foreign Trade

2.1 The Japanese Economy and Trade

World trade (exports) values have continued to increase since World War II under the IMF/GATT system, except in the early 1980s following the second oil crisis. The total amount of exports reached US$3,300 billion in 1990.[1]

Japan's share in world trade is as follows. Its export value ratios in 1980, 1985, and 1990 were 6.8%, 9.7%, and 8.6%, respectively (i.e. third following the F.R. Germany with corresponding export value ratios of 10.1%, 10.1%, and 12.6%, and the US with corresponding export value ratios of 11.8%, 12.0%, and 11.8%). Japan's import value ratios in 1980, 1985, and 1989 were 7.2%, 6.9%, and 7.0%, respectively (i.e. also third following the US with corresponding import value ratios of 13.1%, 18.7%, and 16.4%, and the F.R. Germany with corresponding import value ratios of 9.6%, 8.4%, and 9.0%). Both positions are very significant.[2]

Of course, because the Japanese GNP has been very large, the rates of dependence on foreign trade from 1985 to 1990 were 13.0%, 10.5%, 9.5%, 9.1%, 9.5%, and 9.7% with regard to exports 9.7%, 8.4%, 8.2%, 8.4%, 7.5%, and 7.9% and with regard to imports. These figures are very low. For example, the Japanese rate of dependence on exports in 1989 was 9.5%, which was higher than the rate of 7.0% of the US, but clearly lower than the UK's rate of 18.3%, the F.R. Germany's rate of 28.6%, France's rate of 18.7%, Italy's rate of 16.3%, Belgium's rate of 64.4% and the Netherlands' rate of 48.3%. The Japanese rate of dependence on imports in 1989 was 7.3%, which was lower than the rate of 9.5% of the US, and lower still than rates of the UK (23.7%), the F.R. Germany (22.6%), France (20.2%), Italy (17.8%), Belgium (63.4%) and the Netherlands (46.8%), (Of course, the Japan's dependence rates of both exports and imports were similarly lower in comparison with corresponding rates of Asian NIEs and ASEAN.)[3]

It is obvious, however, that foreign trade (both exports and imports) has a decisive impact on the Japanese national economy because of the fact that the so-called processing trade system has been an important feature in Japanese economic history since prewar times. In particular, the Japanese dependency rates on imports for main resources are, as Table 2.1 shows, absolutely and relatively high compared with other advanced countries. For this reason, and because of the low level of foodstuff self-sufficiency rates mentioned earlier, we must say that the smooth development of

TABLE 2.1 Dependency Rates of Main Resources on Imports in Selected Countries (1982,1988)
(Unit: %)

	Japan		US	F.R. Germany	UK	France
Energy	83.5		12.3	52.1	−10.8	76.1
	90.1[1]		16.4	55.8	−12.0	67.2
Coal	82.9	91.4[2]	−16.9	−0.6	−3.9	56.9
Petroleum	99.8	99.8	32.9	94.7	−26.2	98.3
Natural gas	91.4	95.5	4.1	65.4	24.6	74.5
Iron ore	99.7	99.7	23.8	96.7	95.3	31.8
Copper	95.9	99.6	31.4	99.8	99.8	100.0
Lead	87.0	87.8	52.7	91.1	98.5	97.0
Zinc	64.2	82.5	58.8	71.3	94.4	86.0
Tin	98.3		99.8	100.0	59.6	100.0
Aluminium	100.0		79.9	100.0	100.0	−200.3
Nickel	100.0		96.9	100.0	100.0	100.0
Wood	64.3	54.9	1.2	20.7	68.6	12.2
Wool	100.0		25.7	90.1	43.9	69.4
Raw cotton	100.0		−104.0	100.0	100.0	100.0
Soya Beans	95.1		−70.0	100.0	100.0	97.9
Maize	100.0		−29.8	61.3	100.0	−34.1
Wheat	88.0		−119.2	−0.3	10.9	−83.7

[1] The figures given on the second line of energy are for 1988.
[2] The figures given on the right of Japan are assumed to be for the end of the 1980s, judging from *WPJE*, 1991, pp. 356, 505, but not clearly stated there.
Sources: *WPIT*, 1984, p. 391; *CEFS*, 1991, p. 174.

foreign trade is a matter of life and death for Japan's national economy today. Conversely, Japan is the very country that has most enjoyed the benefits of the IMF/GATT system, which has supported the idea of free, multilateral and equal trading principles after World War II.

Japan's trade balance increased its excess of exports, as shown in Table 2.2, while keeping step with the development of the "high economic growth" period and, furthermore, in spite of the two oil crises (although we can see the reduction of trade surplus for a short term immediately following these crises), the growth of the trade surplus was realized on a larger scale, with the surplus value reaching US$100 billion for 1986–88. The ratio of current balance to GNP reached its maximum point of 4.2% in 1986 (3.6% in 1985 and 1987). This figure was unprecedented. A contributing factor in this increasing Japanese trade surplus was the high exchange rate fluctuation (i.e. its drastic shift to a strong Yen). Of course, other factors also contributed to the trade surplus, including the active technological innovation power of the Japanese economy, the strong competitiveness of its exports based on enterprise's efforts to increase its share in the world market and efforts for energy and resource conservation.[4]

However, the Japanese unilateral accumulation of an enormous trade surplus was criticized by international society, especially the US, and Japan was compelled to make efforts to reduce it (Maekawa Report in April 1986; Economic Management within a Global Context of the Takeshita Cabinet in May 1988).[5] In this situation, in order to reduce the trade surplus and to enlarge domestic demand, the Japanese government

TABLE 2.2 Japan's Trade Balance (1962–95)

(Unit: US$ million)

	Trade balance	Exports	Annual change %	Imports	Annual change %
1962	401	4,861		4,460	
1963	−166	5,391	10.9	5,557	24.6
1964	377	6,704	24.4	6,327	13.9
1965	1,901	8,332	24.3	6,431	1.6
1966	2,275	9,641	15.7	7,366	14.5
1967	1,160	10,231	6.1	9,071	23.1
1968	2,529	12,751	24.6	10,222	12.7
1969	3,699	15,679	23.0	11,980	17.2
1970	3,963	18,969	21.0	15,006	25.3
1971	7,787	23,566	24.2	15,779	5.2
1972	8,971	28,032	19.0	19,061	20.8
1973	3,688	36,264	29.4	32,576	70.9
1974	1,436	54,480	50.2	53,044	62.8
1975	5,028	54,734	0.5	49,706	−6.3
1976	9,887	66,026	20.6	56,139	12.9
1977	17,311	79,333	20.2	62,022	10.5
1978	24,596	95,634	20.5	71,038	14.5
1979	1,845	101,232	5.9	99,387	39.9
1980	2,125	126,736	25.2	124,611	25.4
1981	19,967	149,522	18.0	129,555	4.0
1982	18,079	137,663	−7.9	119,584	−7.7
1983	31,454	145,468	5.7	114,014	−4.7
1984	44,257	168,290	15.7	124,033	8.8
1985	55,986	174,015	3.4	118,029	−4.8
1986	92,827	205,591	18.1	112,764	−4.5
1987	96,386	224,605	9.2	128,219	13.7
1988	95,012	259,765	15.7	164,753	28.5
1989	76,917	269,570	3.8	192,653	16.9
1990	63,856	280,177	3.9	216,321	12.3
1991	77,789	314,525	9.6	236,737	0.8
1992	106,628	339,650	8.0	233,021	−1.6
1993	120,241	360,911	6.3	240,670	3.3
1994	120,858	395,600	9.6	274,742	14.2
1995	106,843	442,937	12.0	336,094	22.3

Sources: *Balance of Payments Monthly*, Bank of Japan, passim; *WPIT*, 1986, p. 104; *ESA*, 1990, p. 233; *White Paper of JETRO* [J], *Foreign Trade Part*, 1996, p. 63.

and the Bank of Japan reduced the official discount rate on a large scale (3.0% at the end of 1986; 2.5% in 1987; 2.5% in 1988) and stimulated internal business activity. Consequently, the bubble economy phenomenon accompanying an extraordinary rise in stock prices and the price of real estate took place and, under these circumstances, imports of manufactured goods from developing countries rapidly increased, as did imports of high-grade durable consumer goods, art works and precious metals from Western countries, thus decreasing the trade surplus.

However, this temporary reduction of the trade surplus depended, in reality, on the overheating of domestic consumption supported by the assets effect during the bubble economy. Practically at the same time when the monetary policy of the Bank of Japan turned to a tight financial position (4.25% at the end of 1989; 6.0% in 1990), excess equipment investment burst the bubble and business conditions moved towards a recession and the trade surplus increased again to US$103.3 billion in 1991.[6] To summarize, we cannot say that the temporary reduction of the trade surplus in 1989 and 1990 arose from an internal change of the Japanese economic structure to contribute to international cooperation and equilibrium.

Notes

1. *WPIT*, 1991, p. 70; *Annual Report on World Economy* [J], 1991. Tokyo: Economic Planning Agency, p. 359.
2. *CEFS*, 1991, p. 131.
3. *Ibid.*, p. 151.
4. *WPJE*, 1991, pp. 279f, 485.
5. Miyazaki I. *The Japanese Economy* [J]. Tokyo: Simul Press Inc., 1990, pp. 103, 151.
6. *ESA*, 1991, p. 233.

2.2 Trade by Commodity Group

Here I would like to look at the features of Japanese exports and imports classified by commodity groups and compare them internationally. First, let us look at exports. As shown in Table 2.3, Japanese exports in 1988 were highly specialized in industrial products, even among advanced countries, with their degree of specialization greater than that of German exports, which had previously been the most specialized. With regard to this, past ratios of machinery and transport equipment exported from Japan in 1955, 1960, 1965, 1970, 1975, 1980, 1985 were 12.3%, 23.2%, 31.2%, 40.5%, 49.2%, 58.6%, and 70.2%, respectively,[1] and we can see that the ratio increased rapidly during and after the period of high economic growth.

Incidentally, although Japanese export values indicated in US$ were, as shown in Table 2.2, increasing after 1985 during the shift to the phase of the strong Yen, their values indicated in ¥ were decreasing or stagnant (i.e. from ¥41.2 trillion in 1985 to ¥34.4 trillion in 1986, ¥32.4 trillion in 1987, ¥33.3 trillion in 1988, ¥37.2 trillion in 1989 and ¥40.4 trillion in 1990).[2] We can regard this situation as the result of the foreign strategy of Japanese enterprise, by which they tried to slough off outdated simple exports as a centric idea after the Plaza agreement at the end of 1985. For example, as Figure 2.1 shows, the exports ratio of manufacturing was reduced in the latter half of the 1980s, although that of electric and general machinery rose a little at the end of the 1980s.

Nevertheless, Japanese export values in US$ continued to increase during the large rise in the Exchange rate of the Yen, during the growth of the sophistication of the export structure and, further, with the increase in higher value-added products during the latter half of the 1980s and thereafter. For example, as shown in Table 2.4, there were many high value-added products from the processing and assembly industries in the higher ranked 20 commodities of the increased contribution ratio for Japanese exports from 1985 to 1990.[3] With regard to this, it is worth noting the strongly

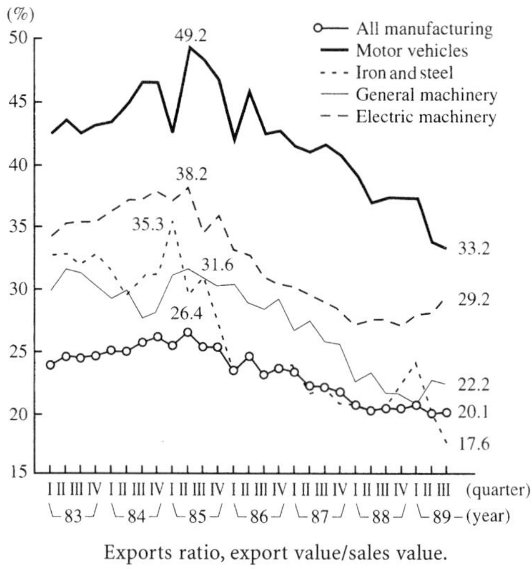

FIG. 2.1 Trends in the Export Ratio of Japan's Main Export Industry
Source: *WPIT* 1990, p. 219

competitive export abilities of Japanese high-technology products. The ratio of high-technology products in Japanese exports was 37.5% in 1987, which was greater than the 31.4% of the US, the 26.3% of the F.R. Germany, the 27.1% of France, and the 30.7% of the UK. In addition, the high-technology. specialization coefficient of Japan, calculated by the balance between imports and exports of high-technology goods/ their imports and exports, was 0.598 in 1987, which was far greater than the 0.097 of the US, the 0.168 of the F.R. Germany, the 0.010 of France, or the 0.004 of the UK.[4] From this, we can say that the strength and competitive superiority of Japan in high-technology goods is clear.

However, it is well known that, due to the above-mentioned situation, Japan has strong export competitive abilities and, consequently, has accumulated the largest trade surplus in the world (a particularly enormous sum of trade surplus value to the US recently amounting to between US$40 and 50 billion a year). This has become one of the biggest issues causing international trade friction today and, furthermore, has become an object of world criticism. With regard to this, it is also well known that certain Japanese goods (i.e. textiles, iron and steel and televisions since the 1960s, machine tools since the 1970s, and automobiles, DAT (digital audio taperecorder), VTR and semiconductors since the 1980s)[5] have caused international trade and commerce issues in the world, especially in Western countries.

Under these circumstances, Japanese manufacturing enterprises, especially those of transportation equipment and electrical machinery, strove to expand overseas production and, as a result, for example, the volume of automobiles exported from Japan to the US has been rapidly approaching the number of vehicles manufactured in the US at the following rate: 1916:50 (thousand) in 1983; 2218:221 in 1985; 2023:766 in 1988; 1719:1395 in 1990.[6] However, we must now note that this increase in overseas production has caused new international investment friction instead of (or in addition to) the former trade friction.[7]

TABLE 2.3 Composition of Exports and Imports by Commodity (1988)

(Units; US$ million, %; figures in parenthesis are for 1983)

	Item	SITC	Japan		US		UK	
				%		%		%
Exports	Foodstuffs	0,1	1,648	0.6 (0.9)	30,647	13.0 (13.8)	9,853	6.8 (7.0)
	Raw materials/fuels	2,3,4	2,611	1.0 (1.3)	31,351	13.3 (15.2)	14,141	9.7 (24.3)
	Industrial products	5,6,7,8	257,070	97.1 (96.8)	151,483	64.4 (68.1)	118,691	81.6 (66.1)
	Chemicals	5	13,904	5.3 (4.6)	21,758	9.3 (10.1)	20,187	13.9 (11.5)
	Machinery and transport	7	185,786	70.2 (63.8)	93,883	39.9 (42.3)	57,189	39.3 (30.3)
	Equipment							
	Motor vehicles	78	61,105	23.1 (22.3)	12,955	5.5 (7.4)	8,895	6.1 (5.1)
	Other i.p.	6,8	57,380	21.7 (28.3)	35,843	15.2 (15.6)	41,315	28.4 (24.3)
	Textiles/clothing	65,84	6,115	2.3 (4.1)	4,266	1.9 (1.7)	5,967	4.1 (3.6)
	Iron and steel	67	15,335	5.8 (8.7)	1,977	0.8 (0.8)	4,261	2.9 (2.2)
	Others	9	3,442	1.3 (1.0)	21,714	9.2 (2.9)	2,709	1.9 (2.6)
Imports	Foodstuffs	0,1	29,083	15.9 (11.9)	26,204	6.5 (7.6)	18,900	10.0 (12.0)
	Raw materials/fuels	2,4	29,156	15.9 (15.0)	10,040	2.5 (4.1)	10,655	5.6 (7.2)
	Fuels	3	38,913	21.2 (47.3)	43,471	10.7 (22.4)	8,970	4.7 (10.8)
	Industrial products	5,6,7,8	84,066	45.9 (25.0)	313,677	77.6 (63.7)	149,116	78.6 (68.6)
	Chemicals	5	14,196	7.7 (5.6)	17,378	4.3 (4.2)	16,583	8.7 (7.8)
	Machinery and transport	7	23,152	12.6 (7.1)	174,820	43.2 (33.2)	71,405	37.6 (30.9)
	Equipment							
	Motor vehicles	78	3,806	2.1 (0.5)	59,400	14.7 (14.0)	20,041	10.6 (8.8)
	Other i.p.	6,8	46,719	25.5 (12.2)	121,479	30.0 (26.3)	61,128	32.2 (29.9)
	Textiles/clothing	65,84	10,673	5.8 (2.5)	25,612	6.4 (5.1)	12,013	6.3 (6.0)
	Iron and Steel	67	4,607	2.5 (1.1)	11,604	2.9 (2.8)	4,218	2.2 (1.2)
	Others	9	2,034	1.1 (0.9)	11,062	2.7 (2.2)	2,106	1.1 (1.4)

	Item	SITC	F.R.Germany		France		Italy	
				%		%		%
Exports	Foodstuffs	0,1	15,293	4.7 (5.0)	24,825	15.4 (15.8)	8,456	6.6 (6.5)
	Raw materials/fuels	2,3,4	10,908	3.4 (5.7)	10,664	6.6 (8.3)	4,690	3.7 (7.2)
	Industrial products	5,6,7,8	293,104	90.9 (86.8)	126,050	78.0 (75.3)	114,702	89.7 (85.8)
	Chemicals	5	43,848	13.6 (13.2)	23,634	14.6 (13.0)	10,170	8.0 (8.4)
	Machinery and transport	7	155,404	48.2 (45.6)	56,877	35.2 (34.1)	45,806	35.8 (32.1)
	Equipment							
	Motor vehicles	78	54,678	17.0 (15.8)	18,155	11.2 (10.6)	9,796	7.7 (6.5)
	Other i.p.	6,8	93,852	29.1 (28.0)	45,539	28.2 (28.3)	58,726	45.9 (45.3)
	Textiles/clothing	65,84	15,903	5.0 (4.7)	7,929	4.9 (5.0)	16,507	12.9 (12.0)
	Iron and steel	67	13,542	4.2 (4.7)	7,805	4.8 (5.3)	4,490	3.5 (4.5)
	Others	9	3,250	1.0 (2.5)	163	0.1 (0.5)	1	0 (0.5)
Imports	Foodstuffs	0,1	26,143	10.5 (11.0)	18,240	10.3 (10.5)	17,689	13.1 (13.1)
	Raw materials/fuels	2,4	17,070	6.9 (7.5)	8,730	4.9 (5.6)	13,044	9.6 (9.4)
	Fuels	3	19,188	7.7 (21.3)	14,583	8.3 (24.6)	14,816	10.9 (31.5)
	Industrial products	5,6,7,8	180,507	72.5 (57.8)	135,076	76.4 (59.2)	89,946	66.4 (44.8)
	Chemicals	5	24,274	9.7 (8.2)	19,619	11.1 (9.1)	16,081	11.9 (9.3)
	Machinery and transport	7	73,027	29.3 (21.9)	58,883	33.3 (24.3)	40,138	29.6 (18.0)
	Equipment							
	Motor vehicles	78	17,831	7.2 (5.0)	15,717	8.9 (6.6)	12,536	9.3 (5.5)
	Other i.p.	6,8	83,206	33.4 (27.6)	56,573	32.0 (25.9)	33,727	24.9 (17.4)
	Textiles/clothing	65,84	23,175	9.3 (7.8)	11,893	6.7 (5.4)	6,691	5.0 (3.6)
	Iron and steel	67	9,339	3.8 (3.4)	6,087	3.4 (3.3)	5,293	3.9 (2.7)
	Others	9	6,071	2.4 (2.5)	116	0.1 (0.1)	4	0 (1.3)

i.p., industrial products.
Sources: *CEFS*, 1991, pp. 139–146; *op.cit.*, 1985, pp. 19f.

TABLE 2.4 The Higher Ranked 20 Commodities of Increased Contribution Ratio for Japanese Exports 1985–1990

	Item	Contribution ratio	Growth rate
1	Passenger cars	14.6	10.4
2	Semiconductors and other electronic components	7.7	22.9
3	Computers	6.8	21.4
4	Car spare parts	5.1	15.7
5	Computer spare parts	4.9	41.5
6	Power generating machines	3.2	17.5
7	TV cameras	3.0	29.2
8	Cable communications equipment	1.9	16.4
9	Buses/trucks	1.5	4.1
10	Electronic measurement equipment	1.5	19.5
11	Machine tools	1.3	13.0
12	Photo materials	1.2	13.5
13	Tankers	1.0	22.3
14	Mechanical shovels/excavators	0.9	15.3
15	Pump for liquids	0.9	24.2
16	Tires and tubes	0.8	9.9
17	Heterocyclic compounds	0.8	18.4
18	Air compressors	0.8	17.6
19	Stainless steel	0.7	12.2
20	Oil products	0.7	27.1
20 Commodities' total		59.0	15.0
Others		41.0	7.1
Total		100.0	10.3

Source: *WPIT*, 1991, p. 139.

Next, imports will be examined according to commodity group. As shown in Table 2.3, comparing the component in 1983 with that in 1988, the ratio of foodstuffs increased from 11.9% to 15.9%, that of raw materials did not change much between 15.0% and 15.9%, while that of fuels fell sharply from 47.3% to 21.2%. Apparently the total ratio of raw materials and fuels in imports fell largely from 62.3% to 37.1% and the ratio of total primary products, including foodstuffs, in imports was reduced from 74.2% to 53.0%. However, the ratio of primary products in Japanese imports is considerably higher. And, in comparison with other advanced countries that are developing horizontal trade, in which industrial products play a central role, Japan still firmly keeps to the classic vertical-type of processing trade, where raw materials and fuels are imported and industrial products are exported.

Yet, it is still epoch making that the ratio of manufactured products in Japanese imports, which was merely 25% in 1983, reached 50.3% in 1989. (Those imports of the EC and the US were over 50% in 1962 and 1964, respectively.) The increase of this ratio in Japanese imports was caused mainly by the increased import of capital goods, intermediate goods and consumption goods from Western countries, NIEs and ASEAN etc. in the boom period of the latter half of the 1980s,[8] and the fact that oil prices had been at a low, stable position in the latter half of the 1980s (the average import price per barrel on a customs clearance basis in 1981, 1985, 1986, 1987, 1988,

1989, and 1990 was US$37.3, 28.7, 16.40, 17.79, 15.6, 16.72, and 22.3, respectively.[9] Although the ratio of manufactured products in Japanese imports was rapidly increasing, the ratio of motor vehicles and electric machinery in imports was still small, at 2.1% (export 23.1%) and 3.9% (export 21.6%), respectively, compared with exports (even though it must be conceded that their import ratios had increased compared with import ratios of 0.5% and 2.0%, respectively, in 1983).[10]

Notes

1. *CEFS*, 1972, p. 93; *op. cit.*, 1982, p. 13; *op. cit.*, 1983, p. 110; *op. cit.*, 1991, p. 142.
2. *ESA*, 1990, p. 231.
3. *WPIT*, 1990, pp. 218–221.
4. *WPJE*, 1991, pp. 282, 486.
5. *WPIT*, 1991, p. 114f.
6. *White Paper of JETRO* [J], *Investment Part*, 1992, p. 72.
7. See: Sasaki K. *Japanese Type Multinational Corporations. From Trade Friction to Investment Friction* [J]. Tokyo: Yuhikaku, 1986.
8. *WPIT*, 1991, pp. 156f.
9. *WPJE*, 1991, p. 292; *The Weekly Toyo Keizai* [J], August 6, 1988, p. 25; *op. cit.*, July 4, 1992, p. 144.
10. *CEFS*, 1991, p. 146.

2.3 Trade by Region and Country

Japanese trade by region in 1989 was as follows. For exports, Japanese trade with North America, Asia and Europe was 38.6%, 32.7% and 22.0%, respectively; for imports, the ratio of Japanese trade with Asia, North America, Europe and Oceania was 41.5%, 28.3%, 18.4% and 6.7%, respectively. Compared with figures for 1980, in terms of exports the positions of North America and Asia were reversed because their ratios had been 29.3% and 38.0%, respectively, in 1980. In terms imports, trade with Asia was greatly reduced and that with Europe and North America was increased, because their ratios in 1980 had been 57.1%, 21.8% and 8.9%, respectively. It is obvious that the increase in the export ratio to North America was caused by the expansion of the export of industrial products from Japan to the US, exported, where transportation equipment and electrical machinery were the main products and that the decrease in the import ratio from Asia was caused by a reduction in the absolute (oil) and relative values of raw materials and fuel imports.[1]

As to Japanese trade ratios by country in 1983 and 1989; as shown in Table 2.5, the US continues to hold a vital position in terms of trade with Japan today. The Japanese trade balance with the US has changed over these 10 years and the respective export values to the US, import values from the US, and Japanese trade balance (US$ billion) arc 38.6, 25.3, and 13.3 in 1981; 36.3, 24.2, and 12.2 in 1982; 42.8, 24.6, and 18.2 in 1983; 59.9, 26.9, and 33.1 in 1984; 65.3, 25.8, and 39.5 in 1985; 80.5, 29.1, 51.4 in 1986; 83.6, 31.5, and 52.1 in 1987; 89.6, 42.0, and 47.6 in 1988, 93.2, 48.2, and 44.9 in 1989; and 90.3, 52.4, and 38.0 in 1990.[2] Japan's trade surplus reached a peak at approximately US$50 billion in 1986 and 1987. Although decreasing after that, Japan's trade surplus remained at the high level of US$38 billion in 1990. Specifically, looking at the upper-

TABLE 2.5 Percentage Distribution of Japanese Trade by Country (1989)

(Unit: %; figures in parenthesis are for 1983)

	Exports		Imports	
1	US	33.9 (29.1)	US	22.9 (19.5)
2	Republic of Korea	6.0 (4.1)	Republic of Korea	6.2 (2.7)
3	F.R. Germany	5.8 (4.0)	Australia	5.5 (5.3)
4	Taiwan	5.6 (3.5)	China	5.3 (4.0)
5	Hong Kong	4.2 (3.6)	Indonesia	5.2 (8.2)
6	UK	3.9 (3.4)	F.R. Germany	4.3 (—)
7	Singapore	3.4 (3.0)	Taiwan	4.3 (2.1)
8	China	3.1 (3.3)	Canada	4.1 (3.5)
9	Australia	2.8 (2.9)	Saudi Arabia	3.3 (12.3)
10	Thailand	2.5 (—)	France	2.6 (—)
	Others	28.9 (38.5)	Others	36.3 (36.6)

Sources: *Statistical Handbook of Japan*, 1991, Tokyo: Management and Coordination Agency, p. 85; *op.cit.*, 1984, p. 85.

level export items to the US in 1990, these Japanese surplus exports were passenger cars (export value US$21 billion), computers (US$5.8 billion), car spare parts (US$5.3 billion), office equipment spare parts (US$4.0 billion), semiconductor integrated circuits (US$2.9 billion), radio receivers and TV cameras (US$2.3 billion), motortrucks (US$2.0 billion), VTR (US$2.0 billion), copying machines (US$1.7 billion), and power generating machines (US$1.6 billion). Durable consumer goods for people's livelihood and microelectronics equipment, where the comparative superiority of Japan is clear, were exported on a large scale. Conversely, Japanese imports of upper-level items from the US included airplanes (import value US$2.4 billion), computers (US$2.2 billion), timber (US$2.0 billion), corn (US$2.0 billion), semiconductor integrated circuits (US$1.8 billion) office equipment spare parts (US$1.4 billion), fish (US$1.2 billion), turbo jet airplanes (US$1.0 billion), aluminum (US$1.0 billion), and cigarettes (US$1.0 billion). Here we see both technologically advanced goods and primary commodities being imported together.[3]

Thus, Japan's trade surplus with the US, besides that with Asian NIEs, Germany, the UK and the Netherlands, was quite large, although, to be sure, there were countries with which the Japanese trade balance was in deficit. The main countries with which the Japanese trade balance deficit was more than US$1 billion in 1990 were, in order of volume, Indonesia (US$7.7 billion), The United Arab Emirates (US$7.5 billion), Saudi Arabia (US$7.1 billion), China (US$5.9 billion), Australia (US$5.5 billion), Iran (US$2.0 billion), Qatar (US$2.0 billion), Brazil (US$1.9 billion), Canada (US$1.7 billion), Italy (US$1.6 billion), Oman (US$1.5 billion), France (US$1.5 billion), Kuwait (US$1.3 billion), Brunei (US$1.2 billion), Switzerland (US$1.2 billion), and Chile (US$1.1 billion).[4] These are mainly countries from which Japan imports raw materials and fuels.

Japanese ratios in terms of export values of the main regions of the world, in 1989 were 12.2% for the US, 2.0% for EC, 14.1% for Asian NIEs, 24.3% for ASEAN, 17.1% for the Middle and Near East, and 6.5% for other regions. Thus, we can judge that, particularly for Asian NIEs and ASEAN countries, the increase in Japanese imports from these countries is important for their economic development.[5]

In connection with this, looking at the export and import ratios of major advanced

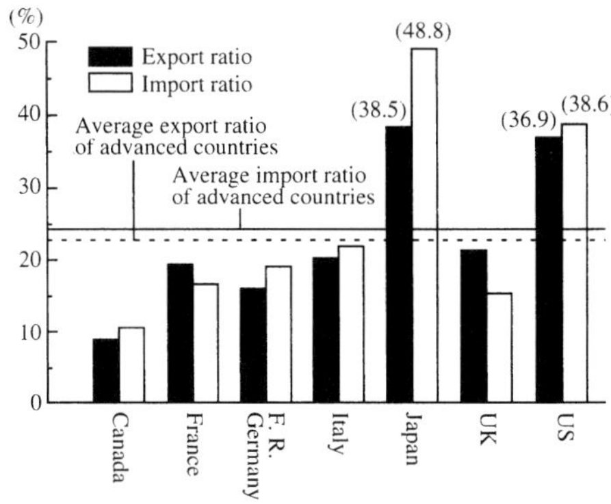

Export ratio, export values for developing countries/total export values ×100; import ratio, import values for developing coutries/total import values ×100

FIG. 2.2 Export and Import Ratios of Major Advanced Countries with Developing Countries (1988)
Source: *WPIT*, 1990, p. 144.

countries with developing countries, as shown in Figure 2.2, those of Japan were considerable higher than those of other countries in 1988 and, in particular, the import ratio of Japan was very high at 48.8%. We can guess that this is deeply connected with the component of Japanese trade through the above-mentioned commodity groups. At the same time, this indicates that it is very important for Japan to build fair and democratic international trade relations with developing countries.

Notes

1. Matsuba M. *An Essay on Contemporary Japanese Capitalism*, *op. cit.*, 1987, p. 41; *Statistical Handbook of Japan*, 1991. Tokyo: Management and Coordination Agency Japan, pp. 86f; *ESA*, 1990, p. 243.
2. *WPIT*, 1991, p. 193.
3. *Ibid.*, p. 380.
4. *Ibid.*, p. 187.
5. *Ibid.*, p. 161.

2.4 The Continuation of the Trade Surplus and the Deindustrialization Problem

2.4.1 Trends in the Trade Balance and Development of the Strong Yen

Japan's trade surplus, which broke the U$100 billion mark to be US$103 billion in 1991, rose further to US$132.3 billion in 1992 and to US$141.4 billion in 1993. Mean while, respective values for Japanese exports and imports were US$306.6 and 203.5 billion in 1991, US$330.9 and 198.5 billion in 1992, and US$351.3 and 209.9 billion in 1993. The "steady" increase of export values and the stagnation of import values is obvious.

However, these figures are in US dollars and the situation is different when viewed in terms of yen. The figures for trade balance, export value, and import value, respectively, were ¥13.84, 41.21 and 27.37 trillion in 1991, ¥16.75, 41.87 and 25.12 trillion in 1992, ¥15.69, 38.97 and 23.29 trillion in 1993. The value of each item in yen decreased from 1992 to 1993, while in terms of US dollars the value increased during the same years. This reflects the rapid rise of the yen's external value (i.e. the rapid and higher yen quotation to US dollars).[1]

In any case, Japan's trade surplus (and current surplus) is enormous and this trends has continued for nearly 10 years, aside from the temporary reduction of the surplus during the bubble economy. This is the fundamental economic basis of the present stronger yen.

Here I would like to introduce an interesting idea from Richard Koo regarding the causal relationship between the strong yen and the enormous trade surplus. Generally speaking, as a countermeasure for the excessively strong yen, an increase in imports because of increased domestic demand and the opening of internal markets, and then a reduction in the trade surplus have been advocated (the Maekawa Report and other economic policies of the Japanese government always state this). However, Koo says that with regard to Japan's trade surplus, this relationship of cause and effect is reversed. Because of Japan's closed domestic market, Japanese imports, which should increase together with the strong yen, do not increase. Therefore, if the closed domestic market is not broken down and an external open market is not enhanced in Japan, imports do not increase and the trade surplus value does not decrease. (There is another way to decrease Japan's trade surplus by reducing exports, but this leads to a balance at a reduced level and causes many larger and more difficult problems both domestically and internationally.) Accordingly, the situation of an excessively strong yen (it is said that the purchasing power parity is US$1 = ¥160–200) is not corrected.[2]

This excessively strong yen has caused serious problems to the Japanese economy itself. One problem is the occurrence of huge appraisal losses in Japanese assets abroad and the other is the deindustrialization problem of the Japanese economy.

Although it is well known that foreign assets are always confronted with the occurrence of appraisal losses by changes in the foreign exchange rate, the following appraisal losses occurred from 1983 to 1992, along with the development of the strong yen (minus signs indicate losses): –¥2 trillion in 1983, 0 in 1984, ¥4 trillion in 1985, –¥14 trillion in 1986, –¥10 trillion in 1987, –¥9 trillion in 1988, –¥7 trillion in 1989, ¥6 trillion in 1990, –¥7 trillion in 1991 and 0 in 1992.[3] Finally, appraisal losses reached the staggering amount of ¥39 trillion. These figures show macroeconomic appraisal losses. Naturally, many major institutional investors in Japan, life insurance companies included, suffered huge appraisal losses (especially of foreign bonds) of their own foreign assets in the latter half of the 1980s. This is why these companies have hesitated to invest in foreign bonds since the 1990s. This then discourages large dollar purchases and reinforces the strong yen.

I will refer to the deindustrialization problem in some detail in Section 2.4.3, and will only briefly touch on this issue here. Because of the excessively strong yen, separated from the purchasing power parity, the Japanese economic sectors and enterprises that hold sufficient competitive power in international markets lose their competitive power and are compelled to transfer their companies and factories to foreign countries. This may lead to the loss of the core of the Japanese economy, with its strong competitive power in manufacturing, especially the assembling and processing sectors, and to very serious problems (including the intensification of the employment problem) for the Japanese economy in the future.

2.4.2 The Closed Nature of the Japanese Domestic Market and the Large Differentials Between Foreign and Domestic Prices

The closed nature of the Japanese market has been frequently commented on both at home and abroad in recent years. This problem will be examined in terms of its external side (i.e. the degree to which the market is open) and its internal side (i.e. the existence of many official regulations).

Is it true that the Japanese market is externally exclusive? The Japanese (MITI, Ministry of International Trade and Industry) bureaucrats strongly deny this on the grounds that the Japanese general rate of tariffs is the lowest among the advanced countries. However, even if we acknowledge this, we cannot help finding that there are still many (de facto) import barriers in Japan that do not accord with Japan's stage of economic development and the demands of the era in all fields of goods, services and funds.

To begin with, I would like to look at the degree to which the market is opened indirectly (but most effectively) by the difficult factors of Japanese direct domestic investment. As discussed in Chapter 3, outstanding direct foreign investment and direct domestic investment were nearly balanced in the US and European advanced countries, while in Japan, in 1990, these values were US$201.4 and 9.9 billion, respectively, and, thus, the import value was only 4.9% of the export value. Determination of the reasons why this imbalance occurred, namely the reason why direct investment to Japan is so difficult for foreign countries, requires an evaluation of the degree to which the Japanese market is open at the levels of goods, services and funds.

Regarding this problem, the regulations created by the Foreign Exchange and Foreign Trade Control Law were abolished except for economic sectors recognized by the OECD and, in this sense, direct regulations by law are not practiced and, therefore, we may be able to say that, de jure, the Japanese market is not exclusive. However, there are many de facto impediments for investment and economic activity, as mentioned below.

First, there are economic factors. (1) Land prices and personnel expenses are very high and these cause investment costs (especially primary costs) to escalate. (2) There are many large rival enterprises in Japan. Relating to this, one should remember that the six large corporation groups have their own enterprises in almost all fundamental economic sectors and these enterprises have already built up their powerful economic and social positions. It is very difficult for foreign entrepreneurs to enter the market and to compete with them. (3) The existence of so-called *Keiretsu* (corporate groups), the complicated distribution and retailing system, and exclusionary business customs are big impeding factors to foreign enterprises. (4) In addition, the generally low profitability of the Japanese market and, relating with this, the low expected earning rate should be taken into account.

Second, there are customary factors. (1) Because the geographic and cultural distance is very large, it is very difficult for foreigners, especially from western countries, to understand and acquire Japanese language skills and customs. (2) With regard to the employment of talented personnel, in the existing Japanese employment system it is extremely difficult for foreign enterprises to get talented new personnel. (3) Demand for the quality of the commodity and service inclusive of aftercare among Japanese consumers is high. Marketing and advertising in the Japanese market will bring about a few difficulties for foreign enterprises.

Third, there are many regulations enforced by ordinances and administrative guidelines. As mentioned earlier, direct regulations by law do not fundamentally exist in Japan, but regulations by ordinances and administrative guidelines concerning certain businesses do exist. Although these regulations are applied equally to both Japanese and foreign enterprises according to the rules, in practice they have a greater restraining effect on foreign enterprises.[4]

These are the factors that present difficulties for direct foreign investment in Japan; however, they work more or less as factors making Japan's imports difficult not only in the case of capital but also in the case of commodity trade.

On the internal side of the closed nature of the Japanese market, there are many official regulations unsuitable for the demands of the present era in Japan. The present situation was examined by trends in the number of administrative permissions and appraisals and it was found that there were 10,054 cases in 1985, 10,169 cases in 1987, 10,441 cases in 1989, 10,717 cases in 1991, and 11,402 cases in 1993. The number of cases has increased consistently. Classified by ministry, the number of cases in 1993 was 1986 cases in (Ministry of) International Trade and Industry; 1893 cases in Transport; 1,427 cases in Agriculture, Forestry and Fisheries; 1,387 cases in Finance; 1,221 cases in Health and Welfare; 910 cases in Construction; 631 cases in Labor; 333 cases in Education; 319 cases in Posts and Telecommunications; 303 cases in Science and Technology Agency; and 188 cases in Environment Agency 188 and so on.[5] Due to government investigation of the economic fields regulated by the relevant laws, 42% of all the value added in Japan is under these regulations. In particular, in the sectors of mining, construction, finance/insurance/securities, and electricity/gas/water, 100% of the value added is under these regulations. Similarly, in transportation/communications, agriculture/forest/fisheries, and in manufacturing 97.3%, 87.1%, and 14.1% of the value added is under these regulations.

Of course, not all these regulations are necessarily injurious and needless. There are social regulations necessary for social security, public welfare, the protection of the environment and the prevention of disaster, as well as economic regulations to counter market failure. However, some regulations have led to the hindrance of newcomers and to the protection of vested interests, and have resulted in economic inefficiency and have disadvantaged consumers. This must also be taken into consideration.

Therefore, we must reexamine in earnest the existing official regulations. In particular, because these regulations were made from the standpoint of protecting producers since the postwar restoration period and the high economic growth period, we must now reexamine them from the standpoint of consumer protection. Then, we must boldly reconsider the official regulations unsuitable for the demands of the present era, and deregulate or abolish them.[6]

Relating to the closed nature of the Japanese market, the differentials between commodity prices at home and abroad became larger. In a macroeconomic perspective,

TABLE 2.6 Cost of Living: an International Comparison of Prices (November 1993; Tokyo prices compared to other cities)

	New York	London	Paris	Berlin
All items	1.48	1.49	1.37	1.41
Rice	2.10	2.12	2.59	2.13
Imported meat	1.86	—	1.20	1.91
Milk	2.50	2.31	1.79	1.94
Orange juice	1.29	1.55	—	1.41
Beer	2.45	1.43	3.25	1.86
Suit	1.35	1.65	1.42	2.36
Blazer for woman	1.97	1.95	1.32	1.45
Briefs for man	1.45	0.76	0.37	0.50
Tennis racket	1.26	1.07	1.05	0.99
Fishing rod	1.35	0.76	0.28	0.63
Hair tonic	1.71	0.95	1.23	1.10
Lipstick	5.33	—	3.72	4.87

For example, rice in Tokyo is 2.1-fold the price of rice in New York.
A survey by the Economic Planning Agency, Japan.
Source: *AE*, August 14, 1994.

when we looked at the price differentials with the figures dividing the purchasing power parity by the exchange rate (US = 1), the figures for Japan increased rapidly since the latter half of the 1980s and were considerably larger than those of Germany, France and the UK. In 1992, Japan's purchasing power parity/exchange rate was 1.50, while in Germany, France, and the UK it was 1.37, 1.24 and 1.14, respectively (Japan's figure reached 1.8 or 1.9 in 1994, assuming that the purchasing power parity is equal to that of 1992).[7]

Table 2.6 shows the price differentials with regard to individual commodities. Apparently, the price level in Tokyo was, as of November 1993, 1.48-, 1.49-, 1.37-, and 1.4-fold that of New York, London, Paris, and Berlin, respectively. All these differentials were higher than those in the previous year. One of the reasons for this was the development of a stronger yen; that is, because of this Japanese domestic prices rose more in terms of US dollars in comparison with foreign prices. However, it is also an obvious fact that factors such as high land prices, exclusive business customs as well as the distribution system and many official regulations etc. have directly and indirectly prevented Japanese consumers from enjoying the benefits of the decrease in the price of imported goods. It is to be desired that these factors are reformed and that Japan's market becomes increasingly more open.

2.4.3 The Continuing Strong Yen and the Deindustrialization Problem

Since the strong yen broke through the level of US$1 = ¥100 in June 1994, export prices for sale below cost of not a few Japanese enterprises have come into the open. The problem of deindustrialization is seriously discussed not only in industrial circles, but also among Japanese people generally.

Although this deindustrialization problem was once intensively discussed in the rapid strong yen phase after the Plaza Agreement in 1985, internal deindustrialization was not realized as a consequence of the arrival of the boom in the latter half of the 1980s.

However, while the recession after the collapse of the bubble boom has lasted beyond all expectations and although business circles do not have a clear view of how to get out of this recession, the strong yen level beyond US$1 = ¥100 has arrived. This situation has increased doubts and fears regarding the deindustrialization of Japanese industry and the economy.

Generally, "deindustrialization" signifies three mutually relevant elements as follows: (1) to substitute imports for internal production as a result of the defeat of internal products in competition by import products; (2) to substitute production abroad for internal production for exports, because exports become unprofitable and production abroad becomes advantageous because of the changing foreign exchange rate; and (3) consequently, because of the reduction of the internal production basis in manufacturing industries, there is a substitution of non-manufacturing for manufacturing (the development of a service economy).[8] Of these, it is the second case that we will deal with here. Many Japanese people are anxious about the reduction of internal production and employment and, furthermore, the increase in bankruptcy and the intensification of the unemployment problem that may be brought about by deindustrialization.

Now, with regard to the manufacturing industry, the ratio of the overseas production value to total domestic sales of Japanese enterprise was at a low level (6.6% in 1992; compared with 27.5% in the US in 1991 and 19.6% in the F.R. Germany in 1989). However, the Japanese ratio classified by industrial sector in 1991 reached 13.7% for transport equipment and 11.0% for electrical equipment.[9]

From these figures, we can forecast that the overseas production ratio of Japanese enterprises will increase further in the future. However, it is a question of under which conditions the situation advances and with what kind of problems and contradictions it develops. Of course, the fact that direct foreign investment is practised in manufacturing sectors does not immediately and directly signify deindustrialization. However, if an industry that originally has adequate international competitiveness under the purchasing power parity is obliged to transfer abroad because of the extremely high exchange rate for the yen too far apart from its purchasing power parity, then there is a significant possibility that the transfer abroad will lead to deindustrialization.[10]

In contrast, if we do not lower the ratio of plant and equipment investment in manufacturing to GDP and succeed in the sophistication of the industrial structure and the creation of new employment there, it is possible for us to avoid deindustrialization of the internal economy.[11]

The Japan of today stands between these two possibilities. The desirable direction and measures are as follows. First, to mitigate or abolish the unsuitable and unnecessary official regulations and to enhance the degree to which the internal market is open for the sake of the adequate return of the macroeconomic strong yen's merit to the consumer. Second, to increase Japanese imports and to correct the differentials between commodity prices at home and abroad and, by this means, to restrain the development of an excessively strong yen. Third, to realize the sophistication of the industrial structure in connection with enlargement of new business frontiers,[12] and to reset the Japanese economy with new and appropriate relations of international specialization.

Notes

1. *ESA*, 1993, pp. 328, 330.
2. Koo R. *Good Strong Yen and Bad Strong Yen* [J]. Tokyo: Toyo Keizai Inc., 1994, Ch. 1.
3. *WPIT*, 1994, p. 167.
4. *WPIT*, 1994, pp. 204–208; *WPJE*, 1994, pp. 118–120; *White Paper of JETRO* [J], *Investment Part*, 1994, p. 89.
5. Iwasaki H. *Japan Controlled by Bureaucrats is in Crisis* [J]. Tokyo: Goma Shobo, 1994, p. 25.
6. *WPJE*, 1994, pp. 363–367.
7. *Ibid.*, pp. 314f, 673.
8. *WPJE*, 1994, p. 279.
9. *White Paper of JETRO*, 1994, *op. cit.*, pp. 65f.
10. See the statement by R. Koo in the interview published in *The Weekly Toyo Keizai* [J], September 10, 1994, p. 20; Tanaka H. Overseas Transfer and Deindustrialization Are Not Directly Connected [J]. In: *NM*, August 9, 1994.
11. Shinpo S. Deindustrialization Arises From the Stagnation of Investment [J]. In: *NM*, August 22, 1994.
12. Suzuki Y. *Future Image of the Japanese Economy* [J]. Tokyo: Toyo Keizai Inc., 1994, p. 95.

Chapter 3
The Development of Foreign Investment

3.1 The Present Stage of Japanese Capital Exports

Japan's long-term capital balance has increased its excess outflow, as shown in Table 3.1, based on its large surplus of current balance, increasing after 1981 and especially in the latter half of the 1980s. The scale of Japan's capital balance reached US$130 billion in 1986/88 (the greater part of it flowed into advanced countries, namely the US and EC, with its main form being securities investment). Japan became the largest capital supplier country during this period. However, the balance decreased rapidly after 1989 (this was caused by a rise on interest rates and an increase in the demand for funds in Japan, the acquisition of Japanese stock by foreigners etc.) to stand at US$43.6 billion in 1990, which was 32% of the maximal value in 1987.[1]

Furthermore, according to statistics on Japanese assets and liabilities abroad, the outstanding amount of direct foreign investments and foreign securities investments in the private sector of long-term assets at the end of 1989 were US$154.4 and 533.8 billion, respectively, and their ratio was 22.4:77.6. Thus, with regard to Japanese capital exports, the ratio of securities investments was much larger than that of direct investments.[2] However, we must not underestimate the position and role of Japanese direct foreign investments in the international economy. As we will soon see, Japanese foreign investment is, with regard to both flow and stock, in the top ranks among major countries and its position is very steady in the world economy. Next, the main trends in direct investment, securities investment and official development assistance will be examined.

First, looking back at the development of Japanese direct foreign investments based on a report to the Ministry of Finance in fiscal year (FY), the values (given as US$) changed as follows: total value for 1951–59 US$196 million, 93 in 1960, 166 in 1961, 99 in 1962, 126 in 1963, 120 in 1964, 159 in 1965, 227 in 1966, 275 in 1967, 557 in 1968, 665 in 1969, 904 in 1970, 858 in 1971, US$2.34 billion in 1972 (the following figures are in billions of dollars), 3.49 in 1973, 2.4 in 1974, 3.28 in 1975, 3.46 in 1976, 2.81 in 1977, 4.6 in 1978, 5.0 in 1979, 4.69 in 1980, 8.93 in 1981, 7.7 in 1982, 8.15 in 1983, 10.16 in 1984, 12.22 in 1985, 22.32 in 1986, 33.36 in 1987, 47.02 in 1988, 67.54 in 1989, and 56.91 in 1990.[3] Obviously the increase in the 1980s, especially in the latter half, was outstanding.

TABLE 3.1 Trends in the Current Balance and Long-term Capital of Japan (1980–94)

(Unit: US$ million, %)

Year	Current balance		Long-term capital		
		Ratio to GNP	Balance	Assets	Liabilities
1980	−10,746	−1.1	2,324	−10,817	13,141
1981	4,770	0.4	−9,672	−22,809	13,137
1982	6,850	0.7	−14,969	−27,418	12,449
1983	20,799	1.8	−17,700	−32,459	14,759
1984	35,003	2.8	−49,651	−56,775	7,124
1985	49,169	3.6	−64,542	−81,815	17,273
1986	85,845	4.2	−131,461	−132,095	634
1987	87,015	3.6	−136,532	−132,830	−3,702
1988	79,631	2.7	−130,930	−149,883	18,953
1989	57,157	2.0	−89,246	−192,118	102,872
1990	35,761	1.2	−43,586	−120,766	77,180
1991	72,901	2.1	37,057	−121,446	158,503
1992	117,551	3.1	−28,459	−57,962	29,503
1993	131,441	3.0	−78,336	−73,608	−4,728
1994	129,333	2.7	−81,857	−109,980	28,123

Sources: *Ministry of Finance Statistics Monthly* [J], August 1991, Tokyo, p. 1; *ESA*, 1994, pp. 332–335; *CEFS*, 1996, p. 32.

The "White Paper of JETRO 1991, Investment Part", which analyzed the trends in these Japanese direct foreign investments, pointed out three periods of expansion, as shown in Table 3.2, and compared them with each other. According to this publication, in direct foreign investments in the latter half of the 1980s, noted as the third period of expansion, we can find the following features. (a) Regionally, the ratio to developing countries decreased and the ratio to advanced countries (e.g. North America and Europe) increased greatly. (b) Classified by industry, the ratio of manufacturing industries fell, but the absolute value of investment in manufacturing increased greatly. The investment branches were shifted from labor-intensive industries and resource-processing industries (e.g. textiles, chemicals, iron and steel and non-ferrous metals etc.) to processing and assembling industries (e.g. machinery, electrical equipment, transportation equipment etc.). (c) In non-manufacturing industries, which increased its share classified by industry, commerce reduced its share, while the ratios of finance and insurance and real estate increased greatly.[4]

The reasons why Japanese direct investment activity was greater during this period (i.e. in the rapid strong yen phase after the Plaza Agreement at the end of 1985) are as follows. (1) The external value of the yen rose. (2) The labor cost in dollar terms in Japan became comparatively more expensive than not only that of developing countries but also that of Western countries. (3) Direct investments toward advanced countries were promoted in a situation where the current balance was largely in surplus to avoid trade friction. (4) Corresponding to EC market integration at the end of 1992, Japanese corporations made efforts to expand and strengthen their business base inside the EC. (5) The globalization strategy of Japanese enterprises was further strengthened. (6) Japanese financial institutions promoted still more globalization

TABLE 3.2 Japan's Direct Foreign Investment During Periods of Expansion (1969–89, s.y.; based on report, FY)

(Unit: US$ million, %)

	First 1969–73		Second 1978–84		Third 1986–89	
	Total	Share	Total	Share	Total	Share
Total	8,259	100.0	49,220	100.0	170,246	100.0
By Region						
North America	1,870	22.6	16,070	32.6	82,028	48.2
Latin America	1,390	16.8	9,262	18.8	21,219	12.5
Asia	2,000	24.2	11,699	23.8	21,002	12.3
Middle East	448	5.4	1,448	2.9	431	0.3
Europe	1,784	21.6	5,997	12.2	33,969	20.0
Africa	193	2.3	2,284	4.6	1,905	1.1
Oceania	572	6.9	2,462	5.0	9,691	5.7
By Industry						
Manufacturing industry total	2,678	32.4	14,911	30.3	41,727	24.5
Food	134	1.6	639	1.3	2,174	1.3
Textiles	637	7.7	769	1.6	1,119	0.7
Chemicals	506	6.1	2,480	5.0	4,667	2.7
Iron and steel and non-ferrous metals	395	4.8	3,755	7.6	4,072	2.4
Machinery	170	2.1	1,106	2.2	4,507	2.6
Electrical equipment	299	3.6	2,385	4.8	10,929	6.4
Transportation equipment	144	1.7	2,208	4.5	5,635	3.3
Non-manufacturing industry total	4,929	59.7	33,073	67.2	126,180	74.1
Mining	2,077	25.1	5,845	11.9	3,455	2.0
Commerce	914	11.0	8,173	16.6	12,482	7.3
Finance and insurance	661	8.0	5,360	10.9	46,412	27.3
Opening and expansion of branch office	364	4.4	942	1.9	2,340	1.4
Real estate	288	3.5	294	0.6	—	(18.9)*

* Not in the original source table, but data provided in the text (p. 15) of the *White Paper of JETRO*.
Source: *White Paper of JETRO* [J]. *Investment Part*, 1991, Tokyo, p. 16.

under the new conditions of deregulation of financial transactions. (7) Real estate prices in foreign countries were considerably cheaper in comparison with the high prices of domestic real estate.[5]

With reference to the development of Japanese direct foreign investments at the level of flow, I would like to compare their remainder with that of other major countries. (Incidentally, the statistical figure used here is based not on a report to the Ministry of Finance but on the balance of payments of the Bank of Japan. We can judge that the figures of the latter source, being "based on practice", are nearer to the real state of affairs.) Referring to Table 3.3, it can be seen that the remainder of Japanese direct foreign investments in 1990 was third after that of the US and the UK. Incidentally, in this regard, the shares of major countries in outstanding world-wide direct investment in 1990 are the USA first at 31.7%, the UK second at 17.6% and Japan at 15.1%. Moreover, as Table 3.3 shows, Japanese direct foreign investment in

TABLE 3.3 Flow and Stock (remainder) of Direct Investments of Selected Countries (1988–90, based on practice)

(Unit: US$ million, %)

	Outward						Inward					
	1988	1989		1990			1988	1989		1990		
	Value	Value	Annual ch. %	Value	Annual ch. %	Remainder (billion)	Value	Value	Annual ch. %	Value	Annual ch. %	Remainder (billion)
Japan	34,210	44,130	29.0	48,024	8.8	201.4	–485	–1,054	n.a.	1,753	n.a.	9.9
USA	17,879	33,388	86.7	33,437	0.1	421.5	59,424	70,551	18.7	37,213	–47.3	403.7
Canada	5,525	4,468	–19.1	1,243	–72.2	72.7	3,580	3,547	–0.9	5,656	59.5	108.5
UK	37,196	35,288	–5.1	20,885	–40.8	233.6	18,208	28,113	54.4	33,904	20.6	190.2
Switzerland	8,695	7,850	–9.7	6,374	–18.8	31.1	42	2,254	5,266.7	4,430	96.5	14.4
F.R. Germany	11,419	14,078	23.3	22,329	58.6	114.5	1,132	6,710	492.8	1,529	–77.2	121.1
Netherlands	4,032	11,269	179.5	11,806	4.8	91.9	3,966	6,444	62.5	7,678	19.1	57.8
France	12,754	16,752	31.3	24,184	44.4	68.4	7,203	9,025	25.3	8,348	–7.5	63.9
Italy	5,450	2,003	–63.3	7,053	252.2	52.9	6,839	2,528	–63.0	6,318	149.9	54.7
Spain	1,358	1,592	17.3	3,170	99.1	9.6	9,130	14,615	60.1	18,106	23.9	57.2
Sweden	7,231	9,683	33.9	14,137	46.0	43.1	1,497	1,523	1.7	2,328	52.9	7.3
Finland	2,610	3,106	19.0	3,023	–2.7	11.5	530	488	–7.9	823	68.6	5.0
Austria	289	898	210.2	1,605	78.8	4.8	447	558	24.9	619	10.9	5.5
Australia	8,242	4,912	–40.4	2,196	–55.3	26.6	6,395	9,262	44.8	5,219	–43.7	70.9
Republic of Korea	151	305	102.0	820	168.9	2.1	871	758	–13.0	715	–5.7	4.9
Taiwan	4,120	6,951	68.7	5,418	–22.1	17.6	959	1,604	67.3	1,330	–17.1	6.7
World (estimated)	167,877	207,701	23.7	217,240	4.6	1330.7	141,184	183,733	30.1	159,194	–13.4	1,181.5

Source: *White Paper of JETRO* [J], *Investment Part*, 1992, p. 3.

1989 and 1990 was, in both cases, the highest in the world. Outstanding direct foreign investment and direct domestic investment were balanced in the US, UK, F.R. Germany and France, while in Japan the remainder of direct foreign investment was overwhelmingly excessive compared with direct domestic investment. In the 1980s, Japanese direct foreign investment, based on the practice mentioned above, was (in US$ billion) 2.39 in 1980, 4.89 in 1981, 4.54 in 1982, 3.61 in 1983, 5.97 in 1984, 6.45 in 1985, 14.48 in 1986, 19.52 in 1987, 34.21 in 1988, 44.13 in 1989, and 48.02 in 1990.[6]

Under these circumstances, the ratio of Japanese enterprise's overseas production value to total domestic sales has been rapidly increasing and reached 6.3% (US$73.9 billion) in 1990 after being 3.2%, 4.0%, and 4.8% in 1982, 1987 and 1988, respectively. However, this figure is still considerably low in comparison with the 21.0% of the US and the 17.3% of the F.R. Germany in 1986 (21.1% and 17.0%, respectively, in 1982; both figures changed negligibly) and we can predict that the Japanese figure will increase in the future.[7]

With regard to trends in direct domestic investments from foreign countries to Japan, these values "based on report" in the 1980s were as follows (given in US$ billion for each FY): 0.3 in 1980, 0.43 in 1981, 0.75 in 1982, 0.81 in 1983, 0.49 in 1984, 0.93 in 1985, 0.94 in 1986, 2.21 in 1987, 3.24 in 1988, 2.86 in 1989, and 2.78 in 1990. The values "based on practice" were (given in US$ billion for each FY): 0.28 in 1980, 0.19 in 1981, 0.44 in 1982, 0.42 in 1983, 0.01 in 1984, 0.64 in 1985, 0.23 in 1986, 1.17 in 1987, −0.49 in 1988, −1.05 in 1989, and 1.75 in 1990.[8] As features of direct domestic investments in the latter half of the 1980s, we can indicate the following. (1) Classified by region, the value from Western countries was more than 70%. (2) Classified by industry, the manufacturing industry was in the center and, recently, the non-manufacturing industry has come to the fore. (3) In the manufacturing industry, the center of investment was shifted from chemicals to machinery. (4) In the non-manufacturing industry, the ratio of commerce and foreign trade was large.[9]

However, comparing values of Japanese direct domestic investments with those of foreign investments, we can at once find that the values of domestic investments were between one-tenth and one-twentieth of those of foreign investments in the 1980s, namely the former were much smaller than the latter. (Moreover, this tendency expanded more with the figures based on practice. The deficits there in 1988 and 1989 were caused by the release of stocks held by foreign enterprises and their capital evacuation.)

Table 3.4 shows the outstanding values (based on report) of direct domestic investment and its development classified by region and industry. Its total amount in 1990 reached US$18.43 billion and was approximately 6% of the outstanding value (based on report; i.e. US$310.8 billion of direct foreign investment in the same year).[10] Its breakdown is as follows: regionally three-quarters of all value was invested by North America and Europe. Classified by industry, in the manufacturing industries, machinery (33.5%) and chemicals (17.1%) were in the main position and, in non-manufacturing industries, commerce and foreign trade (16.0%), services (5.8%), real estate (4.4%) and finance and insurance (3.7%) were in the main position. Incidentally, the outstanding value (based on practice) of direct domestic investments was US$9.16 billion and approximately 6% that (based on practice) of direct foreign investments (i.e. US$157.37 billion) in the same year.[11]

TABLE 3.4 Direct Investment to Japan by Companies, Classified by Region and Industry (1989, 90, based on report; FY)

(Unit: US$ million)

	1989	1990			Remainder 1950–90	
By Region	Value	Value	Distribution ratio	Annual change %	Value	Distribution ratio
US	1,642	664	23.9	–59.6	8,573	46.5
Canada	35	142	5.1	305.7	329	1.8
North America	1,677	806	29.0	–51.9	8,902	48.3
UK	81	54	1.9	–33.3	652	3.5
F.R. Germany	144	259	9.3	79.9	950	5.2
France	25	74	2.7	196.0	301	1.6
Switzerland	87	142	5.1	63.2	1,157	6.3
Netherlands	248	734	26.4	196.0	1,464	7.9
Others	40	98	3.5	145.0	475	2.6
Europe	625	1,361	49.0	117.8	4,999	27.1
Hong Kong	63	62	2.2	–1.6	515	2.8
Japan	198	231	8.3	16.7	2,082	11.3
Others	297	317	11.4	6.7	1,933	10.5
Total	2,860	2,778	100.0	–2.9	18,432	100.0

	1989	1990			Remainder 1950–90	
By Industry	Value	Value	Distribution ratio	Annual change %	Value	Distribution ratio
Manufacturing						
Foods	17	29	1.0	70.6	312	1.7
Textiles	0	18	0.6	—	69	0.4
Rubber/leather	29	1	0.0	–96.6	77	0.4
Chemicals	203	438	15.8	115.8	3,159	17.1
Petroleum	8	30	1.1	275.0	722	3.9
Glass/stone	6	6	0.2	0.0	148	0.8
Metals	40	151	5.4	277.5	648	3.5
Machinery	808	806	29.0	–0.2	6,176	33.5
Others	61	92	3.3	50.8	461	2.5
Subtotal	1,172	1,570	56.5	34.0	11,771	63.9
Non-manufacturing						
Construction	9	9	0.3	0.0	90	0.5
Real estate	647	24	0.9	–96.3	818	4.4
Commerce/trade	544	730	26.3	34.2	2,944	16.0
Services	138	263	9.5	90.6	1,061	5.8
Transportation	47	12	0.4	–74.5	139	0.8
Communication	23	21	0.8	–8.7	148	0.8
Finance and insurance	180	109	3.9	–39.4	681	3.7
Others	100	40	1.4	–60.0	780	4.2
Subtotal	1,688	1,208	43.5	–28.4	6,661	36.1
Total	2,860	2,778	100.0	–2.9	18,432	100.0

Source: *Ibid.*, p. 519.

With regard to trends in Japanese securities investment, in the 1980s, the annual values of securities investment based on the statistics of balance of payments and "securities" of assets were as follows: US$3.75 billion in 1980 (1.75; this figure is a magnification of the ratio of securities investment value to direct investment value in the same year), US$8.87 billion in 1981 (1.79), US$9.74 billion in 1982 (2.15), US$16.02 billion in 1983 (4.44), US$30.8 billion in 1984 (5.16), US$59.77 billion in 1985 (9.26), US$101.98 billion in 1986 (7.04), US$87.76 billion in 1987 (4.50), US$86.95 billion in 1988 (2.54), US$113.18 billion in 1989 (2.56), and US$39.68 billion in 1990 (0.83).[12] Evidently Japanese securities investment increased rapidly in the latter half of the 1980s, corresponding to the large excess outflow of long-term capital regulated by the large surplus of the Japanese current balance during the same period.

The overwhelming majority of Japanese securities investment consisted of investments in equity bonds issued by Japanese enterprises in Europe and in US bonds.[13] In addition, the contraction of securities investment in 1990 was due to Japanese institutional investors reducing their foreign bonds investment as a consequence of the retrenchment of a spread between domestic and foreign interest rates and an increased domestic demand for funds.[14]

As a result of the accumulation of annual vast securities investments, their remainder has reached an enormous value. Outstanding foreign securities investments in the private sector in Japanese long-term assets reached US$533.8 billion at the end of 1989 and were approximately 3.5-fold the value of outstanding foreign direct investments in the same year (i.e. US$154.4 billion). Because outstanding securities investments from abroad in the private sector in Japanese long-term liabilities reached US$374.0 billion at the same time, the balance of Japanese long-term securities investments was favorable (US$159.8 billion for Japan at the end of 1989).[15]

Refering to the trends in Japanese official foreign economic cooperation funds, total Japanese foreign economic cooperation expenditure in 1989 reached US$24.1 billion and was 0.85% of GNP, and its breakdown is shown in Figure 3.1. Looking at official development assistance (ODA), this reached US$8.9 billion in 1989 (although its value increased over the year in terms of yen because of the lower yen quotations, the dollar value of the ODA was reduced from US$9.1 billion in 1988). This value was more than that of the US, which was reduced compared with that of the previous year. The ODA value of Japan is, as shown in Figure 3.2, No.1 in absolute value in the world. However, its ratio in GNP was 0.32% in 1989, which was 12th position in the list of Development Assistance Committee (DAC) nations. Moreover, the ratios of both donations and the grant element in the ODA were the lowest of all DAC nations.[16] With regard to the substance of Japanese ODA, a rapid improvement in both quality and quantity to favorable conditions for developing countries is now necessary.

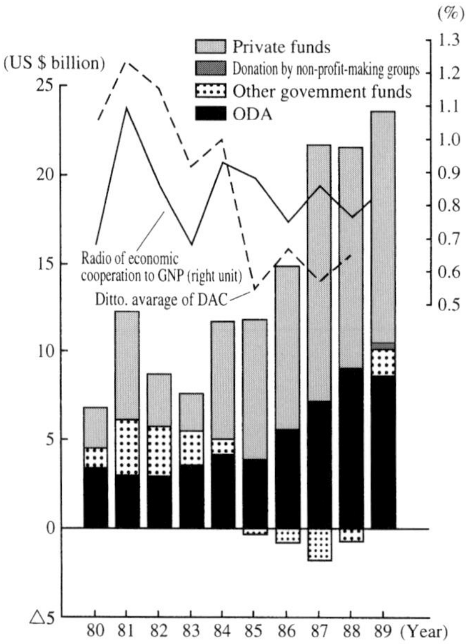

DAC, Development Assistance Committee; ODA, Official Development Assistance.

FIG. 3.1 Trends in Japan's Economic Cooperation Abroad Based on Net Expenditure
Source: *WPIT*, 1991, p. 60.

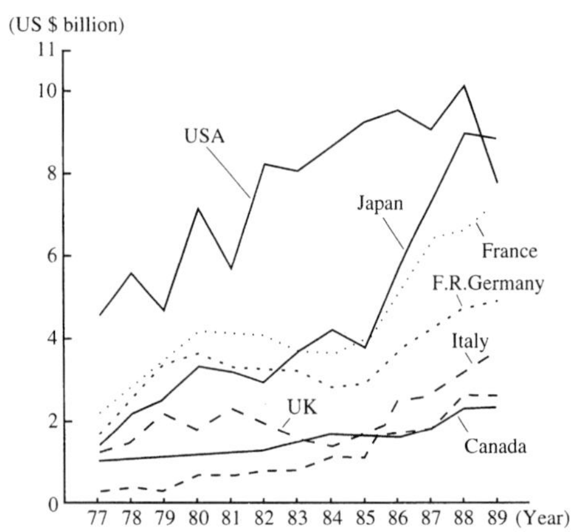

FIG. 3.2 Trends in ODA Expenditure of Selected Countries
Source: *WPIT*, 1991, p. 61.

Notes

1. *WPIT*, 1991, pp. 40f; *Ministry of Finance Statistics Monthly* [J]. Tokyo, August 1991, p. 1.
2. *ESA*, 1990, pp. 250. Because the ratio between them in 1983 was 36.5:63.5, the Japanese feature was strengthened in the meanwhile. Incidentally, the ratios for the US, UK and F.R. Germany in 1983 were 72.7:27.3, 52.2:47.8 and 54.2:45.8, respectively (Matsuba M. *An Essay on Contemporary Japanese Capitalism*, *op. cit.*, 1987, p. 58.)
3. Matsuba M. *op. cit.*, p. 47; *Ministry of Finance Statistics Monthly*, op. cit., p. 9.
4. *White Paper of JETRO* [J], *Investment Part*, 1991, p. 15.
5. *Ibid.*, p. 16; *Ministry of Finance Statistics Monthly*, op.cit., p. 8.
6. *Ministry of Finance Statistics Monthly*, op.cit., p. 9.
7. *WPIT*, 1991, p. 212; *WPJE*, 1989, p. 580.
8. *Ministry of Finance Statistics Monthly*, op.cit., p. 9; *ESA*, 1990, p. 235; *ESA*, 1985, p. 243.
9. *White Paper of JETRO*, 1992, *op.cit.*, p. 85.
10. *Japanese Overseas Investment. A Complete Listing by Firms and Countries* [J]. 1992. Tokyo: Toyo Keizai Inc., pp. 1212f.
11. *ESA*, 1990, p. 250.
12. *Ministry of Finance Statistics Monthly*, op.cit., p. 9; *ESA*, 1985, p. 243; *ESA*, 1990, p. 235.
13. *WPIT*, 1991, pp. 41f; *White Paper of JETRO*, 1992, *op.cit.*, p. 22.
14. *Ministry of Finance Statistics Monthly*, op.cit., p. 2.
15. *ESA*, 1990, p. 250.
16. *WPIT*, 1991, pp. 60f.

3.2 International Development of Japanese Enterprises

Continuing the study on Japanese capital export in the previous sections, this section will deal with direct foreign investments and will focus on the international development of Japanese enterprises.

First, the international development of Japanese direct foreign investments based on reports classified by region and industry after World War II will be examined. Refering to Table 3.5, with regard to outstanding Japanese direct investment in 1989, it can be seen that regionally, the ratio of investment in North America was 42.9%, while that in Europe was 17.7%; namely, these two advanced regions reached approximately 60% of the total direct investment. In addition to these, the direct investment ratio in Asia was 15.9%, South and Central America was 14.5%, Oceania was 5.5%, Africa was 2.1%, and the Middle and Near East was 1.3%. Compared with the situation[1] in the former half of the 1980s, the ratio of direct investment in North America increased markedly (the outstanding ratio in 1983 was 29.3%) and the ratio of investment in Europe increased too (cf. 11.6% in 1983); however, the ratios of investment in Asia and South and Central America decreased considerably (cf. 26.8% and 17.5%, respectively, in 1983). Here, it is shown that the ratio of direct investments from Japan to advanced regions increased remarkably during this period. Classified by country, the ratio of investment to the US was a remarkable 41.1% (27.0% in 1983), which was followed by the UK at 6.2%, Panama at 5.9%, Australia at 4.9%, Indonesia at 4.1% and the Netherlands at 4.0%.

Classified by industry, as shown in Table 3.6, in the non-manufacturing industry, the outstanding ratio in 1989 of finance and insurance was 22.6%, real estate was 13.7%, commerce was 9.9%, and services was 9.2%, while in the manufacturing

TABLE 3.5 Japan's Direct Foreign Investment, Classified by Region (1988, 1989; based on report; FY)

(Unit: Case, US$ million, %)

	1988			1989			Remainder 1951–89		
	No. cases	Value	Distribution ratio	No. cases	Value	Distribution ratio	No. cases	Value	Distribution ratio
US	2,434	21,701	46.2	2,668	32,540	48.2	20,675	104,400	41.1
Canada	109	626	1.3	180	1,362	2.0	1,124	4,593	1.8
Subtotal North America	2,543	22,328	47.5	2,848	33,902	50.2	21,799	108,993	42.9
Panama	327	1,712	3.6	263	2,044	3.0	3,649	14,902	5.9
Brazil	48	510	1.1	39	349	0.5	1,446	5,946	2.3
Cayman	53	2,609	5.5	41	1,658	2.5	227	6,743	2.7
Bahamas	12	737	1.6	14	620	0.9	106	3,338	1.3
Mexico	1	87	0.2	9	36	0.1	260	1,707	0.7
Subtotal South and Central America	507	6,428	13.7	421	5,238	7.8	6,858	36,855	14.5
Indonesia	84	586	1.2	140	631	0.9	1,718	10,435	4.1
Hong Kong	335	1,662	3.5	335	1,898	2.8	3,499	8,066	3.2
Singapore	197	747	1.6	181	1,902	2.8	2,420	5,715	2.3
Republic of Korea	153	483	1.0	81	606	0.9	1,793	3,854	1.5
China	171	296	0.6	126	438	0.6	694	2,474	1.0
Thailand	382	859	1.8	403	1,276	1.9	2,088	3,268	1.3
Malaysia	108	387	0.8	159	673	1.0	1,340	2,507	1.0
Taiwan	234	372	0.8	165	494	0.7	2,298	2,285	0.9
Philippines	54	134	0.3	87	202	0.3	792	1,322	0.5
Subtotal Asia	1,737	5,569	11.8	1,707	8,238	12.2	17,135	40,465	15.9

Saudi Arabia/ Kuwait*	—	20	0.1	—	32	0.0	4	1,415	0.6
Iran	0	1	0.0	—	1	0.0	108	1,006	0.4
Subtotal Middle and Near East	10	259	0.6	5	66	0.1	339	3,404	1.3
UK	211	3,956	8.4	285	5,239	7.8	1,864	15,793	6.2
Netherlands	105	2,359	5.0	112	4,547	6.7	642	10,072	4.0
Luxembourg	13	657	1.4	13	654	1.0	143	5,383	2.1
F.R. Germany	67	409	0.9	119	1,083	1.6	1,053	3,448	1.4
France	148	463	1.0	168	1,136	1.7	1,157	2,899	1.1
Switzerland	27	454	1.0	19	397	0.6	288	1,829	0.7
Spain	32	161	0.3	58	501	0.7	277	1,546	0.6
Subtotal Europe	692	9,116	19.4	916	14,808	21.9	6,469	44,972	17.7
Liberia	68	648	1.4	72	643	1.0	880	4,301	1.7
Subtotal Africa	74	653	1.4	88	671	1.0	1,388	5,275	2.1
Australia	357	2,413	5.1	448	4,256	6.3	2,353	12,394	4.9
Subtotal Oceania	514	2,669	5.7	604	4,618	6.8	3,385	13,933	5.5
Total	6,077	47,022	100.0	6,589	67,540	100.0	57,373	253,896	100.0

* Investment in joint enterprises of both countries.
Source: *Japanese Overseas Investment. A Complete Listing by Firms and Countries* [J]. 1991, Tokyo: Toyo Keizai Inc., p. 60.

TABLE 3.6 Japan's Direct Foreign Investment, Classified by Industry (1988, 1989; based on report; FY)

(Unit: case, US$ million, %)

	1988			1989			Remainder 1951–89		
	No. cases	Value	Distribution ratio	No. cases	Value	Distribution ratio	No. cases	Value	Distribution ratio
Manufacturing									
Foods	169	419	0.9	143	1,300	1.9	1,632	3,265	1.3
Textiles	146	317	0.7	174	533	0.8	1,634	3,203	1.3
Timber/pulp	82	604	1.3	82	555	0.8	745	2,654	1.0
Chemicals	180	1,292	2.7	196	2,109	3.1	1,886	8,649	3.4
Iron and steel and non-ferrous metals	194	1,367	2.9	198	1,591	2.4	1,892	9,261	3.6
Machinery	253	1,432	3.0	229	1,762	2.6	2,172	6,479	2.6
Electrical equipment	316	3,041	6.5	303	4,480	6.6	2,925	14,676	5.8
Transportation equipment	128	1,281	2.7	148	2,053	3.0	981	9,009	3.5
Others	331	4,051	8.6	356	1,901	2.8	3,136	8,932	3.5
Subtotal	1,799	13,805	29.4	1,829	16,284	24.1	17,003	66,127	26.0
Non-manufacturing									
Agriculture/forestry	89	162	0.3	74	151	0.2	1,175	1,205	0.5
Fisheries	53	94	0.2	40	47	0.1	745	678	0.3
Mining	83	1,013	2.2	84	1,262	1.9	1,190	15,211	6.0
Construction	81	309	0.7	94	646	1.0	1,042	2,089	0.8
Commerce	1,064	3,204	6.8	895	5,148	7.6	13,743	25,159	9.9
Finance and insurance	340	13,104	27.9	316	15,395	22.8	2,154	57,271	22.6
Services	671	3,732	7.9	933	10,616	15.7	4,517	23,375	9.2
Transportation	457	2,372	5.0	428	2,927	4.3	3,926	15,269	6.0
Real estate	1,348	8,641	18.4	1,808	14,143	20.9	4,802	34,742	13.7
Others	3	3	0.0	11	180	0.3	3,143	7,515	3.0
Subtotal	4,189	32,634	69.4	4,683	50,517	74.8	36,437	182,516	71.9
Opening and expansion of branch offices	89	584	1.2	77	739	1.1	1,395	4,659	1.8
Immovable	—	—	—	—	—	—	2,538	595	0.2
Total	6,077	47,022	100.0	6,589	67,540	100.0	57,373	253,896	100.0

Source: *Ibid.*, p. 61.

industry the ratios were electrical equipment at 5.8%, iron and steel and non-ferrous metals at 3.6%, transportation equipment at 3.5%, chemicals at 3.4%, and machinery at 2.6%. Comparing these figures with those in the former half of the 1980s, the ratios of finance and insurance (in 1983 they were 8.1%) and of real estate (in 1983 it was 1.5%) increased rapidly.

The distributions by region and industry together are shown in Table 3.7 (where the outstanding figures in the end of FY 1989 (i.e. on March 1990) are indicated). According to Table 3.7, in North America (actually almost equivalent to the US) the ratio (to all investment values in this region) of real estate was 22.6%, finance and insurance was 15.6%, commerce was 13.0%, and services was 11.0%; thus, the ratio of non-manufacturing industries was very large, followed by the manufacturing industry, electrical equipment (8.0%), transportation equipment (4.1%), iron and steel and non-ferrous metals (3.4%), chemicals (3.3%), and machinery (3.0%).

In Europe, the ratio of finance and insurance was 47.3%, commerce was 12.0%, real estate was 8.2%, services were 5.5%, and mining was 3.1%; thus, the ratio of non-manufacturing industries was overwhelming, followed by electrical equipment (4.5%), machinery (3.0%), transportation equipment (3.0%), and chemicals (2.5%).

In Asia, the ratio of mining was 17.6%, services were 11.9%, followed by finance and insurance (8.9%), electrical equipment (8.3%), iron and steel and non-ferrous metals (6.4%), commerce (6.4%), real estate (5.8%), chemicals (5.1%), and textiles (3.9%).

In South and Central America, the ratios of finance and insurance and transportation were 37.2% and 29.5%, respectively, followed by iron and steel and non-ferrous metals (5.5%), commerce (4.8%), and mining (4.2%).

In Africa, the ratio of transportation was projected at 51.2%, and the rest consisted of services at 13.5% and mining at 11.0%. In the Middle and Near East, the ratios were mainly as follows: opening and expansion of branch offices at 41.7%, chemicals at 33.2% and mining at 11.7%. Last, in Oceania, in non-manufacturing industries the ratio of real estate was 27.4%, mining was 16.1%, services were 14.7%, finance and insurance was 11.2%, and commerce was 8.7%, while in manufacturing industries, transportation equipment was 5.6%, and iron and steel and non-ferrous metals were 3.1%.

Here I would like to point out some interesting facts that are relevant to the active development of Japanese direct foreign investments. One point is the rapid development of Japanese companies' offshore manufacturing investment in the US. That is, following the model of the production of color television sets, in which the number of products produced by offshore Japanese companies has exceeded the number exported from Japan since the end of the 1970s (incidentally, in 1989, the former was 6.56 million sets, while the latter was only 0.23 million sets),[2] with regard to the number of products exported from Japan and the number of automobile products produced by offshore Japanese companies, the former was much higher than the latter in the first half of the 1980s, as shown in Table 3.8, but these numbers have approached each other in the early 1990s. Each position changed in 1993 (1,328,000 to 1,510,000).

The other point is the problem of the positions of Japanese and US companies in Asia. As Table 3.9 shows, in the latter half of the 1980s, in addition to the share in sales and employment, in the field of outstanding investments the ratio of Japanese

TABLE 3.7 Japan's Direct Foreign Investment, Classified by Region and Industry (based on report, remainder in March 1990)

(Unit: Case, US$ million)

Region / Industry	North America		South and Central America		Asia		Middle East	
	No. cases	Value	No. cases	Value	No. cases	Value	No. cases	Value
Manufacturing								
Foods	595	1,485	139	234	684	1,049	1	0
Textiles	190	651	164	440	986	1,569	3	4
Timber/pulp	150	1,847	46	202	430	450	—	—
Chemicals	439	3,581	134	602	1,077	2,077	23	1,130
Iron and steel and non-ferrous metals	349	3,656	97	2,010	930	2,578	11	66
Machinery	705	3,277	134	393	1,001	1,387	7	11
Electrical equipment	854	8,686	130	536	1,637	3,348	6	15
Transportation equipment	356	4,453	77	1,070	423	1,326	6	4
Others	841	5,894	114	143	1,837	1,807	22	46
Subtotal	4,479	33,529	1,035	5,633	9,005	15,591	79	1,276
Non-manufacturing								
Agriculture/forestry	233	430	251	208	407	297	4	2
Fisheries	94	158	126	147	289	177	5	1
Mining	353	1,889	152	1,557	251	7,124	16	399
Construction	301	1,015	72	219	518	643	55	40
Commerce	6,969	141,146	621	1,759	2,923	2,575	63	44
Finance and insurance	440	16,996	427	13,715	434	3,588	22	123
Services	2,076	12,038	274	1,271	1,169	4,815	19	5
Transportation	263	411	2,819	10,873	271	982	6	2
Real estate	3,218	24,637	52	200	547	2,351	—	—
Others	956	2,215	870	1,203	531	1,632	32	87
Subtotal	14,903	73,935	5,664	31,153	7,340	24,183	222	705
Opening and expansion of branch offices	412	1,044	60	46	628	654	37	1,421
Immovable	2,005	485	99	23	162	37	1	2
Total	21,799	108,993	6,858	36,855	17,135	40,465	339	3,404

TABLE 3.7 *Continued*

Industry / Region	Europe		Africa		Oceania		Total	
	No. cases	Value	No. cases	Value	No. cases	Value	No. cases	Value
Manufacturing								
Foods	84	311	29	8	100	177	1,632	3,265
Textiles	226	489	51	39	14	11	1,634	3,203
Timber/pulp	12	17	3	1	104	137	745	2,654
Chemicals	177	1,110	13	24	23	126	1,886	8,649
Iron and steel and non-ferrous metals	362	395	27	127	116	428	1,892	9,261
Machinery	286	1,339	2	1	37	70	2,172	6,479
Electrical equipment	272	2,016	9	8	17	66	2,925	14,676
Transportation equipment	83	1,352	6	17	30	786	981	9,009
Others	254	917	8	7	60	118	3,136	8,932
Subtotal	1,756	7,947	148	231	501	1,919	17,003	66,127
Non-manufacturing								
Agriculture/forestry	13	8	13	7	254	253	1,175	1,205
Fisheries	11	18	91	99	129	79	745	678
Mining	33	1,416	129	582	256	2,244	1,190	15,211
Construction	35	84	25	22	36	65	1,042	2,089
Commerce	2,490	5,404	30	14	647	1,218	13,743	25,159
Finance and insurance	726	21,258	25	37	80	1,554	2,154	57,251
Services	460	2,487	87	710	432	2,050	4,517	23,375
Transportation	78	157	449	2,702	40	142	3,926	15,269
Real estate	233	3,669	5	69	747	3,816	4,802	34,742
Others	234	1,056	353	798	167	523	3,143	7,515
Subtotal	4,313	35,556	1,207	5,040	2,788	11,945	36,437	182,516
Opening and expansion of branch offices	220	1,430	12	1	26	62	1,395	4,659
Immovable	180	38	21	2	70	7	2,538	595
Total	6,469	44,972	1,388	5,275	3,385	13,933	57,373	253,896

Source: *Ibid.*, p. 62.

TABLE 3.8 Production and Sales by Japanese Automobile Manufacturers in the US (1980–94, s.y.)
(Unit: 1,000 Vehicles, %)

	1980	1982	1984	1986	1988	1990	1992	1994
Import of finished cars	1,911	1,802	1,906	2,383	2,023	1,719	1,452	1,239
Cars produced in the US	0	0	134	466	766	1,395	1,443	1,768
Total	1,911	1,802	2,040	2,848	2,789	3,115	2,895	3,007
Share (%)	21.3	22.6	19.6	24.9	26.5	33.5	35.3	33.5

Sources: *White Paper of JETRO*, 1992, *op. cit.*, p. 72; *Handbook of Automobile Industry* [J], 1997, Tokyo: Nikkan Jidosha Shinbunsha, pp. 542f.

TABLE 3.9 Position of Japanese and US Companies in the Asian Economy (1980–89, s.y.)
(Unit: %)

	1980	1985		1986		1987		1988		1989		
	Japan	US	Japan	US	Japan	US	Japan	US	Japan	US	Japan	US
Sales (A)	1.5	NA	1.8	1.2	2.1	1.2	3.0	1.4	3.6	1.5	NA	NA
Employment (B)	0.31	NA	NA	0.3	NA	0.2	0.3	0.2	0.3	0.2	0.5	NA
Investment (C)	24.1	45.8	25.8	43.8	27.9	45.8	29.1	45.1	30.5	31.1	34.0	22.9

(A), ratios of gross sales of Japanese and US manufacturing industries in Asian GNP; (B), ratios of native employees working in Japanese and US companies of all employees; (C), ratios of outstanding investment of Japanese and US companies of all main countries (i.e. Republic of Korea, Taiwan, Singapore, Malaysia, Thailand and Philippines).
Source: *WPIT*, 1991, p. 224.

companies in Asia became greater than that of US companies. Thus, the presence of Japanese companies is expanding further into Asia.

Of the main Japanese companies that undertook capital exports and direct foreign investment mentioned above, Table 3.10 shows their overseas loans and investments and Table 3.11 shows their sales value of overseas affiliated companies (needless to say, because both tables are based on the results of a questionnaire, we must take care that companies that did not respond are not included in the survey).

The number of native employees working in Japanese companies abroad reached more than 2.30 million in 1991, increasing from 0.24 and 0.70 million people in 1972 and 1981, respectively. Table 3.12 shows the development of the number of native employees in Japanese companies abroad classified by region and industry in 1991. Regionally, the number of native employees (in thousands) working in Asia was 1,107 thousand (927; here and below, numbers in parenthesis indicate the number of employees in the manufacturing industry) and its ratio in the world was 48% (both figures are approximate); this was followed by North America with 529 (310) or 23%, and Europe with 323 (133) or 14%. Classified by country, numbers for the US were highest (i.e. 429 (287) in Asia, 208 (184) in Korea, 189 (164) in Thailand, 176 (163) in Taiwan, 129 (110) in the Federation of Malaysia, and 97 (79) in Indonesia. In Europe, these figures were 90 (5) in Italy, 76 (37) in the UK, 51 (29) in Germany, 27 (14) in France, and 25 (22) in Spain. Furthermore, there were 190 (82) in Brazil, and 53 (35) in Australia. Classified by industry, there were 1.59 million people working in the manufacturing industry, and its ratio overall was 68%; this was followed by commerce with 342 thousand people (15%), and finance and insurance with 170 thousand people (7%).

TABLE 3.10 Overseas Loans and Investments Ranking of Major Japanese Companies[1] (1989)
(Unit: outstandings, ¥100 million; others, real number)

Rank	Company[2]	Outstandings	No. OS companies invested in	No. delegated Japanese staff	Of which, directors
1	Nippon Life Insurance	38,228	21	56	7
2	Asahi Mutual Life Insurance	12,195	8	26	5
3	Dai-ichi Mutual Life Insurance	5,873	14	35	15
4	Saitama Bank	4,662	10	18	9
5	Mitsubishi Corporation	4,647	289	0	0
6	Nissan Motor	4,350	46	432	50
7	Toho Mutual Life Insurance	4,311	9	17	10
8	Sumitomo Mutual Life Insurance	4,191	22	36	8
9	Daido Mutual Life Insurance	3,647	6	9	2
10	Tokio Marine and Fire Insurance	3,522	29	77	27
11	Nippon Dantai Life Insurance	3,462	1	0	0
12	Fukoku Mutual Life Insurance	3,330	1	0	0
13	Nippon Asahan Aluminum	2,709	1	21	4
14	Mitsui and Co.	2,515	554	0	0
15	Tokyo Lease	2,385	4	10	4
16	Bank of Tokyo	2,036	72	638	52
17	Sony Corporation	1,957	59	0	0
18	Nissho Iwai Corporation	1,919	168	449	58
19	Mitsui Fudosan	1,830	13	18	18
20	C. Itoh and Co.	1,673	265	1,081	0
21	Marubeni Corporation	1,616	307	1,076	6
22	Sumitomo Corporation	1,616	254	564	115
23	Kumagai Gumi.	1,459	44	152	0
24	Matsushita Electric Industrial	1,367	100	1,000	300
25	Meiko Trans Kaisha, Ltd	1,362	10	30	4
26	Honda Motor Co.	1,308	70	0	0
27	Mitsui Mutual Life Insurance	1,228	7	15	3
28	Sanwa Bank	1,200	37	450	0
29	NEC Corporation	1,180	70	692	65
30	Sanyo Electric Co.	1,138	85	597	120
40	Yasuda Fire and Marine Insurance	887	21	52	24
50	Asahi Glass Co.	680	29	200	50
60	Fuji Photo Film Co.	466	18	0	0
70	Oji Paper	398	3	20	3
80	Konica Corporation	351	27	128	20
90	Yoshida Kogyo	304	53	360	0
100	Sumitomo Metal Industries	255	8	15	8

[1] Because data presented in this table are based on the results of a questionaire, companies that did not respond have been excluded. [2] In this table, many companies listed in the original source have been omitted. OS, overseas.
Source: *Japanese Overseas Investment* [J], 1990, *op. cit.*, p. 36.

TABLE 3.11 Sales Ranking of Japanese Overseas Affiliated Companies[1] (FY 1988, in Manufacturing)

(Unit: sales, US$ million; others, real number)

Rank	Company[2]	Sales[3]	No. OS companies invested in	No. delegated Japanese staff	Of which, directors
1	Sony Corporation	10,615	59	0	0
2	NKK	2,865	43	154	27
3	Tyota Motor	2,614	40	433	67
4	Isuzu Motors	2,411	24	138	32
5	Tray Industries	1,746	44	198	73
6	Tomen Corporation	1,626	1	6	2
7	Nippon Oil Co.	1,578	6	23	9
8	Bando Chemical Industries	1,576	13	39	1
9	Asahi Glass Co.	1,426	29	200	50
10	Sharp Corporation	1,351	28	400	42
11	Ajinomoto Co.	813	30	154	49
12	Nikon Corporation	707	13	123	10
13	Yoshida Kogyo	690	53	360	0
14	Kenwood Corporation	673	12	67	12
15	Makita Corp.	663	15	50	18
16	Funai Electric Co.	662	9	50	1
17	Seiko Denshi Kogyo[4]	602	14	55	12
18	Asahi Chemical Industry	487	24	78	35
19	Hino Motors	486	12	54	16
20	Kawasaki Steel Corporation	466	38	0	0
21	Sumitomo Electric Industries	388	54	126	31
22	Mitsumi Electric Co.	386	16	108	12
23	Oji Paper	385	3	20	3
24	Matsushita Refrigeration Co.	360	3	20	4
25	Nichirei Corporation	337	17	52	18
26	Furukawa Electric Co.	337	25	60	18
27	Clarion Co.	336	15	60	14
28	Daihatsu Motor	336	9	17	10
29	Rohm Co.	331	15	43	15
30	Matsushita Elec. Components	330	8	102	0
40	Fujisawa Pharmaceutical Co.	262	8	19	7
50	Taiyo Yuden Co.	217	11	74	15
60	Rinnai Corporation	172	10	17	6
70	Toyobo Co.	148	17	43	20
80	Nisshin Steel Co.	127	13	13	1
90	Terumo Corporation	103	5	13	1
100	Fuji Oil Co.	93	5	18	3

[1] Because data presented in this table are based on the results of a questionaire, companies that did not respond have been excluded. [2] In this table, many companies listed in the original source have been omitted. [3] Total of sales of companies in which the Japanese subscriber's share of the capital was over 25%. [4] The English translation of this company's name cannot be found in the Japan Company Handbook (Autumn 1992, Tokyo: Toyo Keizai). OS, overseas.
Source: *Ibid.*, p. 34.

TABLE 3.12 Development of the Number of Native Employees in Japanese Companies Abroad,[1] Classified by Region and Industry (1991)

(Unit: persons)

	Total World[2]		Subtotal Asia		Republic of Korea		Taiwan	
	Employees[3]	Delegated Japanese staff[3]	Employees	Delegated Japanese staff	Employees	Delegated Japanese staff	Employees	Delegated Japanese staff
All industries	2,356,646	46,668	1,121,333	14,461	208,667	502	178,141	2,091
Agriculture/forestry/fishery	16,318	552	7,949	66	—	—	72	2
Mining	18,805	314	3,062	48	30	—	—	—
Construction	33,116	1,724	21,261	884	660	7	907	130
Manufacturing	1,585,463	18,260	935,377	8,350	184,138	425	164,610	1,533
Commerce	357,624	15,365	74,296	3,017	7,505	30	8,446	350
Finance and insurance	172,687	2,799	23,375	714	1,094	5	29	3
Securities/investment	9,180	1,646	1,289	281	—	—	6	1
Real estate	9,446	487	1,402	95	—	—	26	10
Transportation	47,263	1,713	16,798	417	4,516	1	505	20
Services	71,474	2,817	34,019	456	10,724	34	3,490	30
Stockholding etc.	35,270	991	2,505	133	—	—	50	12

	Thailand		Malaysia		Indonesia		Subtotal Middle East	
	Employees	Delegated Japanese staff	Employees	Delegated Japanese staff	Employees	Delegated Japanese staff	Employees	Delegated Japanese staff
All industries	191,647	2,755	130,805	1,425	97,982	1,208	8,791	289
Agriculture/forestry/fishery	1,583	11	744	1	1,544	37	—	—
Mining	2	1	92	32	2,271	4	3,202	41
Construction	5,077	307	1,991	94	2,711	136	134	34
Manufacturing	165,685	1,736	111,407	1,093	79,681	850	4,160	45
Commerce	12,975	496	8,651	119	7,056	37	938	129
Finance and insurance	2,033	37	4,543	19	2,039	94	129	17
Securities/investment	117	4	306	—	136	18	62	20
Real estate	148	24	15	4	433	9	—	—
Transportation	2,599	85	1,239	43	173	4	66	1
Services	1,270	50	1,667	18	1,938	19	100	2
Stockholding etc.	158	4	150	2	—	—	—	—

TABLE 3.12 *Continued*

	Subtotal Europe		UK		France		F.R. Germany	
	Employees	Delegated Japanese staff	Employees	Delegated Japanese staff	Employees	Delegated Japanese staff	Employees	Delegated Japanese staff
All industries	332,814	9,439	79,270	3,494	27,355	764	53,153	2,314
Agriculture/forestry/fishery	21	1	4	1	2	—	—	—
Mining	143	46	141	45	—	—	—	—
Construction	873	223	280	99	21	5	215	35
Manufacturing	135,138	2,064	38,043	746	13,912	223	29,764	357
Commerce	152,911	4,246	25,510	1,070	10,814	404	17,813	1,548
Finance and insurance	22,650	1,000	4,203	426	30	6	624	136
Securities/investment	3,501	780	2,985	619	223	59	17	13
Real estate	256	40	69	24	12	3	5	2
Transportation	7,771	342	3,034	129	207	30	3,405	109
Services	5,704	454	1,661	233	1,909	28	1,232	89
Stockholding etc.	3,836	243	3,340	102	225	6	78	25
	Spain		**Italy**		**US**		**Subtotal Latin America**	
	Employees	Delegated Japanese staff	Employees	Delegated Japanese staff	Employees	Delegated Japanese staff	Employees	Delegated Japanese staff
All industries	25,103	406	90,411	297	509,576	17,608	252,506	1,985
Agriculture/forestry/fishery	—	—	—	—	2,120	20	2,369	219
Mining	—	—	—	—	55	31	3,211	17
Construction	123	12	—	—	2,528	423	7,752	71
Manufacturing	22,725	272	5,219	69	293,668	6,210	133,050	990
Commerce	1,997	97	83,084	191	101,618	6,370	7,744	509
Finance and insurance	18	1	1,987	9	29,849	791	94,935	85
Securities/investment	46	12	64	19	4,006	490	3	3
Real estate	93	1	—	2	6,501	260	207	17
Transportation	78	7	34	3	18,318	850	2,115	26
Services	23	4	23	4	22,632	1,584	1,068	36
Stockholding etc.	—	—	—	—	28,281	579	52	12

	Brazil		Subtotal Africa		Australia	
	Employees	Delegated Japanese staff	Employees	Delegated Japanese staff	Employees	Delegated Japanese staff
All industries	191,348	943	25,285	321	53,821	1,186
Agriculture/forestry/fishery	446	17	2,135	183	82	1
Mining	708	6	2,035	—	3,227	112
Construction	6,873	18	138	16	300	37
Manufacturing	82,465	575	20,314	86	35,399	202
Commerce	3,445	178	400	24	10,405	551
Finance and insurance	94,283	84	222	—	941	117
Securities/investment	—	—	—	—	155	44
Real estate	154	16	—	—	424	47
Transportation	1,965	9	—	4	1,018	24
Services	989	32	41	8	1,302	33
Stockholding etc.	20	8	—	—	568	18

[1] Companies in which the Japanese subscriber's share in the capital was under 10% are excluded. [2] In this table, some countries listed in the original source have been omitted. [3] The number of employees includes the delegated Japanese staff. However, in the latter group there is a small number of directors that is not included as employees.

Source: *Op.cit.*, 1992 [J], pp. 34–40.

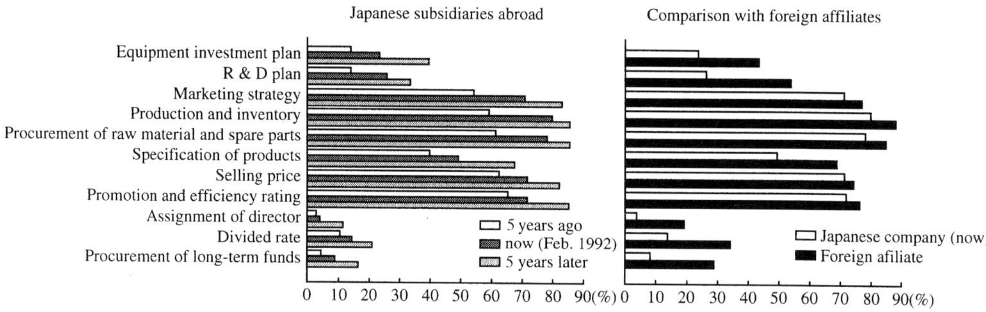

R&D, research and development.

Source: *WPIT*, 1991, p. 225.
FIG. 3.3 Delegation of Authority in Japanese Subsidiaries Abroad

Finally, I would like to refer to one of the management problems in Japanese companies abroad, namely the present situation of the delegation of authority. It is shown in Figure 3.3 that the delegation of authority has developed in Japanese companies abroad over the past 5 years and it will develop still further. However, although the delegation of authority certainly developed in the fields of production, marketing and efficiency rating, it has hardly developed in the essential fields of investment, research and development, assignment of directors, distribution of net profit and funds procurement. On this point, we can also see from Figure 3.3 that, at the present time, the delegation of authority (localization, *genchika*) in companies with foreign capital is progressing more than in Japanese companies abroad.

Notes

1. Matsuba M. *An Essay on Contemporary Japanese Capitalism*, *op. cit.*, 1987, pp. 48f.
2. *WPIT*, 1991, p. 217.

3.3 Expansion of Japanese Foreign Net Assets and Investment Income

Because of the rapid development of capital exports on the flow basis mentioned earlier, as shown in Table 3.13, both the assets and liabilities of Japan have recently increased and the outstanding net foreign assets have expanded to (US$ billion) 129.8 in 1985, 180.4 in 1986, 240.7 in 1987, 291.7 in 1988, 293.2 in 1989, and 328.0 in 1990.

The outstanding values of Japan's net foreign assets were in ranked first in the world from 1985 to 1989.[1] At the end of 1990, as shown in Table 3.14, Germany took over the world's top rank. However, taking account of the relatively small scale of Germany's assets and liabilities, judging from the large scale of Japan's assets and liabilities and net assets, it is no wonder that Japan is one of the biggest countries in terms of net foreign assets. In actual fact, at the end of 1991, Japan regained its top ranking in the world with total assets of US$2,006.5 billion, total liabilities of US$1,623.4 billion and net assets of US$383.1 billion.[2]

TABLE 3.13 Japanese Assets and Liabilities Abroad (1985–1993, at the end of year)

(Unit: US$ billion)

Item	1985	1986	1987	1988	1989	1990	1991	1992	1993
Assets									
Long-term assets	301.3	476.1	646.2	832.7	1,019.2	1,096.1	1,247.8	1,315.6	1,412.9
Short-term assets	136.4	251.2	425.5	636.7	751.8	761.8	758.7	719.7	768.0
Total assets	437.7	727.3	1,071.6	1,469.3	1,771.0	1,857.9	2,006.5	2,035.2	2,180.9
Liabilities									
Long-term liabilities	122.3	192.3	236.2	311.6	447.5	464.0	647.4	658.5	711.8
Short-term liabilities	185.6	354.6	594.7	866.0	1,030.3	1,065.8	976.0	863.2	858.3
Total liabilities	307.9	547.0	830.9	1,177.6	1,477.8	1,529.8	1,623.4	1,521.6	1,570.1
Total net assets	129.8	180.4	240.7	291.7	293.2	328.1	383.1	513.6	610.8

Source: *ESA*, 1991, p. 250; *op.cit.*, 1994, p. 341.

TABLE 3.14 Balance of Assets and Liabilities Abroad of Selected Countries (1985, 90)

(Unit: US$ billion)

	US		UK		Japan		F.R. Germany	
Year	1985	1990	1985	1990	1985	1990	1985	1990
Total assets	1,173.8	1,764.1	866.1	1,885.5	437.8	1,857.8	339.5	1,098.1
Total liabilities	1,109.6	2,176.1	750.0	1,671.6	307.8	1,529.8	288.6	739.7
Net assets	64.2	−412.0	116.1	216.9	130.0	328.0	50.9	358.4

Source: *Annual Report on World Economy* [J], 1991, Tokyo: Economic Planning Agency, p. 259.

The features of Japan's outstanding foreign assets and liabilities are as follows.[3] First, recently both the foreign assets and liabilities of Japan expanded rapidly. Although Japan's total assets and liabilities in 1985 were a little less than the 40% and 30%, respectively, of US, in 1990 both Japan's total assets and liabilities were the largest in the world. This also shows that Japan grew into one of the largest worldwide financial centers in the latter half of the 1980s. Second, securities investment increased remarkably in terms of both outflow and inflow. Japan's institutional finance and insurance investors actively invested in US and equity bonds during the period of deregulation of foreign securities investments. Third, compared with other countries, as mentioned earlier, Japan's outstanding value of direct domestic investments is very small. As reasons for this, we can put forward the fact that in addition to the tendency for a strong yen in recent years, high land prices and mutual retained stocks among Japanese companies in Japan prevented foreign capital from coming into the Japanese market through investment or mergers and acquisitions etc.

Looking at the trends in investment income as the fruit of Japanese capital exports or foreign assets, Table 3.15 shows Japan's investment income values after 1970. Before 1970, both the balance of direct investments and the balance of total foreign investments were in deficit.[4] However, after 1972, as shown in Table 3.15, the balance of total foreign investments has been in the black except for a few years after the two oil crises (restricted only to direct investment income, its balance has been consistently in the black since 1974). Moreover, the surplus value has become very large in recent years, being (in US$ billion) 6.84 in 1985, 9.47 in 1986, 16.67 in 1987, 21.03 in 1988, 23.44 in 1989, 23.2 in 1990, 26.72 in 1991, 36.22 in 1992, 41.41 in 1993, and 40.93 in 1994.[5]

TABLE 3.15 Japanese Investment Income (1970–1990)

(Unit: US$ million)

	Balance		Credits		Debits	
	Investment income	Direct investment income	Investment income	Direct investment income	Investment income	Direct investment income
1970	−209	−23	710	87	919	110
1971	−47	−24	980	115	1,027	139
1972	367	−3	1,622	169	1,255	172
1973	490	−72	2,655	223	2,165	295
1974	−451	59	3,562	349	4,013	290
1975	−273	208	3,616	506	3,889	298
1976	−204	306	3,460	630	3,664	324
1977	115	464	3,738	841	3,623	377
1978	900	376	5,278	782	4,378	406
1979	2,011	345	8,965	931	6,954	586
1980	854	809	11,115	1,340	10,261	531
1981	−763	816	15,761	1,440	16,524	624
1982	1,718	992	18,320	1,589	16,602	597
1983	3,082	1,354	15,601	2,040	12,519	686
1984	4,231	1,428	18,768	2,201	14,537	773
1985	6,840	1,711	22,107	2,538	15,267	827
1986	9,473	1,412	29,086	2,670	19,613	1,258
1987	16,670	2,004	49,245	3,548	32,575	1,544
1988	21,032	1,749	74,837	3,750	53,805	2,001
1989	23,442	2,299	101,785	4,577	78,343	2,278
1990	23,204	2,568	122,167	4,821	98,963	2,253

Source: *Balance of Payments Monthly*, January 1992, Bank of Japan, pp. 29–48; *op.cit.*, June 1985, passim.

Notes

1. *NM*, January 5, 1992.
2. *NE*, May 26, 1992.
3. *Annual Report on World Economy* [J], 1991. Tokyo: Economic Planning Agency, p. 262.
4. Matsuba M. *An Essay on Contemporary Japanese Capilatism*, *op.cit.*, 1987, pp. 60f.
5. *ESA*, 1994, p. 336.

Part 2 The Internal Structure of the Large Corporation System

Chapter 4
The Structure and Position of the Six Large Corporation Groups

4.1 The Position of the Six Large Corporation Groups in the Japanese Economy

It is well known that in the basic industries and in many economic sectors a few huge corporations rule the greater part of production in their industrial sectors. For example, the concentration of production in 1990, looking at the shares of the five higher-ranked companies in each sector, were as follows: pig iron 93.5% (1989 figures), crude steel 63.9% (1989 figures),[1] heavy plate 84%, band steel 98.4%, seamless pipe 99.5%, NC (numerical control) engine lathe 69%, hydraulic shovel 98%, fork lift 87.5%, VTR 75%, color TV 75%, air conditioner 73%, refrigerator 79%, general-purpose motor 89%, personal computer 93%, scientific calculator 98%, word processor 72%, semiconductor 64%, four-wheel drive car 79.4%, passenger car 85.2%, two-wheel drive vehicle 100%, railway rolling stock 90.9%, 35 mm camera 90.8%, wristwatch 100%, piano 99.8%, styrene monomer 78.5%, polypropylene 57.6%, polystyrene 59.2%, synthetic rubber 74.6%, coating 58.6%, synthetic detergent 95.5%, color film 100%, tire and tube 98.3%, plate glass 100%, roof tile 100%, ceramic fiber 100%, polyester long/short fiber 78.4%/97.8%, nylon long fiber 92.1%, acrylic short fiber 84.1%, polypropylene staple 100%, printing paper A/B/C 70.2%/82.4%/92.8%, sensitive paper 100%, and beer 100%.[2]

In this sense, we can safely say that a few large (huge) corporations have decisive ruling power in the Japanese economy. Let us refer to Tables 4.1 and 4.2. For example, in FY 1990 the corporations with a capital of ¥1 billion and over (only 0.19% of all corporations) accounted for 19.30% of all employees, up to 60.11% of all net worth (this item has increased markedly over the past 10 years), up to 44.03% of all liabilities and net worth, up to 36.33% of all sales, up to 46.65% of all current profit, and up to 47.81% of all net profit (the latter two items are for FY 1989); thus, the large corporations with a capital of ¥1 billion and over have a very strong economic influence in the Japanese economy (the figures mentioned above are for corporations other than those involved in finance and insurance).

These large or huge corporations, of course, do not exist as isolated and dispersed cases. They exist and work as large corporation groups that themselves consist of certain oligopolistic industrial capital, certain oligopolistic bank capital and certain

TABLE 4.1. Position of Large Corporations in All Japanese Incorporated Businesses (1960, 70, 80, 90)

Item	By scale of capital	FY 1960	FY 1970	FY 1980	FY 1990
Corporations	All	497,206	874,692	1,567,764	2,020,455
	¥1 billion and over	415	1,185	2,020	3,805
	Of which (%)	0.08	0.14	0.13	0.19
Employees	All (1,000 persons)	14,216	22,087	27,962	34,537
	¥1 billion and over	2,262	4,323	4,639	6,666
	Of which (%)	15.91	19.57	16.60	19.30
Net worth	All (1,000 persons)	6,329.1	23,725.8	76,212.1	218,642.5
	¥1 billion and over	3,388.5	12,383.0	37,057.3	131,435.7
	Of which (%)	52.91	52.19	48.62	60.11
Liabilities and net worth	All (1,000 persons)	27,965.4	147,512.7	499,405.8	1,142,106.8
	¥1 billion and over	11,867.5	68,945.2	209,053.1	502,866.4
	Of which (%)	42.43	46.73	41.86	44.03
Sales	All (1,000 persons)	45,510.9	213,945.9	819,818.9	1,428,180.7
	¥1 billion and over	12,361.9	75,272.8	292,820.6	518,819.0
	Of which (%)	28.04	35.18	35.72	36.33

Excludes finance and insurance.
Sources: Nakamura T. *Huge Corporations in Japan* [J]. Tokyo: Iwanami Shoten, 1983, p. 7; *Annual Report on Financial Statements of Incorporated Businesses* [J], 1991, Tokyo: Ministry of Finance, pp. 46f.

oligopolistic commercial capital, and as the capitals relating to these, in the contemporary Japanese economy. The ruling capitals in Japan, which are discussed in more detail in the next paragraph, consist of the following six large corporation groups: Mitsui, Mitsubishi, Sumitomo, Fuyo (Fuji), Sanwa and Ichikan. (Note, the term "large corporation group" signifies a group of large, independent and equal corporations belonging to one (or more) of the six president's clubs shown in Table 4.5.) Of the many large corporations mentioned, the huge corporations, which belong to these six large corporation groups, stand at the center. They have decisive and ruling economic power over other large corporations and, furthermore, over many medium and small enterprises through stockholdings, credit accommodation and director delegation.

Looking at the position of these six large corporation groups in the Japanese economy, as shown in Table 4.3, their ratios in 1980, 1983, 1987 and 1990 were 15.09%, 14.44%, 15.00%, and 17.35% of all equity capital values, respectively. Similarly, during 1980, 1983, 1987 and 1990, they employed 4.91%, 4.87%, 4.14%, and 4.05% the workforce, respectively, held 15.34%, 15.30%, 12.96%, and 15.03% of all assets, respectively, and accounted for 15.59%, 16.18%, 14.35%, and 15.16% of all sales, 12.08%, 14.57%, 11.70%, and 13.71% of all current profits and 12.84%, 17.58%, 11.88%, and 15.13% of all net profits, respectively. The absolute values of these items (i.e. the total figures and values of the six large corporation groups regarding these items) changed from 1980 to 1985 and to 1990 as follows: employees 1.37 to 1.43 and to 1.34 million persons, respectively (ratio 1990 to 1980 data: 0.98); total assets ¥77 to 100 and to 155 trillion (2.01); equity capital ¥3.8 to 4.9 and to 9.3 trillion (2.45); sales ¥128 to 170 and to 217

TABLE 4.2 Financial Circumstances of Japanese Corporations (FY 1989)

(Unit: ¥ billion)

	Corporations	Total assets	Current assets	Fixed assets	Current liabilities	Fixed liabilities	Net worth	Capital	Sales	Current profit	Net profit
All industries	1,937,322	1,061,353	626,391	432,604	536,764	323,116	201,362	52,630	1,307,850	38,915	17,982
Manufacturing	414,636	337,653	207,152	129,997	155,024	80,444	102,180	22,528	388,571	18,193	8,835
By scale of Capital											
All industries											
<¥2 million	556,936	28,052	15,030	12,958	13,451	11,849	2,751	495	42,904	834	404
¥2–5 million	583,188	52,025	31,717	20,215	26,737	18,091	7,197	1,586	87,988	1,725	730
¥5–10 million	397,117	58,139	34,762	23,175	31,392	17,517	9,229	2,367	91,522	2,102	1,162
¥10–50 million	348,416	254,114	153,097	100,081	137,149	83,169	33,781	7,228	330,924	8,690	3,853
¥50–100 million	29,335	68,909	42,851	25,879	40,035	19,491	9,382	1,919	94,823	2,636	1,039
¥100 million to ¥1 billion	18,916	144,955	92,356	52,366	85,344	39,875	19,736	4,354	182,204	4,774	2,198
¥1 billion or more	3,414	455,159	256,578	197,930	202,656	133,124	119,285	34,681	477,485	18,154	8,597
Manufacturing											
<¥2 million	118,935	5,437	3,349	1,987	2,926	1,628	793	106	8,588	185	107
¥2–5 million	121,193	11,243	6,978	4,250	5,268	3,336	2,638	332	16,037	496	257
¥5–10 million	82,302	16,754	10,314	6,400	9,134	4,802	2,818	493	20,516	732	342
¥10–50 million	76,973	56,663	36,530	19,929	28,959	16,116	11,582	1,655	78,837	2,852	1,397
¥50–100 million	7,956	19,079	11,954	7,069	9,872	4,849	4,358	529	26,011	999	439
¥100 million to ¥1 billion	5,605	37,655	23,212	14,382	20,737	8,107	8,811	1,397	50,668	2,036	933
¥1 billion or more	1,672	190,913	114,815	75,980	78,128	41,604	71,181	18,017	187,913	10,893	5,360

Exludes finance and insurance.
Source: *Economic Statistics Yearbook* [J]. 1991, Tokyo: Toyo Keizai Inc., p. 284.

TABLE 4.3 The Position of the Six Large Corporation Groups in the Japanese Economy (1970–90, s.y.)

(Unit: %)

FY	Employees	Total assets	Capital	Sales	Current profit	Net profit
1970	5.87	17.52	18.92	14.95	13.61	13.24
1975	5.11	15.76	14.74	14.94	8.29	18.55
1980	4.91	15.34	15.09	15.59	12.08	12.84
1983	4.87	15.30	14.44	16.18	14.57	17.58
1986	4.41	13.73	14.36	14.23	11.41	12.44
1987	4.14	12.96	15.00	14.35	11.70	11.88
1988	3.95	12.84	15.54	13.62	12.57	12.27
1989	4.00	13.52	17.24	16.17	13.30	14.00
1990	4.05	15.03	17.35	15.16	13.71	15.13

Excludes finance and insurance.
Sources: *A Comprehensive Survey of Japanese Corporate Groups* [J], 1985, Tokyo: Toyo Keizai Inc., p. 15; *op.cit.*, 1992, p. 33.

TABLE 4.4 The Position of the Six Large Corporation Groups in the Corporations with a Capital of ¥1 Billion and over (FY 1990)

Item	Six large corporation groups	Corporation capital ¥1 billion and over
Employees (1,000 persons)	1,339 (21.0%)	6,666
Total assets (¥ trillion)	155.1 (30.8%)	502.9
Capital	9.4 (25.0%)	37.6
Sales	216.5 (41.7%)	518.8
Current profit	5.2 (27.7%)	18.8
Net profit	2.7 (30.3%)	8.9

Excludes finance and insurance.
Sources: *A Comprehensive Survey of Japanese Corporate Groups* [J], 1992, op. cit., p. 33; *Annual Report on Financial Statements of Incorporated Business* [J], 1991, op. cit., pp. 46f.

trillion (1.70); current profit ¥2.4 to 3.1 and to 5.2 trillion (2.17); and net profit ¥1.2 to 1.5 and to 2.7 trillion (2.25).[3] It should be noted that the number of employees from 1980 to 1990 hardly changed (ratio 0.98; a small decrease), while the other items increased significantly (1.7–2.45-fold) in the 1980s. This suggests that, relatively speaking, the wage costs of the large corporation groups' enterprises were reduced considerably during this period.

From these figures, we can conclude that the economic power of the six large corporation groups is not small, but we may not be able to conclude decisively that it is strong. However, as Table 4.4 shows, the position of the six large corporation groups among the corporations with a capital of ¥1 billion and over was very strong in 1990 given that they employed 21.0% of the workforce, and accounted for 30.8% of total assets, 25.0% of equity capital, 41.7% of sales, 27.7% of current profit, and 30.3% of net profit. Moreover, these figures exclude those of finance and insurance. Therefore, taking account of the strong financial power of the six large corporations, we can say that their economic ruling power is actually much stronger. From these facts and the content of Tables 4.1 and 4.2, we can easily find that the huge corporations belonging to the six large corporation groups, which stand at the center of large corporations with a capital of ¥1 billion and over, and have real ruling power, from the top of a pyramidal structure, over other large corporations, and medium and small enterprises and, furthermore, the Japanese economy as a whole.

Notes

1. *Toyo Keizai Monthly Statistics* [J], September 1990, p. 29.
2. *Op. cit.*, November 1991, pp. 16–25; *op. cit.*, December 1991, pp. 30–39.
3. *A Comprehensive Survey of Japanese Corporate Groups* [J], 1987. Tokyo: Toyo Keizai Inc., p. 15; *op. cit.*, 1992, p. 33.

4.2 The Six Large Corporation Groups and the Large Corporation System

Refering to Table 4.5 (i.e. the list, by sector, of representative corporations (corporations making their own president's club) belonging to the six large corporation groups), it can be seen that the corporation groups that include these large corporations as main members stand in the center of the Japanese large corporation system. Of course, there are other huge corporations and affiliated groups in addition to these that have important economic significance and should not be passed over. These include: (1) independent huge trusts, such as Nippon Steel Corp., Matsushita Electric Industrial Co., Nippon Telegraph and Telephone Corp. and Hitachi Ltd (which simultaneously belongs to three different groups, as shown in Table 4.5) etc.; (2) huge banks, such as the Industrial Bank of Japan, Tokai Bank and Daiwa Bank etc., and huge life insurance companies, such as Nippon Life Insurance and Dai-ichi Mutual Life Insurance etc.; and (3) huge public utility corporations, such as the Tokyo Electric Power Co., Kansai Electric Power Co., Tokyo Gas Co. and Osaka Gas Co. etc. Of these, the representative independent large corporations and their corporate companies are shown in Table 4.6. Because well-known Japanese securities companies have recently played an important role in the capital market at home and abroad, the following companies can be nominated as the four largest securities companies in Japan: Nomura, Daiwa, Nikko and Yamaichi Securities Co. (Incidentally, each of these has a relatively close relationship with the major banks: Nomura Securities Co.—Sakura Bank; Daiwa Securities Co.—Sumitomo Bank; Nikko Securities Co.—Mitsubishi Bank; and Yamaichi Securities Co.—Fuji Bank.) Semilarge securities companies (and their affiliations) include Kokusai (affiliated with Nomura Securities), New Japan (IBJ, Industrial Bank of Japan), Kankaku (Dai-ichi Kangyo Bank), Sanyo (Nomura Securities Co.), Wako (IBJ), Okasan (IBJ), Cosmo (Daiwa Bank), Tokyo (Nikko Securities Co.), Taiheiyo (Yamaichi Securities Co.), Universal (Daiwa Securities Co.), Dai-ichi (Long-Term Credit Bank of Japan), Yamatane Securities Co. (Taiyo Kobe Mitsui (Sakura) Bank), Meiko (Sumitomo Bank), Daito (Fuji Bank), Ryoko (Mitsubishi Bank), Towa (Sanwa Bank), Maruman (Tokai Bank), and Chiyoda (Asahi Bank).[1]

However, of the large corporation groups that comprise huge bank capital, huge industrial capital and huge commercial capital ("Sogo Shôsha"; general trading firm),

TABLE 4.5 President Club Members of the Six Large Corporation Groups (November 1991)

Sector	Mitsui Gr. (Nimokukai, 26 Co.) inaug. Oct. 1961	Mitsubishi Gr. (Kinyokai, 29 Co.) inaug. 1954	Sumitomo Gr. (Hakusuikai, 20 Co.) inaug. April 1951
Banking insurance	Taiyo Kobe Mitsui Bank Mitsui Trust and Banking Mitsui Mutual Life Ins.[1] Mitsui Marine and Fire Ins.	Mitsubishi Bank Mitsubishi Trust and Banking Meiji Mutual Life Ins.[1] Tokio Marine and Fire Ins. (Nippon Trust Bank)[5]	Sumitomo Bank Sumitomo Trust and Banking Sumitomo Life Ins.[1] Sumitomo Marine and Fire Ins.
General trading	Mitsui and Co.	Mitsubishi Corp.	Sumitomo Corp.
Mining	Mitsui Mining Co. Hokkaido Tanko Kisen[1,2]		Sumitomo Coal Mining Co.
Construction	Mitsui Construction Co. Sanki Engineering Co.	[1]Mitsubishi Construction Co.	Sumitomo Construction Co. Sumitomo Forestry Co.
Foods and beverages	Nippon Flour Mills Co.	Kirin Brewery Co.	
Textiles	Toray Industries	Mitsubishi Rayon Co.	
Paper and pulp	Oji Paper Co.	Mitsubishi Paper Mills	
Chemicals	Mitsui Toatsu Chemicals Denki Kagaku Kogyo[3] Mitsui Petrochemical Ind.	Mitsubishi Kasei Corp. Mitsubishi Gas Chemical Mitsubishi Petrochemical Co. Mitsubishi Plastics Ind.	Sumitomo Chemical Co. Sumitomo Bakelite Co.
Petroleum		Mitsubishi Oil Co.	
Rubber			
Glass; Cement	Onoda Cement Co.	Asahi Glass Co.	Nippon Sheet Glass Co. Sumitomo Cement Co.
Iron and Steel	Japan Steel Works	Mitsubishi Steel Mfg.	Sumitomo Metal Industries
Non-ferrous metals	Mitsui Mining and Smelting	Mitsubishi Materials Corp. Mitsubishi Shindoh Co. Mitsubishi Cable Ind. Mitsubishi Aluminum Co.[1]	Sumitomo Metal Mining Co. Sumitomo Light Metal Ind. Sumitomo Electric Ind.
Machinery		Mitsubishi Kakoki	Sumitomo Heavy Industries
Electric equipment	Toshiba Corp.	Mitsubishi Electric Corp.	NEC Corp.
Transportation equipment	Mitsui Engineering and Shipbuilding Ishikawajima-Harima Heavy Ind.[3] Toyota Motor Corp.[4]	Mitsubishi Heavy Ind. Mitsubishi Motors Corp.	
Precision instrument		Nikon Corp.	
Department stores	Mitsukoshi		
Finance			
Real estate	Mitsui Fudosan Co.	Mitsubishi Estate Co.	Sumitomo Reality and Development
Transporatation communication	Mitsui OSK Lines Mitsui Soko Co.	Nippon Yusen Mitsubishi Warehouse and Transportation	Sumitomo Warehouse Co.
Others		Mitsubishi Sogo Kenkyusho[1,2]	

[1] Unlisted company. [2] The English translation of the company name cannot be found in the *Japan Company Handbook* (Tokyo: Toyo Keizai, Autumn 1992). [3] The company belongs to several groups. [4] Toyota Motor is the observer of the Mitsui group, but is added to the company's number of the group. [5] Companies given in parentheses are not members of the group and have been added for reference only.

Source: *A Comprehensive Survey of Japanese Corporate Groups* [J], 1992, Tokyo: Toyo Keizai Inc., p. 50.

Fuyo Gr. (Fuyokai, 29 Co.) inaug. Jan. 1966	Sanwa Gr. (Sansuikai, 44 Co.) inaug. Feb. 1967	Ichikan Gr. (Sankinkai, 47 Co.) inaug. Jan. 1978
Fuji Bank Yasuda Trust and Banking Yasuda Mutual Life Ins.[1] Yasuda Fire and Marine Ins.	Sanwa Bank Toyo Trust and Banking Nippon Life Ins.[1] (Daido Mutual Life Ins.[1])	Dai-Ichi Kangyo Bank Asahi Mutual Life Ins.[1] Fukoku Mutual Life Ins.[1] Nissan Fire and Marine Ins. Taisei Fire and Marine Ins.
Marubeni Corp.	Nichimen Corp. Nissho Iwai Corp.[3] Iwatani International Corp.	C. Itoh and Co. Kanematsu Corp. Nissho Iwai Corp[3] Kawasho Corp.
Taisei Corp.	Obayashi Corp. Zenitaka Corp. Toyo Construction Co. Sekisui House	Shimizu Corp.
Nissin Flour Milling Co. Sapporo Breweries Nichirei Corp.	Itoham Foods Inc. Suntory[1]	
Nisshinbo Ind. Toho Rayon Co.	Unitika Teijin	Asahi Chemical Ind.
Sanyo Kokusaku Pulp		Honshu Paper Co.
Showa Denko Kureha Chemical Ind. Nippon Oil and Fats Co.	Tokuyama Soda Co. Sekisui Chemical Co. Ube Industries Hitachi Chemical Co. Tanabe Seiyaku Co. Fujisawa Pharmaceutiacal Co. Kansai Paint Co.	Denki Kagaku Kogyo[3] Kogyo Kyowa Hakko Kogyo Nippon Zeon Co. Asahi Denka Kogyo Sankyo Co. Shinseido Co. Lion Corp.
Tonen Corp.	Cosmo Oil Co.	Showa Shell Sekiyu
	Toyo Tire and	Yokohama Rubber Co.
Nihon Cement Co.	Osaka Cement Co.	Chichibu Cement Co.
NKK Corp.	Kobe Steel[3] Nisshin Steel Co. Nakayama Steel Works Hitachi Metals	Kawasaki Steel Corp. Kobe Steel[3] Japan Metals and Chemicals Co.
	Hitachi Cable	Nippon Light Metal Co. Furukawa Co. Furukawa Electric Co.
Kubota Corp. Nihon Seiko Co.	NTN	Niigata Engineering Co. Iseki and Co. Ebara Corp.
Hitachi Ltd.[3] Oki Electric Ind. Yokogawa Electric Corp.	Hitachi Ltd.[3] Iwatsu Electric Co. Sharp Corp. Kyocera Corp. Nitto Denko Corp.	Hitachi Ltd.[3] Fuji Electric Co. Yasukawa Electric Corp. Fujitsu Nippon Columbia Co.
Nissan Motor Co.	Hitachi Zosen Corp. Shin Meiwa Ind. Daihatsu Motor Co.	Kawasaki Heavy Ind. Ishikawajima-Harima Heavy Ind.[3] Isuzu Motors
Canon Inc.	Hoya Corp.	Asahi Optical Co.
	Takashimaya Co.	Seibu Hyakkaten[1,2]
	Orix Corp.	Orient Corp. Kankaku Securities Co.
Tokyo Tatemono Co.		
Tobu Railways Co. Keihin Elec. Exp. Railway Showa Line	Hankyu Corp. Nippon Express Co.[3] Navix Line	Nippon Express Co.[3] Kawasaki Kisen Shibusawa Warehouse Co.
		Tokyo Dome Corp.

TABLE 4.6 Typical Independent Large Corporations and their Affiliated Companies (1991)

(Units: ¥ million, %)

Comany name	No. Affiliated Companies	Affiliated Co. Loans and investments	Stocks (book value)	Lending	Stock holdings (book value)	Total assets	a	b
Toyobo Co.	87	54,167	33,661	15,077	74,461	399,149	13.57	45.21
Nippon Oil Co.	60	151,769	56,067	95,702	101,316	2,084,184	7.28	55.34
Nippon Steel Corp.	195	210,109	152,560	49,640	457,345	3,353,463	6.27	33.36
Hitachi Ltd	242	332,282	230,188	46,357	319,569	3,813,377	8.71	72.03
Matsushita Elec.	385	1,287,550	1,164,945	87,424	1,285,209	3,903,496	32.98	90.64
Sony Corp.	114	1,055,522	882,478	201,007	904,190	2,488,056	44.43	97.60
Honda Motor Co.	295	319,065	276,535	42,530	311,497	1,464,559	21.79	88.78
Seiko Corp.	55	66,146	37,530	26,447	65,553	254,257	26.02	57.25
Daiei	130	165,019	130,940	34,079	178,209	911,060	18.11	73.48
Seibu Railway Co.	22	95,634	87,905	7,729	97,000	633,091	15.11	90.62
NTT	152	77,303	77,267	0	154,228	10,928,978	0.71	50.10

(a) The ratio of the value of loans and investments to total assets of the large corporation; (b) the ratio of the value of affiliated companies' stocks value to the stock holdings of the large corporations.
Source: *Ibid.*, p. 54.

TABLE 4.7 Trends in the Interlocking Stockholding Ratio and the Financing Ratios to Group Companies in the Six Large Corporation Groups (1975–95, s.y.)

(Unit: %)

FY	Interlocking stockholding ratio 1975	80	83	87	90	95	Financing ratio to group companies 1975	80	83	87	90	95
Mitsui Gr.	17.50	17.62	17.67	17.10	16.54	16.26	21.20	19.05	18.85	21.94	19.62	20.50
Mitsubishi Gr.	27.84	29.26	24.39	27.80	26.89	26.94	29.17	24.88	23.06	20.17	19.43	19.26
Sumitomo Gr.	25.94	26.74	25.06	24.22	24.06	22.33	30.52	27.78	29.97	24.53	21.49	20.44
Fuyo Gr.	13.77	16.26	15.74	15.61	15.44	14.12	22.37	18.76	17.50	18.20	17.42	16.92
Sanwa Gr.	14.14	16.78	16.56	16.47	16.40	15.72	20.20	20.97	19.88	18.51	18.19	17.35
Ichikan Gr.	11.80	14.12	13.72	12.49	12.06	11.50	13.90	13.15	12.41	11.18	12.52	13.94

Gr., group.
Source: *Op.cit.*, 1985, p. 28; *op.cit.*, 1992, pp. 40–49; *op.cit.*, 1997, pp. 38–47.

and that have both strong cohesive force and multilateral development power because of interlocking stockholdings, financing of group companies and mutual delegations of directors, we should indicate the six large corporation groups mentioned earlier (see: Table 4.5).

Table 4.7 shows the changes in the interlocking stockholding ratios and the financing ratios of group companies. In 1990, the order of interlocking stockholdings was Mitsubishi, Sumitomo, Mitsui, Sanwa, Fuyo and Ichikan. The order of financing ratios to group companies was Sumitomo, Mitsui, Mitsubishi, Sanwa, Fuyo and Ichikan. With regard to both indices, the figures for corporation groups of *Zaibatsu* (old Japanese combine) descent were larger than those of corporation groups from a bank descent.

Considering the figures for interlocking stockholdings and their significance, looking at each group as a whole, these figures are in the minority. In addition, separately, these figures are very different for each company and seldom are higher than 50%. As a matrix, the quota of each company is, at most, several percent (insurance and finance company etc.; of course, there are legal limits for stockholding, for example, in the case of the former it is 10%, while for the latter it is 5%). However, these figures of interlocking stockholdings make practical and stable business control over corporations possible in the contemporary economy, particularly in the Japanese economy after World War II. In this sense, interlocking stockholdings within a group are the economic basis that make the group and its companies, both in peacetime and particularly in situations of crises, behave as if a "pseudo-holding system"[2] existed. On this basis, financing by financial institutions of the same group to group companies and the mutual delegation of directors in the same group form other important economic conditions that strengthen the unification and development of the corporation group.

The actual mechanisms of interlocking stockholdings and financing to group companies of each group, although it cannot be shown as a matrix because of limitations of space, are shown for two groups (Mitsubishi and Fuyo) in Tables 4.8 and 4.9.

Furthermore, on the theme of combinations within the large corporation group, it should be noted that such combinations not only consist of the president's club, which is surely the most representative organization, but are complemented by meetings at different levels (e.g. of vice-presidents, of directors, of heads of departments etc.), and that, as a whole, multilayer relations are formed within the large corporation group.[3]

On this most important matter of the "president's club", Professor Okumura Hiroshi, who is a famous proponent of the "corporate capitalism theory", after analyzing the actual situation of the Japanese interlocking stockholdings mentioned above, estimated it to be a "de facto large shareholders' club" and concluded that "the coexisting system of mutual rule and mutual reliance" and "the system of multilateral reciprocal rule" exists among the corporations that form the president's club.[4] I think this is an insightful observation.

Finally, Table 4.10 shows the number of director delegations of major banks, main corporations and government departments to other listed companies. In Table 4.10 (i.e. in the development of director participation networks), the summit of the Japanese large corporation system, including political society (state), is shown, even if only partially.

TABLE 4.8 Interlocking Stockholding and Financing within the Mitsubishi Group (FY 1990, 1987)
(Unit: %)

No.	Passive Co.	Stocks issued (million shares)	Total (incl. others)	do. FY 1987	a			
					b	c	Total	do. FY 1987
1	Mitsubishi Bank	2,875.3	25.34	25.67	—	—	—	—
2	Mitsubishi Trust and Banking	1,302.1	28.58	28.98	—	—	—	—
3	Nippon Trust Bank	216.6	14.39	14.36	—	—	—	—
4	TokioMarine and Fire Insurance	1,544.7	22.91	23.31	—	—	—	—
5	Mitsubishi Corp.	1,563.1	32.92	31.75	6.47	3.85	12.48	13.13
6	Kirin Brewery Co.	1,002.3	19.49	18.77	26.53	11.05	46.43	41.65
7	Mitsubishi Rayon Co.	627.4	23.40	25.52	24.47	10.65	40.45	30.56
8	Mitsubishi Paper Mills	323.7	31.53	33.65	23.18	12.83	50.88	39.66
9	Mitsubishi Kasei Corp.	1,407.6	22.31	22.75	14.49	8.86	26.11	26.54
10	Mitsubishi Gas Chemical	498.0	24.84	26.55	15.68	15.70	36.89	30.66
11	Mitsubishi Petrochemical Co.	492.4	32.77	34.36	19.07	9.49	29.83	29.83
12	Mitsubishi Plastics Ind.	219.1	56.86	59.93	18.48	17.01	46.37	38.61
13	Mitsubishi Oil Co.	345.2	42.96	45.63	23.24	7.52	31.40	30.38
14	Asahi Glass Co.	1,166.0	27.94	28.60	0	0	0	7.12
15	Mitsubishi Steel Mfg	144.0	36.92	35.92	25.64	17.32	55.45	43.48
16	Mitsubishi Materials Corp.	1,088.8	24.71	21.37	13.70	11.67	30.46	28.46
17	Mitsubishi Shindoh Co.	46.0	52.65	50.52	23.65	24.47	50.88	51.07
18	Mitsubishi Cable Ind.	189.2	48.37	52.10	23.95	19.13	43.35	32.63
19	Mitsubishi Kakoki	79.1	34.14	35.77	14.79	14.54	34.54	33.34
20	Mitsubishi Electric Corp.	2,140.1	17.02	17.65	24.62	12.74	41.39	36.67
21	Mitsubishi Heavy Ind.	3,362.6	20.56	20.76	16.38	8.11	26.49	21.18
22	Mitsubishi Motors Corp.	853.8	53.63	—	17.37	8.88	32.37	—
23	Nikon Corp.	369.6	28.79	27.73	13.89	7.45	47.79	38.79
24	Mitsubishi Estate Co.	1,284.4	27.40	25.06	12.26	11.10	29.68	44.06
25	Nippon Yusen Co.	1,147.7	26.37	25.70	4.86	4.22	16.80	11.81
26	Mitsubishi Warehouse and Transportation	167.6	42.08	41.08	22.72	9.96	36.03	36.25
Average ratios		24,457.6	26.89	—	10.23	6.04	19.43	—
(do. FY 1987)		21,391.7	—	27.80	10.69	6.63	—	20.17

(a) Financing ratio of the group's financial institutions; (b) Mitsubishi Bank; (c) Mitsubishi Trust and Banking.
Source: *A Comprehensive Survey of Japanese Corporate Groups* [J], 1992, pp. 42f.

TABLE 4.9 Interlocking Stockholding and Financing within the Fuyo Group (FY 1990, 1987)

(Unit: %)

No.	Passive Co.	Stocks issued (million shares)	Total (incl. others)	do. FY 1987	a: b	a: c	a: Total	a: do. FY 1987
1	Fuji Bank	2,894.9	26.99	27.92	—	—	—	—
2	Yasuda Trust and Banking	1,102.9	28.94	28.27	—	—	—	—
3	Yasuda Fire and marine Ins.	887.7	17.63	17.79	—	—	—	—
4	Marubeni Corp.	1,490.0	19.37	22.45	7.19	4.74	13.95	12.83
5	Taisei Corp.	1,018.9	8.70	9.28	18.40	10.23	31.50	35.38
6	Nisshin Flour Milling Co.	204.6	9.19	8.75	14.30	4.29	18.59	17.18
7	Sapporo Breweries	333.8	21.68	15.94	6.37	15.24	30.91	25.74
8	Nichirei Corp.	309.2	10.27	9.20	26.42	4.58	30.99	27.78
9	Nisshinbo Ind.	235.5	13.73	11.32	36.75	4.05	40.80	42.56
10	Toho Rayon Co.	91.7	40.43	41.67	16.15	5.13	21.28	40.38
11	Sanyo-Kokusaku Pulp.	449.3	13.09	14.69	8.33	6.59	20.95	21.51
12	Showa Denko	1,037.8	19.31	19.65	19.82	11.70	33.32	27.80
13	Kureha Chemical Ind.	221.6	21.42	21.59	11.06	8.73	22.79	17.09
14	Nippon Oil and Fats Co.	218.0	23.63	22.63	27.75	13.57	41.31	32.61
15	Tonen Corp.	646.5	10.15	9.97	13.28	2.57	15.85	8.92
16	Nihon Cement Co.	326.6	19.14	15.97	17.13	13.18	31.18	32.83
17	NKK Corp.	3,523.5	12.79	12.87	10.35	9.07	21.68	21.10
18	Kubota Corp.	1,408.6	10.37	10.19	1.27	—	4.10	11.52
19	Nihon Seiko Co.	556.9	19.91	23.27	12.11	6.89	20.87	44.94
20	Hitachi, Ltd.	3,273.6	5.24	6.76	9.13	3.45	12.59	13.32
21	Oki Electric ind.	607.8	21.43	20.17	13.89	7.80	23.97	29.23
22	Yokogawa Electric Corp.	259.2	10.92	8.65	15.39	3.30	18.69	22.23
23	Nissan Motor Co.	2,511.4	14.64	15.51	10.28	4.15	15.04	16.98
24	Canon Inc.	746.7	9.86	9.94	18.30	1.26	19.56	29.23
25	Tokyo Tatemono Co.	227.9	25.95	29.26	15.00	9.40	30.78	34.37
26	Tobu Railway Co.	813.9	5.61	5.30	5.34	8.76	15.12	15.29
27	Keihan Elec. Exp. Railway	492.4	10.97	11.47	6.74	6.66	14.63	14.51
28	Showa Line	273.4	32.26	32.90	2.43	1.98	5.76	15.53
Average ratios		26,165.4	15.44	—	9.31	6.13	17.42	—
(do. FY 1987)		22,659.6	—	15.61	10.23	6.36	—	18.20

(a) Financing ratio of the group's financial institutions; (b) Fuji Bank; (c) Yasuda Trust and Banking.
Source: *Ibid.*, pp. 44f.

TABLE 4.10 Number of Delegated Directors of Major Banks, Main Firms and Government Departments and Public Corporations to Other Listed Companies (1990; in case of firms, 15 persons and over)

Delegating company	FY 1990			Delegating company	FY 1990		
	No. delegated companies	No. directors	a		No. delegated companies	No. directors	a
Financial Institution				Matsushita Electric Ind.	18	43	10
Industrial Bank of Japan	104	149	51	Sony Corp.	10	34	7
Dai-Ichi Kangyo Bank	143	239	43	Hitachi Zosen Corp.	9	63	15
Taiyo Kobe Mitsui Bank	131	182	30	Mitsubishi Heavy Ind.	30	49	9
Mitsubishi Bank	128	178	29	Nissan Motor Co.	31	113	12
Fuji Bank	130	176	39	Isuzu Motors	14	36	6
Sumitomo Bank	89	178	49	Toyota Motor Corp.	34	139	45
Sanwa Bank	108	171	31	C. Itoh and Co.	48	91	15
Tokai Bank	80	144	31	Marubeni Corp.	29	55	8
Dai-ichi Mutual Life Insurance	48	51	0	Kanematsu Corp.	10	34	6
Nippon Life Insurance	52	55	1	Mitsui and Co.	51	114	26
				Sumitomo Corp.	23	57	9
Firm				Mitsubishi Corp.	67	110	15
Taisei Corp.	19	49	11	Nissho Iwai Corp.	24	59	14
Misawa Homes Co.	7	33	3	Daiei	10	76	10
Toyobo Co.	11	34	16	Tokyu Corp.	14	57	9
Toray Ind.	18	33	4	Odakyu Electric Railway	7	39	6
Asahi chemical Ind.	20	48	10	Kinki Nippon Railway	12	34	7

Showa Denko	11	34	8	Hankyu Corp.	13	33	5
Sumitomo Chemical Co.	16	45	12	Mitsui OSK Lines	11	40	11
Mitsubishi Kasei Co.	20	65	7	NTT	75	212	28
Asahi Glass Co.	10	37	7	Tokyo Electric Power	33	65	15
Nippon Steel Co.	63	207	29	Kansai Electric Power	22	47	6
NKK Corp.	17	51	6				
Sumitomo Metal Ind.	22	73	19	Government and Public			
Kobe Steel	17	60	10	Bank of Japan	87	114	46
Nippon Mining Co.	11	35	6	Ministry of Finance	115	144	58
Sumitomo Electric Ind.	15	89	16	National Tax Adm. Agency	42	46	2
Komatsu Ltd	8	41	5	Ministry of Agriculture, F.a.F.	46	50	1
Hitachi Ltd	49	216	22	Ministry of Int. Trade and Industry	88	96	28
Toshiba Corp.	28	84	13	Ministry of Transport	31	49	11
Mitsubishi Electric Ind.	19	63	9	Ministry of Construction	88	123	22
NEC Corp.	24	97	17	Ex-Japanese National Railways	49	101	21
Fujitsu Ltd	19	90	11	Housing and Urban Dev. Corp.	38	45	2
Oki Electric Ind.	11	32	8	Japan Highway Public Corp.	57	59	3

(a) Of which, the number of directors who have authority to represent a company.
Source: *Ibid.*, p. 91.

Notes

1. *The Financial Business* [J]. Tokyo: Toyo Keizai Inc., April 1992, pp. 42f.; *The Weekly Toyo Keizai* [J], March 26, 1994, p. 18; *AM*, October 20, 1994. It should be noted that Yamaichi Securities Co. went bankrupt in November 1997.
2. Koga Y. and Tanaka T. "The sophistication of industrial structure and the ruling structure of corporation groups". In: Fujii M. and Maruyama Y. (eds). *The Structure of Japanese-style Management* [J]. Tokyo: Otsuki Shoten 1985, pp. 98–106.
3. For more details, see: *Japanese Six Large Corporation Groups. Their Organization and Behavior* [J]. Fair Trade Commission (ed.). Tokyo: Toyo Keizai Inc., 1992, pp. 6–11.
4. Okumura H. *Corporate Capitalism. A System for Company* [J]. Tokyo: Asahi Bunko 1991, pp. 200, 229f.

   For reference, the historical trends in the composition of stockholders in Japan is shown. Apparently, as shown in Table 4.11, although the ratio of individuals reached approximately 70% in 1949, it declined constantly after World War II and fell to nearly 20% at the end of the 1980s. In contrast, the ratio of corporations, especially of financial institutions, increased markedly.

TABLE 4.11 Trends in Stockholdings Ratio by Holder (1949–1995, s.y.)

(Unit: %)

FY	Government and local government	Financial institutions	Investment trusts	Securities companies	Other business corporations	Individuals	Foreigners (corporations and individuals)
1949	2.8	9.9	—	12.6	5.6	69.1	—
1950	3.1	12.6	—	11.9	11.0	61.3	—
1952	1.0	15.8	6.0	8.4	11.8	55.8	1.2
1954	0.5	16.7	7.0	7.1	13.0	54.0	1.7
1956	0.3	21.7	3.9	7.1	15.7	49.9	1.5
1958	0.3	22.4	6.6	4.4	15.8	49.1	1.5
1960	0.2	23.1	7.5	3.7	17.8	46.3	1.4
1962	0.2	21.5	9.2	2.5	17.7	47.1	1.8
1964	0.2	21.6	7.9	4.4	18.4	45.6	1.9
1966	0.2	26.1	3.7	5.4	18.6	44.1	1.9
1968	0.3	30.3	1.7	2.1	21.4	41.9	2.3
1970	0.3	30.9	1.4	1.2	23.1	39.9	3.2
1972	0.2	33.8	1.3	1.8	26.6	32.7	3.5
1974	0.2	33.9	1.6	1.3	27.1	33.4	2.5
1976	0.2	35.1	1.4	1.4	26.5	32.9	2.6
1978	0.2	36.6	2.2	1.8	26.3	30.8	2.1
1980	0.2	37.3	1.5	1.7	26.0	29.2	4.0
1982	0.2	37.7	1.2	1.8	26.0	28.0	5.1
1984	0.2	38.5	1.1	1.9	25.9	26.3	6.1
1986	0.9	41.7	1.8	2.5	24.5	23.9	4.7
1988	0.7	42.5	3.1	2.5	24.9	22.4	4.0
1990	0.6	41.6	3.6	1.7	25.2	23.1	4.2
1992	0.6	41.3	3.2	1.2	24.4	23.9	5.5
1995	0.6	39.3	2.1	1.4	23.6	23.6	9.4

Sources: Okumura H. *The Structure of Corporate Capitalism* (New Edition) [J]. Tokyo: Shakai Shiso Sha, 1991, p. 326; *ESA*, 1996, p. 252.

4.3 Characteristics of Japanese-Style Management

The Japanese economy successfully overcame each recent serious "crisis" (i.e. two oil crises in 1973/74 and 1979/80 and the rapid and large shift to a strong yen in 1985/86) and, conversely, with these opportunities further heightened its international position in the world economy. It can be said that Japanese-style management was an important factor that made the success and development of the Japanese economy possible. This has attracted world-wide attention.

The fundamental features of Japanese-style management include lifetime employment; a seniority system; an enterprise labor union; ability-, performance- and results-based selection and integration after giving laborers (blue-collar) and staff (white-collar) single employee status; flexibility in duties performed through job rotation; the development of multiskilled workers through job training; quality control (QC) circles and small group activities centered on the productive process and the development of total quality control (TQC) in the company; a personnel assessment system that estimates not only business achievements but also the personality of the employee; realization of high efficiency and extreme cuts in inventory by the Kanban system (Just in Time System); affiliated groupings of related sub-contractors with an outside supplier-ordering system; the ascending character of the decision making process (*Ringi* System); the selection of managers (directors) from among employees; the predominance of large corporate stockholders and the relative absence of owner-managers.[1]

Japanese-style management, as characterized by these factors, was realized and has been developing mainly in large corporations that have stable industrial relations and a solid accumulative foundation. There, the latest technological and productive equipment in the world and the above-mentioned production management and employment system are united, high productivity and labor density are realized, and high quality and low-priced goods with strong international competitiveness are produced.[2]

The Japanese employment system is one of the fundamental conditions making the development of Japanese-style management possible. As is well known, Japanese workers, especially those of large corporations, acquire stable employment and considerably high income even in comparison with workers of other advanced countries; however, they live under the following conditions: a relatively low level of labor's share in the macroeconomy; long-term and high-density labor (which, on occasion, leads to "*karoshi*" (death from overwork)); difficult commuter conditions; a frequent relocation of workers and a change in workplace, and, on occasion, making married employees work alone apart from their families; and neglect, ignorance or oppression of fundamental human rights in the company.

Particularly in large corporations, employees are apt to silently obey their chief and manager as if the interests of capital and labor were almost the same. Conversely, we can say that managers rarely encounter essential and critical resistance from the workforce when they carry out their management plan. In actually fact, during each of the two oil crises and the transition period to a strong yen, the "*genryo keiei*" (reduction in the number of employees) in large corporations of structurally depressed industries occurred smoothly under the hegemony of capital interests and with the agreement of the labor unions, or at least without active resistance from the latter (e.g. from

1975 to 1985 the number of employees in large corporations with a capital of ¥10 billion and over decreased in the following industries as follows: in textiles, from 147 to 85 thousand people; in shipbuilding, from 194 to 128 thousand people; in chemicals from 125 to 94 thousand people; and in iron and steel from 251 to 219 thousand people).[3]

The integration of employees into capital like this was made possible only because of the following conditions: (1) the sweeping exclusion of the political left from companies; (2) military discipline and organization of human relations within the company;[4] (3) remarkable differentials of wages and labor conditions between large corporations and medium and small enterprises; the lack of rights and low wages of part-time workers, casual workers and contingency workers in so-called "middle" or "peripheral" labor markets; (4) the feeling of identification of employees belonging to large corporations with their companies through satisfaction with their high income and fringe benefits (incidentally, the business entertainment expenditure of all Japanese corporations in 1990 reached ¥5.6 trillion according to an investigation of the National Tax Administration Agency Japan);[5] (5) employees of large corporations have been organizing themselves in enterprise unions (moreover, only of formal employees) and have lost the sense of social and universal solidarity; and (6) a lack of powerful social counterprinciples and counterthoughts against capitalism in Japan.[6]

Naturally, there are many diverse opinions about the questions of why have the employees of large corporations been firmly integrated into their companies? Why has their strong loyalty to capital come into being and how is it maintained? Has it been compelled by capital? Or has it been spontaneous? Of course, compulsion and spontaneity occur together to a greater or lesser extent. Also, with regard to the grounds for integration into the company, there are many separate opinions among scholars ranging from an emphasis on labor's autonomous participation to an emphasis on competition among labor organized by capital.[7]

With regard to the grounds for the integration of employees in large corporations into capital, I want to first make note of its material basis. As already mentioned and as will discussed in more detail in Chapter 7, employees working in large corporations have been guaranteed a relatively high income, inclusive of various fringe benefits, and stable employment in comparison with employees working in medium and small enterprises. This is the biggest factor in the integration of employees into capital. On these grounds, both competition among labor and their autonomous participation are important factors. With regard to the problem of compulsion and spontaneity, I affirm, of course, the existence of both elements. However, the spontaneity of labor in Japanese-style management is in the frame set up by capital and to pursue the object set up from the outside by capital.

To the question whether this Japanese-style management is a new system having universal character that is adaptable to countries other than Japan, my answer is negative, for the following reasons: (1) Japanese-style management is connected with the neglect or ignorance of fundamental human rights; (2) it denies the existence of a labor union independent of capital; (3) it sets remarkable differentials in labor conditions between employees in large corporations and other employees; and (4) it compels the employees concerned to be so enterprise-centric as to forget that they are also members of families, regions, states and international society.[8] These conditions are indispensable for the existence of Japanese-style management. Although Japanese-style management is surely a very efficient way in which to pursue business profit, we cannot say that it is a universal system for mankind.

Notes

1. Shibagaki K. The Sublation of Commoditized Labor-Power. Welfare State, Japanese Management and Socialism [J]. In: *The Journal of Social Science* 43 (1), August 1991, p. 160.
2. Aoyama S. "The Development of Overseas Production of Japanese-Style Management." In: Business Administration Society of Japan (ed.). *Reexamination of Japanese-Style Management* [J]. Tokyo: Chikura Shobo, 1990, p. 4.
3. Ito M. "In the Strong Yen and Economic Friction." In: Society for the Study of History (ed.). *Japan. Its Contemporary History*, Vol. 5 [J]. Tokyo: Aoki Shoten, 1991, p. 200.
4. Also, Ronald Dore wrote that "... Japan's peculiarity lies in the fact that a type of organization which in most Western countries is considered suitable only for the army or the civil service is adapted in Japan to industry" (do. *British Factory–Japanese Factory. The Origins of National Diversity in Industrial Relations.* Berkeley: University of California Press, 1973, p. 275) and successively compared the order and principles of a Japanese firm with those of the British army.
5. For more detailed information regarding this, see: Honma M, Atoda N. What Makes the Employees Subordinate to Their Company? [J]. In: *Weekly Economist*, March 17, 1992, pp. 60–63.
6. Hirowatari S. "What is the Today's Problem?" In: Institute of Social Science (ed.). *Contemporary Japanese Society*, Vol. 6, [J]. Tokyo: University of Tokyo Press, 1992, pp. 4, 6.
7. Watanabe O. *The Structure of an "Affluent Society" Japan*, [J]. Tokyo: Rodo Junposha, 1990, p. 56.
8. Kato M. Undiscussed Effects of the "Heterogeneous Japan" Theory [J]. In: *Chishiki* (Knowledge), August 1990, Tokyo: p. 101; Tadokoro M. "Something is Wrong" in Japanese Employment System [J]. In: *Weekly Economist*, October 2, 1990, pp. 78–83.

Chapter 5
Accumulative Structure of the Large Corporation System

5.1 The Earning Capacity and Retained Profit of Large Corporations

First, we will examine the fundamental items of accumulation of Japanese large corporations with a capital of ¥1 billion and over in the 1980s. As shown in Table 5.1, except for the increasing rate of employees (44%), which was below that of the number of corporations (88%), the increasing rates of retained profit (295%), of net worth (255%), of equity capital (182%), of total assets (141%), and of current profit (101%) were over that of the number of corporations for these 10 years. In particular, the increasing rates of retained profit and net worth were conspicuously large. This indicates provisionally, so we can say, that the material basis of the large corporation system was increasingly strengthened throughout the 1980s.

In addition, the trends in current profit (of corporations with a capital of ¥1 billion and over, excepting finance and insurance) relate closely to the above-mentioned fact and represent the typical earning capacity (in ¥ trillion) of corporations in the 1980s as follows: 9.3 (no. corporations: 2,020) in 1980, 8.0 (no. corporations: 2,088) in 1981, 7.9 (no. corporations: 2,195) in 1982, 9.0 (no. corporations: 2,298) in 1983, 11.1 (no. corporations: 2,458) in 1984, 11.4 (no. corporations: 2,598) in 1985, 10.3 (no. corporations: 2,691) in 1986, 12.6 (no. corporations: 2,846) in 1987, 16.1 (no. corporations: 3,088) in 1988, 18.2 (no. corporations: 3,414) in 1989, and 18.8 (no. corporations: 3,805) in 1990.[1]

Apparently after the second oil crisis in 1979/80 and the temporary rapid transition stage to a strong yen phase as a result of the Plaza Agreement in 1985, business income declined a little. However, later on, business activity recovered favorably. In particular, in the latter half of the 1980s, businesses enjoyed an increase in their earnings as never before, because enterprises strove for labor cuts, energy conservation, rationalization investment and new global business strategies corresponding to the strong yen; because the government and the central bank promoted an ultra-low interest policy for the increase of domestic demand; and because as a result of these actions, there was a prolonged boom with stock inflation.

The trends in business results in the latter half of the 1980s will now be examined from a few different angles (the annual trends in current profit mentioned above were also affected by an increase in the number of corporations concerned. Figure 5.1 was created from the main 929 corporations (excepting finance and insurance) of the approximately 2000 corporations listed in the Japanese stock market). As shown in Figure 5.1, the current profit of the main corporations increased smoothly and its

TABLE 5.1 Indices of Large Corporations' Accumulation (with capital of ¥1 billion and over; FY 1980, 1985, 1990)

(Units: ¥ billion, %)

	FY		Growth for 5 years	Growth for 10 years
No. corporations	1980	2,020		
	1985	2,598	29	
	1990	3,805	46	88
Total assets	1980	209,053		
	1985	292,924	40	
	1990	502,886	72	141
Capital	1980	13,319		
	1985	19,765	48	
	1990	37,602	90	182
Net worth	1980	37,057		
	1985	68,714	85	
	1990	131,436	91	255
Retained profit	1980	23,738		
	1985	48,949	106	
	1990	93,834	92	295
Current profit	1980	9,321		
	1985	11,373	22	
	1990	18,780	65	101
Employees 1,000 persons	1980	4,639		
	1985	5,556	20	
	1990	6,666	20	44

Excludes finance and insurance.
Sources: *Annual Report on Financial Statements of Incorporated Business* [J], Tokyo: Ministry of Finance 1981, 1986, 1991, passim.

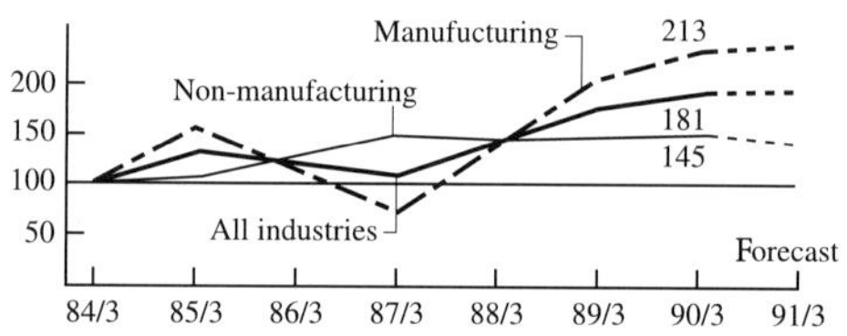

The objects are 929 listed companies, excluding finance and insurance.

FIG. 5.1 Trends in the Current Profit of Main Corporations (FY, 1983–1989; Index, March 1984 = 100)
Source: *NM*, October 23, 1990.

index reached 181 in 1990 (where 1984 = 100). With regard to the non-manufacturing industry, its index of current profit increased to 145 in 1990 without falling below 100 during this period. However, with regard to the manufacturing industry, a reduction in current profit occurred once due to the transition phase to a strong yen in 1985/86, and, after that, because of a business recovery, its index increased to 213 in 1990.

TABLE 5.2 Top 50 Companies Ranked in Terms of Current Profit (FY 1990)

(Unit: ¥ billion)

Rank	Company name	
1	Toyota Motor Corp.	733.8
2	NTT	414.3
3	Matsushita Electric Industrial Co.	276.5
4	Sumitomo Bank	251.6
5	Nomura Securities Co.	233.5
6	Sanwa Bank	226.7
7	Fuji Bank	205.9
8	Hitachi Ltd	205.8
9	Dai-Ichi Kangyo Bank	190.9
10	Mitsubishi Bank	184.0
11	Toshiba Corp.	175.4
12	Taiyo Kobe Mitsui Bank	170.3
13	Nissan Motor Co.	164.7
14	Nippon Steel Corp.	160.9
15	Fuji Photo Film Co.	160.2
16	Mitsubishi Heavy Industries	152.6
17	NEC Corp.	140.5
18	Nintendo Co.	140.3
19	Mitsubishi Electric Corp.	136.3
20	Industrial Bank of Japan	132.9
25	Sony Corp.	114.5
30	Tokio Marine and Fire Insurance	99.7
35	House Food Industrial Co.	89.3
40	Honda Motor Co.	85.0
45	Mitsubishi Trust and Banking	80.2
50	Asahi Chemical Industry	75.5

Source: *NM*, June 4, 1991.

According to recent statistics, the top 50 companies for FY 1990 (generally from April 1990 to March 1991), ranked in terms of current profit, are shown in Table 5.2. Representative companies from the automobile, electrical machinery, banking, securities, electric power, construction and related sectors appear and each company earned a vast sum of current profit. Comparing this current profit ranking in 1990 with that of 1987, it is very clear that the position of the banks and securities companies declined. For example, while there were 14 banks and securities companies in the top 20 companies in 1987, and similarly 20 in the top 30 companies in the same year, their number decreased in 1990 to eight in the top 20 companies and 10 in the top 30 companies.[2]

The top 30 companies for FY 1990, ranked in terms of financial balance (here, surplus) between interest and dividend received etc. and interest and discount payable etc., are shown in Table 5.3. There were many large corporations related with the automobile and electrical machinery industries in the upper ranks (conversely, many corporations dealing with electric power, real estate and the iron and steel industry, which all usually borrow large sums of money, had a general financial deficit). The top three companies, namely Toyota, Matsushita and Hitachi, had vast financial

TABLE 5.3. Top 30 Companies Ranked in Terms of Financial Surplus (FY 1990)

(Unit: ¥ billion)

Rank	Company name		Rank	Company name	
1	Toyota Motor Corp.	165.4	16	Mitsubishi Heavy Industries	19.5
2	Matsushita Electric Ind. Co.	121.4	17	Sekisui Chemical Co.	18.5
3	Hitachi Ltd	70.0	18	Takeda Chemical Industries	17.2
4	Sharp Corp.	28.9	19	Kyocera Corp.	17.1
5	Kirin Brewery Co.	27.6	20	Fanuc Ltd	15.7
6	Toshiba Corp.	27.2	21	Sekisui House	15.2
7	Fuji Photo Film Co.	25.7	22	Komatsu Ltd	14.9
8	Nippon Oil Co.	25.7	23	Asahi Glass Co.	14.5
9	Nissan Motor Co.	24.5	24	House Food Industrial Co.	14.0
10	Hanwa Co.	24.1	25	Ricoh Co.	13.9
11	Nippondenso Co.	23.1	26	Murata Manufacturing Co.	13.3
12	Sanyo Electric Co.	21.6	27	Matsushita Electric Works	12.8
13	Sumitomo Corp.	21.4	28	Ajinomoto Co.	12.8
14	Sony Corp.	21.3	29	Honda Motor Co.	12.4
15	Mitsubishi Electric Corp.	20.9	30	Dai Nippon Printing Co.	12.2

Source: *NM*, June 5, 1991.

surpluses (¥165, 121 and 70 billion, respectively), and these contributed greatly to the increase in their current profits (incidentally, the top 10 companies for FY 1990 ranked in terms of non-operating balance (here, surplus), which consists of financial balance, foreign exchange gain or loss and profit or loss on securities sold etc., were (in order from highest to lowest): Toyota Motor (¥195.1 billion), Matsushita Electric Industries (¥121.7 billion), Nissan Motor (¥45.0 billion), Sony (¥42.2 billion), Hitachi (¥34.7 billion), Nippon oil (¥32.7 billion), Sharp (¥30.0 billion), Sumitomo Corp. (¥24.9 billion), Sanyo Electric (¥23.1 billion), and Kirin Brewery (¥21.7 billion)).[3]

To estimate the earning potential or the economic power of these large corporations, I want to examine the latent assets (or latent profits) of stocks, securities and land possessed by these corporations. Figure 5.2 clearly shows that the prices of stocks and land increased markedly in the latter half of the 1980s because of favorable business performance and the extended low interest policy of the government and the Bank of Japan (however, these extraordinarily high prices of stocks and land began to break down because of their own weight and fell rapidly (in the case of stocks) and steadily (in the case of land) with the increase in the official discount rate at the end of 1989). Under these circumstances, the latent assets of the business corporations, which were the balance between the book value and the current price of stocks and land, grew markedly, as shown in Table 5.4, in the latter half of the 1980s. The latent assets of land and stocks in the macroeconomy reached ¥342 trillion and ¥170 trillion, respectively, in 1988.

The top 50 enterprises and top 20 banks for FY 1990, ranked in terms of latent assets of securities, are shown in Table 5.5 (the Nikkei stock average at the end of March 1991 was ¥26,458). In Table 5.5, traditional and representative companies of the electrical machinery industry, the automobile industry, heavy industries, general trading firms (Sogo Shosha) and banks are listed, and there were eight enterprises

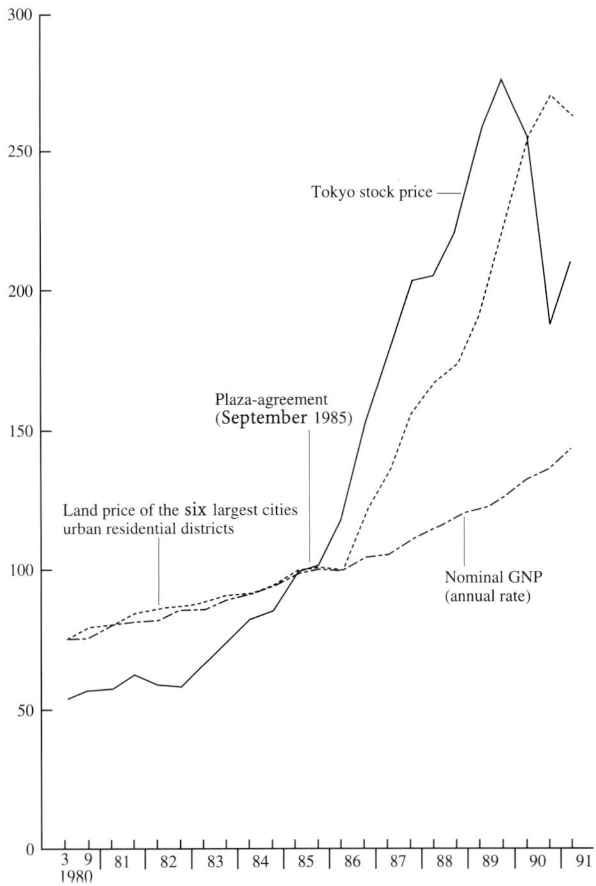

FIG 5.2 Extraordinary Price Rises in Land and Stock (1980–1991; Index, September 1985 = 100)
Source: *The Weekly Toyo Keizai* [J], September 7, 1991, p. 14

TABLE 5.4 Latent Assets of Business Corporations (1976–1988, s.y.)

(Unit: ¥ billion)

Year	Land			Stock		
	Current price	Book value	Latent assets	Current price	Book value	Latent assets
1976	106,813.0	25,782.1	81,030.9	28,945.0	18,036.8	10,908.2
1978	127,796.0	31,445.8	96,350.2	40,266.0	23,211.9	17,054.1
1980	181,371.0	37,754.6	143,616.4	45,951.0	25,436.4	20,514.6
1982	217,699.0	44,746.9	172,952.1	44,767.0	31,512.8	13,254.2
1984	235,050.0	56,906.3	178,143.7	75,451.0	38,227.3	37,223.7
1986	320,802.0	77,805.0	242,997.0	141,080.0	50,887.4	90,192.6
1988	452,388.0	110,462.8	341,925.2	248,705.0	79,120.2	169,584.8

Source: *WPJE*, 1989, p. 591.

TABLE 5.5 Top 50 Enterprises and 20 Banks Ranked in Terms of Latent Assets of Their Holding Securities (FY 1990)

(Unit: ¥ billion)

Rank	Company name	Latent assets	Rank	Company name	Latent assets
	Enterprise			Bank	
1	Hitachi Ltd.	2,343.0	1	Taiyo Kobe Mitsui Bank	3,250.7
2	Matsushita Electric Industrial Co.	2,099.9	2	Industrial Bank of Japan	3,065.5
3	Mippon Steel Corp.	1,672.2	3	Mitsubishi Bank	2,688.9
4	Mitsubishi Corp.	1,413.2	4	Dai-Ichi Kangyo Bank	2,631.7
5	Mitsubishi Heavy Industries	1,182.5	5	Sanwa Bank	2,446.7
6	Fujitsu Ltd	1,060.2	6	Fuji Bank	2,316.6
7	Mitsui and Co.	1,028.6	7	Long-Term Credit Bank of Japan	2,287.6
8	Nissan Motor Co.	1,023.6	8	Sumitomo Bank	2,269.2
9	NEC Corp.	879.5	9	Tokai Bank	1,964.6
10	Toshiba Corp.	765.6	10	Mitsui Trust and Banking	1,524.0
11	Sumitomo Corp.	690.9	11	Mitsubishi Trust and Banking	1,318.3
12	Mitsubishi Electric Corp.	666.6	12	Daiwa Bank	1,303.2
13	Sumitomo Metal Industries	663.2	13	Sumitomo Trust and Banking	1,290.4
14	Marubeni Corp.	661.6	14	Kyowa Saitama Bank	1,217.8
15	Kubata Corp.	594.5	15	Nippon Credit Bank	1,048.2
16	C Itoh and Co.	569.4	16	Yasuda Trust and Banking	984.4
17	Sumitomo Electric Industries	554.4	17	Bank of Tokyo	932.5
18	Kajima Corp.	531.9	18	Toyo Trust and Banking	757.7
19	Asahi Chemical Industry	525.4	19	Hokkaido Takusyoku Bank	535.6
20	Tokyu Corp.	511.7	20	Bank of Yokohama	513.0
25	Kinki Nippon Railway Co.	467.9			
30	Nippon Express Co.	430.8			
35	Mitsui Fudosan Co.	378.5			
40	Kobe Steel Ltd	344.1			
45	Nippon Suisan	313.3			
50	Nagoya Railroad Co.	269.2			

Regarding the latent assets of Toyota Motor Corp. and Ito-Yokado Co., whose accounting terms are different, compared with those of other companies in the first half of FY 1991, they were ¥1,933.0 billion and ¥1,157.4 billion, respectively. The first-ranked company in this period (from April to September 1991) was still Hitachi Ltd (¥2,086.6 billion) and Toyota was second. Incidentally, the Nikkei Stock average prices at the end of March and September were ¥26,458 and ¥23,039, respectively.

Sources: *The Weekly Toyo Keizai* [J], June 29, 1991, p. 37; *op.cit.*, January 11, 1992, p. 142.

(actually 10; refer to the note in Table 5.5 regarding Toyota Motor Corp. and Ito-Yokado Co.) with latent assets of securities over ¥1 trillion, 13 enterprises with latent assets totalling from ¥500 billion to ¥1 trillion and 15 banks (i.e. city banks, long-term credit banks and trust banks) with over ¥1 trillion latent assets (although not shown in the Table 5.5, insurance companies also have vast sums of latent assets; for example, Nippon Life Insurance, the largest insurance company, not only in Japan but also in the world, had latent securities assets of ¥6.9 trillion in March 1991).[4]

The exact value of the latent land assets owned by each company are not published and are unknown, being different from the above-mentioned latent assets of securities the values of which have been officially announced since FY 1990. Therefore, I refer only to the ranking of the latent land assets required for factories in the Tokyo metropolitan area according to the "Toyo Keizai Monthly Statistics" survey of 1989. As shown in Table 5.6, there was a vast sum of latent land assets held by large corporations, especially the heavy, machinery, material and related industries (it should be kept in mind that the most valuable latent land assets owned by large companies in the commercial center of Tokyo are not included here).

However, because the latent assets are the balance between book value and current price, those of securities (stocks) and land always change with fluctuations of current prices and decrease occasionally. So, we must be careful in estimating their content. For example, the total assets of securities owned by 25 life insurance companies decreased rapidly from a maximum value of ¥52 trillion in December 1989 to ¥16 trillion in September 1990 due to a fall in stock prices.[5] The total latent assets of securities owned by city banks decreased from ¥40 trillion in September 1989 to ¥28 trillion in March 1990 and to ¥11 trillion in March 1992.[6] We may be able to identify a decrease in land latent assets values because of the downward tendency in land prices since 1990.

Nevertheless, we must recognize that the values of latent assets that large corporations possess are still significant and they continue to be an important source of security (mortgage) and fund raising for the companies concerned.

The above are observations on the development of and results for large corporations mainly in the 1980s. We will now examine new trends in the development of these corporations since 1990 (i.e. after the collapse of the so-called "bubble boom"). It is obvious that the 1980s, especially the latter half, were years of a long and extraordinary boom period for the Japanese economy.

However, this very boom, with a dramatic rise in stock and land prices, converted to a depression phase because of the increase in the official discount rate (from 2.5% to 3.25% in May 1989, with further increases to 6% in August 1990). The current profits for FY 1990 and FY 1991 of the main listed companies in Japan decreased for 2 years running.[7] Of course, even during this depression (although it can be said that a certain reduction in the economic growth rate or in business results in comparison with those of the latter half of the 1980s during the extraordinary bubble boom, is actually a return to normal economic levels), the effective job opening ratio (i.e. the ratio of job offers to applicants) was still over 1 (as of February 1992) and the economic damage to production and consumption was still not serious. We can say that this depression after the collapse of the bubble boom was related, first, to problems in the fields of banking, securities companies,

TABLE 5.6 Top 30 Companies Ranked in Terms of Latent Assets of Land Required for Factories in the Tokyo Metropolitan Area (1989)

(Unit: ¥ billion)

Rank	Company name	Book value	Current price	Latent assets	Rank	Company name	Book value	Current price	Latent assets
1	NKK	78.0	3,020.7	2,942.7	16	Tonen Corp.	8.6	466.5	457.9
2	Nippon Steel Corp.	74.8	2,106.8	2,031.9	17	Mitsubishi Electric Corp.	1.6	396.6	394.9
3	Kawasaki Steel Corp.	44.7	2,014.5	1,969.7	18	Showa Denko	30.5	425.4	394.8
4	Toshiba Corp.	4.4	1,269.4	1,265.0	19	Sony Corp.	3.1	341.0	337.9
5	Nissan Motor Co.	17.3	1,263.1	1,245.7	20	Fuji Heavy Industries	0.2	332.6	332.4
6	Hitachi Ltd	8.3	881.4	873.1	21	Sumitomo Heavy Industries	5.9	324.2	318.2
7	Tokyo Gas Co.	9.3	879.6	870.2	22	Fujikura Ltd	1.3	255.3	254.0
8	Dai Nippon Printing Co.	11.7	795.3	783.6	23	Taisho Pharmaceutical Co.	2.5	250.8	248.2
9	Chichibu Cement Co.	2.9	785.4	782.5	24	Sankyo Co.	2.8	241.4	238.5
10	Tachihi Enterprise Co.	0.4	569.1	568.7	25	Mitsubishi Steel Manufacturing Co.	0.7	228.5	227.7
11	NEC Corp.	13.2	578.2	565.0	26	Mitsubishi Motors Corp.	28.0	254.2	226.2
12	Hino Motors	1.8	554.7	552.8	27	Mitsubishi Oil Co.	6.7	227.8	221.1
13	Ishikawajima-Harima Heavy Industries	1.8	538.8	537.0	28	Fuji Electric Co.	0.9	219.3	218.3
14	Isuzu Motors	2.5	478.5	476.0	29	Hitachi Metals	2.0	219.3	217.2
15	Bridgestone Corp.	5.0	479.1	474.1	30	Oki Electric Industry	0.7	211.0	210.3

Source: *The Weekly Toyo Keizal* [J], March 10, 1990, p. 27.

insurance companies and related businesses; in short, the financial institution and system.

For example, in banking businesses, overdue loans and bad loans had increased as a result of easy financing for real estate; therefore, with regard to the annual settlements for FY 1991 of 11 city banks, in March 1992 the current profits fell 17% from the previous year (from ¥1.66 trillion to ¥1.38 trillion) and the after-tax net profits similarly fell 29% (from ¥885.4 billion to ¥632.8 billion), although the net operating profits increased from the previous year due to a reduction in the lending rate because the appraisal losses of securities and reserves for uncollectable accounts increased.[8]

The securities companies business income itself was reduced largely because of the large fall in stock prices; furthermore, additional tax collection and reparation payments for *hoten* (the making good, privately and illegally, by securities companies of the losses incurred by large corporate stock customers) and *tobashi* (a special method for the camouflaging of such losses) came into force, and the mistake of excessive investments became clear. Consequently, 20 companies among the 25 listed securities companies had a deficit in their current profits in March 1992 and their total deficit values reached ¥216.2 billion. There were only five companies that had a surplus of current profits (Nomura, ¥44.1 billion; Daiwa, ¥9.3 billion; Nikko, ¥3.1 billion; Kosei, ¥1.9 billion; and Kokusai, ¥0.2 billion) but, with regard to net profit for the term, Daiwa, Nikko and Kosei had deficits of ¥43.5, 25.8 and 12.2 billion, respectively.[9]

Next, we will examine the trends in stock prices and the accumulation of bad loans, which are closely related to the banking situation and the securities business. With regard to stock prices, as it is known, since the Nikkei stock average reached a ¥38,915 maximum at the end of 1989, it decreased nearly constantly for more than 2 years and fell to a level between ¥17,000 and ¥18,000 in April 1992. So, the total value of current prices of listed stocks in the Tokyo Stock Exchange decreased from ¥611 trillion at the end of 1989 to ¥377 trillion at the end of 1991.[10] The main reasons for this fall in stock prices were the over-supply of stocks because of an increase in equity finance in the latter half of the 1980s, the reduction of funds from the stock market caused by the raising of the official discount rate and, consequently, the extreme deterioration of relationships between the demand and supply of stocks. However, the rate of fall of stock prices at this time was 54.2% from the maximum value to the value in early April 1992, and this is the largest fall in Japan since World War II.[11]

Why is it that stock prices have been almost constantly decreasing until now (as of May 1992)? And why it is so difficult for stock prices to rise again? Maybe, the underlying reasons include the following: symptoms of doubt regarding the Japanese-style management system, accompanied by unopened interlocking stockholdings among corporations; long hours of labor, including unpaid overtime; the view of competition solely as an enlargement of market share; and the extraordinarily low dividend rate of stocks etc. Furthermore, there is anxiety regarding the lack of long-term management perspectives of Japanese enterprises in the new international atmosphere since 1989. However, apart from these social and historical problems, I want to refer to two economic factors that make the recovery and rise of stock prices difficult in the capital and securities market (i.e. the problem of designated money in trust/fund trust and the repayment problem of warrant bonds and convertible bonds).

First, with regard to the designated money in trust/fund trust, which rapidly became widespread as one measure of the financial technologies of enterprises and became one of the main causes for the inflow of large funds into the securities market in the latter half of the 1980s, amounts reached approximately ¥40 trillion maximum at the end of 1989. However, after that, along with the fall in stock prices, trust contracts were canceled one after another, with amounts decreasing to ¥26 trillion in March 1992.[12] Nevertheless, the designated money in trust/fund trust that has not been canceled can still be found in large amounts in the securities market, holding its own latent losses because of the large fall in stock prices during this period (as is known, the designated money in trust/ fund trust can be invested in terms of business accounting independent of the book value of trustee's securities). It can be speculated that contracts will be canceled along with a certain recovery of stock prices. Then, as the funds are pulled out of the securities market because of their cancellation, they will necessarily become a new factor for another fall in stock prices at this time. In this sense, the designated money in trust/fund trust at present has come to be called the dead weight of the securities market, although this money had been an important factor in raising stock prices.

The other problem concerns Warrant bonds and convertible bonds, which were issued largely as a means of financial technology in the latter half of the 1980s. Because of the fall in stock prices in the meantime, most bonds must be redeemed hereafter as debentures without being converted to stock. Their total value for redemption will reach approximately ¥20 trillion for 3 years from 1992 to 1994.[13] This is a factor that will reduce the inflow of funds to the stock market and will make recovery and a rise in stock prices difficult.

Finally, the problem of increasing bad claims following the collapse of the bubble economy will be examined. In April 1992, the Japanese Ministry of Finance reported that the value of overdue loans (suspension of interest payments over 6 months) of city banks, long-term credit banks and trust banks may reach ¥7–8 trillion and, therein, the value of bad loans that became uncollectable without mortgage or guarantee may reach ¥2–3 trillion.[14]

However, with regard to the value of these overdue loans, the informal estimation of the Bank of Japan at almost the same time was considerably higher than that of the Ministry of Finance (I think that the former estimate is nearer to fact than the latter) and reached ¥29 trillion. Of course, we must realize that this figure was the total value of overdue loans of all banks, inclusive of related non-banks. The breakdown of this figure is as follows: ¥11 trillion from city banks; ¥5 trillion from long-term credit banks; ¥5 trillion from trust banks; ¥4 trillion from local banks; ¥3 trillion from secondary local banks; and ¥1 trillion from credit associations.[15]

Because the total loan value of all Japanese banks reached ¥584 trillion at the end of 1991, the ratio of overdue loans was approximately 5%. Although claims that were uncollectable without mortgage or guarantee were a part of all overdue loans, if we assume that it is one-third of the same measure as the Ministry of Finance, approximately ¥10 trillion would become the object of cancellation, which is still a considerable sum.[16] The financial institutions, especially city banks, long-term credit banks and trust banks, must seriously strive for a solution to this problem.[17]

Notes

1. *Annual Report on Financial Statements of Incorporated Business* [J]. Tokyo: Ministry of Finance, passim.
2. *NM*, June 1, 1988.
3. *AM*, June 7, 1991.
4. *AM*, June 8, 1991.
5. *AM*, June 7, 1990; *NM*, February 9, 1991; *AM*, June 8, 1991.
6. *NM*, May 29, 1990; *NM*, May 28, 1991; *NM*, May 1, 1992. Incidentally, the total value of latent securities assets owned by city banks was approximately ¥10 trillion in March 1985 (*NM*, August 13, 1985).
7. *MN*, March 16, 1992.
8. *NM*, May 17, 1992.
9. *NM*, May 16, 1992; *AM*, May 16, 1992.
10. *The Financial Business* [J]. April 1992. Tokyo: Toyo Keizai Inc., p. 47.
11. *AM*, April 8, 1992; *AM*, April 9, 1992.
12. *NM*, December 1, 1991; *NM*, May 15, 1992.
13. *The Weekly Toyo Keizai* [J]. April 11, 1992, p. 6; *AM*, October 27, 1991; *NM*, January 31, 1992.
14. *NM*, April 24, 1992.
15. *The Weekly Toyo Keizai* [J]. April 18, 1992, p. 4.
16. Bad loans in foreign countries of the main 21 Japanese banks (i.e. city banks, long-term credit banks and trust banks) totaled approximately ¥5 trillion at the end of 1991. The breakdown of this figure is: ¥2 trillion in Western countries and the rest in cumulative debtor countries and the ex-USSR (*NM*, February 15, 1992).
17. For reference, here I want to show the trends in Japanese personal savings, which have formed an important source of funds for large corporations, especially for large banks for their business development both in and out of Japan. The total value of personal savings, except for stocks, increased from ¥308 trillion in 1980 to ¥479 trillion in 1985 (separate stock values based on market value, in ¥ trillion are given in parentheses; 53), ¥642 trillion (103) in 1988 and ¥754 trillion (81) in 1990. The breakdown in 1990 was as follows: deposit and savings ¥465 trillion, trusts ¥40 trillion, public and corporate bonds ¥52 trillion, investment trusts ¥43 trillion, and insurances ¥155 trillion. This figure of ¥754 trillion, or ¥835 trillion inclusive of stocks in 1990 (which is used for comparison), was approximately 2.5-fold the national income value of Japan of ¥337 trillion in the same year, approximately five-fold the outstanding Japanese government bonds of ¥166 trillion and approximately five-fold the outstanding cumulative debt of developing countries at US$1.26 trillion (approximately ¥174 trillion, calculated on the basis of the average exchange rate in 1989 of US$1 = ¥138). Thus, in spite of personal savings, their total value reached an enormous sum of money. (*ESA*, 1989, pp. 161f; *op. cit.*, 1991, pp. 161f, 225, 336; *WPIT*, 1991, p. 58.)

5.2 The Decline of Business Profit and an Increase in Bad Loans: Before and After the Bubble Economy

The Japanese Economy, enjoying a long boom in the latter half of the 1980s, entered a phase of recession and stagnation with the collapse of the bubble economy at the beginning of the 1990s.

There was a big fall and slump in stock prices, a lasting fall in land prices, a decrease in the annual growth rate of the real GDP (4.3% in 1989, 5.3% in 1990, 3.6% in 1991, 0.4% in 1992, and 0.0% in 1993), a negative annual growth rate in mining and manufacturing production (4.3% in 1989, 5.0% in 1990, –0.7% in 1991, –6.3% in 1992, and –4.0% in 1993), a continuing fall in business profit for four FY (1990–1993), an increase in unemployment rates, a fall in the effective job opening ratio (0.97 in October 1992, 0.65 in November 1993), and an increase in the number of bankruptcies.

Thus, a "combined recession"[1] appeared in Japan, which signifies the combined process of a structural fall in stock prices and a cyclic decrease in the flow of the economic growth rate. This is the first experience for the Japanese economy of this kind of recession in terms of both its form and durability, since the beginning of the high economic growth period. Many different ways of getting out of this situation have been eagerly sought in both official circles and private business. However, no one has yet been able to find an effective solution.

Here, I want to examine this recession phase, while focusing attention on the problems concerning bad loans and the fluctuation of asset prices.

5.2.1 Decrease of Business Profit After the Collapse of the Bubble Economy

Looking at profit trends for corporate enterprises (excluding finance and insurance; capital ¥10 million or more) from FY 1990 to 1993 at the macrolevel, operating profit decreased sharply from ¥49.7 trillion to ¥32.0 trillion (a 35.6% drop) in all industries, and from ¥19.5 trillion to ¥9.7 trillion (a 50.3% drop) in the manufacturing industry. Current profit has also decreased markedly from ¥38.1 trillion to ¥20.5 trillion (a 46.2% drop) in all industries, and from ¥17.5 trillion to ¥7.6 trillion (a 56.6% drop) in the manufacturing industry.[2]

At the microlevel, Tables 5.7–5.9 show the state of business profit in FY 1993. Table 5.7 shows the current profits of the top 50 companies and, relatively speaking, Table 5.8 shows the financial surplus of the top 30 companies. Table 5.9 shows the non-operating balance of the top 10 companies. Comparing these data with those of 1990, which was the last year of the bubble boom, we can find the following differences.

First, in terms of current profit, Toyota is still the top-ranked company. However, the amount of Toyota's profit has decreased greatly from ¥733.8 billion to ¥286.4 billion. In addition, the profit of the 10th-ranked company has fallen from ¥184.0 billion to ¥89.6 billion. Relatively speaking, profit (¥ billion) in the 20th-, 30th-, 40th- and 50th-ranked companies has dropped from 132.9 to 76.6, 99.7 to 62.9, 85.0 to 49.0, and 75.5 to 43.0, respectively. Thus, we can see a general fall in current profits. In terms of economic sectors, the fall in current profits of banks and securities companies is remarkable, and both these sectors are suffering from the management of bad loans and continuing low stock prices.

Second, in terms of financial surplus, Toyota is again the top-ranked company. However, similarly the amount of the financial surplus decreased from ¥165.4 billion to ¥133.8 billion. The decrease in financial surplus (given in ¥ billion) for the 10th-,

TABLE 5.7 Top 50 companies Ranked in Terms of Current Profit (FY 1993)

(Unit: ¥ billion)

Rank	Company name	
1	Toyota Motor Corp.	286.4
2	Tokyo Electric Power Co.	159.9
3	Fuji Photo Film Co.	126.1
4	Shimizu Corp.	119.8
5	Mitsubishi Heavy Industries	119.2
6	Nintendo Co.	115.0
7	Kansai Electric Power Co.	110.4
8	NTT	109.4
9	East Japan Railway Co.	101.5
10	Sanwa Bank	89.6
11	Seven-Eleven Japan Co.	88.1
12	Ito-Yokado Co.	82.0
13	Chubu Electric Power Co.	80.9
14	Sankyo Co.	80.3
15	Kyushu Electric Power Co.	79.8
16	Dai Nippon Printing Co.	79.7
17	Tohoku Electric Power Co.	78.6
18	Takeda Chemical Industries	77.1
19	Kirin Brewery Co.	76.9
20	Tokio Marine and Fire Insurance	76.6
25	Sumitomo Bank	72.6
30	Sakura Bank	62.9
35	Fuji Bank	52.6
40	Kao Corp.	49.0
45	Nippon Express Co.	46.2
50	Shizuoka Bank	43.0

Source: *NM*, June 1, 1994.

TABLE 5.8 Top 30 Companies Ranked in Terms of Financial Surplus (FY 1993)

(Unit: ¥ billion)

Rank	Company name		Rank	Company name	
1	Toyota Motor Corp.	133.8	16	Murata Manufacturing Co.	10.1
2	Hitachi Ltd	51.3	17	Toppan Printing Co.	9.6
3	Hanwa Co.	35.7	18	Sanyo Electric Co.	9.1
4	Matsushita Electric Ind. Co.	24.9	19	Fanuc Ltd	7.7
5	Fuji Photo Film Co.	20.0	20	Tonen Corp.	7.1
6	Sony Corp.	18.2	21	Mitsubishi Corp.	7.0
7	Nippondenso Co.	16.3	22	Dai Nippon Printing Co.	7.0
8	Takeda Chemical Industries	14.5	23	Sumitomo Corp.	6.9
9	Nintendo Co.	14.3	24	TDK	6.4
10	Mitsubishi Electric Corp.	13.1	25	Teijin Ltd	5.7
11	Sharp Corp.	12.3	26	Aoyama Trading Co.	5.7
12	Kirin Brewery Co.	12.1	27	Yamanouchi Pharma. Co.	5.6
13	Nippon Oil Co.	11.5	28	Sony Music	5.4
14	Ito-Yokado Co.	11.2	29	Komatsu Ltd	5.3
15	Kyocera Corp.	10.8	30	Mabuchi Motor Co.	5.3

Source: *NM*, June 2, 1994.

TABLE 5.9 Top 10 Companies Ranked in Terms of Non-Operating Surplus (FY 1993)

(Unit ¥ billion)

Rank	Company name	
1	Toyota Motor Corp.	182.8
2	Nissan Motor Co.	40.7
3	Matsushita Electric Industrial Co.	27.5
4	Sony Corp.	27.5
5	Sanyo Electric Co.	25.4
6	Sumitomo Corp.	21.4
7	Nippon Oil Co.	20.8
8	Toshiba Corp.	19.1
9	Marubeni Corp.	16.0
10	Fuji Photo Film Co.	15.5

Source: *AM*, June 4, 1994.

20th- and 30th-ranked companies was from 24.1 to 13.1, 15.7 to 7.1, and 12.2 to 5.3, respectively. Here too we can see a large fall.

Third, a similar fall in the non-operating balance (given in ¥ billion) can be seen for the first-, second-, fifth- and 10th-ranked companies from 195.1 to 182.8, 121.4 to 40.7, 27.6 to 25.4, and 24.1 to 15.5, respectively.

These figures indicate that the trends in falling business profits for 4 years running at the macroeconomic level apply to individual corporate earnings at the microeconomic level.

5.2.2 Decrease of Latent Assets at the Macroeconomic Level

The fall and stagnancy of stock prices after their peak of ¥38,900 in December 1989 and the subsequent fall of land prices since 1991 have been factors in reducing the latent asset amount of stocks and land in the national economy.

As shown in Table 5.10, large capital losses relating to stocks increased in the sectors of financial institutions, non-financial incorporated enterprises and households after 1990. Large capital losses relating to land increased in the sectors of households and non-financial incorporated enterprises after 1991. For example, in 1992 the total amount of capital losses of stocks and land was ¥406.9 trillion (individually they were ¥178 trillion and ¥228.9 trillion, respectively; these figures are different from those presented in Table 5.10 because of different sources, but these data are corrected figures and more trustworthy), which was approximately 90% of the nominal GDP in the same year. Conversely, the capital gains reached nearly the same percentage of nominal GDP and were generated every year, on average, from 1986 to 1989. In 1993, the capital loss was ¥92.7 trillion because the capital gain of stocks was ¥40.5 trillion due to a certain recovery of the average stock price from a year ago and the capital loss of land was ¥133.2 trillion due to the lasting fall in land prices.[3]

Nevertheless, the latent assets of incorporated enterprises at the level of the macroeconomy have been very large. Admittedly, as shown in Table 5.11, the latent assets of

TABLE 5.10 Trends in Capital Gains/Losses (1980–1992)

Stocks (Unit: ¥ trillion)

	1980	1982	1984	1986	1988	1990	1992
Non-financial incorporated enterprises	−0.5	−5.0	16.4	52.5	66.5	−106.9	−60.9
Financial institutions	1.3	0.7	12.1	36.9	57.0	−123.1	−50.9
General government	0.0	0.0	0.0	0.0	0.0	0.0	0.0
Private non-profit institutions serving households	0.0	0.0	−0.0	−0.0	0.0	0.0	−0.1
Households (includes private unincorporated enterprises	−0.1	−2.8	8.6	31.8	51.3	−76.8	−42.6

Land (Unit: ¥ trillion)

	1980	1982	1984	1986	1988	1990	1992
Non-financial incorporated enterprises	27.1	13.6	7.6	63.0	46.5	69.2	−115.5
Financial institutions	1.7	0.6	0.5	10.2	3.9	14.5	−7.5
General government	4.0	1.3	0.5	7.6	5.4	14.4	−10.5
Private non-profit institutions serving households	0.9	0.4	0.4	4.1	1.0	1.8	−1.9
Households (includes private unincorporated enterprises	76.3	40.8	30.2	168.3	109.9	135.8	−122.9

Source: *WPJE*, 1993, p. 546.

stocks decreased to ¥65 trillion in 1992 because the book value of stock prices owned by enterprises rose because of a lot of new share issues by equity finance and their interlocking stockholdings in the latter half of the 1980s, and the current prices have fallen since 1990, but they remain at a higher level than that of 1985. The latent assets of land were ¥381 trillion in 1992, although land prices have fallen since 1991, and this remain higher than the level in 1985.

5.2.3 *Latent Assets of Individual Corporations*

5.2.3.1 Securities/Stocks

The Nikkei average stock price in September (interim accounting term) 1993 was ¥20,105. This price was more than the ¥18,039 price in March (accounting term) 1993, but was far less than the ¥26,485 price in March 1991, based on which the latent assets' amount of securities (stocks) owned by each corporation were calculated and are presented in Table 5.5. Therefore, it is inevitable that the latent assets of stocks decreased between March 1991 and September 1993. Actually, comparing data presented in Table 5.12 showing the rank in terms of latent assets of securities in September 1993 with the data presented in Table 5.11, we can find that the latent assets of securities owned by each corporation decreased considerably due to the fall in stock prices during this period. Yet, the absolute values of these latent assets are still very large.

TABLE 5.11 Trends in the Latent Assets of Incorporated Enterprises (1984–1992)

Stocks (Unit: ¥ trillion)

	1984	1985	1986	1987	1988	1989	1990	1991	1992
Book value	31.10	35.31	41.62	58.19	69.32	79.91	90.64	99.14	104.34
Current price	75.45	88.25	141.08	181.28	250.71	339.71	235.97	230.85	169.99
Latent profit	44.35	52.94	99.46	123.09	181.39	259.80	145.33	131.71	65.65

Land (Unit: ¥ trillion)

	1984	1985	1986	1987	1988	1989	1990	1991	1992
Book value	57.23	68.09	79.42	104.43	115.30	128.67	139.41	155.15	169.86
Current price	231.54	252.93	318.63	433.04	487.61	582.07	663.71	601.42	550.90
Latent profit	174.31	184.84	239.21	328.61	372.31	453.40	524.30	446.27	381.04

Source: *WPJE*, 1993, p. 549.

TABLE 5.12. Top 30 Corporations Ranked in Terms of Latent Assets of Their Holding Securities (September 1993)

(Unit: ¥ billion)

Rank	Company name		Rank	Company name	
1	Industrial Bank of Japan	2,386.0	16	Mitsui Trust and Banking	1,046.1
2	Sakura Bank	2,243.7	17	Mitsubishi Heavy Industries	1,045.4
3	Mitsubishi Bank	1,909.1	18	Sumitomo Trust and Banking	931.2
4	Hitachi Ltd	1,855.2	19	Daiwa Bank	847.9
5	Dai-Ichi Kangyo Bank	1,770.4	20	Nippon Credit Bank	727.8
6	Sanwa Bank	1,718.2	21	Mitsui and Co.	680.4
7	Long-Term Credit Bank of Japan	1,644.1	22	Fujitsu Ltd	660.0
8	Matsushita Electric Industrial Co.	1,598.4	23	NEC Corp.	647.6
9	Sumitomo Bank	1,516.9	24	Bank of Tokyo	633.2
10	Fuji Bank	1,478.5	25	Nissan Motor Co.	623.0
11	Nippon Steel Corp.	1,260.9	26	Toshiba Corp.	544.8
12	Asahi Bank	1,206.5	27	Mitsubishi Electric Corp.	525.7
13	Tokai Bank	1,177.3	28	Sony Corp.	515.3
14	Mitsubishi Corp.	1,148.5	29	Nomura Securities Co.	496.1
15	Mitsubishi Trust and Banking	1,076.8	30	Toyoda Automatic Loom Works	481.9

Objectives here are limited only to the corporations with the accounting term in March or September.

Source: *NM*, December 8, 1993.

TABLE 5.13 Latent Assets of Stocks in the 21 Major Banks (September 1993)

	A (Unit: ¥ billion)	B (Unit: ¥)	C (Unit: ¥ billion)
City banks			
Dai-Ichi Kangyo Bank	1,666.9	11,669	856
Sakura Bank	2,104.6	11,329	1,120
Sumitomo Bank	1,444.2	11,912	721
Fuji Bank	1,397.8	12,680	625
Mitsubishi Bank	1,921.8	10,213	1,124
Sanwa Bank	1,664.5	11,311	888
Tokai Bank	1,081.8	12,009	533
Asahi Bank	1,150.3	10,172	675
Bank of Tokyo	578.6	13,752	205
Daiwa Bank	798.1	11,941	397
Hokkaido Takusyoku Bank	335.0	11,428	177
Subtotal	14,143.6	11,597	7,320
Long-term credit banks			
Industrial Bank of Japan	2,165.5	9,980	1,288
Long-Term Credit Bank of Japan	1,486.5	10,689	838
Nippon Credit Bank	661.4	11,957	328
Subtotal	4,313.4	10,581	2,454
Trust banks			
Mitsubishi Trust and Banking	928.3	11,499	486
Sumitomo Trust and Banking	818.3	11,033	448
Mitsui Trust and Banking	1,050.6	10,181	616
Yasuda Trust and Banking	478.1	13,549	179
Toyo Trust and Banking	427.6	12,738	189
Chuo Trust and Banking	133.2	15,642	11
Nippon Trust Bank	65.5	13,200	27
Subtotal	3,901.6	11,878	1,955
Total of the 21 major banks	22,358.6	11,471	11,729

A, latent profit; B, the level of the Nikkei stock average price at which the latent profit is zero; C, the amount of latent profit at the Nikkei stock average price of ¥16,000.
Estimation by IBCA Ltd in the UK.
Source: *NM*, December 10, 1993.

Let us consider a hypothetical situation. As is shown in Tables 5.13 and 5.14, even in the case of the representative corporations that have a huge amount of latent assets of stocks (i.e. major banks and life insurance companies), their latent assets become zero when the average Nikkei stock price is between ¥10,000 and ¥15,000.

Is there a danger that this possibility may become a reality (actually, the average Nikkei stock price slipped temporally below ¥15,000 in August 1992.)? The low payout ratio and the low dividend rate of Japanese enterprises have long been recognized as characteristic of Japanese-style management. For example, while the average dividend rate for stock prices (current price) was 2.8% in the US, 3.8% in the UK and 2.7% in Germany as of November 1993, it was only 0.9% in Japan.[4] If the dividend rate of stocks reached the same level as in the US because of pressure brought to bear by

TABLE 5.14. Latent Assets of Stocks in the life Insurance Companies (March 1992)

	A	B
Nippon Life Insurance	3,083.5	13,000
Dai-ichi Mutual Life Insurance	1,488.0	14,000
Sumitomo Life Insurance	569.2	16,000
Meiji Mutual Life Insurance	1,693.7	12,000
Asahi Mutual Life Insurance	649.8	15,000
Yasuda Mutual Life Insurance	484.5	14,000
Mitsui Mutual Life Insurance	262.1	16,000
Kyoei Life Insurance	*	*
Chiyoda Mutual Life Insurance	202.8	16,000
Daido Mutual Life Insurance	72.2	*
Toho Mutual Life Insurance	15.6	*
Taiyo Mutual Life Insurance	690.5	under 10,000
Fukoku Mutual Life Insurance	365.1	under 10,000
Nippon Dantai Life Insurance	*	under 10,000
Daihyaku Mutual Life Insurance	155.2	15,000
Tokyo Mutual Life Insurance	124.6	12,000
Nissan Mutual Life Insurance	*	*
Heiwa Life Insurance	*	10,000
Yamato Mutual Life Insurance	52.0	9,000

At the end of March 1992, the average Nikkei stock price was ¥19,346.

* Unpublished. A, latent profit (unit: ¥ billion); B, the level of the average Nikkei stock price at which the latent profit is zero (unit: ¥)

Source: *The Weekly Toyo Keizai* [J], September 12, 1992.

stockholders and public opinion, the Nikkei average stock price would drop to one-third of ¥18,000, namely ¥6,000 (assuming that the total amount of dividends is invariable), at the same point in time (i.e. November 1993). Then, the latent assets of stocks (securities) owned by large corporations of Japan would almost disappear. However, this cannot be zero, because of the necessity of management to give prominence to stockholders that has recently been advocated in Japan also.

5.2.3.2 Land

Being different from the case of securities (stocks), the latent assets of land owned by large corporations have not been announced officially. However, since the land price tax (0.3% (0.2% in the first year); taxation on roadside value, with many tax-free objects and much basic exemption) was introduced in 1992, the latent assets of land were made public for the first time. Table 5.15 shows the top 50 corporations in terms of the land price tax for 1992. Top real estate companies, financial business, rail-transport business, and traditional heavy industry, which usually have extensive land holdings, and other leading major companies are listed.

The land assets value (current price based on posted prices) can be estimated by calculating back from the assessment value on each company (divided by 0.8 because the assessment value is 80% of the posted price). Meanwhile, there is a

TABLE 5.15 Top 50 Companies Ranked in Terms of Land Price Tax Value (1992)

(Unit: ¥ million)

Rank	Company name	Land price tax	Rank	Company name	Land price tax
1	Mitsubishi Estate Co.	7,573	14	Fuji Bank	2,148
2	Nippon Life Insurance	5,381	15	Japan Tobacco Inc.	2,012
3	Mitsui Fudosan Co.	4,505	16	Sanwa Bank	1,992
4	NTT	3,927	17	Meiji Mutual Life Insurance	1,952
5	Seibu Railway Co.	3,785	18	Kawasaki Steel Corp.	1,923
6	Dai-ichi Mutual Life	3,359	19	Asahi Mutual Life Insurance	1,907
7	Sumitomo Life Insurance	3,033	20	Nissan Motor Co.	1,893
8	Dai-ichi Kangyo Bank	2,786	25	Asahi Bank	1,567
9	East Japan Railway	2,786	30	Matsushita Electric Industrial Co.	1,466
10	Nippon Steel Corp.	2,436	35	Sapporo Breweries	1,261
11	Sakura Bank	2,368	40	Shimizu Corp.	1,150
12	Tokyu Corp.	2,273	45	Matsuzakaya Co.	1,102
13	Mitsubishi Bank	2,247	50	Isetan Co.	1,008

Source: *AE*, April 1, 1993.

book value on the land owned by each company. We can calculate the value of latent assets of land by subtracting the latter figure from the former. Table 5.16 shows the latent assets values of the top 15 companies ranked in terms of land price tax: first, Mitsubishi Estate Co. Ltd with approximately ¥4 trillion; second, Nippon Life Insurance Co. with ¥2.4 trillion; third, Seibu Railway Co. Ltd with ¥2.3 trillion; fourth, NTT Corporation with ¥2.2 trillion. Almost all corporations have latent assets of more than ¥1 trillion. (However, the estimated assets value here is limited only to the part of land for the scope of assessment. The land price tax is free of duty for land of ¥30,000 or less per 1 m^2, for residential land of 1,000 m^2 or less, for land owned by national and local government and for public land, such as hospitals, railways, communications etc. The green tract of factories and others qualifies for a special 50% reduction in tax. Therefore, the practical object for taxation is a part of the owned land. Conversely, the total land assets value owned by each corporation surpasses the estimated value in Table 5.16. Similarly, the value of latent assets shown in Table 5.16 is not the whole, but only a part. The no value given for East Japan Railway is because, except for the above-mentioned reasons, the company is newly established and the book value of its land is remarkably large.)

5.2.4 Bad Loan Problem of Financial Institutions

Eleven city banks, three long-term credit banks and seven trust banks (the three main bank schemes or the 21 major banks, for short) announced officially that the total

TABLE 5.16 Latent Assets of the Top 15 Companies Ranked in Terms of Land Price Tax Value (1992)

(Unit: ¥ billion)

Company name	Book value	Current price	Latent assets
Mitsubishi Estate Co.	701.5	4,794.5	4,093.0
Nippon Life Insurance	992.6	3,430.5	2,437.9
Mitsui Fudosan Co.	1,304.8	2,947.9	1,643.1
NTT	442.6	2,654.5	2,211.3
Seibu Railway Co.	68.9	2,366.0	2,297.1
Dai-ichi Mutual Life	843.8	2,162.2	1,318.4
Sumitomo Life Insurance	598.5	1,932.0	1,333.5
Dai-Ichi Kangyo Bank	98.7	1,761.0	1,662.3
East Japan Railway	2,308.4	1,783.8	—
Nippon Steel Corp.	178.8	1,523.0	1,344.2
Sakura Bank	86.8	1,501.5	1,414.7
Tokyu Corp.	223.5	1,498.4	1,274.9
Mitsubishi Bank	107.2	1,421.2	1,314.0
Fuji Bank	59.8	1,363.0	1,302.2
Japan Tobacco Inc.	120.6	1,452.8	1,332.2

Source: *AM*, April 1, 1993.

value of their bad loans reached ¥13.6 trillion in March 1994. The breakdown for each bank is shown in Table 5.17.

However, we must make note of the fact that the concept of "bad loans" here is limited to loans in bankruptcy and loans with interest that have been overdue for 6 months or more and does not include loans overdue for less than 6 months and interest-reduced or exempted loans.

For example, according to the provisional figures that appeared in the Nihon Keizai Shinbun (Japan Economic Newspaper) dated May 21, 1994, there are unpublished values (¥ billion) of interest-reduced or exempted loans in city banks as follows: Sumitomo Bank 1,050.2; Fuji 877.7; Sanwa 739.1; Daiwa 729.1; Mitsubishi 535.2; Sakura 528.9; Hokkaido-takushoku 452.2; Tokyo 450.7; Tokai 358.2; Asahi 350.7; and Dai-Ichi Kangyo 330.0. The total amount is ¥6.4 trillion.[5]

Furthermore, when we try to examine the total amount of bad loans macroeconomically, we must naturally take regional banks, second regional banks, Shinkin banks (credit associations), credit cooperatives, agricultural financial institutions and other financial institutions (inclusive of non-banks) into account in addition to the above-mentioned three main bank schemes.

In connection with this problem, I want to look at the situation of the eight private housing finance companies established by the financial institution groups. These housing finance companies typically show a side of the bad loans problem generated by the fall of real estate prices after the collapse of the bubble economy. With these companies, as shown in Table 5.18, approximately ¥14 trillion in all is financed by many financial institutions. However, the business of housing finance companies has been completely held up. Now, their reconstruction plans are being carried out by the reduction and exemption of interest as follows: the parent financial companies 0%; the agricultural financial institutions yearly 4.5%; and other financial institutions

TABLE 5.17 Bad Loans of the 21 Major Banks (March 1994)

(Unit: ¥ billion)

Bank name	Value of bad loans
City banks	
Dai-Ichi Kangyo Bank	1,327.1
Sakura Bank	1,458.8
Fuji Bank	1,188.1
Mitsubishi Bank	572.7
Asahi Bank	499.0
Sanwa Bank	909.7
Sumitomo Bank	1,112.6
Daiwa Bank	363.0
Tokai Bank	768.1
Hokkaido Takushoku Bank	508.0
Bank of Tokyo	266.6
Subtotal	8,973.7
Long-term credit banks	
Industrial Bank of Japan	538.7
Long-Term Credit Bank of Japan	744.9
Nippon Credit Bank of Japan	603.9
Subtotal	1,887.5
Trust banks	
Mitsui Trust and Banking	597.9
Mitsubishi Trust and Banking	525.6
Sumitomo Trust and Banking	524.4
Yasuda Trust and Banking	440.0
Toyo Trust and Banking	312.8
Chuo Trust and Banking	180.4
Nippon Trust Banking	130.6
Subtotal	2,712.9
Total	13,574.1

Source: *Weekly Economist* [J], June 14, 1994, p. 44.

2.5%. However, little progress is being made with this practice. The total sum of the reductions and exemptions of interest for the eight housing finance companies reached ¥358.1 billion in FY 1992.

The total amount of bad loans owned by the eight housing finance companies (the definition of "bad loan" here is due to that of the three main bank schemes) had reached ¥6.3 trillion in March 1994.[6] However, one can guess that their true total is more than this reported sum (the problems faced by the agricultural financial institutions, which loaned approximately ¥6 trillion to these housing finance companies, are particularly large). The 21 major banks have lendings (claims) of more than ¥5 trillion, which is not included in the above-mentioned bad loans value of the three main bank schemes.

Naturally, the example of these housing finance companies is a part of the whole. Therefore, we can estimate that the actual total amount of bad loans is two- or three-

TABLE 5.18 Borrowed Money of the Eight Housing Finance Companies (March 1993)

(Unit: ¥ billion)

	Loan value	A
City banks		
Sanwa	298.7	15.0
Sakura	294.0	15.9
Bank of Tokyo	249.1	7.1
Daiwa	110.0	4.9
Asahi	84.1	4.6
Sumitomo	79.6	3.3
Fuji	71.2	2.6
Tokai	67.9	3.0
Mitsubishi	63.2	2.8
Hokkaido Takushoku	32.0	1.7
Subtotal	1,397.8	63.8
Long-term credit banks		
Industrial Bank of Japan	671.2	29.4
Long-Term Credit Bank of Japan	484.5	18.9
Nippon Credit Bank	345.8	14.4
Subtotal	1,501.4	62.8
Trust banks		
Mitsubishi Trust and Banking	520.2	19.5
Sumitomo Trust and Banking	517.1	19.6
Yasuda Trust and Banking	401.5	15.4
Mitsui Trust and Banking	348.8	16.6
Toyo Trust and Banking	230.9	11.3
Chuo Trust and Banking	126.1	5.4
Nippon Trust Bank	56.1	2.9
Subtotal	2,200.8	91.0
Regional banks subtotal	1,100.7	51.2
Norinchukin Bank	1,112.9	8.1
Credit Federations of Agricultural Cooperatives	5,141.8	47.8
Financial institutions for agriculture subtotal	6,254.7	55.9
Insurance subtotal	1,090.0	29.1
Others	169.1	4.0
Total	13,714.4	358.1

A, estimated value of interest reduction and exemption. Note, the figure for Dai-Ichi Kangyo Bank is not written in the original table.

Source: *The Weekly Toyo Keizai* [J], January 1/8, 1994, p. 11.

fold as much as the published figures, also in the case of the three main bank schemes. Including the other financial schemes and the related non-banks, the total value of bad loans for all banks and financial institutions probably reaches approximately ¥60 trillion. Furthermore, there is a view that it reaches as much as ¥100 trillion.

5.2.5 *Writing Off Bad Loans*

The situation of writing off bad loans, especially with regard to the three main bank schemes, will be examined first because they are the largest and most important institutions concerned. Looking at Table 5.19, measures for writing off bad loans have been adopted since 1992, especially in 1993, and the values of such write-offs in 1993 were ¥2.34 trillion in the case of city banks, ¥0.55 trillion for long-term credit banks, and ¥0.5 trillion for trust banks. The total sum of these write-offs reached ¥3.39 trillion.

These write-offs have been implemented by the 21 major banks, which have made good use of the seven-fold consecutive reductions of official discount rates and the accompanying increases in profit margins of interest rates (i.e. the remarkable increase in the net business profit of banks). However, their current profits have decreased remarkably in the meantime because of the large write-offs of bad loans, in spite of the increase in net business profit.

Thus, the 21 major banks tried very hard to write off bad loans in their own way. However, their approach is not as bold as the countermeasures practiced by major banks in the US several years ago, when they did not mind making red figure settlements of accounts to give the write-offs of bad loans priority. So, as mentioned in the previous former paragraph, the large amount of bad loans (i.e. ¥8.97 trillion in the case of city banks, ¥1.89 trillion for long-term credit banks, ¥2.71 trillion for trust banks, and a total of ¥13.57 trillion) still existed officially.

TABLE 5.19 Situation of Bad Loans Write-offs in the three Main Bank Schemes (FY 1989–1993)
(Unit: ¥ billion)

Scheme	FY	Net business profit	Write-off value	Current profit
City banks	1989	1,506.8	86.4	2,164.8
	1990	1,462.0	117.5	1,658.6
	1991	1,922.5	446.4	1,426.3
	1992	2,516.7	1,032.8	964.2
	1993	2,382.2	2,340.1	563.1
Long-term credit banks	1989	188.8	25.9	342.6
	1990	165.9	31.1	279.0
	1991	292.3	49.0	301.0
	1992	401.0	195.2	166.7
	1993	367.6	546.9	106.2
Trust banks	1989	541.1	6.2	604.0
	1990	249.0	21.3	374.8
	1991	217.5	64.4	248.1
	1992	305.7	123.8	181.7
	1993	405.7	501.6	127.9
Total	1989	2,236.7	118.4	3,111.5
	1990	1,876.9	169.9	2,312.4
	1991	2,432.3	559.8	1,975.4
	1992	3,223.4	1,351.8	1,312.7
	1993	3,155.6	3,388.6	797.2

Source: *WPJE*, 1994, p. 222.

In the "White Paper on Japanese Economy 1994", ". . . the strengthening of countermeasures" against bad loans in the three main bank schemes is described on the grounds that the ratio of the outstanding special accounts for loan write-offs to the outstanding amount of bad loans has increased from 13.1% in March 1992 and 14.6% in March 1993 to 22.3% in March 1994.[7] I do not deny this fact, but I do not think that it led necessarily to "the strengthening of countermeasures". The reasons for this are as follows. First, as we have already seen, the published figures themselves of bad loan values are remarkably underestimated. Second, the above-mentioned ratio of the special account (22.3%) is not absolutely high. Third, aside from this special account, surely also the latent assets of stocks owned by banks play a certain role in the write-offs of bad loans. However, the latent assets amount of stocks is unstable because of the change in stock prices and, if many banks tried altogether to realize their latent stock assets, it would necessarily bring about a big fall in stock prices. In addition, the possibility of a big fall in stock prices still remains because of the above-mentioned dividend rate and other causes. Consequently, one had better not put excessive hopes in latent stock assets as a means of solving this problem. Thus, the disposal of bad loans is a very serious and complex problem for financial institutions, inclusive of the major banks.

Here, I would like to refer to the "Joint Claim Purchase Institution", which was established by the joint capital investment of private financial institutions in January 1993 as an important means for the solution of their bad loans problem. This institution purchased 2,327 bad claims, totaling ¥2.3 trillion, from its establishment to July 1994. However, it cannot dispose of real estate as a collateral of claims. Because, on the one hand, the real estate market does not move in the event of a continuing fall in land prices and, on the other, this institution itself hesitates to sell its collateral objects at low prices, these (bad) loans, as it were, are put aside. In addition, the average ratio of the purchasing prices of this institution to the principals of claims decreased from 60–70% in the second-quarter of 1993 to 30% in May 1994. In this situation, the amount of actually recovered loans by sales of the bad loans purchased by this institution was only ¥66.7 billion until July 1994, which was 2.9% of the total.[8]

Above, I have mentioned the problem of the disposal of bad loans held by financial institutions. However, it is not only financial institutions that are confronted with this problem. There are many enterprises that have failed in their own financial transactions and have suffered losses in the trials, including designated money in trust/fund trust, real estate, investment, multidivisional enterprise, restructuring of enterprise, foreign investment and exchange dealing. If we list the representative companies and examples that disposed of bad loans in the settlement of accounts 1993, they are as follows: Hanwa Co. Ltd, ¥120 billion loss (failure of financial transaction and liquidation of its subsidiary); Kabuto Decom Inc., ¥117 billion loss (writing off loans, guarantee of obligation); Showa Shell Sekiyu KK ¥115.3 billion loss (failure to exchange forward contract); Japan Energy, ¥91.2 billion loss (liquidation of subsidiary in the USA); Mitsubishi Corp., ¥80 billion loss (writing off its foreign claims and leasing subsidiaries' bad loans); Matsushita Electric Industrial Co. Ltd, ¥80 billion loss (support for financial subsidiary holding bad loans); Marubeni Corp., ¥80 billion loss (disposal of the designated money in trust/fund trust); Shimizu Corp., ¥75 billion loss (liquidation of subsidiaries abroad); C. Itoh & Co., ¥70 billion loss (liquidation of financial subsidiaries, disposal of the designated money in trust/fund trust); Kajima Corp., ¥62 billion loss (reduction of real estate business abroad); Sumitomo Corp., ¥50 billion loss (disposal of the designated money in trust/fund trust, liquidation of related companies); Sumitomo Realty and Development Co. Ltd, ¥48 billion loss (writing-off bad claims held by subsidiaries); Nissho Iwai Corp., ¥39 billion loss (disposal of the designated money in trust/fund trust, liquidation of related companies); Nittetsu Shoji Co. Ltd., ¥35 billion loss (writing-off overdue claims); Kumagai Gumi Co. Ltd., ¥32 billion loss (liquidation of subsidiaries abroad and related companies); Obayashi Corp., ¥30 billion loss (withdrawal from the real estate business in the US, liquidation of subsidiaries); Fujitsu Ltd, ¥29 billion loss (restructuring costs); Godo Steel Ltd, ¥26.7 billion loss (liquidation of subsidiaries in real estate business); Dainippon Ink and Chemicals Inc., ¥25 billion loss (appraisal loss of subsidiary in the US, withdrawal from unprofitable business); Nissan Motor Co. Ltd, ¥22 billion loss (liquidation of subsidiary in Australia, abolition of domestic production facilities); Kubota Corp., ¥22 billion loss (liquidation of subsidiary for tractor production in Spain); Asahi Breweries Ltd, ¥21.7 billion loss (relinquishment loans owing to subsidiary in Australia and domestic financial subsidiary) and so on.[9]

Obviously, these loss values are not small amounts and the companies that appropriated the above-mentioned amounts of losses do not belong to an exceptional minority. We should consider that many corporations must still dispose of their bad loans and claims after the 1994 March term.

Notes

1. Miyazaki Y. *Combined Recession. For a Prescription of the Post-Bubble Economy* [J]. Tokyo: Chuko Shinsyo, 1992.
2. *Economic Statistics Yearbook* [J], 1999. Tokyo: Toyo Keizai Inc., p. 435.
3. *WPJE*, 1994, pp. 196f.
4. *AM*, January 19, 1994.
5. *NM*, May 21, 1994.
6. *NM*, August 6, 1994.
7. *WPJE*, 1994, pp. 221, 627.
8. *NM*, June 29, 1994; August 20, 1994.
9. *NM*, April 8, 1994.

5.3 The Bad Loan Problem in Early 1996

The bad loan problem in Japan does not relate only to financial institutions, real estate businesses or the construction industry, but it has become a universal problem that relates to the whole structure and development of the Japanese economy. This problem is also an unstable and disturbing factor not to be ignored by the international financial system and the world economy.

This is also the biggest and most difficult problem that the postwar Japanese economy has had to deal with. With regard to postwar reform by the American Occupation Army and the overcoming of the Dodge deflation by special procurement for the Korean War, these two big crises of the postwar Japanese economy were conquered by external factors. The two oil crises and then the rapid strong yen phase after the Plaza Agreement in 1985 were crises brought about by external factors and were overcome by the excellent adaptability of the Japanese economy to crisis. Compared with these examples, this bad loan problem is a result of internal development of the Japanese economy during the 50 years since World War II. Here, the net of vested interests formed for half a century gets entangled and one cannot easily discern the internal crystallization and formation of the social, economic and political ability for the solution of the problem.

We cannot expect a national economy that is not led, not reinforced and not supported by sound financial institutions to develop smoothly. Either the form of the solution or the unsolved situation of this bad loan problem will affect the developing process of the Japanese economy for several decades in the future.

5.3.1 The Writing-off of Bad Loans and Its Core Problem

The Ministry of Finance Japan (MOF) officially announced the present situation of bad loans held by all domestic financial institutions on November 14, 1995, which is shown in Table 5.20. According to this announcement, the loans in bankruptcy and overdue loans amounted to ¥24.43 trillion, the interest-reduced or exempted loans amounted to ¥12.96 trillion, and these bad loans together totaled ¥37.39 trillion.

TABLE 5.20 Situation of Bad Loans Held by Financial Institutions (September 1995)

(Unit: ¥ billion)

	Bad loan value			Reserve for uncollectable account		
Bank name	Total	Bankruptcy/ overdue	Interest-reduced or exempted	Total	Of which, claim write-off special account	Latent assets of securities
City banks	13,094	8,058	5,036	4,179	3,273	8.096
Long-term credit banks	3,970	2,116	1,854	1,038	842	2,504
Trust banks	5,420	2,797	3,499	950	767	2,234
Regional banks	4,946	3,288	1,658	1,268	845	5,071
Regional banks II	2,789	2,208	5,810	600	439	838
All banks, subtotal	31,095	18,467	12,628	8,035	6,166	18,743
FI established by credit unions	6,295	5,963	332	1,518	793	1,595
Total	37,390	24,430	12,960	9,553	6,959	20,338

FI, Financial institutions.
Source: *The Weekly Toyo Keizai* [J], February 3, 1996, p. 50.

However, these official figures obviously underestimated the actual situation of the bad loans because of the following. First, loans overdue for less than 6 months are not included here. Second, interest-reduced or exempted loans here mean loans with interest that is under the official discount rate at the contract date. Conversely, loans with paid interest that is higher than the official discount rate at the contract date, even if under the originally contracted interest, are not included as bad loans. Third, the ¥5.5 trillion loans from the agricultural financial institutions (AFI) to *jusen*, and bad loans of bankrupt financial institutions in the meantime (i.e. Cosmo Credit Association, Kizu Credit Association and Hyogo Bank with bad loans of ¥0.38 trillion, ¥1 trillion and ¥1.5 trillion, respectively) are not included in these figures. Fourth, the ¥1 trillion latent losses owned by the Joint Claim Purchase Institution are not included. Fifth, a part of the bad loans held by bank-affiliated non-banks or subsidiaries are not included and those of insurance companies are also not included.

Taking account of these circumstances (also inclusive of the additional loans of banks for borrowers' interest payments), the real total amount of bad loans held by all financial institutions is considerably greater than the figure announced by the MOF.[1]

Of these officially announced bad loans, the MOF estimated the loss value that cannot be recovered as ¥18.3 trillion (its breakdown: loans in bankruptcy and overdue loans ¥8.4 trillion; interest-reduced or exempted loans ¥2.2 trillion; and unrecovered loans of *jusen* ¥7.7 trillion). Certainly, the loss value of *jusen* are under consideration in this unrecovered value. However, it is too optimistic for us to think that the total value is within ¥18.3 trillion, taking account of the real total amount of bad loans and the downward trend of collateral prices.

Considering some important economic factors relating to trends in this bad loan problem, for a start, the large increase in net business profit of the financial institutions, especially of city banks and long-term credit banks, is of note. The net business profit of 11 city banks reached ¥1.86 trillion, while that of three long-term credit banks reached ¥0.33 trillion at the interim accounting term in September 1995, increasing by 71.1% and 101.7% compared with the corresponding period of the previous year. Taken all together, of the three main bank schemes or the 21 major banks, the net business profit reached ¥3.37 trillion in the same interim accounting term (this value surpassed the net business profit ¥2.77 trillion in the previous 1-year accounting term), while in the case of all financial institutions it reached ¥4.12 trillion. This increase of the net business profit was mainly caused by an increase in the profit margin of interest rates, due to the large fall in the deposit rate, and the increase in capital gains, due to the rising price of bonds, which were supported by the super-low interest policy of the Government and the Bank of Japan (successive reductions of the official discount rate from 2.5% to 1.75% on September 21, 1993, to 1% on April 14, 1995 and to 0.5% on September 8, 1995). Of course, the increase of this net business profit did not lead directly to an increase in current profit and net profit, but it did lead to an increase in reserves for uncollectable accounts for the write-off of bad loans.[2]

Looking at the situation of the latent assets of banks' holding securities, which are one more important resources for the writing-off of bad loans; the recovery of stock prices from the latter half of 1995 (monthly average ¥18,948 in January 1995, ¥16,447 in March, ¥15,039 in June, ¥18,097 in September and ¥19,418 in December) caused the

Table 5.21 Latent Assets of Stocks in the 21 Major Banks (1995/96)

(Unit: billion)

Bank name	March 1995	September 1995	January 1996
(Nikkei average)	(¥16,447)	(¥17,913)	(¥20,618)
Dai-Ichi Kangyo Bank	627.2	980.3	1,531.4
Sakura Bank	763.4	1,172.7	1,832.6
Fuji Bank	343.5	679.7	1,210.4
Mitsubishi Bank	878.8	1,104.6	1,664.4
Asahi Bank	487.9	734.0	1,068.9
Sanwa Bank	795.4	1,088.1	1,619.4
Sumitomo Bank	406.5	729.7	1,235.7
Daiwa Bank	198.6	314.0	574.5
Tokai Bank	434.8	651.9	1,018.6
Hokkaido Takushoku Bank	38.4	78.5	176.6
Bank of Tokyo	274.0	422.3	676.5
City banks, Subtotal	5,248.5	7,956.0	12,609.1
Industrial Bank of Japan	1,218.5	1,538.2	2,123.3
Long-Term Credit Bank of Japan	382.8	569.4	971.9
Nippon Credit Bank	129.5	215.2	427.6
Long-term Credit Bank, Subtotal	1,730.8	2,322.9	3,522.9
Mitsui Trust and Banking	385.5	516.5	801.3
Mitsubishi Trust and Banking	384.7	539.4	837.1
Sumitomo Trust and Banking	317.5	445.6	688.6
Yasuda Trust and Banking	135.9	192.9	376.6
Toyo Trust and Banking	155.5	221.4	376.1
Chuo Trust and Banking	8.6	39.9	119.9
Nippon Trust and Banking	15.0	22.9	42.2
Trust banks, subtotal	1,402.7	1,978.6	3,241.7
The 21 major banks, total	8,382.0	12,257.4	19,373.7

Sources: *AM*, January 5, 1996; *NM*, November 28, 1995.

situation of latent assets of securities in corporations and financial institutions to improve. With regard to the latent assets of stocks owned by the 21 major banks, as shown in Table 5.21, they increased in total from ¥8.38 trillion in March 1995, to ¥12.26 trillion in September to ¥19.37 trillion in January 1996. The latent profits of securities owned by all financial institutions (141 companies) reached ¥20.27 trillion in September 1995, up 43% from half a year before. Incidentally, the latent profits of securities owned by all listed companies (the corporations with the accounting term in March, except for non-life insurance companies) reached ¥55.66 trillion in September 1995, up 25% from March of the same year.[3]

Thus, it appears that the conditions for financial institutions to write off their bad loans improved. However, the following important problems lay concealed in this process. First, although the 21 major banks wrote off ¥8.7 trillion in bad loans, as David Atkinson[4] has made clear, ¥4.7 trillion (54.6%) was written off by profit realization due to cross-transactions of stocks, that is, not by the selling-off of stocks, but by the sale and repurchase of the same stocks. This writing-off method, dependent on the latent profits of stocks, means that items labeled as "bad loans" in the balance sheet were simply transferred as new items to "securities". It does not bear new cash flow and, accordingly, it does not change the profitability of the bank.

Second, because there is a possibility in Japan for banks to lay the bad debts reserve as untaxable, banks are apt to prefer indirect writing-off methods. Also, in the case of this method, cash flow does not come about from the balance sheet of the bank to the outside, and it brings no real improvement in economic activities. In addition, following the establishment of the Joint Claim Purchase Institution, the banks have been able to write-off their bad loans as untaxable, leaving their debts alone for borrowers and not putting up the realized loss. This has led to a decrease in the Government's tax revenue and has meant the actual introduction of official funds to the bad loan problem. According to an estimation, between March 1993 and September 1996, these tax-free write-off values reached ¥7.47 trillion and the exempted tax value reached ¥3.6 trillion.[5]

The third problem is, in fact, the flip-side of the second: the current profit and the self-assessed income of the banks decreased largely in the meantime, despite an increase of their net business profit. For example, comparing the net business profit of the 21 major banks in March (accounting term) 1989 with that in March (accounting term) 1995, although their net business profit increased from ¥2.3 trillion to ¥2.7 trillion, their current profit and self-assessed income decreased from ¥3.1 trillion to ¥0.2 trillion and from ¥4 trillion to ¥0.4 trillion, respectively. The reduction of tax revenue due to these circumstances is practically equal to official funds aid to the banks.[6]

Thus, there are very serious problems in the process of bad loan disposition. Namely, neglecting to make the real nature of the problem clear and the parties responsible, and the actual introduction of official funds started by installments, while the problem of bad debts, which are the reverse of bad loans, has not yet been addressed entirely. The core of the problem's solution is the direct disposition of properties that have caused bad loans and their liquidation. Unless a practical advance in this respect occurs, the change of circumstances is only in the balance sheet of financial institutions. It does not cause any improvement in the real economy.

In the next section I will examine the reverse side of bad loans (i.e. the problem of bad debts).

5.3.2 Bad Loans/Bad Debts and the Real Estate Business and Construction Industry

The core of the bad loan problem is not in the rewriting of the balance sheet, but in the practical disposition of the bad loans, namely in stimulating the actual buying and selling of lands in the frozen real estate market; in short, it is the mobilization problem of land. It was David Atkinson that systematically pointed out this fact for the first time.

The outline of his argument is as follows:

1. The main problem of the Japanese economy at present is not the crisis of banks, but the crisis created by banks.
2. The banks are getting maximal net business profits on record and an advance towards the solution of their bad loan problem has been determined. However, the

reverse side of the bad loans (i.e. the problem of bad debts and the excessive amount of money borrowed by the real estate business and construction industry) are neglected entirely.
3. The banks must renounce their claims to bad loans (at least ¥15 trillion) for the real estate business and construction industry to support their reconstruction. With regard to the influence on the real economy, the number of employees in both industries is approximately 7 million and, based on the assumption that the average household contains 3.6 people, the situation in both industries directly concerns the lives of approximately 25 million people.
4. Banks should renounce their claims to bad loans and assist in the refinancing of the real estate business, while undertaking the allocation of new shares to a third party (in cases where the company is not bankrupt), or taking collateral (in cases where the company is bankrupt).
5. Not only the banks, which now one-sidedly receive benefits from the super-low interest rate policy and the factual introduction of official funds, but also borrowers and people in general should share the burdens and gains.
6. Both the real estate business and the construction industry hold enormous borrowed money (¥126 trillion) and bad debts and it is difficult for them to recover alone. The banks must support the reconstruction of both industries. After that, land development that leads to the mobilization of lands and the generation of cash flow can be undertaken, and the development of the national economy and the fulfillment of national life can be realized.[7]

I think that Atkinson's ideas outlined above are right and point clearly to the essence of the problem.

However, the following two conditions must be added to his argument, also in order to realize it. First, illegal acts carried out by companies in both industries during the bubble economy must be neither exempted nor pardoned. The pursuit of responsibility in this respect must also apply to financial institutions as creditors.

Second, the whole situation regarding the bad loans held by the financial institutions must be made clear to the public through open access to information. Although the present one-sided benefit of the banks itself is not justified, if the real nature of the problem remains unclear, we cannot take accurate and effective measures to tackle the situation. Even if the introduction of official funds is necessary, it must be approached from a "minimal scale and maximal effect" point of view.

At any rate, we must remember that the real solution to the bad loan problem is not a superficial improvement of the balance sheet of the financial institutions, but the liquidation of the bad financial institutions and the mobilization (sale with loss) of lands becoming bad debts.

5.3.3 Composition of the Bad Loan Problem

Socially, there is no objection in Japan to the fact that the disposal problem of enormous bad loans held by financial institutions is the biggest problem for the recent Japanese economy. This is also the biggest problem that the postwar Japanese economy has confronted as a result of its internal developing process.

However, when one tries to investigate the internal structure of this problem, one comes up against a definitive shortage of information. Confidential information is insufficient. It is not difficult to offer a precise numerical value itself. It is rather easy for people concerned to know the value of their own bad loans within each financial institution. It may not be so much more difficult for financial authorities, such as the MOF and the Bank of Japan, to collect such information and to get an almost exact numerical value.

However, until now, people in both private and official circles have provided little specific information to the public. The action of the authorities concerned has been passive and limited. For example, the extent of bad loans grew to include not only bankruptcy and overdue loans, but also interest-reduced and exempted loans. The disclosure of bad loans also spread from the 21 major banks to include regional banks and credit associations. Although this much has been gradually revealed to the public, the complete picture remains unclear.

It is evident that, as long as the true situation remains unclear, we cannot take effective action to solve the problem. In fact, the Government, the MOF and the financial institutions concerned have taken only ad hoc measures for each bankrupt financial institution and have not shown any comprehensive and systematic strategy towards solving this problem. Certainly, if one dares to point it out, there is a sort of policy to deal with the problem. It is the super-low interest rate policy. After decreasing the official discount rate from 6% to 5.5% in July 1991, there were nine successive reductions of the official discount rate to 0.5% in September 1995. It is apparent that these reductions support the increase of net business profit for financial institutions by lowering the interest rate for fund procurement (it always precedes the corresponding loan rate and enlarges the profit margin of the interest rates of banks).

Thus, the biggest beneficiaries of this super-low interest rate policy are the 21 major banks and other financial institutions. As is mentioned above, it is certain that they received maximal and unprecedented net business profit in FY 1995. The profit brought about by this policy is practically an introduction of official funds, together with other special loans by the Bank of Japan (over ¥1 trillion at the end of 1995)[8] and the transfer of funds from the deposit insurance organization to the bankrupt financial institutions (not to depositors, and amounting to more than ¥0.5 trillion in January 1996; because the ¥876 billion liability reserve was expected to run out by the end of March 1996, a large increase in the insurance rate from 0.012% to 0.084% was planned and effected in 1996).[9]

Because of this super-low interest rate policy which has been implemented on the pretext of "the stabilization of the financial system", inferior financial institutions and bad real estate and construction companies that had originally faced bankruptcy and liquidation continue to exist. This creates a negative pressure on solving the bad loan problem and the future of the Japanese economy.

In the process of this super-low interest rate policy, an enormous income transfer from working people and rentiers to financial institutions has occurred. For example, the interest income of the household sector was reduced by approximately ¥5 trillion in each FY 1994 and 1995 (¥10 trillion in total).[10] Because the guaranteed yield of life insurance companies fell from 4.5% to 2.5% in April 1996, the premiums paid by policyholders increase. The activity of many academic and cultural foundations is jeopardized because of the decreases in the interest their funds accrue. Furthermore, we cannot ignore the fact that the delay in business recovery because of this financial insecurity accelerates the public financial crisis because of a reduction in tax revenue and the issue of deficit-financing bonds. Thus, the shadow created by the bad loan problem and the super-low interest rate policy is large and dark.

Where does responsibility for this bad loan problem, which has become one of the most serious problems for the Japanese economy and its future, lie? With the Government, the MOF, the Bank of Japan, 11 city banks, the 21 major banks, all financial institutions, non-banks, the real estate business, the construction industry, the economic world in general, people who took part in the bubble economy, a majority of people, or all people? Who should bear responsibility for the bubble economy?

When thinking about this problem, one must distinguish between people who set the stage for the bubble economy (i.e. its economic and social framework) and the people who danced, acted and performed on the stage. Of course, larger responsibility rests with the former. For, it is fundamentally the former who can decide and regulate the number, extent and content of the latter, although the converse by no means applies. Therefore, the responsibility of the Government, the MOF and the Bank of Japan, which left the official discount rate at 2.5% from February 1987 to May 1989 for 2 years and 3 months, is large and serious, in spite of the fact that business activity was then booming (in F. R. Germany, the official rate became 2.5% in December 1987; however, after approximately 6 months it changed to 3% in July 1988 and to 3.5% in August 1988). As a result, both stock prices and land prices, which were rising at the time, rose further, while large corporations involved received a vast sum of low-cost funds because of equity finance, the financial institutions, the real estate business/the construction industries, men of property and farmers living near big cities, and many people who were situated in the high- and middle-income brackets. This cycle caused further steeply rising trends in the price of stock and land.

It is right that all people concerned are equal participants with self-responsibility in a market economy. However, this is only one side of the situation, and by emphasizing it one can fall into a trap of formal logic. With regard to the responsibility of the government authorities who regulate the economic and social conditions, the responsibility of the directors of large corporations and financial institutions who can mobilize a vast sum of funds, and the responsibility of individuals who take part in the market with limited financial means, they cannot be discussed on the same level. They have equal rights. However, among people having equal rights, larger self-control and responsibility is expected from the socially strong (i.e. rich people). To repeat, in addition to government authorities, the responsibility of large corporations and large financial institutions is not small, because, it is clear that their fund capacity moved and regulated the financial and capital market. Those people who ignored commercial law and criminal law must be punished. However, the social pursuit of this problem has not yet been achieved on a large-scale in Japan.

Relating to this problem of responsibility, important system reforms come to the surface, namely the reform of the MOF and the banking business. I would like to refer to this problem here. The MOF has wide powers in all fields of public financial policy and monetary policy in Japan being involved in the preparation of the budget (Budget Bureau), the collection of taxes (Tax Bureau, Customs House), the management of national assets and government bonds (Financial Bureau), supervision of banking businesses and financial institutions (Banking Bureau, International Finance Bureau), supervision of securities business (Securities Bureau), as well as having the right of supervision and order over the Bank of Japan (it should be noted that under the new law relating to the Bank of Japan that came into force in April 1998, the supervisory right of the MOF over the Bank of Japan was sharply curtailed and its power to issue directives to the Bank of Japan was limited to the right to request to postpone decisions made by the bank; consequently, the Bank of Japan's independence from the MOF and the Government was considerably strengthened). Of other advanced countries, there is no other ministry of finance that has such extensive power. Although the power of the Ministry of Home Affairs and the military authorities were balanced with that of the MOF in prewar Japan, because the former organizations were dissolved after World War II, the power of the MOF was strengthened in postwar Japan and the MOF has been situated in a leading position in all bureaucratic organizations.

The main cause of the bubble economy and the bad loan problem was the failure of the financial policy practiced by the MOF, judging from the above-mentioned policy content, the famous practice method of policy of "*goso sendan hoshiki*" (the "convoy of transport ships" method), which is a back-scratching alliance between all sorts of financial institutions and the MOF, and the close relationships between this ministry and private financial institutions. I think that the MOF should be reformed in the direction of limiting its sphere of activity to the collection of taxes and the administration of national assets. In addition, the bastion of the ministry, the Budget Bureau, should be moved to an organization under the immediate control of the Prime Minister or the Cabinet. The bureaus relating to financial policy should be reorganized and integrated into another organization (partly the Bank, of Japan) independent of the MOF.[11] (It should be noted that in July 2000 the Financial Services Agency, formerly the Financial Supervisory Agency, was established and all finance-related responsibilities were transferred from the MOF to that Agency.)

Incidentally, there is serious doubt that the MOF continues to play a leading role in the process of seeking and creating a solution for the bad loan problem. The MOF is the decisive organization concerned and, as it were, a defendant who had responsibility for the occurrence of the bubble economy and the bad loans. Having the MOF create a solution plan is equivalent to allowing the accused sit in judgment at a trial. This is logically unreasonable. Much more, the MOF cannot take the lead in the execution process of the plan. My proposal is as follows: neither the MOF nor the Cabinet (the latter is too closely related with the former), but the Diet must play a leading role. The Diet should create a time-limited financial supervisory authority independent of the MOF and give it strong power to draw up and enforce a solution plan for the bad loan problem.[12]

With regard to reforms of the banking system from the viewpoint of stabilization of the system; the proposal of Professor Kikuchi Hidehiro is very effective: for the development of the Japanese Economy in the future, it is necessary to secure the stabilization of the financial system, and also banks that can compete equally with banks of Western countries in the international financial market. To realize this objective, the old-type constitution of the Japanese banks, where the fluctuation of stock and land prices is connected directly with the profit structure, and credit creation must be drastically reformed. Specifically: (1) the stock's latent profit from equity capital must be eliminated; (2) there should be a restriction of stock investment of banks; (3) valuation of owned real estates should be at market prices and these should be writen-off in each accounting term; (4) large deposits should be regulated; and (5) risk and responsibility should be defined by the foundation of a financial holding company.

Professor Kikuchi proposed an early introduction of these recommendation.[13] I think that his proposals are appropriate except for the last point (because holding companies have a harmful effect on the enlargement of oligopolic rule not only in the financial sector, but also in general).

The main causes of the Japanese bubble economy in the latter half of the 1980s are as follows. (1) Domestically, while the tight budget for the reconstruction of public finance was situated in the center of all economic policy subjects, the excessive dependence on monetary policy (i.e. the request for a low-interest rate policy) occurred to recover from the strong yen recession after the Plaza Agreement. (2) Internationally, as a part of the international cooperation to prevent Black Monday on October 19, 1987 from developing into a world security and financial crisis, Japan continued its low-interest rate policy. (3) In addition, because of interlocking stockholdings among the *keiretsu* (affiliated companies, corporate groups), few stocks are traded on the market. (4) Real estate is respected as collateral for bank loans. (5) The power of stockholders and outside directors is weak, and also the supervision for enterprise activities from outside is weak. (6) Both the common expectations of a continuous rise in land prices and the market view of a lasting rise in stock prices accelerated buying.[14]

The bubble created by these factors burst and a vast amount of bad loans occurred. However, the essence of these bad loans is the problem of land prices, and the essence of the latter lies with the problem of the postwar Japanese socioeconomy, where people tried to allow land to be a source for capital gain, considering that the possession of land is more important than its utilization. This socioeconomic system of Japan has been up-held by the following: banks (financial institutions), which deal with housing and land as a source of profit; business managers, who support the large corporation system and corporate capitalism; the upper and middle strata of working people, who follow them; trade union members in large corporations; national and local government officials; and farmers owning their land (especially neighboring big cities). The bad loan problem has become a legacy that condenses the negative side of the postwar Japanese socioeconomy.

In addition, the economic, political, administrative and social irresponsibility and incompetence of the people concerned, which has been demonstrated in the activities under taken for the disposal process of the bad loan problem, seriously undermines the confidence in the social contract relations based on self-responsibility, which is at the center of any market economy and credit economy (in addition to self-responsibility, as one more core of a market economy, I want to point out mental openness). (The above-mentioned irresponsibility and incompetence calls to mind the situation until the defeat of Japan at the end of World War II: injustice or absence of strategic value or purpose; shifting the responsibility among persons concerned; the gradual and successive throwing of fighting power or funds (or retreats and losses); failure to find a solution for individual problems based on the standard of general judgment, but an accumulation of problems after successive temporary measures, etc.)

A vast social effort akin to that of postwar reform is necessary for a proper solution to this bad loan problem. It is very difficult in Japan to punish the responsible persons for the occurrence of the bubble economy and the bad loans[15] and to undertake administrative and fiscal reforms, inclusive of the reform of the MOF.

There is no doubt that it will be necessary to spend vast sums of official funds to solve the bad loan problem; however, this does not justify the unfettered spending of official funds for the disposal of *jusen*. The following criteria are necessary for the spending of official funds: the reform of the supervisory system for financial administration; the clear announcement of the total amount of official funds necessary; and public announcement of the introduction period of official funding.[16] It is also desireable that the burden on the people accompanies structural reform of the Japanese economy and the reconstruction of the idea of social justice.

Notes

1. *The Weekly Toyo Keizai* [J], February 3, 1996, p. 50; *NM, AM*, November 15, 1995.
2. *NM*, November 25, 28, 1995; *AM*, October 17, 1995; *AM*, November 25, 1995.
3. *NM*, December 15, 1995.
4. Atkinson, D. The writing-off of bad loans is now only in the balance sheet [J]. In: *NM*, June 1, 1995; do., The actual situation of the bad loans' write-off [J]. In: *Weekly Economist*, June 13, 1995, pp. 42–44.
5. *AM*, January 31, 1996; Atkinson, D. The waiting stance of the banks is permitted only in Japan [J]. In: *Weekly Economist*, October 10, 1995, pp. 70f.
6. *WPJE*, 1994, p. 222; *AM*, October 17, 1995; *NM*, May 27, 1995.
7. See Atkinson's articles in: *Weekly Economist* [J], April 11, 1995, pp. 48–51; *op. cit.*, July 18, 1995, pp. 26–29; *NM*, August 1, 1995; *NM*, February 9, 1996. Articles written by David Atkinson and Murayama Rie in: *Weekly Economist* [J], October 16, 1995, pp. 142–147; *op. cit.*, November 21, 1995, pp. 60–63.
8. *NM*, December 7, 1995.
9. *Weekly Economist* [J], January 30, 1996, p. 57; *op. cit.*, March 4, 1996, pp. 64f, 68f.
10. *NM*, January 5, 1996.
11. On the organization, competence and problems of the MOF, for the present, refer to articles in the following journals: *Weekly Economist* [J], January 10, 1995, pp. 50–53; *op. cit.*, April 4, 1995, pp. 26–45; *The Weekly Toyo Keizai* [J], April 22, 1995, pp. 112–121.
12. See: Takenaka H. Reasonable ground is necessary for the introduction of official funds [J], *NM*, December 10, 1995.
13. Kikuchi H. The drastic reform is necessary for the banking business [J]. In: *NM*, December 18, 1995.
14. *NE*, August 26, 1995.
15. A list of the main people responsible in both the governmental and non-government world during the bubble economy is shown in: *The Weekly Toyo Keizai* [J], July 22, 1995, pp. 32–36.
16. Takenaka H. *op. cit.* In: *NM*, December 10, 1995.

5.4 The Problem of Bad Loans at the End of the 1990s

The definition of "bad loan" went through a series of changes during this period. Briefly, these were as follows:

(a) Japanese Bankers Association's definition, March 1993:

Bankrupt + Overdue for 6 months or more

(b) Japanese Bankers Association's definition, September 1995:
Bankrupt + Overdue for 6 months or more + Interest-reduced or exempted (loans with interest under the official discount rate at the contract date)

(c) so-called "risk management loans", Japanese Bankers Association's definition, March 1998:

Bankrupt + Overdue for 3 months or more + Restructured

(d) a definition based on credit quality assessment, Financial Supervisory Agency (FSA), March 1998:

I, normal; II, needs attention; III, seriously doubtful; IV, loss. Of these, II + III + IV constitute problematic loans.

What distinguished this from previous definitions was a focus on the business administrative and financial situation of debtors and not just on debtors' interest payments.

(e) a definition based on the Financial Revitalization Laws, March 1999:

Needs attention and management + Seriously doubtful + Loss. With regard to the difference from definition (c), see the previous note for definition (d).

We cannot deny that these repeated changes in the definition of "bad loans" made it difficult to grasp the actual situation as regard to these loans. With this in mind, the trend of the bad loans problem at the end of the 1990s will be examined.

5.4.1 Bad Loans of All Financial Institutions as of March 1998, 1999

Looking back over the 1990s from the vantage point of July 1999, the most comprehensive government announcement on the actual situation of the bad loans was the official report published by the FSA[1] in July 1998. This brought together the results of a self-assessment of asset quality produced by all Japanese financial institutions at the end of March 1998.

Table 5.22 summarizes these results. The total of loans in category II (loans in need of attention for collection) and category III (seriously doubtful loans for collection) was ¥87.5 trillion. This amount is approximately 2.5-fold as much as the ¥35.2 trillion[2]

TABLE 5.22 Results of Self-Assessment of Asset Quality by All Financial Institutions (March 1998)

(Unit: ¥ trillion)

	Total credits	Category II	Category III
Major banks[1]	452.4	45.4	4.8
Regional banks	145.5	14.4	0.8
Regional banks II	50.6	5.9	0.4
All banks, subtotal	648.5	65.8	6.1
Cooperative-type Financial institutions	146.6	14.8	0.8
Total of all[2]	795.1	80.6	6.9

[1] City Banks, Long-term Credit Banks, Trust Banks.
[2] The bankrupt financial institutions are excluded from these data.
Source: *NM*, July 18, 1998.

of risk management loans of all financial institutions at the same time and was 11% of all ¥795.1 trillion loans (however, bankrupt loans (i.e. uncollectable loss) were not included in the ¥87.5 trillion problematic loans; the FSA indicated that the reason for this was that the bankrupt loans concerned were wholly secured by thereserve/ allowance).

At the end of July 1999, the FSA also published aggregate figures on the problematic loans as of March 1999 (data of bankrupt financial institutions, such as the Long-Term Credit Bank of Japan and Nippon Credit Bank, were excluded from this announcement). According to these figures, the total credits of all financial institutions was ¥694.3 trillion, while category II loans totalled ¥76.6 trillion, and category III loans totalled ¥3.9 trillion. The total amount of problematic loans was ¥80.5 trillion or 11.6% of total credits. This ratio of problematic loans to all credits was higher than in the previous year.[3] Incidentally, according to the same FSA report, the total amount of risk management loans at the same point in time was ¥38.7 trillion. This figure had increased not only in absolute terms, but also proportionately when compared with the previous year.

5.4.2 Bad Loans of the 17 Major Banks as of March 1999

The amount of bad loans of the 17 major banks is shown in Table 5.23 (there were formerly 21 major banks in Japan; however, Mitsubishi Bank and the Bank of Tokyo merged in April 1996, and Hokkaido Takushoku Bank, Long-Term Credit Bank of Japan and Nippon Credit Bank were declared bankrupt in November 1997, October 1998 and December 1998, respectively; consequently, the number of major banks in Japan is 17).

According to Table 5.23, the total amount of bad loans was ¥20.8 trillion in terms of the standard based on the Financial Revitalization Laws and ¥19.9 trillion in terms of the standard based on risk management loans. Because the bad loan value held by the 19 major banks was ¥22 trillion in March 1998, it may appear to have been decreasing. However, if we exclude the ¥1.4 trillion bad loan value of the Long-Term Credit Bank of Japan and the ¥1.7 trillion bad loan value of Nippon Credit Bank, which were both included in the total for March 1998, the bad loan value of the 17 major banks in 1998 was ¥18.9 trillion. Therefore, it can be seen that there was a substantial increase in the amount of bad loans during this 1 year period after all.[4] In addition, many commentators agree that these official figures underestimate the actual extent of bad loans and this corresponds to the results in Table 5.22 (many people suspect that even these figures on problematic loans are still too low).

The major banks have stated repeatedly that they kept reserves for uncollectable accounts and prepared funds to write-off and are able to cope with the situation (covered ratio is 53% on average; 79% at maximum and 31% at minimum). The banks announced that they wrote-off ¥10.4 trillion of bad loans in FY 1998. However, the main part of the written-off value is still shown only indirectly in the balance sheet (of the ¥58.8 trillion total disposal value of bad loans from FY 1992 to FY 1998, the direct written-off value in the narrow sense that was exempted from the debtor account and led to fix losses totalled ¥7.1 trillion, only 12% of the total disposal value[5]), in the continuous falling of land prices, and additional losses will be compelled in the

TABLE 5.23 Situation of Bad Loans Held by the 17 Major Banks (March 1999)

(Unit: ¥ billion, %)

	Bad loans				
	e[1]	c[1]	Ratio[2]	Repaid tax	Public fund
Dai-Ichi Kangyo Bank	2,253.4	2,204.8	6.7	613.7	900.0
Sakura Bank	1,800.0	1,760.5	5.5	677.7	800.0
Fuji Bank	1,388.6	1,361.7	4.6	732.6	1,000.0
Bank of Tokyo-Mitsubishi	2,160.7	2,077.6	5.3	622.6	0
Asahi Bank	929.9	920.1	4.4	334.2	500.0
Sanwa Bank	1,730.9	1,686.2	4.3	592.6	700.0
Sumitomo Bank	2,013.7	1,959.9	5.8	719.9	501.0
Daiwa Bank	794.0	743.4	7.2	211.2	408.0
Tokai Bank	753.2	476.0	2.5	365.1	600.0
City banks, subtotal	13,824.4	13,190.2	5.1	4,873.2	5,409.0
Industrial Bank of Japan	1,872.4	1,844.2	8.2	406.3	600.0
Mitsui Trust and Banking	768.9	762.2	9.9	243.6	350.2
Mitsubishi Trust and Banking	1,361.8	1,300.7	12.1	275.8	300.0
Yasuda Trust and Banking	665.6	551.1	9.1	253.9	0
Toyo Trust and Banking	898.3	899.4	12.5	183.0	200.0
Chuo Trust and Banking	238.0	203.1	5.0	689.0	200.0
Nippon Trust and Banking	242.8	239.3	24.1	200.0	0
Sumitomo Trust and Banking	950.3	946.4	8.6	287.7	200.0
Trust banks, subtotal	5,125.7	4,900.2	11.6	1,332.9	1,250.2
The 17 major banks, total	20,825.5	19,936.6	8.3	6,612.4	7,259.2

[1] e and c mean that the standard used to calculate the figures is definition (e) and (c) for bad loans; respectively.

[2] The ratio of bad loans in total loans.

Source: *Weekly Economist* [J], June 8, 1999, pp. 26f.

case of direct writing-off (i.e. through sales of collaterals). In this sense, many difficulties are waiting until the effective solution of the bad loan problem.

In addition, we have to consider that the write-off value of ¥10 trillion in FY 1998 occurred under special conditions. The major banks, whose management was preoccupied with the bad loan problem, were strongly supported by the super-low interest policy of the Government and the Bank of Japan and, specifically, by the increase in net business profit by the profit margin of interest rates and commission for the buying and selling of securities. Furthermore, in this term, they could get both direct capital injections from public funds and the recognition of the owned capitalization of the repaid tax (see: Table 5.23, made by Professor Kyuno Masao).

With regard to capital injections from public funds, the 15 major banks, except for the Bank of Tokyo-Mitsubishi (excluding its subsidiary Nippon Trust Bank and Fuji Bank's subsidiary Yasuda Trust and Banking, and including the largest regional bank, Bank of Yokohama), applied for these to the Deposit Insurance Corporation (DIC). Consequently, after recognition by the Financial Reconstruction Commission[6] (FRC), a total amount of more than ¥7 trillion was injected separately into each bank in March 1999. The government undertook 75% of these capital injections, ¥5.5 trillion in terms of convertible preferred stock (which includes the right to take part in management; the rest was subordinated debentures etc.). The time until this stock converts to ordinary stock ranges from 3 months at the shortest to 7 years and 6 months at the longest. The average yield of the dividend is annually between 0.54% and 1.73%.[7]

The owned capitalization of the repaid tax was first recognized by the government in FY 1998. This is an accounting system that, on the assumption that the excessive paid tax (prepaid tax) at the disposal of bad loans will be returned, permits it to count in the balance sheet as owned capital.[8]

Capital injections from public funds or the recognition of the owned capitalization of repaid tax are examples of the state giving strong support to the banks that have been exhausting their management power (i.e. damaging their owned capital) in coping with the bad loan problem.

5.4.3 Framework for Injecting Public Funds and Related Problems

Following the bankruptcy of Hokkaido Takushoku Bank in autumn 1997, Long-Term Credit Bank of Japan and Nippon Credit Bank went bankrupt in autumn/winter 1998. Moreover, five Banks, four Shinkin Banks and 32 credit cooperatives had gone bankrupt by June 1999.[9]

Prompted by these bankruptcies, the Government, which had officially promised not to make any pay offs and to fully protect all deposits until the end of March 2001 [in May 2000, postponed until March 2002], tried to build a new framework to protect the deposits and to stabilize the financial system.

The most important measure in this regard was the approval of the Financial Revitalization Laws in October 1998 and the new public fund injections to the DIC based on this. Consequently, ¥60 trillion of public funds was newly set aside in the DIC. This comprised: (a) a ¥17 trillion account for special business (¥7 trillion in government bonds and ¥10 trillion government-guaranteed bonds); (b) a ¥18 trillion account for financial revitalization (government-guaranteed bonds); and (c) a ¥25 trillion account for the early rebuilding of sound financial functions (government-guaranteed bonds). The respective aims and content of each account are: (a) the fund aims for the full protection of deposits; (b) the business of the bridge banks and the special officially controlled banks, the business for the purchase of bad loans by the Resolution and Collection Bank and (c) strengthening the capital of financial institutions.[10]

Here, I will refer to the account for special business. The total amount of public funds used for the full protection of deposits in bankrupt financial institutions had already reached more than ¥7 trillion in July 1999. As a result, the funds procured by government bonds were used up. Hereafter, funds had to be newly procured by a new issue of government-guaranteed bonds. It must be recognized that the public funds injected to make up the excessive liabilities of assets are impossible to repay in principle and are sure to become a burden on taxpayers.

Relating to this, we must note the fact that, in the meantime, the amount of excessive liabilities of bankrupt financial institutions has changed (increased) largely before and after bankruptcy.

It was said that Hokkaido Takushoku Bank, which went bankrupt on November 17, 1997, still had net assets of ¥296.1 billion 3 days prior to its bankruptcy. However, according to the inspection for liquidation at the end of June 1998, the bank had net liabilities exceeding ¥1.77 trillion.

It was announced that the Long-Term Credit Bank of Japan, which went bankrupt on October 23, 1998, and came under special public management (temporary nationalization) had net assets of ¥160 billion following an inspection by the FSA at the end of September 1998. However, the Stock-Price Evaluation Commission of the FRC announced that the bank had excessive liabilities of ¥2.6 trillion as of October 28, 1998. Furthermore, as of July 1999, this figure appears to have increased to ¥3.5 trillion.

It was said that Nippon Credit Bank, which went bankrupt on December 13, 1998, had excessive liabilities of only ¥94.4 billion according to an inspection of the FSA at the end of March 1998. However, later, on December 17, 1998, the Stock-Price Evaluation Commission calculated the figure to be ¥3 trillion.[11]

The remarkable increase in the losses (i.e. the amount of the excessive liabilities) of bankrupt financial institutions over a relatively short period shows that, on the one hand, financial inspection by government authorities was both irresponsible and lax. On the other hand, it casts severe doubt on the reliability of officially announced values regarding the bad loans of the not yet bankrupt financial institutions. The actual amount of bad loans is probably far larger than the officially published figures, and the problems faced by each financial institution must be far more serious than commonly thought.

Notes

1. The FSA is the institution that took over the division of financial inspection and supervision in the MOF and was founded by the Prime Minister's Office in June 1998. In July 2000, the FSA integrated also the division of financial planning in the MOF and was reorganized to the Financial Services Agency.
2. *NM*, July 18, 1998.
3. *NM*, July 24, 1999.
4. Kyuno, M. Aspects of the Banks Losing the Reserve Power to Dispose of the Bad Loans [J]. In: *Weekly Economist*, June 9, 1998, p. 25.
5. http://www.fsa.go.jp/news/newse/ne_018b.html, p. 3.
6. This commission consists of five members and its chairman is a minister of the cabinet. It started in December 1998. The FSA is systematically under the leadership of this commission. However, this commission will cease to exist in January 2001 and its function will be transferred to the Financial Services Agency (as of August 2000).
7. *NM*, March 5, 1999.
8. *NM*, May 25, 1999.
9. *NM*, June 15 and July 10, 1999.
10. *NM*, July 1, 1999.
11. See: *NM*, July 9 and 16, 1999.

Chapter 6
Trends and Problems in Central Government Finance

6.1 Trends in Central Government Finance

Trends in the scale of central and local public finance (expenditure) of Japan are shown in Table 6.1. The ratio of the general accounts expenditure of the central government to GNP has changed in recent years by approximately 20%–15% and, if local government expenditure is included, by approximately 30%–25% (incidentally, in 1989, the ratio of national and local taxes to national income was 27.9% and, if social security contributions are included, 38.3%; these ratios, including social security contributions, of other advanced countries were: US 34.9% in 1988; UK 50.3% in 1987; F.R. Germany 50.2% in 1988; France 59.5% in 1988; and Italy 46.2% in 1988).[1]

The decreases in these ratios were caused by factors including the following. Although an active fiscal policy aimed at expanding domestic demand was necessary in the latter half of the 1980s, on the one hand, efforts to restrict expenditure continued in order to solve the problem of outstanding government bonds, on the other, the national economy expanded well, with the economic growth rate reaching over 5% almost successively for 10 years.

The breakdown of general account expenditure in recent years is shown in Table 6.2. In 1991, the ratio of government debt expenses for the redemption and interest payments on cumulative government bonds was a maximum of 22.8%; similarly, social security expenses were 17.4%, public works expenses were 9.4%, expenses for education and culture, and promotion of science and technology were 7.7% and national defense expenses were 6.2%.

With regard to the rate of change of each principal item from 1986 to 1991, in a situation where the total expenditure increased 31% on average, expenses for local finance, government debt expenses and expenses for economic cooperation increased considerably, by 64%, 50% and 41%, respectively. National defense expenses increased 31% on average. Conversely social security expenses and expenses for education and culture etc., showed only modest increases of 21% and 10%, respectively. Public works expenses, small enterprises assistance expenses and foodstuff control expenses decreased 5%, 14% and 39%, respectively.

Next, the problem of cumulative government bonds (i.e. one of the biggest problems in the fiscal structure of Japan) will be examined. Refering to Figure 6.1, it can be seen that dependence rates of budget revenue on government bond issues, looking

TABLE 6.1 Scale of Central and Local Public Finance (Expenditure) for 1981–94 (s.y.)

(Unit: ¥ billion)

FY	General account of central government		Ordinary account of local government		Net total		GNE		Ratio to GNE		
	Value (A)	Annual change (%)	Value (B)	Annual change (%)	Value (C)	Annual change (%)	Value (D)	Annual change (%)	A/D (%)	B/D (%)	C/D (%)
1981	46,921.2	8.1	49,165.3	7.4	76,496.1	7.8	260,334.3	5.9	18.1	18.9	29.5
1982	47,245.1	0.7	51,133.3	4.0	79,770.7	4.3	273,461.5	5.0	17.3	18.7	29.2
1984	51,480.6	1.7	53,870.0	3.0	85,705.8	1.1	305,725.3	6.9	16.8	17.6	28.0
1986	53,640.4	1.2	58,717.1	4.3	92,174.9	3.7	339,685.3	4.4	15.8	17.3	27.1
1988	61,471.1	6.5	66,401.6	5.0	104,263.7	5.3	378,963.0	6.4	16.2	17.5	27.5
1990	69,268.7	5.2	78,473.2	7.9	123,932.4	6.6	441,640.3	7.7	15.7	17.8	28.1
1992	70,497.4	−0.1	89,559.7	6.9	134,803.8	4.0	477,264.8	2.2	14.8	18.8	28.2
1994	73,430.5	−2.2	93,817.8	0.8	141,441.0	1.1	482,419.8	0.4	15.2	19.4	29.3

Settlement figures for 1992 and, before, supplemented budget figures for 1994.
Sources: *Economic Statistics Yearbook* [J], 1991, Tokyo: Toyo Keizai Inc., p. 330; *op. cit.*, 1996, p. 495.

TABLE 6.2 Breakdown of Expenditure Budget of General Accounts (FY 1986–1994; s.y.)

(Unit: ¥ billion)

Principal items	1986	1988	1990	1992	1994
Social security expenses	10,090.3 (18.7)	11,801.4 (19.1)	11,544.5 (16.6)	12,196.5 (17.8)	13,565.1 (18.5)
Expenses for education and culture, promotion of science and technology	4,886.6 (9.1)	4,981.9 (8.1)	5,359.4 (7.7)	5,854.3 (8.2)	5,893.6 (8.0)
Government debt expense	10,664.3 (19.8)	12,030.7 (19.5)	14,493.3 (20.7)	15,181.8 (21.2)	13,605.5 (18.5)
Expenses for pensions	1,850.1 (3.4)	1,879.7 (3.0)	1,837.5 (2.6)	1,783.7 (2.5)	1,761.6 (2.4)
Expenses for local finance	9,734.7 (18.1)	13,031.1 (21.1)	15,930.8 (22.9)	14,203.6 (19.9)	12,068.7 (16.4)
National defense expenses	3,337.9 (6.2)	3,728.2 (6.0)	4,254.0 (6.1)	4,577.8 (6.4)	4,651.8 (6.3)
Public works expenses	6,946.3 (12.9)	6,682.9 (10.8)	7,013.1 (10.1)	9,941.3 (13.9)	12,770.6 (17.4)
Expenses for economic cooperation	602.0 (1.1)	718.9 (1.2)	802.0 (1.2)	900.4 (1.3)	992.3 (1.4)
Small enterprises assistance expenses	225.6 (0.4)	257.6 (0.4)	240.8 (0.3)	259.6 (0.4)	270.1 (0.4)
Expenses for measures for energy	570.5 (1.1)	458.3 (0.7)	547.0 (0.8)	630.6 (0.9)	670.7 (0.9)
Transfer to industrial Investment special account	—	458.0 (0.7)	1,300.0 (1.9)	216.6 (0.3)	172.5 (0.2)
Foodstuff control expenses	613.8 (1.1)	480.3 (0.8)	404.6 (0.6)	352.8 (0.5)	264.8 (0.4)
Sundry expenses and others	4,102.4 (7.6)	4,300.0 (7.0)	5,642.7 (8.1)	4,641.2 (6.5)	5,047.8 (6.9)
Reserve funds	200.0 (0.4)	200.0 (0.3)	325.0 (0.5)	200.0 (0.3)	150.0 (0.2)
Total	53,824.8 (100.0)	61,851.7 (100.0)	69,651.1 (100.0)	71,489.6 (100.0)	73,430.5 (100.0)

All figures are based on supplemented budgets and figures in parentheses denote the percentage of the total budget.
Sources: *ESA*, 1991, p. 218; *op. cit.*, 1996, p. 281.

at them individually for each year, decreased steadily during this period from a maximum of 34.7% in 1979 to 7.6% (this value based on the original budget; ¥5.3 trillion) in 1991. However, their outstanding value continued to increase consistently during this period and reached the vast sum of ¥168 trillion (adding in government-guaranteed bonds and borrowings to government bonds, the total amount reached approximately ¥224 trillion in 1990; the outstanding value of local government bonds reached ¥52 trillion).[2] Regulated by the increase of the outstanding value of cumulative government bonds, the ratio of government debt expenses in annual total government expenditure continued to increase each year and reached 22.8% in 1991, as mentioned earlier. Although the ratio of the value of the outstanding government bonds to GNP decreased somewhat after 1987, it remained at a high level of 36.7% in 1991[3] and its ratio to total government expenditure of general accounts reached 240% in 1991.

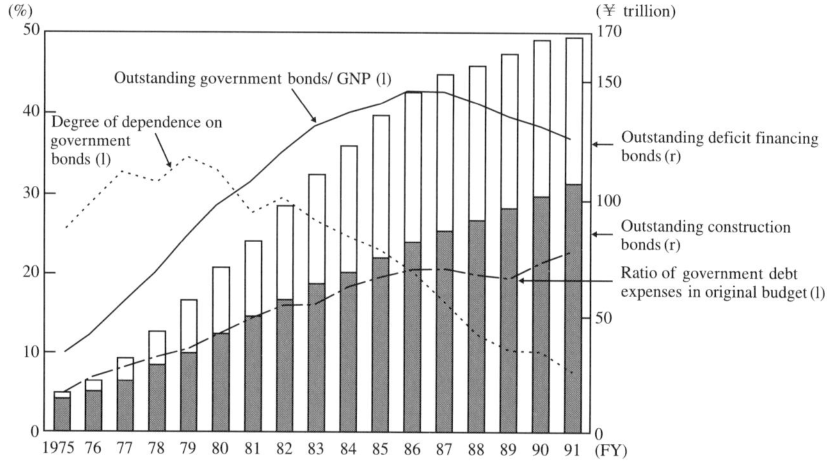

FIG. 6.1 Central Public Finance and Government Bonds (FY 1975–1991)
(r) right. (l) left.
Source: *WPJE*, 1991, p. 113.

By way of comparison, the respective ratios of outstanding long-term government liabilities to GNP and of interest payment expenditure to total government expenditure of general accounts in advanced countries in 1989 were 47.1% and 16.0% in Japan, 47.7% and 14.8% in the US, 31.8% and 8.0% in the UK, 21.2% and 11.1% in the F.R. Germany and 13.6% and 11.0% in France.[4] Obviously, we can see that the problem of cumulative government bonds in Japan has been as serious as that in the US.

The structure of revenue of general accounts is broken down into its main components in Table 6.3. In recent years, a decreasing ratio of government securities and borrowings and an increasing ratio of tax revenue have become evident. The breakdown of this tax revenue from 1988 to 1991 was as follows: income tax 34.4%, 37.4%, 39.4%, and 39.9% for FY 1988, 1989, 1990 and 1991, respectively (of which, with-holding tax constituted 24.9%, 26.8%, 29.6%, and 31.1%, respectively, and self-assessment was 9.5%, 10.6%, 9.8% and 8.7%), corporation tax 35.3%, 33.2%, 30.1%, and 29.8% for FY 1988, 1989, 1990 and 1991, respectively, and commodity tax (after 1989, consumption tax) 3.9%, 5.7%, 7.9%, and 7.7% for FY 1988, 1989, 1990 and 1991, respectively.[5] Apparently, during this period, the ratio of income tax, especially the with-holding tax section, increased and the ratio of corporation tax decreased. The ratio of commodity tax, or consumption tax (the latter was introduced generally at a tax rate of 3% during the tax reform of 1989), rose by approximately 4% during this period.

Looking at these data, the respective ratios of direct and indirect tax in Japan were 70.1% and 29.2% in 1981, 73.1% and 26.9% in 1986, 73.2% and 26.8% in 1988, 74.2% and 25.8% in 1989, 72.5% and 27.5% in 1990 and 72.9% and 27.1% in 1991.[6] Although the general consumption tax mentioned earlier was introduced in 1989, there are still no changes evident as a result of its introduction. For comparison, the respective ratios of direct and indirect tax in selected countries were: US 91.7% and 8.3% in 1990; UK 58.2% and 41.8% in 1989; F.R. Germany 44.1% and 55.9% in 1989; and France 37.3% and 62.7% in 1988.[7]

TABLE 6.3 Breakdown of Revenue of General Accounts (FY 1981–1993, s.y.)

(Unit: ¥ billion)

FY	Total	Tax and stamp revenue	Of which, Tax	Of which, stamp	Government monopolies	Government enterprise profit and receipts	Receipt from liquidation of government property	Miscellaneous	Surplus during previous FY	Public bonds (%)	
1981	47,433.3	28,952.1	27,779.2	1,172.9	787.4	12.2	78.1	1,583.2	635.6	12,899.9	27.2
1982	48,001.3	30,511.1	29,248.4	1,262.7	769.3	15.6	73.2	2,065.2	522.2	14,044.7	29.3
1984	52,183.4	34,908.4	33,573.8	1,334.5	1,030.8	16.8	94.7	2,333.8	1,017.6	12,781.3	24.5
1986	56,489.2	41,876.8	40,301.0	1,575.8	12.5	25.3	143.6	2,189.0	987.1	11,254.9	19.9
1988	64,607.4	50,826.5	49,894.3	1,932.3	10.8	19.8	155.8	2,784.4	3,657.6	7,152.5	11.1
1990	71,703.5	60,105.9	58,211.8	1,894.0	11.1	22.4	162.0	2,701.1	1,388.9	7,312.0	10.2
1992	71,466.0	54,445.3	52,874.7	1,570.6	13.2	22.3	123.5	3,337.6	2,443.4	9,536.0	13.3
1993	77,731.2	54,129.2	52,227.1	1,599.1	14.3	24.7	122.9	5,734.2	968.6	16,174.0	20.8

All figures are settlement figures.
Sources: *Economic Statistics Yearbook*, 1991, op. cit., p. 330; *op. cit.*, 1996, p. 483.

In the present discussion of tax reform, with regard to the relationship between direct and indirect tax in Japan, there has been considerable political pressure, led by the MOF, for an increase in consumption tax and reduced income tax. The reasons for this are the need for an increase in consumption tax to secure stable financial resources for social welfare in the steadily aging society and to reduce income tax rates for those in the upper and middle income brackets, namely those who feel a heavy tax burden, in order to maintain their will to work and social vitality.

However, we cannot directly conclude that the income tax burden is relatively heavier in Japan, on the grounds that the ratio of direct to indirect tax is larger in Japan than in European countries. Naturally, income tax is merely a part of direct tax. Therefore, if we compare the weight of the income tax burden internationally, we must compare not the ratios of direct and indirect tax, but the ratios of individual income tax revenue to the GDP of the countries concerned. These indices are shown in Figure 6.2.

Apparently, Japan's ratio of income tax revenue to GDP was the second lowest (next to France) in selected countries of the OECD in 1989 (it increased to 8.3% in 1991, but the position of Japan did not change). Furthermore, in the case of income tax rates for the middle-income earners, for people whose annual earnings are ¥20 million or less, Japan's effective tax rate (income tax + inhabitants tax) is lower than that of the US, the UK and F.R. Germany (more specifically, for incomes less than ¥25 million the effective tax rate is lower in Japan than the UK, and for incomes less than ¥35 million the rate is lower in Japan than in Germany).[8]

Accordingly, on the pretext of correcting the direct and indirect tax ratios, truly for the realization of an increase in consumption tax, to emphasize the necessity for a decrease in the income tax rate is a consciously misleading opinion. At least, one must not substitute (or confuse) correction of the direct and indirect tax ratios with a discussion on income tax as it ought to be.

Furthermore, it cannot be denied that the financial situation of the Japanese central government is critical. At the end of FY 1994, the outstanding value of government bonds reached ¥207 trillion, and adding in the value of government-guaranteed bonds and borrowing to government bonds, the total amount reached ¥262 trillion. (In addition, there were concealed borrowings of ¥38.7 trillion, including the long-term debts of the former Japanese National Railways of ¥26 trillion.)[9] [For the figures for FY2000, see the preface.]

As mentioned earlier, the emergence of a society dominated by the elderly in the near future and a large increase in social security expenses is inevitable. Any tax reform aiming at fiscal reconstruction under these circumstances, must address the following points: fair and strict collection of taxes (including accurate accounting of income and the prevention of tax evasion, the introduction of a taxpayer's number to allow horizontal impartiality); the achievement of real social fairness (a highly progressive tax rate is equivalent to vertical impartiality); stricter taxation on unearned compared with earned incomes (the strengthening of assets taxation); and the protection of and provision of relief to the socially weak.

Finally, the financial resources and purposes of the fiscal investment and loan program, also known as the second national budget, which accounts for approximately 10% of the GNP and approximately 50% of the general account, will be examined. Referring to Tables 6.4 and 6.5, it can be seen that the main resources consist of postal

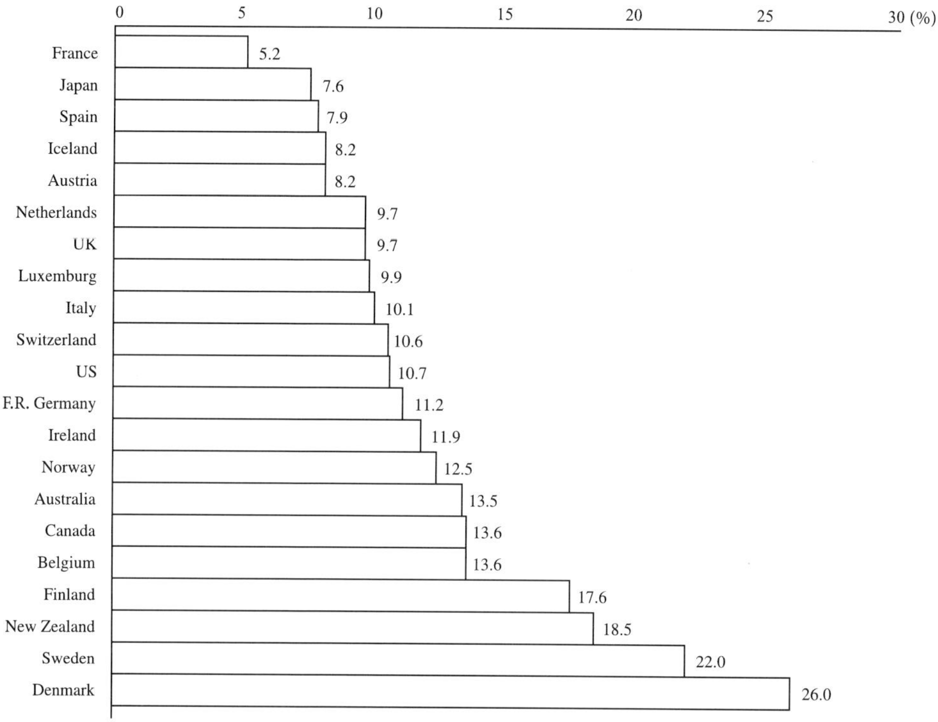

FIG. 6.2 Ratios of Income Tax Revenue to GDP in Selected OECD Countries (1989)
Source: *Weekly Economist* [J], November 2, 1993, p. 29.

savings, welfare pensions, national pensions (these resources are concentrated in the Trust Fund Bureau of the Government and the MOF), and the postal insurance of the Ministry of Posts and Telecommunications. With regard to its purpose, although the preparation and maintenance of an industrial foundation was the central focus during the high economic growth period, recently housing, life environment improvement and medium and small enterprises have become the main concerns. The item listed as "Fund application" in Table 6.5 is a fund used at the discretion of the Ministry of Posts and Telecommunications and the Pension Welfare Service Public Corporation. Its ratio in total value of the program was 12% in the first year 1987 and increased to 20% in 1991.

TABLE 6.4 Financial Resources of the Fiscal Investment and Loan Program (FY 1981–1993, s.y.)

(Unit: ¥ billion)

FY	Total (A)	Special account for ind. investment	Trust Fund Bureau	Of which, postal savings	Of which, welfare pension, national pension	Of which, withdrawal money etc.	Postal insurance	Government-garanteed bonds/ borrowings	GNP (B)	A/B (%)
1981	23,540.2	18.5	20,034.7	7,599.7	4,660.4	..	1,886.6	1,600.4	259,668.8	9.1
1982	24,223.6	18.9	20,008.4	8,354.4	4,551.2	7,410.3	1,976.4	2,219.9	273,461.5	8.9
1984	27,283.1	4.0	21,670.1	7,797.0	5,198.8	8,674.3	2,576.5	3,032.5	305,725.3	8.9
1986	29,579.2	61.1	23,423.7	7,547.2	4,491.9	11,384.9	3,098.6	2,995.8	339,685.3	8.7
1988	32,223.9	82.4	25,674.4	8,463.3	5,866.9	11,344.2	4,221.1	2,246.0	381,998.2	8.5
1990	35,813.9	63.8	27,817.5	4,594.7	6,802.6	18,420.2	6,033.3	1,899.3	441,640.3	8.1
1991	38,153.5	62.6	29,903.9	18,706.7	7,789.5	14,781.6	6,287.9	1,899.8	467,099.1	8.2
1993	52,457.7	99.0	43,035.8	10,400.0	7,413.1	20,069.5	6,976.7	2,346.2	480,622.8	10.9

All figures are settlement figures.

Sources: *Economic Statistics Yearbook*, 1991, op. cit., p. 332; *op. cit.*, 1996, p. 493.

TABLE 6.5 Purposes of the Fiscal Investment and Loan Program (FY 1987–1993, s.y.)

(Unit: ¥ billion)

Item	1987	1988	1989	1990	1991	1993
Total	27,081.3	29,614.0	32,270.5	34,572.4	36,805.6	45,770.6
Housing	6,328.2	6,921.5	7,460.6	8,365.9	9,474.5	10,798.9
Life environment improvement	3,998.7	4,450.9	4,371.3	4,222.0	4,293.3	6,069.6
Welfare	627.7	661.8	736.0	851.9	1,026.1	1,397.1
Educational institution	784.1	637.6	520.2	554.1	582.4	649.9
Medium and small enterprises	3,985.6	4,030.6	4,176.4	4,337.8	4,494.5	5,341.6
Agriculture, Forestry and Fisheries	907.8	979.4	924.4	876.0	908.2	914.5
Land maintenance/disaster relief	493.0	409.8	357.9	328.5	330.6	531.8
Road	2,363.0	2,512.1	2,576.8	2,700.1	2,983.2	3,626.9
Transport and communications	2,264.1	2,229.9	2,361.6	2,304.1	1,468.1	2,889.8
Regional development	657.7	652.2	676.6	682.5	709.0	981.5
Industrial technology	630.9	687.2	758.7	796.5	937.7	1,289.0
Trade/economic cooperation	690.5	1,171.0	1,420.0	1,603.0	1,898.0	2,105.0
Fund application	3,350.0	4,270.0	5,930.0	6,950.0	7,700.0	9,175.0

All figures are settlement figures.
Sources: *op. cit.*, 1991, p. 334; *op. cit.*, 1996, p. 493.

Notes

1. *CEFS*, 1991, p. 91.
2. *ESA*, 1991, p. 223; *White Paper on Local Government Finance* [J], 1991. Tokyo: Ministry of Home Affairs, p. 23.
3. *WPJE*, 1991, pp. 113f, 435f.
4. *Fiscal Statistics* [J], Ministry of Finance, 1991, p. 19.
5. *Economic Statistics Yearbook* [J], 1991. Tokyo: Toyo Keizai Inc., p. 330.
6. *Ibid.*, p. 331.
7. *CEFS*, 1991, p. 89.
8. Hatta T. Now Is the Chance to Introduce the Taxpayer Number [J]. In: *Weekly Economist*, November 2, 1993, pp. 28–31; do., Six Myths Concerning the Consumption Tax [J]. In: *NM*, May 20–26, 1994; *Weekly Japan* [J]. Tokyo: Prime Minister's Office, August 1, 1994.
9. *NM* and *AM*, March 26, 1994.

6.2 The Problems in the Dissolution Process of the Private Housing Finance Companies

This section aims to examine the problems of the dissolution process of the seven private housing finance companies[1] (*jusen*) as a typical example of the bad loan problem following the collapse of the bubble economy, focusing on the *jusen* dissolution draft (bill) of the government proposed as part of the FY 1996 budget bill end of 1995.

Needless to say, the bad loan problem of the *jusen* itself is only a part of all Japanese bad loan problems. However, the relations surrounding the *jusen* and the trends of the social groups (i.e., the *jusen* companies, their parent banks, financial institutions in general, Agricultural Financial Institutions (AFI), the MOF, the Ministry of Agriculture, Forestry and Fisheries (MAFF), the Government and the political parties) in this *jusen* dissolution process hold an important key to solving the questions of who has the power to decide on economic policy in today's Japan, what are the mutual relations of social influences surrounding state power, what are the relations between state and civil society (especially the latter's immaturity) and, furthermore, what are the historical and structural characteristics of Japanese capitalism? Therefore, the object of this section is of interest. However, the objective term of the investigation in this section is limited from December 1995 to April 1996 because of the shortage of material during the preparation of this section.

6.2.1 The Content of the Dissolution Plan of the Bankrupt Jusen

After the collapse of the bubble economy, the *jusen* were in management crisis. In order to save them, under the leadership of the MOF, the first and second reconstruction plans were created in October 1991 and February 1993, respectively. However, it was obvious to everyone that the *jusen* were actually in (or near) bankruptcy at that time. It was not until December 19, 1995, that the Government officially published its dissolution plan for the bankrupt *jusen*.

Before we examine the contents this dissolution plan, let us look at the scale and content of the bad loans held by the *jusen*. Their outstanding loans amounted to ¥0.72 trillion in June 1995, of which, bad loans accounted for ¥8.13 trillion (76%), and the estimated loss value was ¥4.95 trillion (46%). The bad loans, which totalled ¥4.65 trillion (38% of their outstanding loans then) in 1991/92, had increased by 75% in 4 years. Their outstanding assets value, inclusive of their owning securities and real estates, was ¥12.93 trillion, of which, bad assets accounted for ¥9.56 trillion (74%) and the estimated loss value was ¥6.27 trillion (49%).[2] If we look at the loan values regarding the top 50 borrower companies of the *jusen*, outstanding loans totalled ¥4.4 trillion, of which the bad loan value reached ¥4.17 trillion (95%) and the estimated loss value was ¥2.77 trillion (63%). The deterioration of the prime borrowers in the real estate business was marked.[3]

Examining the Government's dissolution plan for the bad loans of the *jusen*, the plan was decided on December 19, 1995, along with the FY 1996 budget bill. According to this plan, the estimated loss value of the *jusen*'s bad loans was ¥6.41 trillion. The disposal method was as follows: (a) the parent banks relinquish all their claims, amounting to ¥3.5 trillion; (b) the general banks give up ¥1.7 trillion of their claims to ¥3.8 trillion; (c) the AFI, having ¥5.5 trillion worth of claims, receive repayment for all their claims (¥5.5 trillion) and subsequently donate ¥0.53 trillion to the organization for *jusen* dissolution; (d) with regard to the shortage following these measures, ¥0.685 trillion will be spent and covered by the FY 1996 budget.[4]

Apparently, compared with the burden of the parent banks and the general banks, that of the AFI is remarkably light. Looking at the suffering loss ratio for all claims, that of the parent banks is 100%, that of general banks is 44.7%, while that of the AFI is actually 9.6% after full repayment. Surprisingly, the method of calculating the fiscal burden value of ¥0.685 trillion was not made clear by the Government itself. It was obvious that this dissolution plan gave remarkably favorable treatment to agricultural interests.

In addition, this plan was not for the total disposal of all losses held by the *jusen*. It (the primary loss value is ¥6.4 trillion) concerns only the balance between the book value of the assets (¥12.9 trillion) owned by the *jusen* and the current value of the collateral real estate (¥6.5 trillion) estimated by the "roadside value". It is inevitable that the latter will bring new losses, so-called secondary losses. The breakdown of the latter ¥6.5 trillion is as follows: normal claims of ¥3.3 trillion (supposedly recoverable); doubtful claims of ¥2 trillion (supposedly difficult to recover); and almost unrecovered claims of ¥1.2 trillion. This ¥1.2 trillion was originally to be included in the primary losses, but was excluded because of political considerations. Furthermore, because of falling land prices, the loss value as a whole will also increase in the future.

The Government passed a recovery plan to tackle these secondary losses on January 26, 1996. Accordingly, half the losses will be covered by fiscal expenditure and the rest by private financial institutions. The latter losses will be covered by the working interest of the *jusen* account, which is made up of special funds (maximum ¥0.9 trillion) inside of the Deposit Insurance Organization. If a shortage arises, it will be covered by the working interest of the low-interest loans (they are the purchasing funds for the assets of the *jusen*), which financial institutions will offer to the *jusen* dissolution organization. The principal ¥6.7 trillion of this loan will be paid by the parent banks, the general banks and the AFI (each paying approximately ¥2.2 trillion) and the Deposit Insurance Organization guarantees the principal. The disposal of these secondary losses will be carried out over 15 years, according to the Government plan. Regarding the estimated amount of secondary losses, it is now virtually certain that the above-mentioned ¥1.2 trillion, originally classified as a part of the primary losses, will constitute a part of the secondary losses. If land prices continue to fall in the future, a part of the doubtful claims of ¥2 trillion, and even a part of the normal claims, will change to losses. Therefore, the secondary loss value will reach a considerable amount.[5]

This dissolution plan of the bankrupt *jusen* by the Government gives rise to various doubts. (a) Why is fiscal expenditure necessary for the liquidation of private companies, and is it legally and morally permissible? (b) Although the Government emphasized the necessity of the stabilization of the financial system, the *jusen* are only money-lending companies and do not have their own depositors. If they become bankrupt, public panic does not occur. (c) The actual purpose in saving the AFI is conspicuously transparent. The private banks lending to the *jusen* write off ¥5.2 trillion (70%) themselves out of their loan value of ¥7.4 trillion. After the AFI receives repayment of all its claims of ¥5.5 trillion, it donates only ¥0.53 trillion (10%). (d) Why is the fiscal expenditure for the primary losses ¥0.685 trillion? The grounds for determining this figure for primary losses has not been made public. (e) Leaving the true facts and responsibility of the borrower companies unclear, only the dissolution plan was submitted. (f) Is the legal liquidation by bankruptcy procedures a more justifiable solution than this obscure disposal plan of the Government? (g) What is the responsibility of the MOF, which delayed the disposal of the *jusen*'s bad loans and consequently enlarged their losses? (e) What is the management responsibility of the AFI, which loaned a vast sum of money without careful scrutiny to the *jusen* that were actually bankrupt? These issues will be examined in the next section.

6.2.2 Problems of the Dissolution Plan of the Bankrupt Jusen

Here, the process and problems that led the *jusen* to bankruptcy will be examined in due order of the related factors concerned.

6.2.2.1 *Jusen* (Private Housing Finance Company)

The seven *jusen* companies were founded by the joint capital investment of the parent financial institutions successively from June 1971 (at first, Nippon Housing Loan Co. Ltd) to June 1976. Already early in the period, the positions of president and other important directors were mostly occupied by the "*amakudari*" (coming from heaven) people from parent banks and the MOF. Needless to say, the *jusen* are money-lending companies that do not conduct deposit business.

The *jusen* engaged mainly in the area of personal housing loans, which the parent banks did not positively deal with from the 1970s to the first half of the 1980s. After that time, the parent banks themselves began to search for new loans customers because of excessive funds in their banks and advanced aggressively into the field of personal housing loans. Furthermore, the Housing Loan Corporation advanced more aggressively into the same field. Consequently, the *jusen* were deprived of their sphere of operation. (Because the *jusen* originally lent money to individuals with funds that the *jusen* borrowed from the parent banks, it is theoretically impossible for the *jusen* to present more favorable (i.e. lower) interest rates to customers than that of the parent banks. Therefore, the disadvantage of the *jusen* in this respect is self-evident. With regard to the competition with the Housing Loan Corporation, the situation is essentially the same. The Housing Loan Corporation can use low-cost funds from treasury investment and loan under the control of the MOF. The share of the *jusen* in credit for the personal housing loans changed from 3.8% in 1975, to 7.2% in 1980, 5.2% in 1985 and 1.7% in 1994.)[6]

Under these circumstances, the *jusen* engaged in imprudent loans to real estate businesses and went bankrupt simultaneously with the burst of the bubble economy. As mentioned earlier, the *jusen* made personal housing loans with funds that the *jusen* themselves borrowed from parent banks. Therefore, when parent banks advanced into the personal housing loan arena, it was inevitable that the *jusen* would go bankrupt. In this sense, in the bubble period, when the parent banks were earnestly engaged in the personal housing loan business, the historical role of the *jusen* was virtually over and their life came practically ended.

6.2.2.2 The Parent Banks

The main parent banks of the seven *jusen* companies are as follows. Nippon Housing Loan (founded June 1971): Sanwa, Sakura, Daiwa, Asahi, Mitsui Trust, Toyo Trust, Chiba, etc. Housing Loan Service (founded September 1971): Dai-Ichi Kangyo, Fuji, Mitsubishi, Sumitomo, Asahi, Sakura, Tokai, etc. Juso (founded October 1971): seven trust banks. Sogo Housing Loan (founded July 1972): the secondary regional banks. Daiichi Housing Loan (founded December 1975): Long-Term Credit Bank of Japan, Nomura Securities. Chigin-Seiho Housing Loan (founded June 1976): regional banks, life insurance companies. Japan Housing Loan (founded June 1976): Industrial Bank of Japan, Nippon Credit Bank, Daiwa Securities, Nikko Securities, Yamaichi Securities.[7]

In the case of the dissolution of the bankrupt *jusen*, why did the parent banks accept the Government's plan, which was one-sidedly in favor of the AFI and was disadvantageous to themselves? Why did the parent banks not choose the legal liquidation method of the *jusen*, which was not only favorable to themselves but also conformed to the principle of social fairness? Surely, this was (and is) the biggest enigma surrounding the dissolution of the *jusen* (although the parent banks suggested a legal liquidation of assets, it does not appear that they pushed hard for this course of action).

Reasons why the parent banks did not or could not take advantage of legal liquidation of the *jusen* may include the following. First, as a general reason, many managers of the parent banks thought that to reject the Government's plan and to make relations with the MOF worse would hinder the management of the banks in the long run. Second, there is a problem of settled accounts. If the parent banks accepted the Government's plan, they could totally write off the bad loans to the *jusen* as untaxable during the accounting term in March 1996. However, in the case of legal liquidation, they would only be able to write-off half their claim value with no tax for the present and must additionally write-off the rest of the value at the time when the withdrawal value is decided. Third, many managers of parent banks were afraid of a counterattack by the AFI. One of the important causes of the *jusen*'s bankruptcy is the existence of many loans introduced by parent banks. It is said that a lot of memorandums relating to these loans were handed to the AFI.[8] Their public disclosure would lower the credit of the banks. If parent banks pressed for legal liquidation of the *jusen*, the truth in the actual process would be made clear and judged under the administration of justice. It is supposed that the parent banks were also afraid of this happening and tried to avoid it.[9]

6.2.2.3 Agricultural Financial Institutions

At the end of March in 1995, loans to the *jusen* according to financial group were as follows: 11 city banks loaned ¥1.5 trillion, three long-term credit banks loaned ¥1.5 trillion, seven trust banks loaned ¥2 trillion (the total for the 21 major banks was ¥5 trillion), regional banks loaned ¥1.1 trillion, the AFI loaned ¥5.5 trillion, life insurance companies loaned ¥0.8 trillion, and others had loaned ¥0.6 trillion.[10]

If the bankrupt *jusen* were subject to the process of legal liquidation, the original loss value of the parent banks, general banks and the AFI would be ¥2.1 trillion, ¥2.3 trillion and ¥3.3 trillion, respectively, because of the rule of "equality of creditors".[11]

It was due mostly to the political power of the AFI that their burden was limited to only ¥0.53 trillion. In this sense, it is clear that the essence of the Government's dissolution plan was to save the AFI (especially a part of the "*shinren*" (prefecture organization of the AFI) and individual agricultural cooperatives), which would be successively bankrupt in the case of legal liquidation of the *jusen*.

Now, what is the reason for the political strength of agricultural interests, given that the agricultural sector accounts for only 2% of the GDP and its ratio in terms of all employed people is only 5%? The traditional political power cultivated in the former multimember constituency system is well known. A considerable amount of this power is likely to survive under the new system (i.e. the new parallel system of both single-member constituency and proportional representation). In addition, the voting rate in rural communities is twice as high as that in urban communities, and the number of Diet members in comparison with the population ratio is also doubled, therefore the total weight of a vote in rural communities is four-fold that of a vote from urban communities. This amounts to strong political pressure on present Diet members.

Of course, there are difficult and serious problems for the AFI too. First, the yearly interest on ¥250 billion (high deposit rate 4.5%, despite a super-low interest rate era) that came from the *jusen* would become zero after dissolution of the *jusen*. Second, the loan value of the AFI to non-banks other than the *jusen* reached ¥7.7 trillion in March 1995, and it is supposed that a considerable part of this is made up of irrecoverable loans.

6.2.2.4 Ministry of Finance and the Ministry of Agriculture, Forestry and Fisheries

The MOF played a decisive role at least twice in the bankruptcy process of the *jusen* after 1990.

First, a notification was released by the chief of the Banking Bureau (Mr. Tsuchida Masakane) dated March 27, 1990, "On the Control of Loans Relating to Lands".[12] This demanded that the financial institutions regulate loans for the real estate business at a time when the bubble economy had begun to collapse. It consisted of two parts, namely "The Regulation of Total Amount" and "The Regulation to the Three Business Sectors". The former demanded that general financial institutions and the AFI (regarding the AFI under the joint signature of the chief of the Economic Affairs Bureau of the MAFF, Mr. Kawai Junji) control the increase in the loan rate with regard to real estate business under the increase in the rate of total loans. The *jusen*, strangely, were excluded from the object of this notification. The latter demanded that general financial institutions report their loan situation regarding the real estate business, the construction industry and non-banks (exclusive of the *jusen*). The AFI, strangely, were excluded from a duty to make such a report.

Consequently, what happened? "The framework was formed as follows: funds flow from the AFI, which were excluded from the object by the regulation of the three business sectors, to the *jusen*, which were excluded from the object by the regulation of the total amount. As a result, the *jusen* came to depend strongly on the AFI, because the *jusen* faced restrictions on borrowing money from general financial institutions. In addition, the AFI willingly accepted the wishes of the *jusen*, because the AFI did not have good loan customers and experienced fund operation difficulty."[13] The outstanding amount of the AFI's loans to the *jusen* increased rapidly from ¥1.9 trillion in March 1989 to ¥4.9 trillion in March 1991.[14]

Second, a memorandum was exchanged between the chief of the Banking Bureau of the MOF (Mr. Teramura Nobuyuki) and the chief of the Economic Affairs Bureau of the MAFF (Mr. Manabe Takenori) on February 3, 1993.[15] This memorandum was made when the business difficulties of the *jusen* became apparent to everybody and continued to increase. The main contents of the memorandum were as follows: (1) the parent banks have the responsibility to reconstruct the *jusen*; (2) the new interest rates after the interest-reduced and exempted measures are 0% for parent banks, 2.5% for general banks and 4.5% for the AFI; and (3) if necessary, the Bank of Japan will accommodate funds to the Norin Chukin Bank (this third clause was secret).[16]

On the basis of this memorandum, a second reconstruction plan for the *jusen* was drawn up. This replaced the first reconstruction plan made in October 1991, the content of which consisted of a reduction in the parent bank's interest rate and maintaining the balance of other banks' loans. The MOF required the parent banks to draft and offer a covenant, the contents of which respected the memorandum and guaranteed the principal of the AFI's loans.[17]

However, the behavior of the MOF is questionable. Even the MOF has no right to make a promise to guarantee the principal instead of the parent banks, and, in this sense, the behavior of the MOF may be considered criminal abuse on the part of the MOF officials. In addition, the third secret clause is illegal. Although the Minister of Finance certainly had the right to supervise and order the Bank of Japan, the Bank of Japan was, itself, independent of the MOF. Therefore, this memorandum apparently exceeded the authority of the MOF.[18]

The most important point is that the solution to the *jusen* problem was delayed by this memorandum and the second reconstruction plan. The bankruptcy of the *jusen* and the impossibility of their reconstruction was obvious to everyone concerned as of 1991/92 when the MOF first became involved and inspected the *jusen*.

Nevertheless, because this memorandum delayed solution of the problem, when the MOF entered and inspected the *jusen* for a second time in August 1995, their bad loans had increased from ¥4.6 trillion (the ratio to total loan value 37.7%) at the first inspection to ¥8.1 trillion (75.9%), up 1.8-fold.[19]

6.2.2.5 Others

With regard to prime borrowers of the *jusen* (i.e. their company names, the sum borrowed, the ratio of bad loans and the estimated loss values, etc.), much information was made public during the discussion process on disposal plans of the Government in the Diet.[20] Furthermore, a considerable amount of material was published regarding the loans introduced by the parent banks to the *jusen*,[21] and a relationship between the bad loans held by the *jusen* and organized groups of gangsters was exposed.[22]

Although a detailed investigation into these problems is also very important, I can only indicate subjects for consideration here.

6.2.3 Location of Responsibility and the Direction Towards a Solution for the Problem

The dissolution plan of the *jusen* was created by a "*dangou*" (unofficial consultation in private closed circles) of people concerned who were responsible for the problem in the first place. This is a sort of "*tobashi*", a special method for camouflaging losses, of the bad loans.[23] The unfair disposal and the easygoing fiscal expenditure (i.e. the introduction of official funds) are a state swindle.

It is the AFI that benefitted the most, and the strength of their political influence continued to be prominent. However, the AFI could not get the approval and sympathy of the public. The feeling that the AFI consists of organizations that devote themselves to protecting vested interests continues to spread.

It has been made clear that the power of the MOF is very strong in both political and civil society, but the compensation that it has paid has been very large. Everyone has come to know that the elite bureaucrats of the MOF are far removed from the idea of social fairness and lack the ability to solve the problem. The myth that these bureaucrats are the most clever and elite in the Japanese bureaucracy has almost disappeared. In addition, public confidence in the other groups concerned has also been more or less lowered.

For a proper solution of the problem, it is not the "dangou", mentioned above, but a legal dissolution among the people concerned (i.e. the legal liquidation of the *jusen*) that is most desirable. The Government's plan says that it will take 15 years for a complete solution to be effected. However, experts in the field of the administration of justice and business administration say that it would take approximately 5 years to solve in the case of legal liquidation. Above all, it is desirable that the people concerned who gave rise to the problem do not work on its solution alone (this is unfair and impossible), rather the justice administration should decide a fair burden of losses for each party according to the law.

In the solution process of the bad loan problem in the US from 1988 to 1995, 6,405 people (4,513 cases) were indicted as economic criminals, of which, 5,506 were declared guilty and 3,793 served custodial sentences.[24] In Japan, cases where economic criminals in the bubble economy have been accused are few, inclusive of the *jusen* problem. Economic criminals (i.e. those guilty of legally unjust deeds), including those from both political and official worlds, should receive strict legal judgment.

Once all people concerned strive for a solution to the *jusen* problem, it is possible that the introduction of official funds may still be necessary. Then, the following criteria are indispensable: the reform of the supervisory system for financial administration; a clear announcement of the total amount of official funds necessary; and a public announcement of the introduction period of official funds.[25]

On April 11, 1996, the Government's budget bill, containing the expenditure of ¥685 billion for the dissolution of the *jusen*, was passed in the House of Representatives. However, regarding this expenditure of ¥685 billion, a conditional clause of "taking measures after preparation of the system" was added to the general budget provision. In addition, the prospect of approval of the following laws, namely "a bill for the dissolution of the *jusen*" and five bills relating to financial reform (a bill for the reform of the deposit insurance law, a bill to secure the soundness of financial institutions and a bill for the special rehabilitation procedures of financial institutions etc.), which are indispensable premises for the execution of the expenditure of ¥685 billion, were obscure at that time. The introduction of official funds for the disposal of the *jusen* fell into temporary difficulty. The unfairness of the Government's disposal plan for the *jusen* is a fundamental cause for this confusion.

However, after the budget bill passed in the House of Councilors on May 10, 1996, the Government and the MOF strove to achieve their original aim. Consequently, "a bill for the dissolution of the *jusen*" as well as five bills relating to financial reform passed in their original form without amendment in the House of Representatives on June 7, and in the House of Councilors on June 18, 1996.

Notes

1. Specifically: Nippon Housing Loan Co. Ltd; Housing Loan Service Co. Ltd; Juso Co. Ltd; Sogo Housing Loan Co. Ltd; Daiichi Housing Loan Co. Ltd; Chigin-Seiho Housing Loan Co. Ltd; and Japan Housing Loan Co. Ltd. Except for these seven companies, there is one more company, Kyodo Housing Loan Co. Ltd, which was established by the AFI. However, this company is exempted from one of the objects in bill at this time. It is clear that the reason for this exception is in order to set the responsibility of the parent banks of the seven above-mentioned companies (i.e. financial institutions except for the AFI) in this draft (bill) at the forefront.
2. Takarabe S. *Jusen*. Its Birth, Bankruptcy and Disposal [J]. In: *Ushio*, special number, March 1996. Tokyo: Ushio Shuppansha, p. 58; Ikuta T. The True Grounds for the Policy Bankruptcy of the Banking Bureau of the MOF [J]. In: *Ushio*, *op. cit.*, p. 143; *NM*, March 4, 1996.
3. *NE*, February 7, 1996.
4. Goto S. The Structure of the Financial Bankruptcy [J]. In: *Sekai*. Tokyo: Iwanami Shoten, April 1996, pp. 38f; *AM*, January 23, 1996.
5. *Weekly Economist* [J], March 4, 1996, p. 62; *NM*, January 25–27, 1996.
6. Goto S. *op. cit.*, p. 36; *NM*, January 20, 1996.
7. Takarabe S. *op. cit.*, p. 29; *NM*, January 20, 1996.
8. Cf. *AM*, August 19, 1995; *AM*, January 19, 1996; *AM*, February 22, 1996; *AE*, February 23, 1996.
9. *NM*, January 20, 1996; *Weekly Economist* [J], February 13, 1996, p. 40.
10. *NM*, January 20, 1996.
11. Goto S. *op. cit.*, pp. 38f.
12. The original text, see in: Takarabe S, *op. cit.*, pp. 34f.
13. Ikuta T. *op. cit.*, p. 142.
14. Takarabe S. *op. cit.*, pp. 34f; Goto S, *op. cit.*, pp. 36f.
15. The original text, see in: *NM*, January 20, 1996.
16. Takarabe S. *op. cit.*, pp. 50f; Goto S, *op. cit.*, p. 37.
17. Domon T. The irresponsible covenant is more important than the memorandum [J]. In: *Weekly Economist*, January 23, 1996, pp. 36–39; do., The irresponsibility of the AFI [J]. In: *Ushio*, March 1996, p. 110; *AM*, August 19, 1995; *AM*, February 17, 1996; *AM*, February 22, 1996.
18. Takarabe S. *op. cit.*, pp. 26, 51; Domon T. *op. cit.* In: *Ushio*, p. 110; Ikuta T. *op. cit.*, p. 143.
19. Goto S. *op. cit.*, p. 37; *NM*, February 6, 1996.
20. See: Japanese newspapers dated January 20, 23 and February 5–7, 1996.
21. See: Japanese newspapers dated March 2, 1996.
22. Miyawaki R. Politician, police and media must fight against gang [J]. In: *Weekly Economist*, January 30, 1996, pp. 39–41; Tamura K. Why was the Nagoya branch manager of Sumitomo Bank shot to kill? [J]. In: *Ushio*, March 1996, pp. 84–89; Ino K. The depths of financial circles and the dark people [J]. In: *Ushio*, March 1996, pp. 90–99.
23. Tateishi T. Nonbanks have begun to march to the death [J]. In: *Weekly Economist*, February 27, 1996, p. 36.
24. *The Weekly Toyo Keizai* [J], January 27, 1996, p. 19.
25. Articles by Professor Takenaka Heizou, *NM*, December 10, 1995; *AM*, January 30, 1996.

Part 3 The Large Corporation System and the Life of the People

Chapter 7
The Internal Composition of Workers and Employees

7.1 Differential Wage Structure

As already seen in section 1.2, the rate of compensation for employees in Japan has been low in comparison with other countries.

However, regarding the level of wages, as shown in Table 7.1, the annual wages of production workers in manufacturing industries in Japan in 1989 were higher, taking into consideration the exchange rate conversion, than those of the US and the F.R. Germany and were one of the highest in the world. However, because of the high commodity prices in Japan, this "high" level of wages in Japan was less than that of the US and the F.R. Germany when purchasing power parity is considered. This situation can be seen more clearly in the case of hourly wages, on account of the long working hours in Japan. According to this criterion, in 1989; in regard to both purchasing power parity and also exchange rate conversion, the wage level in Japan was less than that of the F.R. Germany and the US (in 1990, the wages per working hour, in terms of exchange rate conversion, if Japan = 100, were US = 109, and F.R. Germany = 156; in the case of purchasing power parity, if Japan = 100, US = 144, and F.R. Germany = 147).[1]

Taking this into consideration, the wage characteristics in Japan will be examined, especially their differential structure. First, looking at wage differentials by industry; in 1989, setting the average for all private sectors as 100, they were: public utilities (electric power, gas and water, including public enterprises) 148, finance and insurance 142, real estate 110, transportation and communication (inclusive of public enterprises) 106, construction 102, wholesale, retail and restaurant 98, mining 97, service 96, and manufacturing 95. These figures are based on scheduled earnings. We can find no small differentials there.[2]

Next, wage differentials will be examined according to the size of enterprise, which seems to be most important. Look at Table 7.2, the monthly earnings by size of enterprise in manufacturing can be seen. Setting the earnings of enterprises with 500 employees and over as 100, and looking at total cash earnings, enterprises with between five and 29 employees were 46.3 in 1960, 63.2 in 1965, 61.8 in 1970, 60.2 in 1975, 58.0 in 1980, 54.9 in 1985, and 56.6 in 1987. With regard to contractual cash earnings, those were 54.2 in 1960, 72.6 in 1965, 71.4 in 1970, 70.3 in 1975, 67.6 in 1980, 64.7 in 1985, and 66.1 in 1987. Apparently, and as is often pointed out, the wage differen-

TABLE 7.1 International Comparison of Wages (1989, manufactuing, production workers)

Item	Japan	US	F.R. Germany
Total yearly wages	¥3,192,000	$22,448	DM42,116
Exchange rate	¥3,192,000 (100)	¥3,097,000 (97)	¥3,090,000 (97)
Purchasing power parity	¥3,192,000 (100)	¥4,400,000 (138)	¥3,563,000 (112)
Wages per working hour	¥1,478	$11.52	DM25.77
Exchange rate	¥1,478 (100)	¥1,589 (108)	¥1,810 (122)
Purchasing power parity	¥1,478 (100)	¥2,258 (162)	¥2,180 (151)
1989 Exchange rate		137.96 ¥/$	73.38 ¥/DM

Index values are given in parentheses.
Source: *Handbook of Labour Statistics in Japan* [J], 1991, Tokyo: Ministry of Labour, p. 219.

TABLE 7.2 Monthly Earnings by Size of Enterprise (1960–87, s.y.; manufacturing)

(Unit: ¥ 1,000)

	Total cash earnings				Contractual cash earnings			
Year	500 employees and over	100–499 employees	30–99 employees	5–29 employees	500 employees and over	100–499 employees	30–99 employees	5–29 employees
1960	28.7	20.3	16.9	13.3	22.4	16.5	14.7	12.1
1965	42.2	34.1	29.9	26.6	32.5	27.2	25.5	23.6
1970	83.6	68.1	58.2	51.7	61.0	50.8	46.5	43.6
1975	191.4	158.6	131.4	115.2	137.7	118.0	104.3	96.8
1980	296.1	238.3	193.5	171.7	215.4	176.4	151.8	145.7
1982	329.0	259.6	210.9	186.6	238.8	193.6	167.0	158.9
1983	340.9	269.4	218.1	192.8	248.7	202.0	173.6	165.4
1984	357.3	284.1	225.3	204.8	261.5	213.0	179.8	173.3
1985	369.8	285.0	232.7	203.0	270.2	214.5	185.7	174.7
1986	371.7	288.8	240.0	212.8	272.9	218.6	192.1	182.1
1987	378.9	297.3	248.9	214.3	280.3	224.9	198.4	185.3

Source: *Op. cit.*, 1988, p. 105.

tials by size of enterprise decreased during the "high economic growth period", but after the 1970s they expanded again. (Incidentally, in the case of the total cash earnings, the values are 55.9 in 1988, 55.0 in 1989 and 55.2 in 1990.[3] So, we cannot find a definite reduction in the latter half of the 1980s). The reason why the differentials are larger in the case of total cash earnings rather than contractual cash earnings is that the differentials of special cash payments (bonuses etc.) are larger. The differentials of total cash earnings between enterprises with 500 employees or more and those with between five and 29 employees in all industries were 57.9 in 1985, 59.7 in 1986, 59.6 in 1987, 58.3 in 1988, 57.9 in 1989 and 57.5 in 1990,[4] and were smaller to some extent than in manufacturing.

TABLE 7.3 Average Yearly Cash Earnings by Size of Enterprise (1978–95, s.y.; manufacturing)

(Unit: ¥ 1,000)

Year / Size of enterprise	1978	1980	1982	1984	1986	1988	1989	1992	1995
1–3 employees	1,137*	1,317*	—	—	—	—	—	—	—
4–9 employees			1,870	2,018	2,193	2,329	2,500	2,972	2,985
10–19 employees	1,781	2,041	2,279	2,447	2,643	2,801	2,944	3,442	3,557
20–99 employees	1,942	2,218	2,470	2,629	2,824	2,993	3,126	3,570	3,759
100–299 employees	2,354	2,643	2,938	3,071	3,306	3,481	3,631	4,114	4,366
300–999 employees	2,818	3,200	3,558	3,807	4,105	4,315	4,523	5,000	5,367
1,000 employees and over	3,361	3,823	4,274	4,607	5,039	5,344	5,583	6,087	6,485

* Figures for the enterprises with 1–9 employees.
Source: *WPSE*, 1991, appendix p. 11; *op. cit.*, 1997, app. p. 11.

The differentials mentioned above are greater between larger enterprises with over 500 employees and small and very small enterprises. Table 7.3. shows the yearly cash earnings per employee in manufacturing. Setting the earnings of enterprises with 1,000 employees and over as 100, those of enterprises with 1–9 employees were 33.8 in 1978, 34.3 in 1979, and 34.4 in 1980. Because of changes in statistical standards, after 1981 the comparison is made for enterprises with 4–9 employees. The differentials were 43.9 in 1981, 43.8 in 1982, 42.9 in 1983, 43.8 in 1984, 43.4 in 1985, 43.5 in 1986, 44.1 in 1987, 43.6 in 1988, 44.8 in 1989, 48.8 in 1992 and 46.0 in 1995. Obviously, the earnings of employees in small and very small enterprises in Japan have ranged from approximately one-third to, at most, half of those of employees in large enterprises and are, as such, very low.

In addition to these facts, in 1989, setting the earnings of enterprises with 1,000 employees and over as 100, those of enterprises with 300–999, 100–299, 20–99, 10–19 and 4–9 employees were 81.0, 65.0, 56.0, 52.7 and 44.8, respectively. It can clearly be seen from these figures that, in Japan, the wage differentials have been closely related to the size of the enterprise or establishment.

We can also find these wage differentials, as a matter of course, in severance payments. If we look at non-production workers who graduated from upper secondary school, the average severance pay for an employee working for 35 years or more in 1989 was ¥24.13 million in an enterprise with 1,000 employees and over, ¥17.92 million in an enterprise with 100–999 employees and ¥10.11 million in an enterprise with 30–99 employees. As shown, the differentials are considerably large. In addition, taking into account educational attainment, severance pay in 1989 was ¥26.67 million for workers who had graduated from college or university and worked in enterprises with 1,000 employees and over, ¥17.92 million (as mentioned above) for non-production workers who had graduated from upper secondary school and worked in enterprises with 100–999 employees and ¥8.35 million for production workers who had graduated from lower secondary school and worked in enterprises with 30–99 employees. In this way, differentials in average severance payments by size of enterprise increased.[5]

TABLE 7.4 International Comparison of Wage Differentials by Age Group (male, 21–24 years = 100; manufacturing, production workers)

	Age, less than 18 years	18–20	21–24	25–29	30–34	35–39	40–44	45–49	50–54	55–59	60 years or more
Japan (1989)*	60.7	83.8	100.0	118.4	137.0	154.7	166.2	173.1	168.0	147.8	105.4
US (1969)	—	—	100.0	124.1	124.1	122.6	122.6	122.6	122.6	115.6	115.6
UK (1989)	51.1	77.9	100.0	109.9	118.3	118.3	119.6	119.6	113.8	113.8	104.9
F.R. Germany (1972)	58.5	88.1	100.0	105.5	108.0	108.2	106.9	105.4	103.0	99.8	95.9
France (1972)	70.5	87.2	100.0	108.8	113.0	113.9	111.6	109.9	106.6	102.5	106.7
Italy (1972)	70.5	88.6	100.0	108.5	111.7	112.7	111.6	111.0	110.2	109.3	101.2

Years in parentheses indicate the year in which investigations were made.
Source: *WPJE*, 1990, pp. 170, 500.

Examining the wage differentials by age group, Table 7.4 shows wage differentials by age group of production workers in the manufacturing industries of selected countries. As shown, setting the earnings of 21–24-year-old male workers as 100, the maximum value of earning differentials was 173.1 (45–49 years) in Japan, 122.6 (45–54 years) in the US, 119.6 (40–49 years) in the UK, 113.9 (35–39 years) in France, 112.7 (35–39 years) in Italy and 108.2 (35–39 years) in the F.R. Germany. Although we must take into consideration the difference in years in which these data were collected, the earning differentials of Japan remain outstandingly large.

If we examine earnings of non-production workers, namely staff, the earning differentials by age group were maximum at 226.8 (50–54 years) in Japan, 220.2 (55 years over) in Italy, 187.7 (45–49 years) in France, 177.4 (40–49 years) in the UK, 171.4 (35–44 years) in the US and 156.5 (40–44 years) in the F.R. Germany.[6] As shown, the differentials in countries in addition to Japan have become larger, being different from those of production workers. Nevertheless those of Japan remain highest.

Let us combine wage differentials by age group with those by size of enterprise in Japan. As shown in Table 7.5, wage differentials became larger as the size of the enterprise grew. (Earnings were at a maximum in the 50–54-year-old group in enterprises with 1,000 employees and over (index 223.9 for 20–24-year-olds = 100), in the 45–49-year-old group in enterprises with 100–999 employees (196.4) and with 10–99 employees (171.0).)

With regard to the earning differentials of male employees in industries in terms of size of enterprise and age groups, they were less in younger men and largest in men in their 50s in Japan (in 1989, setting the earnings of men in their 50s in enterprises with 1,000 employees and over as 100, the differential was approximately 80 for enterprises with 100–999 employees and approximately 67 for enterprises with 10–99 employees).[7]

TABLE 7.5 Wage Differentials by Size of Enterprise and by Age Group (1989, all industries; male workers, age 20–24 years = 100)

Size of enterprise, age group	Contractual earnings	Scheduled earnings	Size of enterprise, age group	Contractual earnings	Scheduled earnings
Total for all sizes of enterprise	158.0	166.1	100–999 employees	155.7	164.8
≤17 years	62.8	71.8	≤17 years	64.1	74.0
18–19	81.7	82.6	18–19	82.8	84.0
20–24	100.0	100.0	20–24	100.0	100.0
25–29	122.6	123.3	25–29	121.8	123.7
30–34	146.8	150.8	30–34	145.0	150.1
35–39	167.9	175.1	35–39	166.0	174.4
40–44	185.0	196.8	40–44	183.1	197.0
45–49	197.8	212.1	45–49	196.4	213.0
50–54	194.4	209.0	50–54	195.5	211.4
55–59	168.2	181.8	55–59	173.3	188.8
60–64	129.9	145.3	60–64	140.6	158.4
65+	116.2	132.3	65+	124.8	142.2
1,000 employees and over	173.3	185.7	10–99 employees	143.6	148.1
≤17 years	54.1	64.9	≤17 years	65.7	71.6
18–19	83.1	83.0	18–19	80.3	81.1
20–24	100.0	100.0	20–24	100.0	100.0
25–29	123.0	123.7	25–29	120.6	121.8
30–34	153.8	158.6	30–34	139.0	142.7
35–39	179.8	189.9	35–39	153.4	158.4
40–44	200.6	218.9	40–44	164.7	170.4
45–49	218.2	241.4	45–49	171.0	176.9
50–54	223.9	249.0	50–54	164.3	170.5
55–59	199.1	221.0	55–59	148.4	154.9
60–64	146.4	171.0	60–64	126.3	134.9
65+	134.4	159.2	65+	116.9	127.2

Source: *Handbook of Labour Statistics in Japan* [J], 1991, pp. 114f.

Wage differentials can also be seen between public and private sectors in Japan. Of course, with civil servants there are earning differentials regulated by position, function and specialty. However, as shown in Table 7.6, the average earnings of civil servants in Japan have surpassed, on average, those of employees in general and also non-official staff in the private sector. We can estimate that the earnings of civil servants have been generally located on a high–middle level, at least in the Japanese labor market, even if not on a high or the highest level.[8]

Finally, looking at wage differentials by sex, refering to Table 7.7, in 1989, setting the earnings of male employees as 100, the earnings of female employees were, in case of the scheduled earnings, 60.2, contractual earnings 57.0 and special earnings 49.1. The differentials were very large. With regard to this problem, even the elements of educational level, size of enterprise and length of service are equalized for male and female workers, the wage differentials by sex were, in the case of scheduled earnings,

TABLE 7.6 Average Monthly Earnings of Household Head by Type of Worker (1975–89, s.y.)

(Unit: ¥)

Year	Average	Regular laborer	Non-official staff	Official staff
1970	105,468	89,709	115,902	125,186
1975	222,455	181,398	235,736	298,982
1980	330,587	277,271	353,317	428,050
1985	419,610	342,030	453,211	514,596
1989	466,564	378,736	502,081	572,076

Source: *Statistics on Japanese Standard of Living* [J], 1991, p. 56.

TABLE 7.7 Average Earnings for Women Compared with Men (1970–90, s.y.; average wages of male employees = 100)

	Scheduled earnings	Contractual earnings	Special earnings
1970	55.6	51.3	44.2
1975	58.4	56.0	47.7
1980	58.9	55.3	48.1
1985	59.6	56.1	48.9
1986	59.7	56.6	50.3
1987	60.5	57.6	50.5
1988	60.5	57.2	49.5
1989	60.2	57.0	49.1
1990	60.2	57.1	—

Source: *WPL*, 1991, appendix, p. 52.

71.5 (female; male = 100) in 1975, 74.5 in 1980, 75.9 in 1985 and 76.2 in 1989.[9] Thus, we can find clear differentials also in this field.

Notes

1. *The Weekly Toyo Keizai* [J], March 28, 1992, p. 9.
2. *WPJE*, 1990, pp. 298, 538.
3. *WPSE*, 1991, p. 35.
4. *Ibid.*
5. *Handbook of Labour Statistics in Japan* [J], 1991. Tokyo: Ministry of Labour, p. 153.
6. *WPJE*, 1990, p. 500.
7. *Handbook of Labour Statistics in Japan*, 1991, op. cit., p. 142.
8. On the grounds, see: Matsuba M. *An Essay on Contemporary Japanese Capitalism*, *op. cit.*, 1987, p. 114.
9. *WPJE*, 1990, p. 302.

7.2 Differential Structure of Labor Conditions

Following on from the wage problems outlined in the previous section, here I would like to survey other labor conditions, while making an international comparison. It is well known that the working hours of Japanese employees have been outstandingly

TABLE 7.8 International Comparison of Yearly Working Hours etc. (1988, manufacturing, production workers)

(Unit: hours, days)

	Japan	US	UK	F.R. Germany	France
Total yearly working hours	2,189	1,962	1,961	1,642	1,647
Scheduled	1,936	1,759	1,774	1,559	—
Non-scheduled	253	203	187	83	—
Total yearly days off	117	139	147	155	154
Weekends	85	104	104	104	104
Other holidays	20	10	8	11	8
Annual number days paid leave	9	19	24	29	26
Annual number days absent	3	6	11	11	16
Yearly commuter time	281	214	—	159	187

Source: *WPL*, 1990, p. 227.

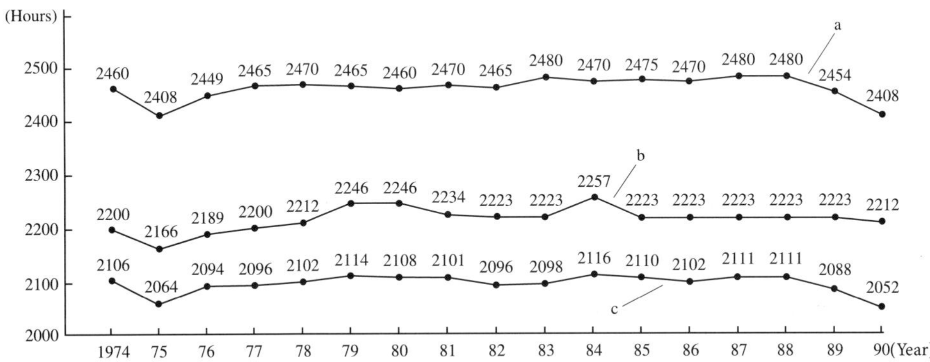

(a) The Labour Force Survey; (b) The Basic Survey on Wage Structure; (c) The Monthly Labour Survey.

FIG. 7.1 Trends in Yearly Working Hours (1974–90)
Source: Morioka K. Japanese Corporate Centricism and the Polarization of Working Hour Structure [J], in: *Keizai* (Economy), March 1992, p. 125.

long in comparison with other advanced countries. For example, as shown in Table 7.8, the annual working hours (manufacturing, production workers) in 1988 were 2189 in Japan, 1962 in the US, 1961 in the UK, 1647 in France and 1642 in the F.R. Germany (in 1994 these figures were 1966, 2005, 1920, 1679 and 1542, respectively).[1] Assuming an 8-hour work day, Japanese workers worked for over 1 month longer than workers in the US and, furthermore, for approximately 3 months longer than those of the F.R. Germany in 1 year.

Figure 7.1 shows the trends in annual Japanese working hours. Three sorts of statistical values published by the Japanese government are shown, and there is an approximate difference of 100–350 hours among them. For example, the actual number of annual working hours in 1990, from "The Monthly Labour Survey" (MLS) was 2,052 hours (from 1991 to 1995 the number of annual working hours in each year was 2016, 1972, 1913, 1904 and 1909, respectively),[2] from "The Basic Survey on Wage Structure" (BSWS) it was 2,212 hours and from "The Labour Force Survey" (LFS) it was 2,408 hours (2,273 hours in 1995).[3]

As to what causes these differences, we can include the following. To begin with, the MLS and BSWS have been prepared by the Ministry of Labour and the LFS has been prepared by the Management and Coordination Agency. The former two are fundamentally surveys practiced in establishments on the grounds of information provided en masse by the company. So, we must consider that the hours for the so-called "service *zangyo*" (unpaid overtime work) are not included therein. In addition, while the BSWS shows the actual working hours of ordinary workers other than part-timers, the MLS shows the working hours inclusive of regular part-timers but does not clearly show the working hours of ordinary workers excluding part-timers. (Incidentally, in the MLS of 1990, the annual working hours for male workers, whose part-time ratio was a low 3.96%, were 2,184 hours, while those of female workers, whose part-time ratio was a relatively high 29.9%, were 1867. There was, on average, a difference of over 300 hours for 1 year between male and female workers.)

Because the LFS is a study based on a questionnaire administered to individual workers, it seems that the results of the LFS are nearer to the real working hours of employees. In addition, regular and non-regular part-timers have been included in the LFS.[4] Taking into account the above-mentioned, I think that the LFS shows more precisely the real state of annual actual working hours of Japanese regular employees than do the other two surveys.

Concerning the differentials of yearly working hours by size of enterprise, until the end of the 1970s, the larger the enterprise was, the shorter the working hours were. Conversely, of course, the smaller the size of the enterprise, the longer the working hours were.[5] However, as shown in Figure 7.2, in recent years the differentials by size of enterprise have declined and, occasionally, have reversed because of the increase of nonscheduled working hours in large enterprises. However, with regard to regular employees, it is still the case that larger the enterprise, the higher the ratio of employees working fewer hours and the lower the ratio of employees working long hours. So, we can judge that the above-mentioned reduction of the differentials by size of enterprise has been caused by the high ratio of the part-time employees in small enterprises.[6]

Next, the types of weekdays off, which is closely related to the problem of working hours, will be examined. As shown in Table 7.9, in 1989, while in enterprises with 1,000 employees and over the ratio of employees working a 5 day week with 2 days off, in the wide sense, was 97.9% and that of a complete 2 days off each week was 64.1%, in enterprises with 30–99 employees, the ratio of employees working in a 6 day working week was 45.9% (i.e. approximately half) and that of a complete 2 days off each week was only 6.5%. Thus, we can easily and clearly find large differentials according to the size of enterprise in the case of the type of weekdays off.

With regard to welfare provisions, we can also clearly find a differential structure according to the size of the enterprise. In particular, as shown in Table 7.10, the differentials between large enterprises and medium and small enterprises are conspicuous regarding the cost of non-legislated welfare, especially housing and medical services.

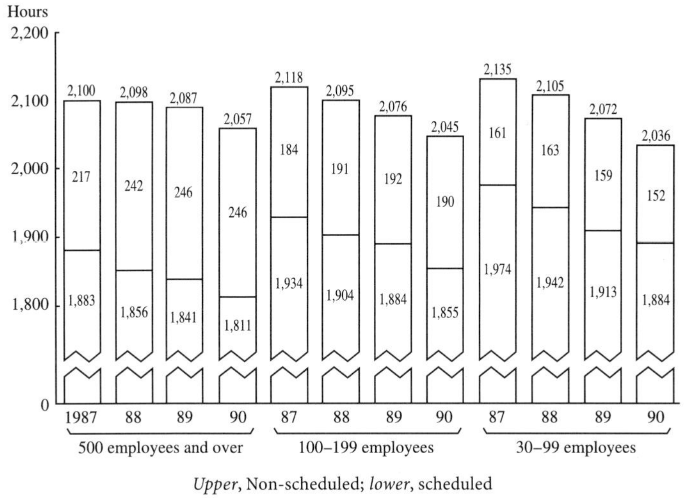

FIG. 7.2 Total Yearly Working Hours by Size of Establishment (1987–90, all industries)
Source: *White Paper on Working Hours in Japan* [J], Tokyo: Ministry of Labour, 1991, p. 12.

Furthermore, in the case of labor accidents, it is shown clearly in Table 7.11 that the casualty toll by labor accidents was less in larger enterprises and, conversely, was higher in smaller enterprises (here, establishments with 100 and more employees).

As we can see from the discussion above, in the Japanese economy, ordinary male employees in the prime of manhood and working in large enterprises (i.e. the employees who are most useful for capital, namely those who are situated at the center of the large corporation system) have been treated most favorably, with all other employees being situated in relatively worse conditions. Of course, the existence of a differential structure like this, in itself, is not peculiar to the Japanese economy, but is common to every national economy of advanced Western countries. However, the extent and minuteness of differentials within the Japanese structure surpass those found in all other countries.

Furthermore, as a more important point, the movement of people has been very fluid in the Japanese differential structure. Although, in reality, an overwhelming number of people in Japan take part in the struggle for a change of positions within the differential structure, the universal movement to abolish this differential structure in itself is socially very weak in Japan.

As a related issue, here I want to refer to the problem of the type of employment (i.e. loan (secondary) employees, part-time engagements, contingency workers, part-time workers, casual workers etc.), which has been increasing since the latter half of the 1970s in Japan and is increasing still more.

In February 1991, the number of employees in Japan increased to 48.77 million (of which, 30.16 million were male and 18.61 million were female; incidentally, the total

TABLE 7.9 Ratio of Workers by Size of Enterprise and Type of Weekly Days off (1975–89, s.y.; all industries)

(Unit: %)

Size of enterprise, year	Total	One day off per week	One and a half days off per week	Two days off per week						Other systems
				Total	Weekly	Three times a month	Bi-weekly	Twice a month	Once a month	
Industries covered										
1975	100.0	27.1	2.6	69.9	21.4	5.5	13.1	16.2	13.9	0.4
1980	100.0	23.7	2.1	74.1	23.0	7.4	11.6	16.9	15.2	0.0
1985	100.0	22.8	0.6	76.5	27.1	7.2	10.3	16.9	14.9	—
1988	100.0	18.9	0.9	79.9	29.5	10.0	13.3	15.2	12.0	0.2
1989	100.0	16.4	0.8	82.7	36.9	10.5	12.9	10.5	12.0	0.1
1,000 employees and over										
1975	100.0	9.0	2.3	88.1	40.8	7.9	13.5	16.9	8.9	0.6
1980	100.0	4.5	1.4	94.0	41.1	10.4	12.4	18.7	11.4	0.0
1985	100.0	3.6	0.2	96.3	50.1	9.2	9.9	18.1	9.0	—
1988	100.0	1.9	0.2	97.4	52.2	12.3	14.0	14.0	4.8	0.5
1989	100.0	1.8	0.1	97.9	64.1	11.4	11.5	6.5	4.3	0.2
100–999 employees										
1975	100.0	29.1	3.3	67.2	10.7	5.0	14.9	17.2	19.6	0.3
1980	100.0	27.1	2.3	70.6	14.8	7.1	12.4	17.6	18.6	0.0
1985	100.0	24.8	0.9	74.3	16.3	7.9	12.8	19.1	18.1	—
1988	100.0	20.1	1.4	78.4	16.2	10.7	15.4	19.0	17.1	0.1
1989	100.0	16.8	0.9	82.2	21.7	12.7	16.5	14.9	16.4	0.1
30–99 employees										
1975	100.0	60.4	1.9	37.7	2.7	1.3	8.6	11.9	13.1	0.0
1980	100.0	54.3	3.2	42.5	2.8	2.4	8.6	12.1	16.6	0.0
1985	100.0	54.7	1.0	44.3	3.2	2.6	7.0	11.2	20.3	—
1988	100.0	52.4	1.3	46.2	4.9	3.9	8.3	11.0	18.2	—
1989	100.0	45.9	1.9	52.3	6.5	4.7	9.6	11.2	20.3	—

Source: *WPL*, 1991, p. 288.

number of employed people was 61.59 million). The breakdown of these figures was as follows: regular employees 36.39 million (74.6%), part-time workers 5.22 million (10.7%) and casual workers 2.12 million (4.3%). (The remainder were part-time engagements, corporate executives etc.) However, with regard to the ratios of part-time workers and casual workers, there has been a large difference between the proportion of male and female workers in these types of employment. In the case of males, the number and ratio of regular employees was 25.18 million (83.5%), part-time workers 0.27 million (0.9%) and casual workers 1.04 million (3.4%). (The total of the latter two types of employment is 1.31 million or 4.3%.) In the case of females, the number and ratio of regular employees was 11.21 million (60.2%), part-time workers 4.95 million (26.6%) and casual workers 1.08 million (5.8%; total 6.03 million

TABLE 7.10 Welfare Expense Differentials by Size of Enterprise (1988, average monthly labor cost per employee)

(Unit: ¥)

Size of enterprise	Cash earnings	Labour cost excepting cash earnings							
					Cost of non-legislated welfare				
		Total*	Cost of severance pay	Legal welfare expenses	Total*	Company housing	Medial and health services	Canteens and other food services	Cultural sporting and recreational facilities
Industries covered	333,638	64,476	16,534	31,330	11,048	4,242	1,144	1,425	1,263
5,000 employees and over	419,579	101,496	32,425	37,982	22,927	9,934	3,905	2,424	2,023
1,000–4,999 employees	364,429	69,892	18,700	33,484	10,539	4,773	588	1,348	1,015
300–999 employees	317,829	54,805	12,069	29,863	7,485	2,771	289	1,176	919
100–299 employees	289,639	47,719	10,238	27,428	6,091	1,880	212	957	1,032
30–99 employees	263,224	41,852	6,372	26,778	5,892	830	168	1,031	1,151

* These total values are written equally as in the original Tables. However, some sub-items that were in the original tables have been omitted here.
Source: *Handbook of Labour Statistics in Japan* [J], 1991, pp. 159f.

Table 7.11 Frequency Rate* of Labor-Related Accidents by Size of the Establishment (1975–93, s.y.)

Size of establishment	1975	1980	1985	1988	1989	1990	1993
Total	4.77	3.59	2.52	2.09	2.05	1.95	2.00
1,000 employees and over	2.67	1.76	0.93	0.53	0.60	0.49	0.46
500–999 employees	3.38	2.14	1.43	1.17	1.13	1.15	0.98
300–499 employees	4.95	3.35	2.27	1.93	1.95	1.90	2.34
100–299 employees	7.38	5.49	4.06	3.56	3.40	3.36	3.29

Frequency rate = No. deaths and injuries due to labor accidents ÷ cumulative hours worked ×1,000,000
Sources: *WPL*, 1991, p. 299; *op. cit.*, 1994, p. 421.

or 32.4%). Apparently, in the case of females, the ratio of temporary workers was very large. Because the ratio of total temporary workers in 1985 was 11.7% (4.99 million people), of which 3.0% were male (0.83 million) and 27.6% were female (4.17 million), the statistical values of each sex increased in 1991. However, regarding the increased contribution ratio for the total value, the value of females was far larger than that of males.[7]

These part-time workers and casual workers, as well as loan employees, part-time engagements and contingency workers, as mentioned above, are an undoubtedly cheap and useful labor force for capital. And, in comparison with regular employees, they are also "unstable employees" who are situated in worse and poorer conditions in terms of employment, wages and welfare provision etc.[8]

With regard to this, we must make note of foreign workers, the numbers of whom have been rapidly increasing in Japan in the latter half of the 1980s. In addition to the existing Korean and Chinese workers, many foreign workers, mainly from Asia and South America, have come to Japan legally and illegally in recent years and they have been situated in the lower strata of the hierarchic labor market in Japan. I will examine this problem in the next section.

Notes

1. *WPL*, 1996, p. 74.
2. *Ibid.*, p. 38.
3. *Annual Report on the Labour Force Survey*, 1985. Tokyo: Management and Coordination Agency, p. 23.
4. Morioka K. Japanese Corporate Centricism and the Polarization of Working Hour Structure [J]. In: *Keizai* (Economy) March 1992. Tokyo: Shinnihon Shuppansha, pp. 124–126.
5. *WPL*, 1991, p. 287; Matsuba M. *An Essay on Contemporary Japanese Capitalism*, *op. cit.*, 1987, p. 115.
6. *WPL*, 1990, p. 225.
7. *Report on the Special Survey of the Labour Force Survey* [J], No.55. Tokyo: Management and Coordination Agency, February 1991, pp. 11–13.
8. Ito M. "In the Strong Yen and Economic Friction." [J]. In: Society for the Study of History (ed.). *Japan. Its Contemporary History*, Vol. 5. Tokyo: Aoki Shoten, 1991, pp. 201f.

7.3 The Current State of the Foreign Worker Problem

The lasting boom in the latter half of the 1980s, the labor shortage, the remarkable economic differentials between Japan and other Asian countries (Japanese national income per capita in 1987 were 99-, 53-, 45-, 27-, 8.8-, and 5.9-fold that of Bangladesh, China, Pakistan, the Philippines, Malaysia and Korea, respectively) and the strong yen were all factors causing the steady increase in the flow of foreign workers to Japan in the latter half of the 1980s.

Of these foreign workers, the number who entered Japan legally for the purpose of work in 1990 was 94,868. This number was 2.2-fold the 43,994 people who entered Japan in 1985. A breakdown of this figure according to occupation is as follows: entertainment 75,091 people; teachers 4,092 people; investment and management personnel 3,807 people; humanities and international work 2,756 people; and intra-company transfers 1,540 people.[1]

However, these figures show only a very small part of the real problem of foreign workers in Japan. In this country, the employment of foreigners for simple work is prohibited by the immigration law. Nevertheless, as a practical matter, many foreign workers who had no special skills came to Japan in the latter half of the 1980s to engage in simple work through various channels, and they have continued to work in this type of employment in Japan. Professor Hiroshi Komai, a notable scholar in the field of foreign workers in Japan, gave a figure of nearly 200,000 foreign workers who were engaged in simple work in Japan in 1990.

The breakdown of this figure according to immigration category is as follows: foreigners who entered on a tourist visa but worked illegally, approximately 70,000 peolpe; "U-turn" Japanese descendants from Latin America, 80,000 people (the Japanese government does not limit the entrance to Japan of these people or their field of employment if they follow the necessary procedures); and covert employment of foreign students and trainees, 60,000 people. According to country, this figure breaks down to: Brazil 65,000 people; Philippines 30,000 people; China 25,000 people; Korea 18,000 people; Pakistan 13,000 people; Bangladesh 10,000 people; Malaysia 10,000 people; and Thailand 6,000. By industry, the breakdown is: manufacturing 100,000 people; entertainment and amusement 40,000 people; service 30,000 people; construction 25,000 people. In this last aspect, the increasing ratio of the number of people in manufacturing and the decreasing ratio of the number of people in entertainment and amusement and construction during the latter half of the 1980s is of note.[2]

It is regrettable that the employment of foreign workers in simple work is legally prohibited, as mentioned earlier, except for the so-called U-turn Japanese descendants and, therefore, the number of foreigners arrested for working illegally has increased rapidly. The number of foreigners arrested increased 5.3-fold from 5,600 people in 1985 to 29,900 people in 1990, as shown in Table 7.12. The decisive factors that have affected the fluctuation of illegal workers according to country of origin have been the necessity of having an entry visa and the difficulty in obtaining one. With regard to the sex of illegal workers, there were more females (mainly in entertainment and amusement) than males until 1987, but the positions were reversed in 1988 and the ratio of males (mainly in manufacturing and construction) was over 80% in 1990.[3]

TABLE 7.12 Trends in the Number of Exposed Illegal Foreign Workers (1985–91, s.y.)

(Unit: people)

	1985	1986	1987	1988	1989	1990	1991 F.H.
Total	5,629	8,131	11,307	14,314	16,608	29,884	12,265
Of which, outside approved status	218	349	372	839	696	751	—
illegal stay (visa expired)	5,411	7,782	10,935	13,475	15,912	29,133	—
Top five countries							
Bangladesh	1	58	438	2,942	2,277	5,925	122
Korea	76	119	208	1,033	3,129	5,534	4,221
Malaysia	—	—	18	279	1,865	4,465	1,290
Philippines	3,927	6,297	8,027	5,386	3,740	4,042	1,426
Pakistan	36	195	905	2,497	3,170	3,886	386
Iran	—	—	—	—	15	652	2,225

The number of illegal foreign workers from other countries in 1990 were: Thailand 1,450; China 1,142; Sri Lanka 831.

For Bangladesh and Pakistan, on and after January 15, 1989, an entry Visa has been required. This is also the case for Iran on and after April 15, 1992.

Sources: Shinozuka Eiko. The Necessity of a Long Term Vision for Foreign Worker Problem [J], in: *Weekly Economist*, April 7, 1992, p. 62; *WPL*, 1991, p. 26.

How should this foreign worker problem be dealt with? This is a political and social problem with difficulties that are common to all advanced countries. However, legal protection on the grounds of fundamental human rights should be given to foreigners who are presently working, even if engaged in simple work, in Japan. In the case of Korean and Chinese people, who were forced to come to Japan as cheap labor before and during World War II, and their descendants living in Japan (i.e. approximately 700,000 Koreans and 140,000 Chinese), they still do not have completely equal legal rights with the Japanese. A solution to this problem is of the utmost urgency for Japan.

Here, I would like to add a supplementary explanation to the present problem of foreign workers in Japan. The population of registered foreigners broke through 1.28 million people, over 1% of the Japanese population, at the end of 1992. Because the number of undocumented foreign workers (illegally overstaying foreigners) was 300,000 in May 1993, the total population of foreigners in Japan was then approximately 1.6 million.[4]

Of these, the number of foreign workers in Japan, namely foreigners who legally entered Japan for work purposes, those of Japanese ancestry and undocumented foreign workers (overstaying illegally) totalled nearly 600,000. This figure is equivalent to over 1% of employees in Japan (as of 1993, there were 64.5 million employed people and 52 million employees). (Incidentally, in addition to illegally overstaying workers, undocumented foreign workers consist of those who entered Japan illegally and those who work outside approved status.)[5]

(a) The number of U-turn Japanese descendants from Latin America, to whom special legal position is given, increased rapidly from 8,450 people in 1988 to 149,000 people in 1991 and 152,000 people in 1992.[6] However, the increased rate of immigration has been abruptly lowered in the transition to the recession phase of the Japanese economy since 1991.

(b) The trends in the numbers of foreign workers who overstay their visa are as follows: 106,000 people in July 1990, 160,000 people in May 1991, 216,000 people in November 1991, 279,000 people in May 1992, 299,000 people in May 1993 and 297,000 people in November 1993. Thus, although the numbers increased rapidly after the beginning of the 1990s, there is an indication of a small decrease in 1993. The breakdown of these figures by nationality in November 1993 is as follows: Thailand 18.1%, Korea 13.8%, China 12.2%, and Philippines 12.2% etc.; the total of these four countries reached 56.4%.[7]

(c) The number of foreign trainees, who, in recent years, have become a large source of foreign workers outside approved status, along with exchange and regular students, increased steadily from 10,000 people in 1982 (when this status was established) to 23,000 people in 1988, 29,000 people in 1989, 38,000 people in 1990 and 44,000 people in 1991. However, the numbers stagnated and decreased a little from 44,000 in 1991 to 44,000 in 1992 and 40,000 in 1993.[8]

(d) Finally, the number of undocumented foreign workers discovered to be working illegally was 33,000 people in 1991, 62,000 people in 1992 and 64,000 in 1993, showing a dramatic increase from 1991 to 1992.[9]

Notes

1. *WPL*, 1991, p. 40.
2. Komai H. The Rapid Change of the Employment of Foreigners by the New Immigration Law [J]. In: *Weekly Economist*, October 23, 1990, pp. 80–83.
3. *WPL*, 1991, p. 26.
4. Komai H. *Japan As a Multi-Ethnic Society* [J]. Tokyo: Kokusai Shoin 1994, p. 11.
5. *WPL*,1994, pp. 53f, 361.
6. *Ibid.*, p. 52.
7. Komai H. *Live Together with Immigrant Workers* [J]. Tokyo: Akashi Shoten 1993, p. 32; *WPL*, 1994, pp. 53f.
8. Komai H. *op. cit.*, p. 34; *WPL*, 1994, p. 57.
9. *WPL*, 1994, p. 53; *WPL*, 1993, p. 46; *WPL*, 1992, p. 31.

Chapter 8
Trends for Farmers and Small Enterprises

8.1 Farmers

I must first point out to the reader that the objective of this section is not to comprehensively examine the agricultural problem in Japan, but to investigate the situation of farm household income, based on fundamental statistics on the agricultural economy, and to compare it with worker household income.

With regard to farm population and the cultivated area in Japan; in 1990, the number of farm households was 3,835,000, of which the number of farm households that received most of their income from other jobs was 2,712,000 (70.7%), accounting for the majority of households; those households whose income was mainly from farming was 531,000 (13.8%), and the number of households who exclusively engaged in farming was 592,000 (15.4%). The total population of farm households was 17.3 million in the same year, but the number of basic farmers was only 3.1 million people.[1]

The cultivated area per farm household in 1990 was quite small, at 0.9 ha on average, apart from 10.8 ha in Hokkaido. To examine this problem in more detail, as shown in Table 8.1, the ratio of farm households with less than 0.5 ha cultivated area in all Japanese farm households, except for Hokkaido, was 41.6%, while those with 0.5–1.0 ha constituted 28.0%; 13.7% had 1.0–1.5 ha (and so the ratio of farm households with less than 1.5 ha was an overwhelming 83.3%); 7.2% had 1.5–2.0 ha, 5.9% had 2–3 ha, 3.4% had 3–5 ha, and 0.7% had 5 ha and over.

With regard to the ratios according to size of cultivated area, except for Hokkaido, in 1990, as shown in Table 8.2, the majority (52.1%) had less than 1.5 ha, those with less than 3 ha constituted 81%, while those with 3 ha and over was only 16.4%.

Alhough the proportion of farm households with a cultivated area of 0.5–1.5 ha and the proportion of farm households with a cultivated area of less than 2 ha has decreased since 1960, the proportion of farm households with 3 ha and over has remained quite small at 3.4% in 1990, and although the proportion of farm households with a cultivated area of 3 ha and over increased to 16.4% in the same year, it remains clearly in the minority.

The main reasons why small farm households have persisted and why the cultivated area per farmer has not increased as a whole in prefectures other than Hokkaido are because of the increase in farmland prices and the holding tendency accompanying

TABLE 8.1. Number of Farm Households and Their Farm Size (1960–90, s.y.)

(Units: thousand %)

	1960	70	80	90
Number				
Total				
Farm households	6,057	5,402	4,661	3,835
Agricultural enterprise	—	9	10	9
Hokkaido				
Farm households	234	166	120	95
Of which, 200 ha and over	0	5	13	16
Agricultural enterprise	—	1	1	1
Prefectures*				
Farm households	5,823	5,236	4,542	3,739
Less than 0.5 ha	2,275	2,030	1,922	1,560
0.5–1.0 ha	1,907	1,619	1,304	1,049
1.0–1.5 ha	1,002	874	652	514
1.5–2.0 ha	404	407	328	268
2.0–3.0 ha	201	244	240	222
3.0 ha and over	36	63	95	126
5.0 ha and over	2	6	13	26
Agricultural enterprise	—	8	8	8
Share				
Prefectures*				
Farm households	100.0	99.8	99.8	99.8
Less than 0.5 ha	39.1	38.7	42.2	41.6
0.5–1.0 ha	32.7	30.9	28.7	28.0
1.0–1.5 ha	17.2	16.7	14.3	13.7
1.5–2.0 ha	6.9	7.8	7.2	7.2
2.0–3.0 ha	3.4	4.7	5.3	5.9
3.0 ha and over	0.6	1.2	2.1	3.4
5.0 ha and over	0.0	0.1	0.3	0.7
Agricultural enterprise	—	0.2	0.2	0.2

* Prefectures except for Hokkaido.

Source: *Statistical Appendix of White Paper on Agriculture in Japan* [J], 1990, Tokyo, p. 53.

this increase, with farmland being viewed by farmers as an asset. Because the assets value of farmland rose due to an increase in demand for land from other industries after the high economic growth period, many farmers looked for other jobs while holding onto their own land.[2]

Also regulated by the small size of the farms, agricultural income of farm households in 1989 was as follows: that of households exclusively engaged in farming ¥2.86 million (in the case of farming households headed by adult males ¥5.02 million); that of households with income mainly from farming ¥4.86 million; and that of households with income mainly from other jobs ¥0.48 million.[3] These statistics show, in part, the critical circumstances of Japanese agriculture, along with the big fall in self-sufficiency rates for foodstuffs.

TABLE 8.2 Cultivated Area of Farm Households and Their Farm Size (1960–90, s.y.)

(Unit: 1,000 ha, %)

	1960	70	80	90
Number				
Total				
Farm households	5,324	5,156	4,706	4,361
Agricultural enterprise	—	100	173	190
Hokkaido				
Farm households	826	890	969	1,032
Of which, 200 ha and over	7	124	414	576
Agricultural enterprise	—	41	85	102
Prefectures*				
Farm households	4,497	4,266	3,737	3,330
Less than 0.5 ha	614	547	501	423
0.5–1.0 ha	1,387	1,161	926	740
1.0–1.5 ha	1,213	1,056	788	620
1.5–2.0 ha	687	692	560	457
2.0–3.0 ha	468	571	569	529
3.0 ha and over	128	239	393	560
5.0 ha and over	9	39	99	196
Agricultural enterprise	—	59	87	89
Share				
Prefectures*				
Farm households	100.0	98.6	97.7	97.4
Less than 0.5 ha	13.6	12.7	13.1	12.4
0.5–1.0 ha	30.8	26.8	24.2	21.6
1.0–1.5 ha	27.0	24.4	20.6	18.1
1.5–2.0 ha	15.3	16.0	14.6	13.4
2.0–3.0 ha	10.4	13.2	14.9	15.5
3.0 ha and over	2.8	5.5	10.3	16.4
5.0 ha and over	0.2	0.9	2.6	5.7
Agricultural enterprise	—	1.4	2.3	2.6

* Prefectures except for Hokkaido.
Source: *Ibid.*, p. 54.

However, when we make note of actual farm households (i.e. total farm household income inclusive of non-agricultural income) and, additionally, the economic power of land ownership, which regulates the practical life of the farmer and his family and their social behavior, what is the actual situation of farm household economy?

As shown in Table 8.3, compared with worker household income in 1989, farm household income was lower only in the case of income per employed person, but was higher in the case of income per household and per household member. So, we can estimate that the absolute value of farm household income created the possibility of a stable life for farmers. In addition, income differentials between farm and worker households have not been reduced in the meanwhile.

Comparing savings of farm households with those of worker households in 1989, as shown in Table 8.4, the savings of farm households were 2.19-fold those of

TABLE 8.3 Comparison of Incomes of Farm Households and Worker Households (1965–94, s.y.)

	Unit	1965	1975	1985	1989	1994
Farm households						
Persons per household ①	People	5.28	4.56	4.34	4.26	4.22
Of which, working ②	People	2.70	2.55	2.46	2.40	2.44
Total income ③	¥1,000	835.10	3,966.5	6,925.8	7,992.5	9,097.6
Disposable income ④	¥1,000	775.1	3,576.8	5,765.0	6,651.1	7,666.4
Income from farming ⑤	¥1,000	365.2	1,146.0	1,065.5	1,111.7	1,593.1
Total income per week ⑥ = ③/②	¥1,000	309.3	1,555.5	2,815.4	3,330.2	3,728.5
Total income per person ⑦ = ③/①	¥1,000	158.2	869.8	1,595.8	1,876.2	2,155.8
Disposable income per person ⑧ = ④/①	¥1,000	146.8	784.4	1,328.3	1,561.3	1,816.7
Income f.f./total income ⑨ = ⑤/③	%	43.7	28.9	15.4	13.9	17.5
Worker households						
Persons per household (1)	People	4.11	3.81	3.79	3.72	3.62
Of which, earners (2)	People	1.52	1.50	1.57	1.63	1.68
Income (3)	¥1,000	797.3	2,897.2	5,387.5	6,003.4	6,817.3
Disposable income (4)	¥1,000	728.2	2,642.4	4,516.5	5,094.5	5,787.9
Wages and salaries (5)	¥1,000	740.9	2,726.2	5,079.2	5,648.4	6,392.5
Income per earner (6) = (3)/(2)	¥1,000	524.5	1,931.5	3,431.5	3,683.1	4,057.9
Income per person (7) = (3)/(1)	¥1,000	194.0	760.4	1,421.5	1,613.8	1,883.2
Disposable income per earner (8) = (4)/(1)	¥1,000	177.2	693.5	1,191.7	1,369.5	1,598.9
Wages and salaries/ income (9) = (5)/(3)	%	92.9	94.1	94.3	94.1	93.8
Ratio of worker household income to farm household income						
Income per household ③/(3)	%	104.7	136.9	128.6	133.1	133.4
Income per week/earner ⑥/(6)	%	59.0	80.5	82.0	90.4	91.9
Income per person ⑦/(7)	%	81.5	114.4	112.3	116.3	114.5
Disposable income per person ⑧/(8)	%	82.8	113.1	111.5	114.0	113.6

Source: *Ibid.*, p. 62; *op. cit.*, 1995, p. 60.

workers households and were 2.84-fold (nearly three-fold!) in the case of net savings deducting debts. (If we take into account the average age of all farm household heads, which is 56 years of age, and look at the class of 55–59-year-old worker household heads, then the savings of the latter grasp was ¥16.2 million and net savings were at ¥14.1 million. The savings of farm households were still more than those of the workers.)

TABLE 8.4 Comparison of Savings and Liabilities of Farm Households and Worker Households (1989, 1994)

(Unit: ¥ 1,000)

	Per household		
	Savings	Liabilities	Net savings
Farm households			
Total (56)	21,136	2,099	19,038
	[29,113]	[2,650]	[26,464]
Exclusively farming (62)	16,546	3,237	13,309
Mainly farming (55)	21,223	4,710	16,514
Mainly other job (55)	22,157	1,672	20,485
With basic male farmer (53)	20,880	5,213	15,667
Worker households (by age group)			
Total (44)	9,646	3,254	6,692
	[12,343]	[4,052]	[8,291]
24 years and under	1,976	667	1,308
25–29 years	4,310	1,236	3,074
30–34 years	5,126	2,980	2,146
35–39 years	7,201	3,423	3,778
40–44 years	8,314	4,350	3,963
45–49 years	11,224	4,644	6,580
50–55 years	11,599	2,718	8,881
55–59 years	16,216	2,081	14,136
60–64 years	18,512	1,193	17,319
65 years and over	19,867	1,001	18,866

Figures in parenthesis give the average age of the household head. Figures in brackets are data for 1994.

Source: *Op. cit.*, 1990, p. 63; *op. cit.*, 1995, p. 51.

In addition to these differentials between farm households and worker households, we must make note of the fact that the economic power of land ownership of farmers in urban areas and their neighborhoods has become much stronger than before because of the extraordinary rise in land prices, mentioned later, in the latter half of the 1980s.

Notes

1. *Statistical Appendix of White Paper on Agriculture in Japan* [J], 1990. Tokyo: Association of Agriculture and Forestry Statistics pp. 42, 44.
2. *White Paper on Agriculture in Japan* [J], 1990, p. 41.
3. *Statistical Appendix of White Paper on Agriculture in Japan*, 1990, *op. cit.*, pp. 64f.

8.2 Small Enterprises

In the government statistics of Japan "small enterprises" generally signify corporations with a capital of less than ¥100 million or with a number of employees fewer than 300 people, or private enterprises with fewer than 300 employees. However, in the case of wholesale, "small enterprise" refers to businesses with a capital of less than ¥30 million or with fewer than 100 employees and in the case of a retail business or service sector, it refers to businesses with a capital of less than ¥10 million or with fewer than 50 employees.[1] Although I do not unconditionally accept this conceptual definition, I use it provisionally as an important reference standard.

First, regarding classification by capital. There was a total of 2,020,455 corporations in Japan in 1990. Of these, the number of corporations with a capital of ¥100 million and over was 23,802 (1.2%), and those with a capital of ¥10 million and over was 430,420 (21.3%).[2] Because almost all private enterprises (not incorporated business) that were not included in these statistics were small enterprises, we can say that the overwhelming majority of Japanese enterprises consist of numerically small enterprises. (Incidentally, in 1983 the number of small establishments in the private sector, as defined above, and large establishments was 6,572,000 (99.2%) and 50,000 (0.8%), respectively.)[3]

Second, regarding classification by employees. Of the total number of employees in non-agricultural industries, which was 45.75 million people (including government employees of approximately 5 million) in 1987, the number of employees who belonged to enterprises with fewer than 300 employees was 27.85 million people or 60.9%. In the case of the manufacturing industry, of a total of 12.71 million employees, 7.82 million (61.5%) were employed by enterprises with fewer than 300 employees.[4] (However, not all employees who work in enterprises with fewer than 300 employees are regular employees. Temporary employees and part-time workers must also be included. On the basis of the size of the establishment, based on the above definition, in 1986 the number people employed (including self-employed and family workers) by small establishments in the private sector and large establishments was 39.51 million (80.6%) and 9.49 million (19.4%), respectively.[5]

The majority of these small enterprises consists of subcontractors in the field of industry, as shown in Figure 8.1; namely 355,000 (58.7%) in 1971, 373,000 (60.7%) in 1976, 465,000 (65.5%) in 1981 and 378,000 (55.9%) in 1987. This parent company—subcontractor relation has brought about certain reciprocal benefits. Namely, the parent company can get cheap and high-quality spare parts because of the low wages paid by the subcontractors and the fierce competition that exists among them, and it can cope flexibly and efficiently with any fluctuations of business and demand (an extreme form of this is the "just in time system" that greatly cuts down on inventory cost), while subcontractors can secure continuous and stable orders and absorb the technology and know-how of the parent company. However, it is evident that the parent company generally holds a dominant position in this relationship.

Both the number and ratio of these small subcontracting enterprises increased from the 1970s to the beginning of the 1980s, as shown in Figure 8.1. However, from 1981 to 1987, both the number and ratio of subcontracting enterprises decreased considerably. As possible causes for this, we can suggest that with the proliferation of microelectronics, a soft economy and drastic globalization a number of small enterprises that were not able to meet the demands of their parent company were compelled to change or close their business, while some small enterprises that had newly strengthened their business capacity consequently reduced their dependency on the parent company and became rather independent.[6]

FIG. 8.1 Number and Ratio of Subcontractors (1971–87)
Source: *WPSE*, 1991, p. 86.

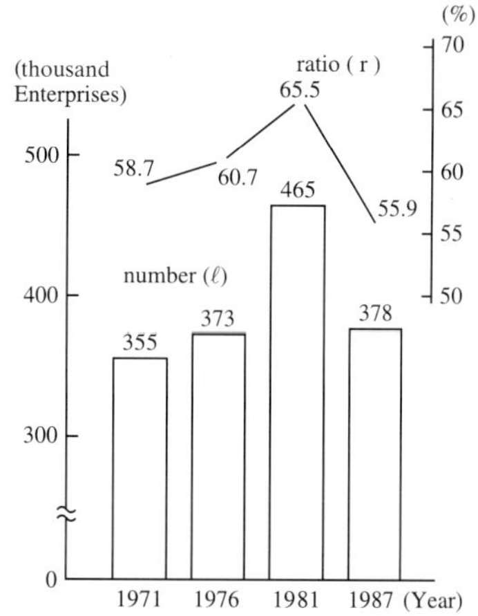

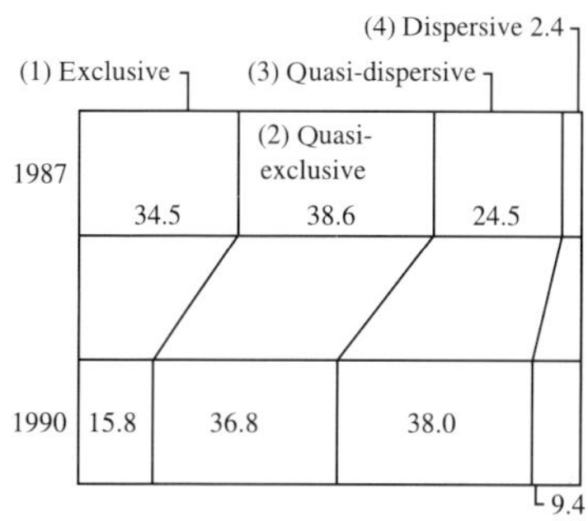

(1)"Exclusive" type, subcontractor has one parent company whose subcontracting transaction ratio is 90% and over; (2) "quasi-exclusive", subcontractor has two to five parent companies whose subcontracting transaction ratio is 90% and over, or has one parent company whose subcontracting transaction ratio is less than 90%; (3) "quasi-dispersire", two to five parent companies with a transaction ratio less than 90%, or six and over parent companies with a transaction ratio less than 70%; (4) "dispersive", six and over parent companies with a transaction ratio less than 70%.

FIG. 8.2 Types of Subcontracting Small Enterprieses and Their Share (1987, 1990) (Unit: %)
Source: *Ibid.*, pp. 89f.

Related to this, the change of shares according to type of small enterprise from 1987 to 1990, as shown in Figure 8.2, is of interest. During this period, the total ratio of "exclusive" and "quasi-exclusive" subcontractors decreased from 73.1% to 52.6%, while the total ratio of "quasi-dispersive" and "dispersive" subcontractors increased from 26.9% to 47.4%. In this sense, we can say that subcontracting small enterprises have been widening their customer base.

However, the fundamental predominance of the parent company over subcontractors is clear, judging from differentials by size, stock possession, financing, delegation

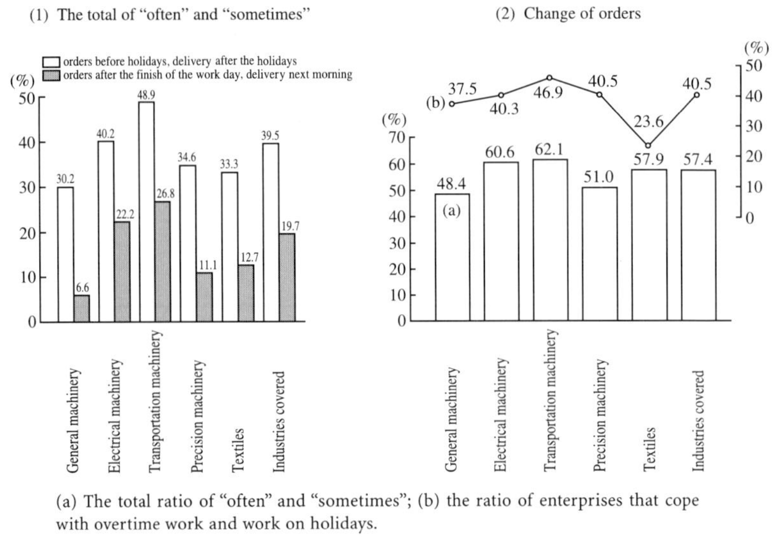

FIG. 8.3. Situation of Order and Delivery in Subcontracting Small Enterprises (1990)
Source: *WPSE*, 1991, p. 315.

of directors and technical guidance. This predominance results in orders before holidays/delivery of goods on the day following holidays, orders after the finish of the work day/delivery of goods the next morning, change of orders and overtime work/work on holiday etc., which are shown in Figure 8.3. These compel the employees in small enterprises to accept long working hours and a high density of labor, which may infringe on fundamental human rights.

Looking at trends in the opening and closure of small business enterprises, as shown in Figure 8.4, the decline in the ratio of businesses opening and the relatively fixed tendency of the ratio of businesses closing are characteristic in the long term for all industries (including large enterprises) in the Japanese economy. Under these conditions, of course, in comparison with large enterprises, the majority of openings and closures were by small enterprises in manufacturing during the 1980s. As Figure 8.5 shows, the ratios of businesses opening and closing were higher in smaller enterprises. In addition, when we examine these ratios of small enterprises in the 1980s separating manufacturing into growth industries and others, the ratio of businesses opening in the former category was 44.0% (closure ratio 37.3%), while that of the latter category was 31.4% (closure ratio 40.4%). We can estimate that active entry to growth industries promoted the conversion and sophistication of the industrial structure.[7]

Finally, I would like to examine the trends in bankruptcy (debt of at least ¥10 million) among small enterprises in recent years. Because of the long boom in the latter half of the 1980s, as Figure 8.6 shows, both the number of bankruptcies and the total debt values decreased remarkably during this period.

However, in 1990, when the bubble economy burst, there was a turning point for small enterprise bankruptcies. The number of bankruptcies decreased steadily during

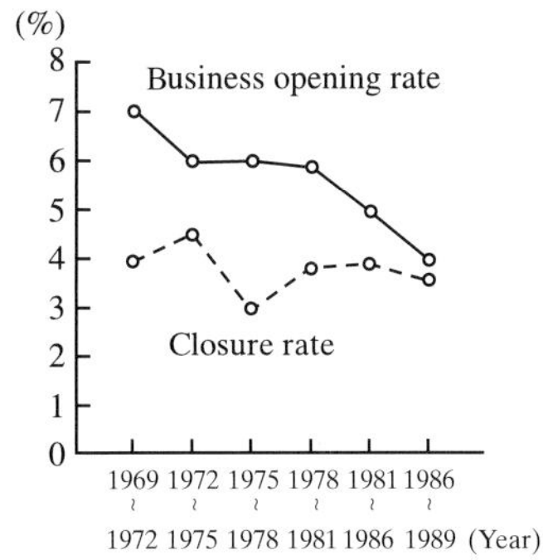

(1) Business opening rate is (the number of establishments that started business between the pervious and present investigation years divided by the number of establishments on the previous investigation divided by the number of years) × 100.
(2) Business closing rate is the business open rate minus the increasing rate.

FIG. 8.4. Trends in Business Openings and Closures (1969–89)
Source: *WPSE*, 1991, p. 49.

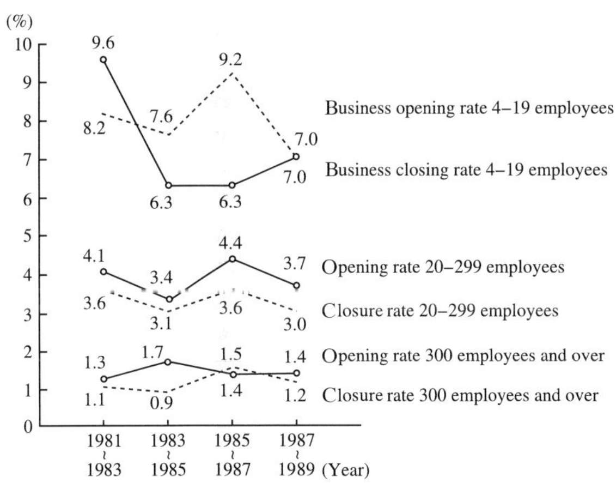

(1) Business opening rate is (the number of establishments opened during the period divided by the number of establishments at the beginning of the period divided by 2) × 100.
(2) Business closing rate is (the number of establishments closed during the period divided by the number of establishments at the beginning of the period divided by 2) × 100.

FIG. 8.5. Trends in the Rates of Business Openings and Closures by Size of Establishment (1981–89; manufacturing, average of years)
Source: *Ibid.*, p. 50.

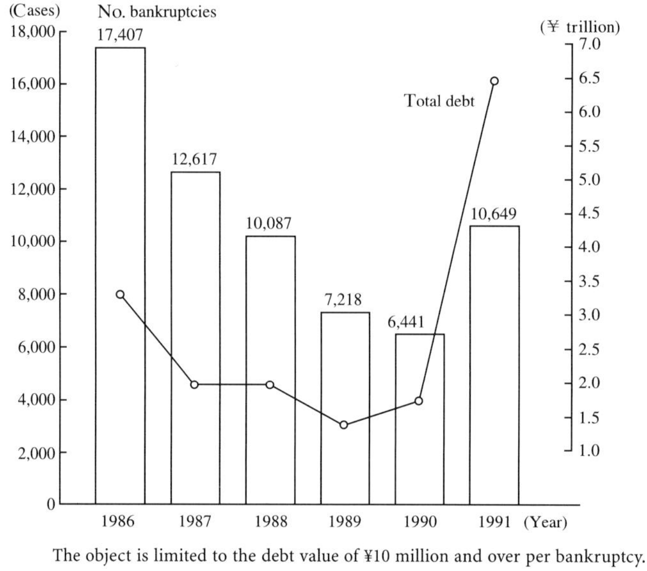

FIG. 8.6. Trends in the Number of Bankruptcies and Total Debt Value of Small Enterprises (1986–91)
Source: *WPSE*, 1992, p. 10.

this year, while the total debt began to increase. Consequently, the debt value per bankruptcy increased to ¥243 million in 1990 from ¥170 million in 1985, from ¥180 million in 1986, ¥144 million in 1987, ¥173 million in 1988 and ¥168 million in 1989.

This conversion was made clearer in 1991, when the number of bankruptcies increased to 10,649 (return to more than 10,000) and the total debt value increased to ¥6.36 trillion. This was three-fold the value in the previous year and the highest of past years. As a result, the debt value per bankruptcy increased greatly to ¥597 million (approximately 2.5-fold of that in the previous year). Thus, we can see the strong effects of the burst of the bubble economy and the subsequent business downturn on small enterprise bankruptcies in 1991.[8]

Notes

1. See: *WPSE*, 1991, explanatory notes. These criteria were partially amended in 1999. For more detail, refer to: *WPSE*, 2000, first appendix, pp. 1f.
2. *Annual Report on Financial Statements of Incorporated Businesses* [J], 1990. Tokyo: Ministry of Finance, p. 46.
3. *WPSE*, 1991, p. 2.
4. *WPL*, 1991, p. 246.
5. *WPSE*, 1991, p. 3.
6. *WPSE*, 1990, pp. 157f.
7. *WPSE*, 1991, p. 50.
8. *WPSE*, 1991, p. 15; *op. cit.*, 1992, pp. 10f.

Chapter 9
Aspects of the Life of the People

9.1 Distribution of Income and Assets

To begin with, the stratified composition of family income in Japan will be examined. As Table 9.1 shows, the ratio of households with a yearly family income of less than ¥1.5 million of total households covered in 1989 was 10.2% (11.6% in 1983), while the ratio of those households with an income of less than ¥2.5 million was 21.6% (26.1% in 1983). In standard households with four people, these values were 1.7% and 7.8%, respectively, in 1988 (2.6% and 7.8%, respectively, in 1983). It must be said that these households have been put in a situation where daily life is materially difficult. The results of improvements to social welfare, security and reform should apply first of all to these social groups.

However, conversely, the ratio of households with a yearly income of ¥3 million and over in 1989 was 72.6% (65.6% in 1983), while the ratio of those households with an income of ¥5 million and over was 47.1% (33.9% in 1983). The average yearly income of total households covered was ¥5.67 million and the median value by which the total households were divided into two groups was ¥4.71 million; these indices clearly show that the economic basis of the contemporary Japanese social system is definitely not fragile.[1]

With regard to family savings, the average amount of savings per worker household at the end of 1990 was ¥10.51 million (liabilities ¥3.4 million; that of savings per household for all households, inclusive of individual proprietors, corporative administrators and independent professionals etc., ¥13.53 million). Then, the median was ¥7.00 million and the mode was ¥2.94 million. This average amount of savings increased 2.2-fold for the 10 year period from 1980. Considering that the average yearly income increased 1.5-fold from ¥4.49 million to ¥6.94 million for the same period, the growth of savings greatly surpassed that of income. The breakdown of the savings figures according to type of savings was as follows: time deposits ¥4.44 million, life and non-life insurance ¥2.94 million, securities ¥1.97 million, demand deposits ¥0.75 million and others at ¥0.41 million.[2]

This savings situation and the distribution of savings over several strata, as shown in Table 9.2, indicates that many workers and people in Japan today possess substantial financial assets. In fact, making an international comparison of outstanding values of financial assets per capita in 1988, the ¥6.46 million in Japan was greater

TABLE 9.1 Stratified Composition of Yearly Family Income (1988, 89)

	All households		Standard households with four people	
	Cumulative %	%	Cumulative %	%
Yearly income groups (¥10,000)	1989		1988	
Total		100.0		100.0
Less than 50	1.1	1.1	—	—
50–100	4.8	3.7	0.5	0.5
100–150	10.2	5.4	1.7	1.3
150–200	15.7	5.4	4.2	2.5
200–250	21.6	5.9	7.8	3.6
250–300	27.4	5.9	13.4	5.6
300–350	34.0	6.6	20.8	7.3
350–400	40.6	6.6	29.8	9.0
400–450	47.0	6.4	39.2	9.4
450–500	52.9	5.9	48.2	9.0
500–550	58.7	5.8	58.4	10.2
550–600	63.7	5.0	66.2	7.7
600–650	68.5	4.8	73.8	7.6
650–700	72.7	4.2	78.8	5.1
700–750	76.6	3.8	83.5	4.6
750–800	79.6	3.0	86.5	3.1
800–850	82.7	3.1	89.1	2.6
850–900	85.0	2.4	90.9	1.8
900–950	87.2	2.1	92.8	1.9
950–1,000	88.6	1.4	93.9	1.1
1,000–1,100	91.5	2.9	95.9	2.0
1,100–1,200	93.6	2.1	96.8	0.9
1,200–1,500	97.1	3.5	98.5	1.7
1,500–2,000	98.6	1.5	99.5	0.9
2,000 and over	100.0	1.4	100.0	0.5
Average (¥10,000)	566.7		554.3	
Median (¥10,000)	471		500	
Ratio under average income (%)	60.7		60.0	

Source: *The Fundamental Survey of the National Life Japan* [J], 1990, Tokyo, p. 135; *op. cit.*, 1989, p. 227.

than that of the F.R. Germany (¥2.93 million), UK (¥3.37 million in 1987) and US (¥6.13 million).[3]

The situation of family assets in Japan will now be examined in more detail. In 1989, family assets (net value) for all households with two or more persons in Japan stood at ¥53.72 million per household and their breakdown by type was as follows: residential land ¥39.94 million (74.4% of all assets), financial assets (savings minus liabilities) ¥6.81 million (12.7%), houses ¥5.09 million (9.5%), and durable goods ¥1.89 million (3.5%). Thereby, with regard to assets of houses and residential land, their average value in 1989 was ¥45.02 million, the median was ¥19.70 million and the mode was ¥15.30 million. (However, in the case of calculations made excluding households

TABLE 9.2 Amount of Savings by City Groups, Profession, Income Bracket and Age (1990)

(Unit: %)

		Total no. households with savings	Amount groups of savings (¥10,000)										Average (¥10,000)
			Less than 100	100 ~ 200	200 ~ 300	300 ~ 400	400 ~ 500	500 ~ 700	700 ~ 1,000	1,000 ~ 1,500	1,500 ~ 2,000	2,000 and over	
	Total	100.0 (3,768)	4.1	6.4	6.2	6.9	5.8	10.5	11.1	11.1	5.0	14.3	1,181
By city groups	12 major cities	100.0 (914)	3.8	6.3	5.8	6.0	5.8	9.5	9.7	12.3	4.8	16.8	1,315
	Middle cities	100.0 (1,254)	3.9	5.9	6.2	7.0	5.2	10.8	11.2	10.5	5.3	13.2	1,179
	Small cities	100.0 (802)	5.1	7.1	6.5	7.1	6.9	11.0	12.2	11.0	3.9	13.2	1,067
	Rural districts	100.0 (798)	3.6	6.5	6.5	7.4	5.6	10.5	11.5	10.9	5.6	14.0	1,150
By profession of household head	Farmers etc.	100.0 (213)	5.2	3.8	5.2	4.7	5.6	11.7	13.6	16.0	6.1	15.5	1,145
	Self-employed	100.0 (786)	4.8	5.5	5.3	6.6	6.6	9.8	8.5	10.6	5.6	15.8	1,285
	Office workers	100.0 (736)	3.4	5.8	8.2	10.5	7.2	11.4	14.7	9.0	5.8	9.5	955
	Non-office workers	100.0 (767)	6.1	11.3	8.3	7.4	6.4	11.9	10.0	9.3	2.6	5.2	703
	Administrator	100.0 (523)	0.2	2.9	2.9	5.0	4.0	10.5	13.6	15.3	5.9	23.5	1,616
	Professional service	100.0 (121)	5.0	5.8	8.3	5.8	4.1	5.0	5.0	8.3	4.1	25.6	1,610
By yearly income	Less than 200 (¥10,000)	100.0 (83)	12.0	19.8	9.6	10.8	4.8	8.4	8.4	4.8	3.6	2.4	478
	200–300 (¥10,000)	100.0 (263)	9.9	15.6	11.0	8.7	4.2	7.2	9.1	10.6	3.4	9.9	820
	300–400 (¥10,000)	100.0 (464)	9.3	10.1	10.6	8.4	8.0	11.4	9.1	10.3	1.7	6.3	727
	400–500 (¥10,000)	100.0 (557)	5.6	8.1	9.2	10.8	7.4	12.0	12.2	7.9	4.5	8.8	870
	500–700 (¥10,000)	100.0 (926)	1.6	4.9	6.0	7.3	7.7	14.4	15.0	12.9	6.3	14.8	1,138
	700 (¥10,000) and over	100.0 (929)	0.8	2.5	2.4	4.8	4.5	9.3	12.3	15.4	8.0	28.6	1,825
By age of household head	20 s	100.0 (110)	20.0	20.0	17.3	8.2	6.4	3.6	3.6	5.5	0.0	2.7	413
	30 s	100.0 (712)	6.0	12.1	9.7	10.7	7.4	12.4	11.2	7.6	3.1	3.5	645
	40 s	100.0 (1,097)	3.8	4.3	6.0	8.0	7.6	13.1	13.8	10.2	5.4	9.7	967
	50 s	100.0 (962)	3.0	5.3	4.6	5.1	4.9	8.1	10.1	12.7	5.1	20.3	1,436
	60 s	100.0 (661)	1.2	3.6	4.1	4.4	3.2	10.1	10.1	13.0	6.4	23.8	1,752
	70 and over	100.0 (226)	4.4	4.9	4.4	3.5	3.1	5.8	9.3	17.3	6.6	23.0	1,669

Source: *Statistics on Japanese Standard of Living* [J], 1991, Tokyo, p. 117.

without houses and residential land, the average value of assets was ¥57.41 million and the median was ¥27.24 million. Incidentally, in 1984 the ratio of households with houses and residential land in a two or more person household was 74.2%, based on the "National Survey of Family Income and Expenditure".)[4] Regarding these family assets, based on the same survey in 1994, the situation was as follows. The average value of family assets (net value) for all households with two or more persons was ¥53.75 million, and their breakdown was residential land ¥36.36 million, financial assets ¥8.47 million, houses ¥6.59 million and durable goods ¥2.33 million. As we can see, although the value of residential land decreased a little, the value of total assets was almost unchanged. This indicates that, up until this time, the collapse of the bubble economy had not damaged the household sector as much as it had the corporate sector.[5]

Looking at land assets whose prices rose extraordinarily in the latter half of the 1980s, the number of households with land assets of ¥100 million and over increased from 153,000 (except for one-person households) in 1984 to 1.15 million in 1987. In addition, the number of households with land assets of ¥50 million and over rose from 1.24 million to 3.26 million, while those with land assets of ¥30 million rose from 3.96 million to 6.24 million. Of course, the increase in the value of land assets was particularly conspicuous in Tokyo. There, the land assets of households living with houses and residential land in Tokyo were ¥130 million on average (median ¥91 million) in 1987. The share of land assets of households with houses and residential land in the four prefectures of the Tokyo metropolitan area (Tokyo, Kanagawa, Saitama and Chiba) of all Japanese land assets was 34% in 1984 and reached 54% (at last, reaching a majority) in 1987, although their share was 23% of the whole country (in 1984) when looking at the number of households and a little less than 15% (in 1984) when looking at land area.[6]

Examining the differential structure of income and assets, which we have seen above, by the trends of Gini's coefficient, as shown in Table 9.3, with regard to income differentials, the figures of Gini's coefficient have been under 0.3. We can say that the degree of equality has been high, as far as these figures show. (However, in the original statistics "Family Income and Expenditure" produced by the Management and Coordination Agency, households of agriculture, forestry and fishery and one-person households have been excluded. In this sense, we must make note of the figures shown.) The differentials in financial assets and land assets have been large in comparison with differentials in income. In particular, the differentials in land assets have increased remarkably in the latter half of the 1980s.[7]

To best illustrate the equal degree of income distribution at present, we can refer to the "Survey Results of Income Redistribution 1990" of the Ministry of Health and Welfare. This survey covered all professions and also included one-person households, like the young or elderly, as samples (total 8,856 households). The trends of Gini's coefficient with regard to original income and redistributive income (= original income – tax – social security insurance + social security benefit) were, on the basis of this material, as follows (figures for original and redistributive income, respectively): 0.3419 and 0.3143 in 1981, 0.3975 and 0.3426 in 1984, 0.4049 and 0.3382 in 1987 and 0.4334 and 0.3643 in 1990.[8]

Gini's coefficients indicating an equal degree of income distribution (the larger the coefficient, the more unequal the situation) rose rapidly in the 1980s and were greater

Table 9.3 Trends in Differentials of Income, Financial Assets and Land Assets (1963–89, s.y., shown by Gini's coefficient)

Year	Income	Financial assets	Land assets
1963	0.2968	0.6489	—
1965	0.2793	0.6150	—
1970	0.2669	0.5447	—
1975	0.2742	0.5390	—
1980	0.2596	0.5205	0.5992
1981	0.2620	0.5138	—
1982	0.2601	0.5215	—
1983	0.2652	0.5124	—
1984	0.2825	0.5101	—
1985	0.2785	0.5097	0.5639
1986	0.2812	0.5107	—
1987	0.2845	0.5210	0.6531
1988	0.2814	0.5128	0.6475
1989	0.2894	0.5146	0.6510

Source: *Annual Report on the National Life* [J], 1990, Tokyo, p. 339.

than 0.4 in the case of original income in 1987 and 1990 (at the level of 0.4, it is said that social inequality begins to become conspicuous). In the case of redistributive income, Gini's coefficients reached a value of 0.36 in 1990. There is a large difference between these figures and the figures of the "Annual Report on the National Life 1990" based on the original statistics of "Family Income and Expenditure" by the Management and Coordination Agency. I think that the figures for Gini's coefficient based on the investigation of the Ministry of Health and Welfare are more precise, taking the scope of the investigation into account.

Based on the results of this survey, Professor Tachibanaki Toshiaki constructed Table 9.4, comparing these values internationally. He arrived at the following conclusion concerning the degree of equality of Japanese income distribution (his conclusions are very interesting, so I will quote from his report at length):

"From this Table [9.4] we can understand the following points. Firstly, the unequal degree of Japanese income distribution has risen rapidly both in the case of original income and redistributive income. Gini's coefficient rose by about 0.1. It is rare in any country for the unequal degree of distribution to rise this rapidly and for such a short period. And it is not easy to believe that Gini's coefficient was over 0.4.

Secondly, the unequal degree of the Japanese income distribution was the highest among the advanced countries in the latter half of the [1980s] and in 1990. Gini's coefficient of the original income in Japan showed a surprisingly high unequal degree and was higher than that of the US, which has been regarded as the country with the highest inequalities of income distribution.

Thirdly, it is surely confirmed that Japan's unequal degree was average or rather lower than other countries' around 1980.

Fourthly, among advanced countries, the countries with equal income distribution are the Northern European countries and the Oceanic countries.

As mentioned above, the unequal degree of Japan's income distribution has risen rapidly in the last 10 years or more and the myth that the equal degree of Japanese

Table 9.4 Unequal Degree of Income Distribution after Taxation by Gini's Coefficient (1981–1990, s.y.)

	Japan		US		UK		France		Australia	
	Original income	Redistributive income	1979	0.37	1981	0.28	1979	0.364	1981	0.31
1981	0.349	0.314	1989	0.40	1988	0.35	1984	0.372	1985	0.32
1984	0.398	0.343	Norway		Finland		Canada		New Zealand	
1987	0.405	0.338	1979	0.346	1981	0.206	1981	0.395	1981	0.29
1990	0.433	0.364	1986	0.330	1985	0.200	1988	0.404	1985	0.30

Only figures for the US show original income.
Original sources: *Investigation Result of Income Redistribution* 1990 [J], Ministry of Health and Welfare Japan, p. 11; Atkinson AB, *What is Happening to the Distribution and Income in the UK?* LSE, Welfare State Program, 1993.
Source: Tachibanaki T. The Myth of the Equal Income Distribution Has Collapsed [J], in: *Sekai* (*World*), March 1994, Tokyo: Iwanami Shoten, p. 73.

income distribution is high has perfectly collapsed. We must newly recognize that Japan is a country with a high unequal degree of income distribution. This fact is very important, when we evaluate the economic system and performance of Japan. The relatively good performance of the Japanese economy advances with the fact of the unequalizing of income distribution and with great social cost."[9]

In order to further consider the equality problem of material life conditions in Japanese society, a part of the present situation regarding property holders or those in high-income brackets will be shown. For example, the top 100 wealthy people who had individual assets of over ¥20 billion (the top 20 people are shown in Table 9.5) and the top 1,000 people who had stock assets of over ¥2.4 billion appeared in the "Men of Property in Japan" investigation (in June 1991) of the "Nikkei Venture" issued in September 1991.[10] The top 50 wealthy people with forestry assets (1. (names have been omitted here) Wakayama prefecture, 4,900 ha, ¥23 billion; 2. Mie-Wakayama, 3,000 ha, ¥21 billion; 3. Mie, 3,400 ha, ¥20 billion; 4. Wakayama, 3,000 ha, ¥15 billion; 5. Shimane, 8,000 ha, ¥14.5 billion; 6. Nara, 1,800 ha, ¥12 billion; 7. Nara, 2,000 ha, ¥9.5 billion; 8. Nara, 2,000 ha, ¥9.5 billion; 9. Wakayama, 2,200 ha, ¥9.5 billion, 10. Tokushima, 3,000 ha, ¥9 billion) and the top 17 wealthy people with art assets appeared in the same "Nikkei Venture" issued in September 1986.[11]

However, these surveys limited the assets only to those under the name of the person himself, as the magazine itself stated. So, of course, assets under the name of one's family member or relatives or the corporations over which one had virtual ruling power were excluded from the survey results. Therefore, factual economic ruling power of the wealthy people mentioned above must be larger than that shown. (For example, as the first-ranked man of property outside of the royal family of Japan and the heads of state in the world, Mr. Mori Taikichiro (president of Mori Building Co.) was listed in the "Forbes" July 1991 issue and his assets were estimated to be US$15 billion (equivalent to ¥2.07 trillion). Similarly, Mr. Tsutsumi Yoshiaki, president of Seibu Railway Co., was ranked second with assets of US$14 billion.[12] However, neither Mr. Mori nor Mr. Tsutsumi appeared even within the top 100 list in the "Nikkei

TABLE 9.5 Top 20 Men of Property (1991)

(Unit: ¥ billion)

Rank[1]	Name	Occupation	Amount of assets
1 (1)		Togensha, president	410.0
2 (4)		Kishu Museum, chairman	330.0
3 (4)		Marugen, president	300.0
4 (8)		Japan Herald Movie, chairman	250.0
5 (3)		Nintendo, president	221.4
6 (6)		THK, president	219.1
7 (2)		Heiwa, president	210.0
8 (19)		Kabuto Decom, president	151.3
9 (9)		Daito Kentaku, president	123.6
10 (10)	Omission	Taisho Pharmaceutical, chairman	114.9
11 (—)		Shima Seiki, president	113.1
12 (11)		Takefuji, president and chairman	104.5
13 (14)		Daishowa Paper Mfg, honorary chairman	100.0
14 (16)		Azabu Motor, president	100.0
15 (13)		Kyocera, chairman	73.6
16 (12)		Obayashi Corp., chairman	72.7
17 (—)		Mabuchi Motor, chairman	70.0
18 (—)		Sega Enterprises, president	69.2
19 (—)		Ito-Yokado, president	68.7
20 (—)		Capcom, president	66.7

(1) Rank for the previous year is given in parentheses; (—) indicates a ranking of 21 or lower in the previous year.
Source: *NM*, August 19, 1991.

Venture" 1991, where the assets surveyed were limited only to those directly under their names. In the "Nikkei Venture" study, the economic power of general land owners remained almost unknown. Considering that the economic power of land owners in urban areas and their neighborhoods is very strong today, we must pay attention to this aspect.) In any case, the above-mentioned shows a part of the top layer of individual wealthy people. However, today there are not a few people in Japan who are situated near the wealthy people mentioned earlier.

Next, when the assets problem is viewed from the angle of large value tax payments (payers), there were 176,000 people (only official number confirmed by final return) who paid income tax (not income) of ¥10 million and over in 1991, of which the top 50 people are shown in Table 9.6. (The number of people in this group was 68,000 in 1984, so it increased 2.5-fold during these 7 years. In spite of a change in tax rates in the reform of 1989, the income tax rate of the marginal part concerned hardly changed.) A large part of the income for these people presumably comes from their possession of assets (i.e. land alienation, securities trading, dividend and interest etc.).

Viewed from the angle of legacy, of the 820,000 people who died in 1990, 48,300 left fortunes over the minimum taxable ceiling of inheritance tax (as of 1990, in cases where the successors were a wife and two children, ¥64 million) and, of these, 35,700 left a fortune of over ¥100 million.[13] The total value of taxable legacy was

TABLE 9.6 Top 50 People Ranked in Terms of Income Tax Value (1991)

(Unit: ¥ million)

	Rank	Name	Occupation	Address (prefecture)	Income tax value	Rank in the previous year
○	1		No occupation	Hyogo	4,131.45	—
○	2		Mortgage credit	Tokyo	3,367.83	—
▲	3		President of company	Gunma	2,947.25	—
○	4		Honorary president of company	Shizuoka	1,561.72	1
▲	5		Member of Parliament	Gunma	1,505.44	—
▲	6		Director	Tokyo	1,486.56	12
○	7		President of company	Tokyo	1,410.05	—
○	8		No occupation	Tokyo	1,301.18	—
○	9		President of company	Hyogo	1,256.30	—
—	10		President of company	Osaka	1,251.46	22
○	11		No occupation	Tokyo	1,178.31	—
○	12		President of company	Tokyo	1,155.41	—
○	13	Omission	Unknown	US	1,151.45	—
○	14		Former member of parliament	Saitama	1,148.70	—
▲	15		Managing director	Tokyo	1,133.45	—
○	16		President of company	Saitama	1,103.83	—
○	17		President of company	Tokyo	1,080.11	—
○	18		President of company	Tokyo	1,049.06	—
○	19		Former ambassador	France	1,040.10	—
○	20		President of company	Tokyo	1,014.20	—
○	25		President of company	Tokyo	922.74	—
○	30		Managing director	Tokyo	821.59	—
—	35		President of company	Tokyo	790.15	87
○	40		Farmer	Kanagawa	740.15	—
○	45		Private administrator	Tokyo	723.03	
▲	50		President of company	Kagawa	701.42	—

○, main income from land transfer; ▲, main income came from stock dealing; (—) ranking 101 or less in the previous year.

Source: *AE*, May 1, 1992.

¥14.05 trillion, including the values shown in Table 9.7, and the amount of inheritance tax reached ¥2.95 trillion in 1990. The breakdown of the total legacy was as follows: land 71.2%, securities 10.2%, cash and deposits 8.2%, and others.[14]

The existence and form of these assets (and the income from these assets) are important problems to be examined in terms of the actual situation of wealth and poverty in Japan.

TABLE 9.7 Top 10 Persons Ranked in Terms of Legacy

(1990) (Unit: ¥ million)

Rank	Name	Occupation	Address (prefecture)	Taxable legacy value
1	Omission	Director of real estate	Tokyo	30,000.00
2		Mortgage credit	Tokyo	25,771.10
3		Director of real estate	Tokyo	18,738.53
4		Former minister	Shiga	18,040.62
5		Honorary chairman of company	Tokyo	15,437.30
6		Director	Tokyo	13,910.98
7		Farmer	Tokyo	13,694.35
8		Director of real estate	Osaka	13,402.04
9		Mortgage credit	Kanagawa	13,397.62
10		Professor	Tokyo	13,140.44

Source: *NM*, June 6, 1992.

Notes

1. *Fundamental Survey of the National Life in Japan* [J], 1990. Tokyo: Ministry of Health and Welfare, p. 135; *op. cit.*, 1989, Vol. 1, p. 227.

   The number of samples in this investigation was 50,000 and 13,000 households in 1989 and 1990, respectively. The survey method consisted of a visit and interview conducted by the investigator. So, it is possible that there is a significant underestimation/under reporting of the actual income of households by the person being interviewed in this kind of survey.
2. *1990 Family Savings Survey*. Tokyo: Management and Coordination Agency, pp. 17–21.
3. *The Weekly Toyo Keizai* [J], November 18, 1989, p. 62.
4. *1989 National Survey of Family Income and Expenditure*, Vol. 8, part 3. Tokyo: Management and Coordination Agency, pp. 33, 47; Takayama N. (ed.), *Stock Economy. An Economic Analysis of Assets Formation and Savings/Pensions* [J]. Tokyo: Toyo Keizai Inc., 1992, p. 56.
5. *1994 National Survey of Family Income and Expenditure (Family Assets, Prompt Report)* [J]. Tokyo: Management and Coordination Agency, May 1996, p. 1.
6. Takayama N. (ed.). *op. cit.*, pp. 50f.
7. International comparisons of Gini's coefficient regarding the value of assets were as follows: Japan 0.52 (in 1984), US 0.72 (1983), and UK 0.78 (1972). The share of assets owned by the top 5% of asset owners was 49% in the US (1983), 55% in the UK (1972) and 25% in Japan (1984). (Takayama N. (ed.), *op. cit.*, pp. 12, 24.)

   The 35% of total net assets (except for durable consumer goods) existed in the top 0.5% households in the US, while 71.7% of total net assets were found in the top 10% households in 1983. In the UK, 22% of total assets were held by the top 1% of individuals (not households; 1983), and 53% of total assets were held by the top 10% of individuals. (Ishikawa T. *Income and Wealth* [J]. Tokyo: Iwanami Shoten, 1991, pp. 18f.)
8. *The Survey Results of Income Redistribution 1990* [J]. Tokyo: Ministry of Health and Welfare, p. 11.
9. Tachibanaki T. The Myth of the Equal Income Distribution Has Collapsed [J]. In: *Sekai* (*World*), March 1994. Tokyo: Iwanami Shoten, p. 74.

10. *Nikkei Venture* [J], September 1991, Tokyo: Nikkei Business Publications, Inc. pp. 80–122.
11. *Op. cit.*, September 1986, pp. 14–113.
12. *Forbes*, July 22, 1991, New York, p. 128; *NE* and *AE*, July 8, 1991.
13. *Statistical Yearbook of the National Tax Administration Agency Japan* [J], 1990, Tokyo, p. 129.
14. *NM* and *AM*, June 6, 1992.

9.2 The Current State of Social Security

This section, cannot, of course, deal with all the problems of social security in Japan. The discussion will be limited to livelihood assistance and pensions and the examination of immanent issues.

Table 9.8 makes international comparisons of the fundamental indices regarding social security. In Japan, regulated by the low ratio of the aged population, in 1989 the ratio of the social security benefit to national income was 14.0% and the ratio of taxes and social security contributions to national income was 38.7%. The level of these indices in Japan was very near to those of the US and was considerably lower than those of European countries.

However, the forecasts for the proportion of the population aged 65 years or older in 2000–2020 are as follows: 16.3%–23.6% in Japan, 16.7%–21.7% in Germany, 14.7%–18.0% in France, 15.3%–17.8% in the UK and 12.0%–15.4% in the US.[1] Because Japan is predicted to become a society with many more elderly people than not only the US but also European countries, both the cost of social security benefits and the ratio of taxes and social security contributions to national income will increase rapidly hereafter.

The number of households and people receiving livelihood assistance in 1990 was 0.62 million and 1.01 million, respectively. In addition, the number of people receiving a livelihood assistance benefit was 0.89 million.[2] The standard values for

TABLE 9.8 Fundamental Indices of Social Security in Selected Countries (1986, 1989)

(Unit: %)

Country	Ratio of social security benefit to national income	Ratio of people 65 years and over	Ratios to national income: Taxes	Social security contributions	Total
Japan	14.3	10.6	25.0	10.7	35.7
1989	14.0	11.6	27.8	10.9	38.7
US	15.2	12.1	25.7	10.1	35.8
UK	25.0	15.3	41.3	11.2	52.5
F.R. Germany	29.1	15.1	30.0	22.4	52.4
France	36.1	13.1	33.6	27.7	61.3
Sweden	39.7	18.1	53.2	19.1	72.3

Source: *White Paper on Health and Welfare in Japan* [J], 1991, Tokyo, p. 391.

TABLE 9.9 Monthly Livelihood Assistance Standard Benefit (1990)

(Unit: ¥)

Type of household	Parent and two children		Mother and two children		Two aged	
Region	Class 1–1	Class 3–1	Class 1–1	Class 3–1	Class 1–1	Class 3–1
Livelihood assistance	177,196	145,306	137,533	112,774	103,958	85,239
Addition	—	—	25,000	23,930	16,030	15,280
Subtotal per household	177,196	145,306	162,533	136,704	119,988	100,519
Subtotal per person	44,299	36,327	54,178	45,568	59,994	50,260
Education cost	1,850	1,850	1,850	1,850	—	—
housing cost	13,000	8,000	13,000	8,000	13,000	8,000
Total per household	192,046	155,156	177,383	146,554	132,988	108,519
Total per person	48,012	38,789	59,128	48,851	66,494	54,260

Class 1–1, metropolitan area. Class 3–1, relatively small city.
Source: *Handbook of Health and Welfare Statistics in Japan* [J], 1990, Tokyo, pp. 190f.

TABLE 9.10 Annuity Value of Old-Age Pension per Beneficiary (1980–94, s.y.)

(Unit: ¥ 1,000)

Scheme	1980	1985	1988	1994
Welfare Pension	1,208	1,450	1,570	1,924
(1)	1,566	1,963	2,079	2,442
(2)	1,689	2,100	2,151	2,456
(3)	1,746	2,202	2,298	2,715
(4)	1,300	1,739	1,838	2,174
(5)	1,090	1,466	1,557	1,890
National Pension	269	334	356	448

(1) Mutual aid pension for government officials; (2) mutual aid pension for quasi-government officials; (3) mutual aid pension for local government officials; (4) mutual aid pension for the staff of private schools; (5) mutual aid pension for the staff of associations of agriculture, forestry and fisheries.
Sources: *Statistics on Japanese Standard of Living* [J], 1991, Tokyo, p. 157; *Handbook of Health and Welfare Statistics in Japan* [J], 1995, Tokyo, p. 276.

1990 for this benefit are shown in Table 9.9. It must be said that these values were very low for those who are socially weak and who have lost their livelihood. However, although these values were such that it would be difficult for one to live on them, they were at a level that prevented social crisis.

Looking at the value of old-age pensions, as shown in Table 9.10, there have been large differentials among public pension schemes. Certainly the annuity values of Mutual Aid Pensions and the Welfare pension, especially those of government employees, have been relatively high. However, the average monthly remuneration of the National Pension was very low, at less than ¥30,000 in 1988, and pensioners cannot live on this alone.

TABLE 9.11 Public Pension Participants and Beneficiaries (1980–94, s.y.)

(Unit: 1,000 persons)

Scheme	1980	1985	1988	1994
	Participants			
Total	59,046	58,237	64,925	69,548
Welfare pension	25,239	27,068	28,769	32,740
Seaman insurance	205	166	(138)*	(104)
(1)	1,179	1,161	1,147	1,128
(2)	788	621	526	471
(3)	3,239	3,295	3,272	3,344
(4)	319	347	375	398
(5)	481	488	494	511
National pension	27,596	25,091	30,342	30,956
	Beneficiaries			
Total	18,397	21,549	24,612	30,578
Welfare pension	6,256	7,246	9,279	12,601
Seaman insurance	88	139	(138)	(120)
(1)	372	511	605	746
(2)	388	565	617	635
(3)	737	1,092	1,284	1,654
(4)	42	69	90	148
(5)	95	152	183	251
National pension (insurance)	6,256	8,837	10,962	13,913
National pension (benefit)	4,163	2,938	1,592	630

(1) Mutual aid pension for government officials; (2) mutual aid pension for quasi-government officials; (3) mutual aid pension for local government officials; (4) mutual aid pension for the staff of private schools; (5) mutual aid pension for the staff of associations of agriculture, forestry and fisheries.

* In 1986, integrated into the welfare pension scheme.

Sources: *Handbook of Health and Welfare Statistics in Japan* [J], 1990, p. 259; *op.cit.*, 1995, pp. 274–289.

In addition, as shown in Table 9.11, there were 30.34 million participants (46.7% in all) and 12.55 million beneficiaries (51.0% in all) in this National Pension scheme in 1988, which was the largest pension scheme in terms of the number of participants of all pension schemes in Japan.

However, on the basis of this we cannot conclude that half the households in Japan with elderly couples have lived by means of an income of, at most, ¥60,000 monthly. This is because, first, both the husband and wife are not necessarily together beneficiaries of the National Pension. Second, the income of the aged is not limited only to the pension. There are other possibilities for earned income, assets income etc. Third, there is a possibility, too, that elderly couples live with their children or with relatives.

Taking account of these points, I want to examine in detail the life conditions of the aged. The annuity income of households with an aged couple in 1989 was as follows: for husband, the average was ¥1.54 million and the median was ¥1.6 million; for wives, the average was ¥0.26 million and the median was ¥0.23 million (here, note the large effect of National Pension benefits); the total as a household was ¥1.8 million for both average and median values.[3] Table 9.12 shows the economic conditions for life of

TABLE 9.12 Economic Conditions of the Households Consisting of Elderly Couples (1989)
(Unit: ¥ 10,000)

Item	Mode	Median	Average
Yearly income (Japan)	280–289	338	430 (33%)[(1)]
Monthly living expenditure (Japan)	14.0–14.9	19.5	22.9 (36%)
〃 〃 (Tokyo)	16.0–16.9	22.1	26.8 (35%)
〃 〃 (local)	14.0–14.9	18.1	21.2 (37%)
Amount of savings (Japan)	300–399	1,135	1,956 (30%)
Residential land/houses[(2)] (Japan)	1,400–1,499	2,728	6,488 (24%)
〃 〃 (Tokyo)	15,100–15,199	15,780	24,063 (33%)

(1) Cumulative percentage from above; (2) only for households having them.
Source: Takayama N. Emerging from the Uniform Image of the Aged [J], in: *NM*, June 20, 1992.

households consisting of elderly couples (number of samples 4,743). Table 9.12 was constructed by Professor Takayama Noriyuki, based on the 1989 National Survey of Family Income and Expenditure by the Management and Coordination Agency Japan. On the basis of data presented in Table 9.12, we can say that households consisting of elderly couples had generally stable economic conditions in cases of income, consumption and assets judging by both the average and median and mode values. (The assets values of residential land and houses in Tokyo are, literally, overwhelming.)

Furthermore, comparing the assets holdings in 1989 of general worker households with those of households with people who are not working and who are aged 65 years and over, looking at the ratio of owned homes, the rate in the former group was 68.7%, while the rate in the latter group was 94.8%; with regard to the amount of savings the figures are ¥8.72 million and ¥12.14 million, respectively; in the case of liabilities they are ¥3.53 million and ¥2.98 million, respectively. Thus, in every case, the assets holdings of households consisting of aged people were larger.[4]

However, this does not signify that there is no individual and social problem for aged people and their households in Japan. Still, 4% of all households consisting of an aged couple receive livelihood assistance in 1989.[5] It has been estimated that, as of 1990, there are 700,000 aged people in Japan who are confined to bed (4.6% of the population aged 65 years and over) and one million aged people with senile dementia (6.7% of those aged 65 years and over).[6] Then, the number of aged people who need to be taken care of is approximately 1.3 million, inclusive of the above-mentioned. Of these, 250,000 were long-term inpatients, 150,000 were in special nursing hospices and 10,000 were in hospices. It is assumed that the remainder, some 900,000 people (approximately 70% of the aged who need to be taken care of) are looked after by their family.[7]

The mental, physical and economic burden on these families has been very serious. Furthermore, the care situation for the aged in hospitals and hospices is regrettably not good because of the shortage of professional nurses. Accompanied by a rapid increase in the ratio of aged people in the population, as of 2000, the number of elderly people confined to bed is estimated to be more than one million. Moreover, the total number of elderly people in delicate health or with senile dementia is currently estimated at 1.5 million and is expected to rise to 2.2 million by 2010. Somehow we must comprehensively strengthen measures to cope with the "elderly dominant society".

Notes

1. *WPJE*, 1989, p. 636.
2. *White Paper on Health and Welfare in Japan* [J], 1991. Tokyo: Ministry of Health and Welfare, p. 343.
3. Takayama N. (ed.), *Stock Economy*, *op. cit.*, 1992, pp. 167, 169.
4. *1989 National Survey of Family Income and Expenditure*, Vol. 6, *op. cit.*, pp. 26f.
5. Miyajima H. *Socio-Economics of the "Elderly Dominant Era". Family, Enterprise and Government* [J]. Tokyo: Iwanami Shoten, 1992, p. 219.
6. *White Paper on Health and Welfare in Japan*, 1991, *op. cit.*, p. 272.
7. Nakamura T. Rich Country But Poor Japanese [J]. In: *Weekly Economist*, January 7, 1992, p. 103.

9.3 Housing and Land Problems

The breakdown of Japanese land use in 1987 was as follows: dwelling area 1.55 million ha (4.1% of all), agricultural land 5.44 million ha (14.4%), forests and fields 25.57 million ha (67.7%) and roads and other 5.22 million ha (13.8%). The breakdown by form of ownership of the former three groups into state or public land, privately owned by individuals, private land of corporations was as follows: 17.4%, 63.9%, and 18.7%, respectively, for dwelling areas; 1.8%, 97.1%, and 1.1%, respectively, for agricultural land; and 42.0%, 49.2%, and 8.8%; respectively; for forests and fields.[1]

With regard to housing, of the total number of 37.6 million households in 1988, the 23.03 million households owned their own house (61.3% of all) and 14.11 million households rented a house (37.5%). The further breakdown of the latter figure was 2.8 million rented a publicly owned house, 9.72 million rented privately owned houses and 1.59 million were issued houses (company housing).[2]

Taking account these indices, I will first examine land problems. Setting the land price (average price of residential land), wages (manufacturing, nominal), deposits (interest rate 7%) and consumer prices in 1955 as 100, these indices, after 30 years, became, in 1985, 5,598, 1,818, 761, and 515, respectively. It can be seen that the increase in land price was remarkable.[3]

Moreover, the low interest rate and the long boom in the latter half of the 1980s promoted this tendency. As Table 9.13 shows, the rising wave of land prices spread rapidly from the commercial land of Tokyo in 1986 to the Tokyo metropolitan area in 1987/88 and, after that, to the metropolitan areas of Osaka and Nagoya, and neighboring local major cities. The following examples show how astonishing the increase in land prices then was. First, setting the land price per 1 m^2 in 1987 of Setagaya Ward (a typical residential area in Tokyo ward) as 100, the residential land prices of other cities were as follows: Paris 45.3, Osaka 21.0, London 4.5, Frankfurt 3.0, and Los Angeles 1.0.[4] Second, the total value of all land assets in Japan reached ¥1,673 trillion in 1987, while that in the US was ¥410 trillion. Thus, the former was four-fold the value of the latter.[5] Third, as one more remarkable example, if we were to try and construct a road (width 40 m × length 1.3 km) between Toranomon and Shimbashi for redevelopment of the Shiodome district in the center of Tokyo, purchasing the land on which to build the road would require ¥1 trillion, or 99.7% of the total project costs.[6]

TABLE 9.13 Trends in the Posted Prices of Land (1985–90, s.y., annual change)

(Unit: %)

	1985	1986	1987	1988	1989	1990
Residential						
Tokyo metropolitan area	1.7	3.0	21.5	68.6	0.4	6.6
Osaka metropolitan area	3.0	2.6	3.4	18.6	32.7	56.1
Nagoya metropolitan area	1.6	1.4	1.6	7.3	16.4	20.2
Average in three major metropolitan areas	2.0	2.7	13.7	46.6	11.0	22.0
Average in local areas	2.4	1.7	1.2	1.9	4.4	11.4
Average in Japan	2.2	2.2	7.6	25.0	7.9	17.0
Commercial						
Tokyo metropolitan area	7.2	12.5	48.2	61.1	3.0	4.8
Osaka metropolitan area	5.0	7.0	13.2	37.2	35.6	46.3
Nagoya metropolitan area	2.7	3.3	6.4	16.8	21.0	22.4
Average in three major metropolitan areas	5.8	9.2	30.1	46.6	14.1	18.6
Average in local areas	2.6	2.5	2.9	5.4	7.6	15.4
Average in Japan	3.8	5.1	13.4	21.9	10.3	16.7

Source: *WP-Land*, 1990, p. 100.

Here, land ownership and its economic power in Tokyo will be examined in greater detail, as this has been the focus of the land problem in Japan. The land assets value per land owner in Tokyo increased rapidly by 3.3-fold from ¥78 million in 1982, to ¥80 million in 1983, ¥83 million in 1984, ¥102 million in 1985, ¥187 million in 1986, and ¥258 million in 1987.[7] It is self-evident that this value of ¥258 million is enormous. However, this is even more obvious when we compare it with the ¥2.59 million average value of savings by securities per Japanese household in the same year.

However, because the above-mentioned values are averaged per capita, their content will be examined more closely. The object here is the residential land in Tokyo wards in 1988. This area consists of 35,000 ha and, in 1988, there were 981,000 land owners (excepting partition owners of common houses). These were divided into 906,000 individual owners (92.4%) and 75,000 corporation owners (7.6%). Although there were significantly more individual than corporation owners, the area owned by the former group was 74%, while the latter owned 26%. With regard to the size of the land owned, there were 762,000 land owners with less than 300 m^2 for their own use (77.7% of all) in the case of individual owners and 42,000 corporations (4.3%) in the case of corporation owners who owned similar sized tracts of land. These ratios totaled 82%. The total value of the land assets of the former was ¥116 trillion, while that of the latter was ¥8 trillion, which totaled ¥124 trillion. Because the land assets value of all Tokyo wards was ¥460 trillion, small land owners, accounting for 82% of all land owners, held 27% of all land assets values. Conversely, for land areas of 10,000 m^2 and over, there were 1,800 people (0.2%) and 1,100 corporations (0.1%) owning these areas, which totaled only 0.3% of all land owners. However, the total value of the land assets of the former was ¥38 trillion (8.3%), while that of the latter was ¥58 trillion (12.6%), which totaled ¥96 trillion and 20.9% of all land assets values. In addition, there are land owners with 300–10,000 m^2 land, between the two above-mentioned groups, which, in the case of individual owners, number 142,000 people

(14.5%; ¥188 trillion) and, in the case of corporation owners, 31,000 corporations (3.2%; ¥52 trillion), accounting for 11.3%.

Next, regarding land assets value per capita, individual owners had ¥0.32 billion and corporation owners had ¥1.52 billion, on average. Looking at it by class, even in the case of small land owners with less than 300 m^2, individual owners had land assets of ¥0.15 billion and corporation owners had land assets of ¥0.19 billion, on average. In the case of land owners with 10,000 m^2 and over, individual owners (the majority of whom are farmers in the urbanization promotion area; incidentally, the ratio of farmland in this area was 2.9% in Tokyo wards, 7.5% in Tokyo, 10.0% in the Tokyo metropolitan area, 9.0% in the Osaka metropolitan area, 13.8% in the Nagoya metropolitan area and 12.1% in the whole country in 1989)[8] had ¥21.3 billion and corporation owners had ¥52.9 billion.[9] Thus, residential land owners, including small plot owners in Tokyo, became owners of large assets, with assets values the owners themselves could not believe, during the course of several years during the latter half of the 1980s.

Throughout Japan, enormous capital gain (including of unrealized gain) rose due to a large increase in land prices during this period. For example, the capital gain value in 1986 was ¥164 trillion in the household sector and ¥72 trillion in the corporate sector, totaling ¥236 trillion and, in 1987, these values were ¥255 trillion, ¥104 trillion and, ¥359 trillion total, respectively (the 1987 total value alone was 1.3-fold the national income value (¥278 trillion) in the same year). Although the increasing rate of land prices reduced a little in 1988, these values were ¥85 trillion, ¥47 trillion, and ¥123 trillion total, respectively.[10]

The impetus behind this land price increase has been the intensive buying of land by corporations. At the level of national accounts, the corporate sector was on the buying side (net value) and the household sector was on the selling side (net value) throughout the 1980s. Their net values for the corporate and household sectors were as follows: ¥3.87 trillion and (−)¥6.92 trillion, respectively, in 1985; ¥3.33 trillion and (−)¥6.48 trillion, respectively, in 1986; ¥4.58 trillion and (−)¥8.41 trillion, respectively, in 1987; ¥6.35 trillion and (−)¥11.01 trillion, respectively, in 1988.[11]

The latent assets value of corporations increased rapidly during this period through intensive land buying and increasing land prices. The current price, the book value and the latent assets value of land owned by corporations became vast, being ¥256 trillion, ¥65 trillion, and ¥191 trillion, respectively, in 1985; ¥321 trillion, ¥78 trillion, and ¥243 trillion, respectively, in 1986; ¥418 trillion, ¥93 trillion, and ¥325 trillion, respectively, in 1987; and ¥452 trillion, ¥110 trillion, and ¥342 trillion, respectively, in 1988.[12]

This intensive land buying by corporations was also connected with the land tax system and the accounting code of the corporations. Namely: (1) the interest on loans for land purchases can be fundamentally appropriated as expenditure. (2) Profit and loss through land transfer and those of the main business can be summed up as a measure of tax retrenchment. (3) The payment of municipal property tax can be appropriated as expenditure, and, in the case of deficit corporations, it was exempted. (4) As long as the assets value registered by book value continues, capital gain due to increasing land prices is not taxed. Being different from individuals, inheritance tax is not imposed on corporations. (5) Because the latent assets of land work as collateral, the credibility of the corporation rises.[13] These factors have become reciprocally causes and results and corporate land purchases have developed intensively. The ratio of "originally no intention to use" in the as yet unused land owned by corporations increased from 15% in 1985 (this is the inquiry year; the land was bought 5 years ago) to 26% in 1987 and 50% in 1989. This fact clearly shows that corporations perceiving the advantage of land as assets pursued the buying and holding of land as a self-purpose measure, so to speak, in those years.[14]

Of course, the above-mentioned extraordinary rise of land prices caused by the extreme low-interest policy with land trading surpassing the practical demand did not continue. Actually, as shown in Table 9.12, land prices in Tokyo reached their first ceiling in 1989 and land prices in the whole country began to fall in 1991. The prices of land posted on January 1, 1992, by the National Land Agency fell 4.6%, on average, from the previous year after an interval of 17 years.[15] The outstanding lending value to real estate businesses from financial institutions increased from ¥14.3 trillion in 1983 to ¥59.2 trillion in the middle of 1991. Also, loans from non-banks reached ¥20 trillion in September 1990.[16] Of these, as mentioned in Chapter 5, approximately ¥30 trillion (at least) came to be overdue claims, which is the cause of the insecurity among the management of financial institutions.

Let us now turn our attention to the housing problem. The owned home ratio in Japan was 61.3% on average in the whole country in 1988. Although this value is lower than the 64.1% (1987) in the UK and 63.5% (1985) in the US, it is higher than the 54.9% (1980) in Sweden, 51.2% (1984) in France and 40.1% (1982) in the F.R. Germany.[17] This relatively high ratio of owned homes has been caused by the fact that Japanese people strove to get their own homes in a situation lacking real urban policy or an earnest government public housing policy. The inclination to own a home has been supported and promoted by low-interest loans for employees of large corporations and the following assistance policies of the government. Namely, low-interest loans using the treasury investment and loan funds of the Government Housing Loan Corporation, the substantially lowered municipal property tax, several kinds of deductions for tax assessment by acquisition of housing and the fact that the inheritance tax of land is calculated not by the current price but by roadside value (the latter is approximately half that of the former; furthermore, compare this with 100% assessment of financial assets).[18]

On average, the size of houses in Japan in 1988 was 89.90 m^2 (owned houses 117 m^2; rented houses 45 m^2). Comparing the average floor space of new housing internationally, that in Japan was 83.1 m^2 (1985), while it was 88.6 m^2 in France (1983), 90.0 m^2 in F.R. Germany (1984), 95.1 m^2 in Sweden (1984) and 134.8 m^2 in US (1984).[19] The figure for Japan is certainly low, but not remarkably lower than those of European countries. However, regarding the floor space of housing per capita, it was 25 m^2 (in 1988) in Japan, 31 m^2 in France (1984), 32 m^2 in F.R. Germany (1982), 35 m^2 in UK (1988) and 61 m^2 in US (1985). The figure for Japan is smaller than those of other countries.[20]

Moreover, in Japan (1988), the cost of housing is 5.7-fold an average person's yearly income (8.7-fold in the Tokyo area) and high, in comparison with the 3.4-, 4.4-, and 4.6-fold in the US (1987), the UK (1987) and F.R. Germany (1986), respectively.[21] This Japanese figure is so high it makes the new acquisition of housing in large cities impossible for working people alone. Also, after 1990, when the bubble economy burst, being different from stock prices, land prices have remained at a high level, although they have fallen a little. We must say that it is very difficult for lower-income groups to acquire good housing under the present situation in which households having their own homes are in the majority.

The main cause of high housing prices is high land prices. The rise of land prices may, certainly for the moment, increase the (latent) assets values of individuals and corporations and raise their vitality. However, in the long term, the rise of land prices frustrates socially balanced consumption, makes new investments difficult, hinders efficient investment and leads to demoralizingly large assets differentials. Consequently, it makes stable economic development impossible.[22]

Therefore, the following measures are desirable, namely: (1) there are five kinds of land prices. They are current price, posted price by the National Land Agency, standard price by the prefectural government, roadside value by the National Tax Administration Agency and value for the assessment of municipal property tax by the Ministry of Home Affairs and local government. They must be unified. (2) To return the gain of increasing land prices caused by urban and rural development to society. (3) To tax heavily gains by land transfer, in comparison with the tax for earned income. (4) To improve the new "land price tax" enforced from January 1992 (0.3% (0.2% in the starting year) taxation to the roadside value, but there are many tax-free objects and much basic exemption) to a more systematic land-holding tax. (5) Last, and most importantly, rational urban planning on a long-term basis, supplying good and low-priced public housing.[23]

Notes

1. *WP-Land*, 1990, p. 31.
2. *Statistics on Japanese Standard of Living* [J], 1991. Tokyo: Center of National Life, p. 134.
3. Hasegawa T. *A Viewpoint for Land Reform* [J]. Tokyo: Toyo Keizai Inc., 1990, pp. 6f.
4. *WPIT*, 1990, p. 259.
5. *ESA*, 1990, p. 342; Noguchi Y. *An Essay on Stock Economy* [J]. Tokyo: Chuko Shinsyo, 1991, p. 9.
6. Hasegawa T. *op. cit.*, p. 11. Incidentally, the ratio of the cost of land purchases of the total cost of the paving of roads in Tokyo were as follows: 48.3% in 1983, 53.9% in 1984, 55.5% in 1985, 58.1% in 1986, 66.0% in 1987, 76.3% in 1988, 79.7% in 1989, 78.2% in 1990, 77.8% in 1991, and 73.6% in 1992. Similarly, those costs in the case of the whole country under the control of the Ministry of Construction were 19.3% (in this case, inclusive of compensation costs) in 1983, 19.4% in 1984, 20.1% in 1985, 19.1% in 1986, 20.3% in 1987, 22.5% in 1988, 23.1% in 1989 and 23.6% in 1990 (*WP-Land*, 1994, p. 132).
7. *Annual Report on the National Life in Japan* [J], 1989. Tokyo: Economic Planning Agency, p. 319.
8. *WP-Land*, 1991, p. 147.
9. Hasegawa T. *op. cit.*, pp. 22–25.
10. *WPJE*, 1989, pp. 271, 273, 590.
11. *WPJE*, 1990, p. 537.
12. *WPJE*, 1989, p. 591.
13. Hasegawa T. *op. cit.*, p. 49; Shimono K. *An Economic Analysis of Wealth Inequality* [J]. Nagoya: Nagoya University Press, 1991, pp. 146–169.
14. *WPL*, 1990, pp. 191, ref. 79.
15. *NM* and *AM*, March 27, 1992.

16. Hasegawa T. *op. cit.*, p. 38; *The Weekly Toyo Keizai* [J], January 11, 1992, p. 14; *WP-Land*, 1991, p. 140.
17. *WP-Land*, 1991, p. 178; *WPL*, 1990, p. 448.
18. Kaneko M. "The Formation of Corporate Centricism and Japanese Society" [J]. In: Institute of Social Science (ed.). *Contemporary Japanese Society*, Vol. 5. Tokyo: University of Tokyo Press, 1991, pp. 136f.
19. *Annual Report on the National Life in Japan*, 1989, op. cit., p. 327; Shimada H. *Japanese Economy. Its Contradiction and Regeneration* [J]. Tokyo: Chikuma Shobo, 1991, p. 68.
20. *WPL*, 1990, p. 447.
21. *WPL*, 1990, p. 449.
22. Hasegawa T. *op. cit.*, p. 8.
23. *Ibid.*, pp. 52f, 86f, 113f, 181–187.

9.4 The Structural Changes in the Conditions for Land Price Formation

9.4.1 Recent Trends in Land Prices

The trend of falling land prices (as of January 1, each year) since 1991 continued in 1995, marking the fifth consecutive year of decline. This was naturally the first experience of such a decline in land prices for the Japanese economy after World War II. The posted prices of land announced by the National Land Agency in 1995 were down 10% for commercial land and down 1.6% for residential land from the previous year. The average land prices in the three metropolitan areas were down 14.8% and 2.8%,[1] respectively. These trends were shown similarly in basic land prices (as of June 1, each year) announced by the local government and were down 6.9% for commercial land and down 0.9% for residential land from the previous year.[2]

However, setting the land prices in 1983 as 100, the respective land price indices for residential and commercial properties in the Tokyo Osaka and Nagoya metropolitan areas, and in provincial areas in January 1994 were as follows: Tokyo 179 (residential) and 210 (commercial); Osaka, 176 and 192; Nagoya, 156 and 169; provinces, 146 and 151. These figures suggest that the absolute value of land is still at a very high level, in spite of the recent decline. (Incidentally, the maximum levels of posted prices for residential and commercial properties in 1991 were as follows: 250 and 341, 296 and 389, 191 and 239, and 150 and 170 (1992) for the Tokyo, Osaka and Nagoya metropolitan areas and provincial areas, respectively.[3])

Meanwhile, land taxation has been revised to promote active land transactions, such as the disposition of public lands, the deregulation of urban planning and the pulling back of the land capital gain tax to 32.5% from 39% in the bubble period.[4] Nevertheless, the situation of stagnant land transactions and continuing falls in land prices has not changed fundamentally.

As a result, for example, the revenue from the land price tax in 1995 decreased to ¥401.6 billion, marking the second consecutive year of decline. (Reported cases of land price tax decreased to 24,623, down 12.6% from the previous year.) Incidentally, the top 10 corporations in terms of land price tax for 1995 (in order from first to tenth) are: Mitsubishi Estate Co. (¥6.08 billion), Nippon Life Insurance (¥4.39 billion), NTT

TABLE 9.14 Latent Land Assets of the 21 Major Banks

(Unit: ¥ billion)

Bank name	January 1992	March 1994	March 1995
Dai-Ichi Kangyo Bank	1,650	1,030	784.7
Fuji Bank	1,300	760	600.1
Sakura Bank	1,400	790	592.2
Mitsubishi Bank	1,300	760	587.6
Sanwa Bank	1,200	640	496.6
Sumitomo Bank	1,050	610	449.9
Asahi Bank	900	520	419.3
Daiwa Bank	650	360	272.3
Tokai Bank	550	320	246.6
Bank of Tokyo	300	n.a.	124.3
Hokkaido Takushoku Bank	250	n.a.	105.5
City banks, subtotal	10,550	6,120	4,679.1
Industrial Bank of Japan			177.3
Long-Term Credit Bank of Japan			63.2
Nippon Credit Bank			56.8
Long-term credit banks, subtotal		370	297.3
Sumitomo Trust and Banking			66.6
Yasuda Trust and Banking			64.3
Toyo Trust and Banking			34.7
Mitsui Trust and Banking			32.9
Nippon Trust and Banking			23.0
Chuo Trust and Banking			6.5
Mitsubishi Trust and Banking			n.a.
Trust banks, subtotal		300	228.1
The 21 major banks, total		6,790	5,204.5

Sources: *NM*, January 18, 1994; *NM*, August 17, 1995; *NM*, January 26, 1996.

(¥4.02 billion), Mitsui Fudosan Co. (¥3.03 billion), Dai-ichi Mutual Life (¥2.91 billion), Seibu Railway Co. (¥2.63 billion), East Japan Railway (¥2.51 billion), Sumitomo Life Insurance (¥2.30 billion), Nippon Steel Corp. (¥2.28 billion), and Dai-Ichi Kangyo Bank (¥2.06 billion).[5]

Regulated by the above-mentioned trends in land prices, the total of Japan's land assets on a macroeconomic level changed from ¥889 trillion in 1983 to a peak of ¥2,389 trillion in 1990 (the difference concerning the maximal figure is based on the grounds that the posted land price is calculated at the beginning of the year, while the statistics on national wealth are calculated at the end of the year). This figure later decreased to ¥2,197 trillion in 1991, down 8% from the previous year, and to ¥1,968 trillion in 1992, down 10.4%.

The value of land latent assets of the major financial institutions has been declining considerably in the meantime. For example, the value of latent land assets of the 21 major banks is shown in Table 9.14. It appears that the total value decreased from ¥6.79 trillion in 1994 to ¥5.20 trillion in 1995. With regard to city banks only, the total amount decreased from ¥10.55 trillion in January 1992 to ¥6.12 trillion in March 1994 and ¥4.68 trillion in March 1995. This reduction is approximately ¥6 trillion in terms of absolute value and nearly half in terms of ratio.

TABLE 9.15 Trends in Condominium Prices (1989–1993)

(Unit: ¥ million; in parenthesis, price per 1 m^2 ¥ 1,000)

Year	1989	1990	1991	1992	1993
Area					
Tokyo metropolitan area	54.11	61.23	59.00	50.66	44.88
	(797)	(934)	(910)	(800)	(704)
Osaka metropolitan area	39.90	52.79	55.52	44.02	38.79
	(562)	(741)	(750)	(573)	(531)
Average in Japan	38.33	44.03	44.88	39.38	37.37
	(579)	(694)	(667)	(576)	(547)
Annual change of the average price in Japan	22.0%	14.9%	1.9%	−12.3%	−5.1%
	(20.6%)	(19.9%)	(−3.9%)	(−13.6%)	(−5.0%)

Source: *WP-Land*, 1994, p. 30.

9.4.2 *Trends in Condominium Prices and the Outbreak of Latent Losses*

After the collapse of the bubble economy, peaking in 1990/91, the prices of condominium units decreased in major urban areas as well as in the whole country, as shown in Table 9.15.

Consequently, the average price of condominiums (for example, in the case of a 70 m^2 condominium) fell rather remarkably from 8.5-fold a worker's average yearly income during the peak year of 1990 to 5.8-fold a worker's annual salary in 1993. However, this figure is still higher than 5.4-fold in 1983, 4.9-fold in 1984, 4.7-fold in 1985 and 4.5-fold in 1986,[6] and, if we take into account an area of 70 m^2, we must say that this absolute value of 5.8-fold is still unreasonably high.

Related to this, according to a survey conducted by the Real Estate Association, 120,000 condominiums, equivalent to 80% of the 148,000 available in the Tokyo metropolitan area between 1988 and 1992, held latent losses as of the end of 1993 and the total value reached ¥2 trillion. In addition, according to results of a survey conducted by the real estate business, in the whole national market, inclusive of privately-owned houses, latent losses of approximately ¥10 trillion were experienced.[7]

Furthermore, affected by falling land prices, decreases in the value of existing housing assets are continuing. In particular, there is a marked decrease in the assets value of condominiums. For example, the latent losses of condominiums purchased in the Tokyo metropolitan area since 1988 reached a total of ¥4 trillion in 1995.[8]

This is the first experience in Japan of falling assets in the field of housing and land problems since Word War II. Hitherto, in cases of both houses and condominiums that are owned privately, latent assets had always developed, while latent losses never developed as a socially significant phenomenon, with some individual exceptions. In reality, the reasons why many people made an effort to acquire a house in spite of their very high values compared internationally are not only because there are few good and low-priced houses for rent, but also because of the continuance after World War II of the fact that even if one purchased one's own house with a loan, one could sell the house, if necessary, at a price that was much greater than the purchase price. In this respect, people owning their own houses, including those with loans, have always been the owners of latent assets (profit). However, at present, after the collapse of the bubble economy, this situation appears to have changed for the first time.

The emergence of the above-mentioned large latent losses of land, caused mainly by the recent fall in land prices, may be the beginning of either the process of self-disintegration of exorbitant housing (land) prices in Japan or of the turnabout of the hitherto ascending price spiral. I think this a reasonable possibility, considering the decreasing proportion of young people in Japan over the long term, a quantitatively excessive supply of housing in recent years and the introduction of a land price tax, as well as the correction of official estimated land prices.

9.4.3 Tendency Towards Excessive Supply of Available Office Space

The primary motive for the extraordinary rise in land prices during the bubble economy in the latter half of the 1980s was the forecast of a shortage of available office space in the near future in the commercial districts of Tokyo, whose international economic position was rising rapidly. This forecast was created by both the government and by non-governmental institutions. Under their guidance, a large amount of money was invested in the purchase of Tokyo real estate. Consequently, the extraordinary rise of land prices began and spread to other large cities and then to the whole of Japan.

The total office floor space both in the Tokyo metropolitan area and in the whole country increased throughout the bubble economy period and the total amount available was approximately double that available in 1983. After 1991, office space started to decrease, but still the total space available in the Tokyo area as well as in the whole country was 1.9- and 1.6-fold, respectively that in 1983.[9]

In this situation, after the collapse of the bubble economy, an excessive supply of office space (buildings) has been realized in Tokyo and other large cities. Particularly, in Tokyo, the office vacancy rates of big high-rise buildings recently constructed have reached an incredible 40%–100% in almost all cases. Furthermore, there are still many plans to construct new buildings and this situation allows us to forecast a more excessive supply of available office space in the future.[10] Especially in Tokyo wards, office vacancy rates reached nearly 1% in mid-1990, but they have became 10% in mid-1994, a figure that was far higher than the proper stock sales ratio (i.e. office vacancy rates) of 5%. Under these circumstances, office building rents in Tokyo and major cities began to drop after 1992 and a "reverse phenomenon" appeared, where rents for office space for new tenants were cheaper than those for old tenants.[11]

9.4.4 Change in Land Prices Over the Long Term and the Burst of the Bubble Economy

To consider the significance of falling land prices in recent years, as mentioned above, I would like to set them in the postwar Japanese economy in the long term.

The recent serious fall of land prices is a first for the Japanese economy, except for the temporary price decline in 1975. Until the collapse of the bubble economy, the following land myths prevailed in Japan: "land prices do not fall absolutely" and "one

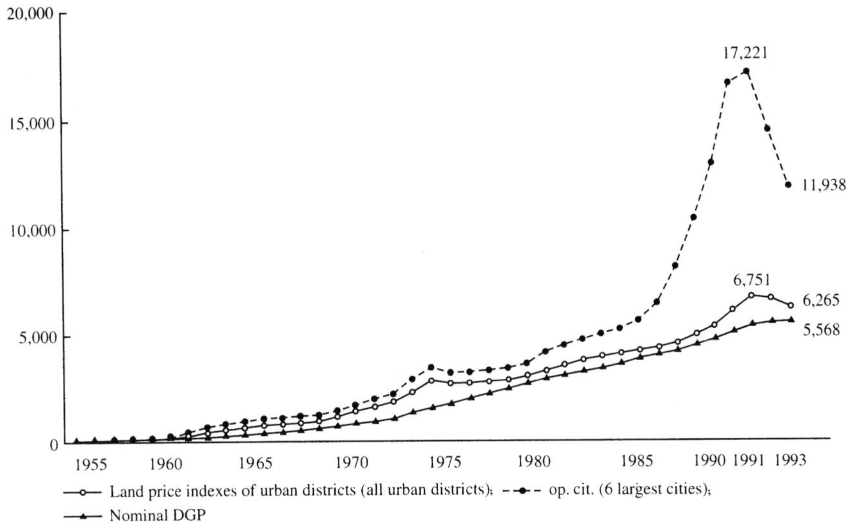

FIG. 9.1 Trends in Land Prices and GDP (Index: 1955 = 100)
Source: *WP-Land*, 1995, p. 93.

who purchases land, even if by borrowed money, never suffers a loss". Actually, there was a real basis for these myths. For example, from 1955 to 1985, in terms of nominal index, while the consumer price index was 5.1-fold higher, deposit money (on the assumption of 7% in a year) was 7.6-fold larger and wages were 17.4-fold higher, while land prices were a surprising 56.1-fold higher. Land prices increased three-fold more than wages, 7.4-fold more than deposit money and 11-fold more than the consumer price index.[12]

There are some reasons why these land myths survived until the end of the bubble economy. Before 1985 (i.e. before the bubble economy), the balance between land prices and other prices was such that economic growth would catch up with preceding land prices even after several years delay. However, this state of equilibrium was definitely destroyed during the period of the bubble economy.[13]

Looking at Figure 9.1, it can be seen that because of the steep rise in land prices in the latter half of the 1980s, the balanced state that had been barely kept between the GDP and land prices was clearly broken. According to trial calculations of Professor Hasegawa Tokunosuke, in order that the GDP could catch up with land prices during the peak period, it would take approximately 30 years (until 2020) to dissolve the bubble, even if one optimistically estimates the nominal growth rate of the GDP to be 4% annually (this figure appears to be almost impossible, as Hasegawa also recognizes[14]). It was inevitable and necessary that these steeply rising land prices could not be sustained.

However, the absolute level of land prices is still very high. It is too high in comparison with profitability for commercial land and with consumer income for residential land. Hereafter, land prices as a whole must move, regulated not by capital gain, but by income gain, towards prices reduced by revenue.[15]

Incidentally, the outstanding amount of loans and discounts by banks to the real estate business reached ¥61.8 trillion in March 1995. If we also add to this the loans and discounts by the private housing finance companies (*jusen*), non-banks and insurance companies, it reached more than ¥100 trillion, with the total amount of loans and discounts by banks to real estate business, non-banks and the construction industry reaching ¥156 trillion at the end of 1994.[16] We must estimate that a considerable part of this figure, at least half, represents bad loans (bad claims). These bad claims (i.e. land stocks) must be disposed of and they will necessarily lower land prices.

However, under the present circumstances, land transactions are stagnant. For example, regarding the bad loans purchased by the Joint Claim Purchase Institution before March 1995, the purchase cases were 5,197 pieces, the purchased value was ¥3.82 trillion and the principal value was ¥8.56 trillion. Its loss rate was 55.3%, which means disposal at approximately half price. The most important aspect is recovery of the principal value. In this respect, the amount of loans actually recovered by sales in the bad loans purchased by this institution was only ¥171.7 billion, which was 2% of the whole principal, 98% of which was put aside.[17]

At any rate, without actual land transactions, there is no real solution to the bad loan problem. This is by no means a question of rewriting the balance sheets of financial institutions. However, actual land transactions remain inactive. The main reason for this is that the absolute level of land prices is still too high.

Although land prices affected by the bubble economy have reduced considerably from the present land prices, they are still very high. Certainly there are some places with lower land prices than during the bubble period. However, as a whole, land prices affected by the bubble economy have not yet reached a reasonable level. In addition, excessively high-priced land, for which price increases surpassed the growth rate of GDP for a long time, will decrease ever further. The tendency, in which the ascending spiral of land prices in the latter half of the 1980s turned into a descending spiral after the collapse of the bubble economy, will continue. Namely, land prices in Japan, which were formed and promoted by the conditions of the large corporation system, the corporation-centered society and corporate capitalism, have begun to disintegrate and will fall further.

9.4.5 Dramatic Changes in the Conditions for the Formation of Land Prices

The fall of land prices after the burst of the bubble economy was caused directly by successive increase in the official discount rate after May 1989, by the notification of the chief of the Banking Bureau in the MOF relating to the regulation of the total amount of the loans for land purchase in March 1990 and by the enactment of the Land Price Tax Law in May 1991. However, the fall in land prices was basically caused by the self-disintegration of the steep rise in land prices formed by the conditions of the large corporation system, the corporation-centered society and corporate capitalism.

In recent years, with regard to the conditions for the formation of land prices, epoch-making changes have taken place.[18] To begin with, on the demand side, speculative demands have almost disappeared and actual demands play a central role in the market. Normally, demand for land/real estate has a stable relationship with the increase in the population and in number of households. In Japan, the ratio of households who own their own house surpasses two-thirds. The average birth rate is 1.5 people and there will be no large increase in household number in the future. In addition, as the Japanese economy enters into a period of maturity, its growth rate will be approximately 3% or less. Furthermore, the large population movements of the past from rural districts to big cities will not recur. Taking account of these factors, there is no possibility for an abrupt increase in demand for land/real estate. Due to the fixation of the strong yen, the economic activities abroad of Japanese enterprise will increase still more. Thus, the demand for collective office/factory area will continue to decrease. Currently, there is almost no structural element in Japan to push up land prices on a long-term basis.

In contrast, the supply pressure of land/real estate is increasing steadily. First, due to the enforcement of the same taxation rate as residential land for farmland within the urbanization promotion area, 30,000 ha farmland neighboring big cities will become residential land hereafter. Only in the Tokyo metropolitan area (Tokyo, Kanagawa, Chiba and Saitama) are the farmers who have a total of 18,500 ha farmland in the urbanization promotion area able to choose the way in which to convert their farmland to residential land. The area involved amounts to 35.9-fold (or years) as much as the average of 515.4 ha, which was made available each year as new residential land in the same region from 1975 to 1984.[19] Second, the 830,000 ha of rice farmland which, due to government policy, is currently lying unused, may be converted for urban use because of the increasing liberalization of the rice market. This area represents an area equal to that of all current residential land in Japan. Third, in contrast with the demand side, because the traditional heavy and chemical industries usually have very extensive land holdings for factories and they must sell these lands for restructuring, their existing collective factory areas and water-front land will convert to residential land. Fourth, the introduction of fixed leaseholds will cause a decrease in the demand for landownership. Fifth, perhaps the strongest supply pressure will come from the mobilization of the massive land holdings that the financial institutions financed and that have now become bad loans/assets.

As a result, the land/real estate market has completely changed from a seller's market to a buyer's market. In this situation, the above-mentioned factors (i.e. the deregulation of land administration by the government, the pulling back of the land capital gain tax and/or the pulling back of the land price tax (after 1996 from 0.3% to 0.15%, after 1998 to 0%)), will not cause a rise in land prices.

What kind of influences do these fundamental changes in the conditions for the formation of land prices have? What is the significance of falling land prices for the Japanese economy? First, they will make the disposition of bad loans for the financial institutions more difficult, because the fall of the collateral value reduces still more a withdrawal of loans. Second, because of the reduction of the latent land assets value of enterprise, there will come about a decrease in the source for the covering of deficits or a shortage of funds for restructuring. Third, these conditions are apparently favorable for people who do not have their own land/real estate to purchase their own house. This then makes greater demands on the construction sector and causes business trends to improve. Fourth, it is obvious that high land prices have made the establishment of promising venture business and the new entry of domestic and foreign capital more difficult. Therefore, the decline in land prices enhances the vitality of the Japanese economy and will benefit consumers because of the establishment of new enterprise in advanced industries and the activation of competition among enterprises.

Thus, "the fall in land prices brings frictional phenomena in the short term, but contributes to the normalization of the Japanese economy in the long term."[20] This means the appearance of new conditions that facilitate the improvement of poor housing conditions in Japan (very conspicuous among advanced countries) and, furthermore, the dramatic improvement of social capital and the environment in cities. The continuous fall in land prices in Japan may become an important lever to convert the corporation-centered society into a civil society.

Notes

1. *WP-Land*, 1995, p. 408.
2. *NM*, September 20, 1995.
3. *WP-Land*, 1994, pp. 88–97.
4. Hasegawa T. Wound by the bubble economy cannot be cured by bubble economy [J]. In: *NM*, July 31, 1995.
5. *AE*, January 16, 1996.
6. *WP-Land*, 1994, p. 137.
7. *NM*, December 11, 1993.
8. *NE*, August 18, 1995.
9. *WP-Land*, 1994, pp. 211f.
10. In more detail, refer to *The Weekly Toyo Keizai* [J], April 9, 1994, p. 13; *Weekly Economist* [J], June 28, 1994, p. 41.
11. *The Weekly Toyo Keizai* [J], *op. cit.*, pp. 10–14; *Weekly Economist* [J], *op. cit.*, pp. 40–43.
12. Hasegawa T. (ed.). *The Collapse of a Land Standard Economy* [J]. Tokyo: Sogo Horei Shuppan, 1995, p. 165.
13. Hasegawa T. The Purchase of Land by Public Body [J]. In: *The Weekly Toyo Keizai*, August 12/19, 1995, pp. 44, 46.
14. *Ibid.*
15. Hasegawa T. *op. cit.*. In: *NM*, July 31, 1995; do., The Irreversible Change and No Soft Landing [J]. In: *Weekly Economist*, November 21, 1995, pp. 69f.
16. Hasegawa T. *op. cit.*. In: *The Weekly Toyo Keizai*, August 12/19, 1995, p. 45; *The Weekly Toyo Keizai* [J], December 9, 1995, p. 13; *ESA*, 1994, pp. 192f.
17. Hasegawa T. *op.cit.*, August 12/19, 1995, p. 46.
18. The description below is mainly based on the following articles: Hasegawa T. *op. cit.*, *NM*, July 31, 1995; Noguchi Y. The fall of land prices is a source for the normalization of Japanese economy [J]. In: *NM*, July 21, 1995.
19. However, with regard to the object of 1,000 m^2 and over, which was provided by private business, see: Koda M. Six important points destroying land myth in Japan [J]. In: *Weekly Economist*, March 21, 1995, p. 36.
20. Noguchi Y. *op. cit.*.

Conclusion

The Japanese large corporation system has developed with its foundation in the stable industrial relations of the internal structure, and involving various social strata, including farmers and the self-employed, within its ruling structure. This large corporation system has evolved, as mentioned above, while developing a minutely differentiated hierarchic structure in all sides of society. However, until now, the social contradictions in Japan have been mitigated by the results and distribution of the benefits of economic development, and the large corporation system is fundamentally stable.

The excess profit acquired by large corporations inside and out of the country has been widely distributed among the upper and middle strata of employees and, with respect to the income levels of Japanese people, there exists a wide middle strata that is socially stable. Today, of course, employees and workers cannot be regarded en masse as weak members of society (i.e. the socially disadvantaged). For example, white collar workers, staff, administrators and technical experts can be designated as the new social middle classes, whose number and social significance increases further with the remarkable development of innovation and information. These classes, or strata, are definitely not the socially weak, as we can see when they are compared with the lower strata, or the periphery, such as the unemployed and employees without stable employment. The situation is the same for the greater part of employees organized in labor unions. As a result of the labor union movement, these employees are no longer in the position of the socially weak.

However, even so, social problems have not disappeared in Japan. First, the unemployed and employees without stable employment do exist, and these groups suffer from a lack of rights and low wages. In addition, there are those literally socially weak, who are including:

"people who cannot live by themselves and need support, 1.2 million persons; the aged in need of support inclusive of those who are bedridden or who live alone, 4.4 million persons; the physically or mentally handicapped (children and adults), 5 million persons; one-parent families, 1.8 million persons; children who need protection, 0.5 million persons; and following them, those with war injuries, tubercular patients, patients with incurable diseases, and so on, with all the above, totaling around 13 million persons. Moreover there are others, whose number we cannot grasp: women in need of protection, men in need of correction and protection, the low-income groups, and so on."[1]

Until now, it has been a basic fact that the development of the large corporation system in Japan, especially of its wide and minute differential structure, has made a majority of diligent and conciliatory Japanese people subordinate to the collective interest but able to enjoy a satisfactory life with respect to material conditions; that is, the majority of Japanese people have become rich. An essential reason for this fact is that the differential structure has been a very favorable objective ground for capital to organize the competition among employees and has offered very efficient conditions in which to organize workshops in factories. In other words, workers and employees have put their confidence for life in the step-by-step improvement of their social positions (compared with their past and with people around them) by cooperating with capital rather than becoming involved with radical labor unions or in the universal solidarity of the people.

However, in the current stagnation and confusion in the Japanese economy following the burst of the "bubble economy", the large corporation system is compelled to reorganize itself. Because the strong counterprinciples to capitalism (e.g. religion with transcendental and absolute values, radical labor movements or social movements etc.) do not exist or are very weak in Japan, a collapse of the existing system and/or a dramatic change to the system are unlikely. However, the reorganization of the system is inevitable if we wish to realize stable and continuous economic development and a genuinely comfortable life for each individual. Maybe the reorganization will proceed tentatively in the form of a gradual coordination of each group's interest. Contemporary Japan is an affluent and conservative society in terms of both income and assets, where wealthy people form a majority and, of course, it is most unlikely that they hope for or will accept a radical social change.

If a change were actually possible, a calm, progressive and democratic change would be desirable. The ideal elements of such a change include the following: internationally, faithful fulfillment of postwar compensation to East Asia, including compensation for individuals; fair and democratic aid to the developing world; a contribution to the solution of worldwide environmental and resource problems; and the coexistence of nations. Domestically, the restoration of civil society instead of a corporation-centered society; specifically, the formation of a society where work values take priority over assets values, democracy takes precedence over authority, and both the freedom of individuals and social solidarity exist together and a fulfilling social security system exists. The appropriate social change can be made possible only through the realization of a political bloc between a majority of employees and the socially weak. The decisive condition for this depends on whether the upper and middle strata of employees and independent individuals who participate in labor union movements, as well as various social movements, do not simply demand an improvement in their own conditions and the rise of their own social positions, but pursue, in earnests, a policy for solidarity with the lower strata of employees and the socially weak. For this purpose, the former group must be ready to make partial sacrifices in the interests of the latter, according to circumstances.

Now, how can we define the contemporary Japanese society from the standpoint of the concept of civil society? On the basis of legal and institutional factors, I would characterize Japanese society on the whole as "a distorted civil society".[2] However, if we look at the country from the viewpoint of the mode of thought and behavior of the individuals who are the subjective factor in the society, I would characterize Japan as essentially "a highly developed industrial society without civil society",[3] which lacks remarkably independent individuals.

It is very difficult for us to judge immediately which definition is correct. My conclusion for the present is to define the Japanese society as an "immature civil society", according to the concept of civil society as the ideal type.

Just as military values were excessively strong in prewar Japan, economic values have been overwhelmingly superior to other social values in postwar Japan. This imbalance in the system of social values disturbs the sound development of society in the long run. Even if economic values are primary or hegemonic in Japan, one should not forget the political dimension. However, the condition of politics in Japan approximates that of brain death.[4] It is once again necessary for us to achieve a balanced and organic development embracing policy, economy, urban and rural life, culture, art and science, civil society and the overall development of individuals within society.

Notes

1. Shinoda T. The Restoration of Solidarity. Asked Social Function of "Federation of Japan Labor Unions" [J]. In: *Sekai* (World), March 1990. Tokyo: Iwanami Shoten p. 91.

2, 3. I am extremely grateful to Professor Bob Jessop of the Department of Sociology at Lancaster University for his advice on these concepts.

4. If a civil society tries to get the hegemony of the political society while maintaining the immanent principles of civil society, the civil society itself must be politicized. More precisely, it must be politically mature. (In this respect, it is significant that both the Latin and Greek words meaning civil society (*societas civilis* and *politikē koinōnia*, respectively) signified originally the community of citizens as political sovereigns of the city state; i.e., the actual political society. See, Murakami J. Civil society. In: *An Encyclopedia of Philosophy and Thought* [J]. Tokyo: Iwanami Shoten, 1998, p. 683. Although politics does not impinge upon all relations in civil society (otherwise, the autonomy of civil society is not secured), politics permeates its economic foundations. This fact has to be recognized. In addition, even if we stress the predominance of civil society vis-à-vis the state and civil society's independence from the state, the problem remains of how civil society gets control of and develops the economic abilities that belong to the state and the strata whose interests are bound up with it. This is one of the most fundamental problems.

Bibliography

1. Statistics, Bulletins and Government Publications

A Comprehensive Survey of Japanese Corporate Groups [J]. Tokyo: Toyo Keizai Inc.

Annual Report on Financial Statements of Incorporated Business [J]. Tokyo: Ministry of Finance.

Annual Report on National Accounts. Tokyo: Economic Planning Agency.

Annual Report on the Consumer Price Index. Tokyo: Management and Coordination Agency.

Annual Report on the Labour Force Survey. Tokyo: Management and Coordination Agency.

Annual Report on the National Life [J]. Tokyo: Economic Planning Agency.

Annual Report on World Economy [J]. Tokyo: Economic Planning Agency.

Balance of Payments Monthly. Tokyo: Bank of Japan.

Comparative Economic and Financial Statistics, Japan and Other Major Countries. Tokyo: Bank of Japan.

Defense of Japan [J]. Tokyo: Defense Agency.

Economic Statistics Annual. Tokyo: Bank of Japan.

Economic Statistics Yearbook [J]. Tokyo: Toyo Keizai Inc.

Employment Status Survey. Tokyo: Management and Coordination Agency.

Family Savings Survey. Tokyo: Management and Coordination Agency.

Fiscal Statistics [J]. Tokyo: Ministry of Finance.

Fundamental Survey of the National Life in Japan [J]. Tokyo: Ministry of Health and Welfare.

Handbook of Health and Welfare Statistics in Japan [J]. Tokyo: Ministry of Health and Welfare.

Handbook of Labour Statistics in Japan [J]. Tokyo: Ministry of Labour.

Indicators of Science and Technology. Tokyo: Science and Technology Agency.

Japan, An International Comparison. Tokyo: Keizai Koho Center.

Japan Company Handbook, Quarterly. Tokyo: Toyo Keizai Inc.

Japan Economic Almanac. Tokyo: The Japan Economic Journal.

Japanese Overseas Investment. A Complete Listing by Firms and Countries [J]. Tokyo: Toyo Keizai Inc.

Ministry of Finance Statistics Monthly [J]. Tokyo: Ministry of Finance.

National Survey of Family Income and Expenditure. Tokyo: Management and Coordination Agency.

Nippon, Business Facts and Figures. Tokyo: Jetro.
Opinion Research on Savings [J]. Tokyo: Central Committee of Public Information for Savings.
Price Indexes Annual. Tokyo: Bank of Japan.
Prices Report [J]. Tokyo: Economic Planning Agency.
Report on the Special Survey of the Labour Force Survey [J]. Tokyo: Management and Coordination Agency.
Securities Market in Japan. Tokyo: Japan Securities Research Institute.
Statistical Appendix of White Paper on Agriculture Japan [J]. Tokyo: Association of Agriculture and Forestry Statistics.
Statistical Handbook of Japan. Tokyo: Management and Coordination Agency.
Statistical Yearbook of the National Tax Administration Agency Japan [J]. Tokyo.
Statistics on Japanese Standard of Living [J]. Tokyo: Center of National Life.
The Investigation Results of Income Redistribution [J]. Tokyo: Ministry of Health and Welfare.
The Weekly Toyo Keizai [J]. Tokyo: Toyo Keizai Inc.
Weekly Economist [J]. Tokyo: Mainichi Newspapers Co.
White Paper of JETRO, Investment Part and *Foreign Trade Part* [J]. Tokyo: Jetro.
White Paper on Agriculture Japan [J]. Tokyo: Association of Agriculture and Forestry Statistics.
White Paper on Construction [J]. Tokyo: Ministry of Construction.
White Paper on Crime Japan [J]. Tokyo: Ministry of Justice.
White Paper on Health and Welfare in Japan [J]. Tokyo: Ministry of Health and Welfare.
White Paper on International Trade Japan [J]. Tokyo: Ministry of International Trade and Industry.
White Paper on Japanese Economy [J]. Tokyo: Economic Planning Agency.
White Paper on Labour in Japan [J]. Tokyo: Ministry of Labour.
White Paper on Land in Japan [J]. Tokyo: National Land Agency.
White Paper on Local Government Finance [J]. Tokyo: Ministry of Home Affairs.
White Paper on Small Enterprises in Japan [J]. Tokyo: Small and Medium Enterprise Agency.
White Paper on Working Hours in Japan [J]. Tokyo: Ministry of Labour.
Yearbook of Labour Statistics. Tokyo: Ministry of Labour.

2. Books and Articles

Abe, Kinya. *What is "Seken"?* [J]. Tokyo: Kodansha Gendai Shinsho, 1995.
Abe, Kinya. *Living in Japanese Society* [J]. Tokyo: Asahi Shinbunsha, 1999.
Abo, Tetsuo. *The Japanese Management and Production System and the United States: International Transfer of the System and the Hybrids* [J]. Kyoto: Minerva Shobo, 1994.
Akai, Shoji. "Civil Society" as Sociological Concept: Contents Analysis of News Stories [J]. In: *RSSR*, Vol. 34, No. 1, June, 1998.
Albert, Michel. *Capitalisme contre Capitalisme*. Paris: Editions du Seuil, 1991.
Aoki, Masahiko. *Information, Incentives and Bargaining in the Japanese Economy*. Cambridge: Cambridge University Press, 1988.

Aoki, Masahiko and Dore, Ronald P. (eds) *The Japanese Firm: Sources of Competitive Strength*. New York: Oxford University Press Inc., 1994.
Aoki, Masahiko, Koike, Kazuo and Nakatani, Iwao. *The Economics of the Japanese Firm* [J]. Tokyo: TBS Britannica, 1986.
Aoyama, Shigeki. "The Development of Overseas Production of Japanese-Style Management." In: The Business Administration Society of Japan (ed.). *Reexamination of Japanese-Style Management* [J]. Tokyo: Chikura Shobo, 1990.
Arato, Andrew and Cohen, Jean. (tr. Akai Shoji, Saito Mao and Shinohara Shoichi) The Rise, Decline and Reconstruction of the Concept of Civil Society, and Direction for Future Research. In: *RSSR*, Vol. 32, No. 4, March, 1997.
Asahi Newspaper, Department of Economic Affairs. *Financial Upheaval: Can We Restore the Economic System* [J]? Tokyo: Asahi Shinbunsha, 1999.
Atkinson, David. The writing-off of bad loans is now only in the balance sheet [J]. In: NM, June 1, 1995.
Atkinson, David. The Actual Situation of the Bad Loans' Write-off [J]. In: *Weekly Economist*, June 13, 1995.
Atkinson, David. The waiting stance of the banks is permitted only in Japan [J]. In: *Weekly Economist*, October 10, 1995.
Baba, Hiroji. *"Fuyu-ka" (Becoming Wealthier) and Financial Capital* [J]. Kyoto: Minerva Shobo, 1986.
Baba, Masao. *Japanese Economy: Observation and Analysis* [J]. Nagoya: University of Nagoya Press, 1988.
Coriat, Benjamin. *Penser a l'Envers: Travail et Organisation dans L'Entreprise Japonaise*. Paris: Christian Bourgois Editeur, 1991.
Domon, Takeshi. The Irresponsible Covenant Is More Important Than the Memorandum [J]. In: *Weekly Economist*, January 23, 1996.
Dore, Ronald P. *British Factory-Japanese Factory: The Origins of National Diversity in Industrial Relations*. Berkeley: University of California Press, 1973.
Dore, Ronald P. (tr. Tamaru, Nobuo.) *Sociology of Trade Friction: Japan and Britain*. Tokyo: Iwanami Shinsho, 1986.
Economic Planning Agency (ed.). *Laying the Track of the Postwar Japanese Economy: The 50-Year History of the Economic Planning Agency* [J]. Tokyo: Printing Bureau, Ministry of Finance, 1997.
Eguchi, Eiichi. *The Contemporary Low-Income Stratum*, (3 Vols.) [J]. Tokyo: Miraisha, 1979.
Fujimoto, Takeshi. *International Comparison: Japanese Worker* [J]. Tokyo: Shinnihon Shuppansha, 1990.
Fukuda, Yusuke and Dore, Ronald *What would Japan be without Japanese-Style Capitalism* [J]. Tokyo: Kobunsha, 1993.
Furukawa, Masanori. *Administrative Capitalism and Heisei Recession* [J]. Kyoto: Minerva Shobo, 1999.
Futatsugi, Yusaku. *Corporate Groups in Contemporary Japan: Towards an Analysis on Large Business* [J]. Tokyo: Toyo Keizai Inc., 1976.
Galbraith, John Kenneth. *The New Industrial State*, 2nd edn. Boston: Houghton Mifflin Co., 1972.
Gendai Kigyo Kenkyu-Kai (ed.). *Inter-Corporate Relations in Japan: Theory and Case Studies* [J]. Tokyo: Chuo-Keizaisha, 1994.

Giner, Salvador. "Civil Society and its Future." In: Hall J.A. (ed.). *Civil Society: Theory, History, Comparison*. Cambridge: Polity Press, 1995.

Goto, Michio. "From the Non-'Civil Society' to the 'Japanese-Style Mass Society'." In: Watanabe Osamu (ed.). *Contemporary Japanese Society* [J]. Tokyo: Rodo Junposha, 1996.

Goto, Michio and Ito, Masanao. *Lectures on Contemporary Japan, Vol. 2: Modern Imperialism and Reorganization of the World Order* [J]. Tokyo: Ohtsuki Shoten, 1997.

Goto, Shin'ichi. The Structure of the Financial Bankruptcy [J]. In *Sekai*, Tokyo: Iwanami Shoten, April, 1996.

Hall, John A (ed.). *Civil Society: Theory, History, Comparison*. Cambridge (UK): Polity Press, 1995.

Hanada, Tatsuro. *The Social Space in the Name of Public Sphere: Public Sphere, Media and Civil Society* [J]. Tokyo: Bokutakusha, 1996.

Hasegawa, Tokunosuke. *A Viewpoint for Land Reform* [J]. Tokyo: Toyo Keizai Inc., 1990.

Hasegawa, Tokunosuke (ed.). *The Collapse of a Land Standard Economy* [J]. Tokyo: Sogo Horei Shuppan, 1995.

Hasegawa, Tokunosuke. Wound by the bubble economy cannot be cured by bubble economy [J]. In: NM, July 31, 1995.

Hasegawa, Tokunosuke. The Purchase of Land by Public Body [J]. In: *The Weekly Toyo Keizai*, August 12/19, 1995.

Hasegawa, Tokunosuke. The Irreversible Change and No Soft Landing [J]. In: *Weekly Economist*, November 21, 1995.

Hasegawa, Tokunosuke. The Coming Explosion in Land Supply [J]. In: *Weekly Economist,* September 22, 1998.

Hashimoto, Juro. *The Japanese Economy: The 20th Century System and Japanese Economy* [J]. Kyoto: Minerva Shobo, 1991.

Hatta, Tatsuo. Now Is the Chance to Introduce the Taxpayer Number [J]. In: *Weekly Economist*, November 2, 1993.

Hatta, Tatsuo. Six Myths Concerning the Consumption Tax [J]. In: *NM*, May 20–26, 1994.

Hayashi, Akira. *Japanese Big Businesses and the Modern Society: Stockholding, Management Systems, Deregulation and Economic Democracy* [J]. Tokyo: Chuo Keizaisha, 1995.

Hayashi, Naomichi (ed.). *Treatises on the Contemporary Capitalism* [J]. Tokyo: Aoki Shoten, 1994.

Hayashi, Naomichi. *The Contemporary Japanese Economy* [J]. Tokyo: Aoki Shoten, 1986.

Hazama Hiroshi, *The Japanese-Style Management: Pluses and Minuses of Groupism* [J]. Tokyo: Nikkei Shinsho, 1971.

Hazama, Hiroshi. *Japanese Employers Associations and Industrial Relations* [J]. Tokyo: Nihon Rodo Kyokai, 1981.

Hirata, Kiyoaki. *Civil Society and Socialism* [J]. Tokyo: Iwanami Shoten, 1969.

Hirata, Kiyoaki. *La Societe Civile et Regulation* [J]. Tokyo: Iwanami Shoten, 1993.

Hirata, Kiyoaki. *Classics and Contemporary Thoughts on Civil Society*. (His posthumous book ed. by Yagi Kiichiro and Ohmachi Mitsuhiro) [J]. Tokyo: Yuhikaku, 1996.

Hirata, Kiyoaki. Yamada Toshio, Kato Tetsuro, et al. *Modern Civil Society and the Corporate-Centered State* [J]. Tokyo: Ochanomizu Shobo, 1994.

Hirowatari, Seigo. "What is Today's Problem?" In: The Institute of Social Science, University of Tokyo (ed.). *Contemporary Japanese Society, Vol. 6* [J]. Tokyo: University of Tokyo Press, 1992.

Hirschmeier, Johannes and Yui, Tsunehiko. *The Development of Japanese Management.* Tokyo: Toyo Keizai Inc., 1977.

Honma, Masaaki and Atoda, Naosumi. What Makes the Employees Subordinate to Their Company [J]? In: *Weekly Economist*, March 17, 1992.

Horiuchi, Akiyoshi. *The Future of the Financial System: Bad Loan Problems and the Big Bang* [J]. Tokyo: Iwanami Shinsho, 1998.

Hosaka, Naomichi. *An Analysis on the Structure of the Bubble Economy* [J]. Tokyo: Nihon Hyoronsha, 1994.

Hoshino, Eiichi. *A Recommendation for Civil Law* [J]. Tokyo: Iwanami Shinsho, 1998.

Hyodo, Tsutomu. *A Postwar History of Labor in Japan* [J]. Tokyo: University of Tokyo Press, 1997.

Ifo Institute for Economic Research and Sakura Institute of Research. *A Comparative Analysis of Japanese and German Economic Success.* Tokyo: Springer Verlag Tokyo, 1997.

Iinuma, Kazumasa and Nagata, Akiya. Japan is Now a Technological Power [J]. In: *The Weekly Toyo Keizai*, April 13, 1991.

Ikeo, Kazuhito. *A Warning for the Financial Industry* [J]. Tokyo: Toyo Keizai Inc., 1995.

Ikuta, Tadahide. The True Grounds for the Policy Bankruptcy of the Banking Bureau of the MOF [J]. In: *Ushio*, special number, March, 1996.

Imai, Ken'ichi. *Competition Among Different Systems in Capitalism* [J]. Tokyo: Chikuma Shobo, 1992.

Imura, Kiyoko. *Contemporary Japanese Economy: From the Defeat and Through to a Super Economic Power* [J]. Tokyo: Yuhikaku, 1993.

Inagami, Takeshi (ed.). *Corporate Unions in the Matured Society* [J]. Tokyo: Nihon Rodo Kenkyu Kiko, 1995.

Ino, Kenji. The depths of financial circles and the dark people [J]. In: *Ushio*, March, 1996.

Ishihara, Shunji. *Civil Society and Worker Culture: Social Origin of the Swedish Welfare State* [J]. Tokyo: Bokutakusha, 1996.

Ishikawa, Tsuneo. *Income and Wealth* [J]. Tokyo: Iwanami Shoten, 1991.

Itagaki, Hiroshi. *The Japanese Management and Production System and the East Asia: The Hybrid Plants in Taiwan, Korea and China* [J]. Kyoto: Minerva Shobo, 1997.

Ito, Makoto. *Japanese Capitalism at a Crossroads* [J]. Tokyo: Aoki Shoten, 1995.

Ito, Masanao. "In the Strong Yen and Economic Friction." In: The Society for the Study of History (ed.). *Japan: Its Contemporary History*, Vol. 5 [J], Tokyo: Aoki Shoten, 1991.

Iwasaki, Hiromitsu. *Japan Controlled by Bureaucrats is in Crisis* [J]. Tokyo: Goma Shobo, 1994.

Iwata, Kikuo. *The Structure of Stock Economy* [J]. Tokyo: Iwanami Shoten, 1993.

Iwata, Ryushi. *Organizing Principles of the Japanese-Style Management* [J]. Tokyo: Bunshindo, 1977.

Iwata, Ryushi. *Controversy Over the "Japanese-Style Management": Results and Looking Forward* [J]. Tokyo: Nihon Keizai Shinbunsha, 1984.

Izu, Hiroshi. *The Japanese Real Estate Market: Theories and Perspectives* [J]. Tokyo: Toyo Keizai Inc., 1997.

Japan Economic Policy Association (ed.). *The Japanese Socio-Economic System* [J]. Tokyo: Yuhikaku, 1995.

Jessop, Bob. (tr. Shinoda Takeshi, Sakurai Junri and Takashima Masaharu) The Future of the National State: Limits to the De-Statization of Politics and to the Governmentalization of Civil Society. In: *RSSR*, Vol. 32, No. 4, March, 1997.

Jinno, Naohiko. *The Political Economy of System Reform* [J]. Tokyo: Iwanami Shoten, 1998.

Kanamori, Hisao and Japan Center for Economic Research (eds). *The Japanese Economy: At a Turning Point* [J]. Tokyo: Nihon Keizai Shinbunsha, 1984.

Kaneko, Masaru. "The Formation of Corporate Centricism and Japanese Society." In: The Institute of Social Science (ed.). *Contemporary Japanese Society*, Vol. 5 [J], Tokyo: University of Tokyo Press, 1991.

Kaneko, Masaru. *Anti-Economics: The Limits of Market-Oriented Liberalism* [J]. Tokyo: Shinshokan, 1999.

Kato, Masaru. Undiscussed Effects of the "Heterogeneous Japan" Theory [J]. In: *Chishiki*, August, 1990.

Kato, Shuichi. (tr. by Chibbett, David and Sanderson, Don.) *A History of Japanese Literature.* (3 Vols.) Tokyo/New York/London: Kodansha International, paperback edition, 1990.

Kato, Tetsuro and Steven, Rob (eds). *An International Debate: Is Japanese Management Post-Fordism?* Tokyo: Mado-sha, 1993.

Kato, Yuji. *Unstable Worker in Contemporary Japan*, (2 Vols.) [J], Tokyo: Ochanomizu Shobo, 1980.

Katz, Richard. (tr. Suzuki, Akihiko.) *Japan: The System that Soured: The Rise and Fall of the Japanese Economic Miracle* [J]. Tokyo: Toyo Keizai Inc., 1999.

Kawahito, Hiroshi. *Karoshi (Death from Overwork), Society and Japan* [J]. Tokyo: Kadensha, 1992.

Kida, Akio. The Concept of "Society" and Japanese Society [J]. In: *RSSR*, Vol. 32, No. 4, March, 1997.

Kikuchi, Hidehiro. The drastic reform is necessary for the banking business [J]. In: NM, December 18, 1995.

Kim, Yeong-Ho. A Proposal to the 21st Century [J]. In: *Asahi Newspaper* (international edition), December 1, 1996.

Kinugawa, Megumi. *The Financial Economy of Contemporary Japan: Around the Bubble Economy and the Heisei Depression* [J]. Tokyo: Chuo University Press, 1995.

Kocka, Jürgen. "The Difficult Rise of a Civil Society: Societal History of Modern Germany." In: Fulbrook, Mary (ed.). *German History Since 1800.* London/New York: Arnold, 1997.

Koda, Masanori. Six important points destroying land myth in Japan [J]. In: *Weekly Economist*, March 21, 1995.

Koga, Eizaburo. "Civil Society." In: *Encyclopedia Nipponica 2001* Vol. 11 [J]. Tokyo: Shogakukan, 1989.

Koike, Kazuo. *Labor Union and Participation in Workplaces: Japan–U.S. Comparison of Industrial Relations* [J]. Tokyo: Toyo Keizai Shinposha, 1977.

Koike, Kazuo. *Economics of Work* [J]. Tokyo: Toyo Keizai Inc., 1991.

Koike, Kazuo. *Japanese Employment System* [J]. Tokyo: Toyo Keizai Inc., 1994.

Komai, Hiroshi. The Rapid Change of the Employment of Foreigners by the New Immigration Law [J]. In: *Weekly Economist*, October 23, 1990.

Komai, Hiroshi. *Live Together with Immigrant Workers* [J]. Tokyo: Akashi Shoten, 1993.

Komai, Hiroshi. *Japan As a Multi-Ethnic Society* [J]. Tokyo: Kokusai Shoin, 1994.

Komiya, Ryutaro. *Contemporary Japanese Economy: Overview from the Macroeconomic Perspective and International Economic Relations* [J]. Tokyo: University of Tokyo Press, 1988.

Koo, Richard. *Good Strong Yen and Bad Strong Yen* [J]. Tokyo: Toyo Keizai Inc., 1994.

Koo, Richard. *A Blueprint for the Recovery of the Japanese Economy* [J]. Tokyo: PHP, 1999.

Koo, Richard and Shinya Nakamura. Adjustment Inflation Does us No Good and Much Harm [J]. In: *Weekly Toyo Keizai*, July 3, 1999.

Kosai, Yutaka. *Era of the Rapid Economic Growth: Notes on the Contemporary Economic History of Japan* [J]. Tokyo: Nihon Hyoronsha, 1981.

Kosai, Yutaka and Ogino, Yoshitaro. (tr. by Thompson, Ralph) *The Contemporary Japanese Economy*. London: Macmmilan Press, 1984.

Kosaka, Shuhei. *Civil Society and Dissolution of the Idea* [J]. Tokyo: Sairyusha, 1994.

Kumazawa, Makoto. *The Bright and Dark Sides of the Japanese-Style Management* [J]. Tokyo: Chikuma Shobo, 1989.

Kume, Ikuo. *Labor Politics in Japan* [J]. Tokyo: Yuhikaku, 1998.

Kurita, Ken. *The Japanese Labor Society* [J]. Tokyo: University of Tokyo Press, 1994.

Kyuno, Masao. Settlements of Accounts of the Major Seventeen Banks in March 1999 [J]. In: *Weekly Economist*, June 8, 1999.

McCormack, Gavan. *The Emptiness of Japanese Affluence*. New York/London: M.E. Sharpe. Inc., 1996.

Maruyama, Yoshinari. *The Japanese-Style Management: Structure and Behavior* [J]. Tokyo: Nihon Hyoronsha, 1989.

Masamura, Kimihiro. *Illustration of the History of Japanese Postwar Economy*, Vol. 7. [J]. Tokyo: Chikuma Shobo, 1988.

Masamura, Kimihiro. *Japanese Economy: Can We Avoid Decline*? [J]. Tokyo: Chikuma Shobo, 1997.

Matsuba, Masafumi. *An Essay on Contemporary Japanese Capitalism: A Survey Based on Statistics* [J]. Kyoto: Minerva Shobo, 1987.

Matsuba, Masafumi. Contemporary Japanese Economy (1): The Position of the Japanese Economy in the World. In: *RSSR* Vol. 28, No. 4, March, 1993.

Matsuba, Masafumi. Contemporary Japanese Economy (2): The Internal Structure of the Large Corporation System. In: *RSSR*, Vol. 29 No. 1, June, 1993.

Matsuba, Masafumi. Contemporary Japanese Economy (3): The Large Corporation System and the Life of the People. In: *RSSR*, Vol. 29, No. 2, September, 1993.

Matsuba, Masafumi. Supplements to My Treatise "Contemporary Japanese Economy". In: *RSSR*, Vol. 31, No. 1, June, 1995.

Matsuba, Masafumi. An Introduction to the Analysis of Contemporary Japanese Economy. The Development and Reorganization of the Large Corporation System. In: *Ritsumeikan Keieigaku* (Ritsumeikan Business Review), Vol. 34, No. 5, Kyoto, January, 1996.

Matsuba, Masafumi. Supplements (No. 2) to my Treatise "Contemporary Japanese Economy". In: *RSSR*, Vol. 33, No. 2, September, 1997.

Matsuba, Masafumi. The Problems in the Dissolution Process of the Private Housing Finance Companies (the *Jusen*). From December 1995 to April 1996. In: *RSSR*, Vol. 33, No. 3, December, 1997.

Matsushita, Keiichi. Civil Society, in: *Lexicon of Economics*, 3rd edn [J]. Tokyo: Iwanami Shoten, 1992.
Minami, Ryoshin. *Economic Developments of Japan* [J]. Tokyo: Toyo Keizai Inc., 1981.
Mitsuhashi, Tadahiro and Uchida, Shigeo. *The Economic History of the Showa Era*, (2 Vols.) [J]. Tokyo: Nikkei Bunko, 1994.
Miyajima, Hiroshi. *Socio-Economics of the "Elderly Dominant Era." Family, Enterprise and Government* [J]. Tokyo: Iwanami Shoten, 1992.
Miyamoto, Ken'ichi. *Environmental Economics* [J]. Tokyo: Iwanami Shoten, 1989.
Miyamoto, Ken'ichi. *The History of the Showa Era 10: Japan as An Economic Power* [J]. Tokyo: Shougakkan Library, 1994.
Miyawaki, Atsushi and Tadayasu Miyashita. *Reform of the Financial System* [J]. Tokyo: Nihon Keizai Shinbunsha, 1995.
Miyawaki, Raisuke. Politician, police and media must fight against gang [J]. In: *Weekly Economist*, January 30, 1996.
Miyazaki, Isamu. *The Japanese Economy: What Makes It Tick*. Tokyo: Simul Press, 1990.
Miyazaki, Yoshikazu. *The Structure and Behavior of Japanese Economy: Track of the Postwar 40 Years*, (2 Vols.) [J]. Tokyo: Chikuma Shobo, 1985.
Miyazaki, Yoshikazu. *Combined Recession: For a Prescription of the Post-Bubble Economy* [J]. Tokyo: Chuko Shinsho, 1992.
Moriguchi, Shinji. *Japanese Economy* [J]. Tokyo: Sobunsha, 1988.
Morioka, Koji. Japanese Corporate Centricism and the Polarization of Working Hour Structure [J]. In: *Keizai*, March, 1992.
Murakami, Jun'ichi. "Civil Society." In: *An Encyclopedia of Philosophy and Thought* [J]. Tokyo: Iwanami Shoten, 1998.
Murakami, Yasusuke, Kumon, Shunpei and Sato, Seizaburo. *The "Ie" Society as a Civilization* [J]. Tokyo: Chuou Koronsha, 1979.
Murakami, Yasusuke. *Era of the New Middle Masses* [J]. Tokyo: Chuko Bunko, 1987.
Murphy, R. Taggart. (tr. Hatamizu, Toshiyuki.) *The Weight of the Yen*. Tokyo: Mainichi Shinbunsha, 1996.
Nagashima, Osamu. *A Handbook of the Contemporary Japanese Economy* [J]. Kyoto: Horitsu Bunkasha, 1993.
Nakakita, Toru. Financial Institutions After the Injection of Public Funds [J]. In: *Weekly Toyo Keizai*, March 6, 1999.
Nakamura, Hideichiro. *A New Theory of Mid-Sized Firms* [J]. Tokyo: Toyo Keizai Inc., 1990.
Nakamura, Keisuke. *Japan's Production System and the Organization of Work* [J]. Tokyo: University of Tokyo Press, 1996.
Nakamura, Takafusa. (tr. Kaminski, Jacqueline) *The Postwar Japanese Economy: Its Development and Structure*. Tokyo: University of Tokyo Press, 1981.
Nakamura, Takafusa. *The Contemporary Economic History* [J]. Tokyo: Iwanami Seminar Books 53, 1995.
Nakamura, Takatosi. *Huge Corporations in Japan* [J]. Tokyo: Iwanami Shoten, 1983.
Nakamura, Tatsuya. Rich Country But Poor Japanese [J]. In: *Weekly Economist*, January 7, 1992.
Nakatani, Iwao. *Japanese Enterprise: Its Conditions for Rebirth* [J]. Tokyo: Toyo Keizai Inc., 1993.

Nihon Keizai Shinbun Inc. (ed.). *My Capitalism Theory* [J]. Tokyo: Nihon Keizai Shinbunsha, 1993.

Nishimura, Kiyohiko and Miwa, Toshiro. *Stock and Land Prices in Japan: The Mechanism for Price Formation* [J]. Tokyo: University of Tokyo Press, 1990.

Nishitani, Satoshi. *Conditions for the "Yutori" Society* [J]. Tokyo: Rodo Junposha, 1992.

Noguchi, Yukio. *An Essay on Stock Economy* [J]. Tokyo: Chuko Shinsyo, 1991.

Noguchi, Yukio. *Japanese Economy: A Reform Plan* [J]. Tokyo: Toyo Keizai Inc., 1993.

Noguchi, Yukio. *The 1940 Regime: Good-Bye, the "Wartime Economy"* [J]. Tokyo: Toyo Keizai Inc., 1995.

Noguchi, Yukio. The fall of land prices is a source for the normalization of Japanese economy [J]. In: *NM*, July 21, 1995.

Nomura, Masami. *Toyotism: Maturity and Transformation of the Japanese-Style Production System* [J]. Kyoto: Minerva Shobo, 1993.

Odaka, Kunio. *Japanese Management: A Forward-Looking Analysis* [J]. Tokyo: Chuko Shinsho, 1984.

Ohara, Yukiko. Semi-nationalize All Major Banks with Fifty Trillion Yen in Public Funds [J]. In: *Weekly Economist*, September 15, 1998.

Ohara, Yukiko. Disappointing Public Rescue: Settlement of Bad Loans Carried over to Fiscal 1999 [J]. In: *Weekly Economist*, March 2, 1999.

Ohashi, Shoichi, Okuda, Kosuke and Okubayashi, Koji. *Ideas of Labor Participation* [J]. Tokyo: Yuhikaku, 1979.

Ohashi, Shoichi, Akira, Oda and Schanz, Günther (eds). *Japanese-Style Management and German-Style Management* [J]. Tokyo: Chikura Shobo, 1995.

Ohishi, Kaichirou. "The Historical Position of the Postwar Japanese Capitalism and the Postwar Reforms" [J]. In: *Contemporary Japanese Capitalism*, Vol. 2. Tokyo: Ohtsuki Shoten, 1981.

Ohtaki, Masayuki. *The Theory of Business Cycle: The Structure of Contemporary Japanese Economy* [J]. Tokyo: University of Tokyo Press, 1994.

Okazaki, Tetsuji. *Japanese Industrialization and the Steel Industry* [J]. Tokyo: University of Tokyo Press, 1993.

Okazaki, Tetsuji and Okuno, Masahiro (eds). *The Origin of the Modern Japanese Economic System* [J]. Tokyo: Nihon Keizai Shinbunsha, 1993.

Okumura, Hirohiko. *Contemporary Japanese Economy: the Appearance and Collapse of the Bubble Economy* [J]. Tokyo: Toyo Keizai Inc., 1999.

Okumura, Hiroshi. *Corporate Capitalism: A System for Company* [J]. Tokyo: Asahi Bunko, 1991 (1st edn 1984).

Okumura, Hiroshi. *The Structure of Corporate Capitalism* (New Edition) [J]. Tokyo: Shakai Shisosha, 1991 (1st edn 1975).

Okumura, Shigetsugu, Yanagida Tadashi, Shimizu Sadatoshi and Morita Kiriro (eds). *Data World Economy* [J]. Tokyo: University of Tokyo Press, 1990.

Ono, Akira. *Japanese Employment Customs and Labor Market* [J]. Tokyo: Toyo Keizai Inc., 1989.

Ono, Kiyomi. "Peukert and the Modern Era." In: Peukert, Detlev. *The Weimar Republic: Crisis of the Classic Modernity* [J]. Nagoya: University of Nagoya Press, 1993.

Onodera, Yoshiyuki. Agricultural Cooperative at the Turning Point [J]. In: *Economic Review*, Tokyo: Nihon Hyoronsha, August, 1982.
Ryu, Shokichi. *The Treasury Investment and Loan of the Modern Japan* [J]. Tokyo: Toyo Keizai Inc., 1988.
Ryu, Shokichi. *A Research on Contemporary Japanese Economy* [J]. Tokyo: Gakubunsha, 1994.
Sakakibara, Eisuke. *Japanese-Type Capitalism as a Civilization* [J]. Tokyo: Toyo Keizai Inc., 1993.
Sakakibara, Eisuke (ed.). *Economic and Social Systems in Japan, Europe and the United States* [J]. Tokyo: Toyo Keizai Inc., 1995.
Sasabe, Yukitaka. "Modern as a Destiny." In: Peukert, Detlev. *Weber: Diagnosis for the Modern Era* [J]. Nagoya: University of Nagoya Press, 1994.
Sasaki, Ken. *Contemporary European Capitalism: Its Structure Centered Around the Economic Integration Policy* [J]. Tokyo: Yuhikaku, 1975.
Sasaki, Ken. *Japanese Type Multinational Corporations: From Trade Friction to Investment Friction* [J]. Tokyo: Yuhikaku, 1986.
Sato, Akira. *Documentary: Financial Collapse* [J]. Tokyo: Iwanami Shoten, 1998.
Sato, Tomoyasu. *Keibatsu (Alliances Centered Around Relatives): New Establishments in Japan* [J]. Tokyo: Rippu Shobo, 1981.
Sato, Toshiki. *Modernity, Organization and Capitalism: Horizon of Modernity in Japan and the West* [J]. Kyoto: Minerva Shobo, 1993.
Sato, Yoshikazu. The Phenomena of the "I": A development of the Problem of "Society and Individual" [J]. In: *RSSR*, Vol. 35, No. 4, March, 2000.
Sawa, Takamitsu. *The Rapid Economic Growth: Contemporary History of the "Ideology" and Policies* [J]. Tokyo: NHK Books, 1984.
Sawa, Takamitsu. *The Political Economy of the Heisei Depression: Conditions for a Matured Society* [J]. Tokyo: Chuko Shinsho, 1994.
Sekiguchi, Sueo, Tanaka, Hiroshi et al. *Foreign Direct Investment and the Japanese Economy*. Tokyo: Toyo Keizai Inc., 1996.
Shibagaki, Kazuo. The Sublation of Commoditized Labor-Power. Welfare State, Japanese Management and Socialism [J]. In: *The Journal of Social Science* (Institute of Social Science, University of Tokyo), Vol. 43, No. 1, August, 1991.
Shimada, Haruo. *Japanese Economy: Its Contradiction and Regeneration* [J]. Tokyo: Chikuma Shobo, 1991.
Shimizu, Shinzo (ed.). *Postwar History of the Labor Movements* [J]. Tokyo: Nihon Hyoronsha, 1982.
Shimono, Keiko. *An Economic Analysis of Wealth Inequality* [J]. Nagoya: Nagoya University Press, 1991.
Shinoda, Takeshi. The Crisis of the Japanese Style of After-Fordism and Neoliberalism [J]. In: *RSSR*, Vol. 32, No. 4, March, 1997.
Shinoda, Toru. The Restoration of Solidarity. Asked Social Function of "Federation of Japan Labor Unions" [J]. In: *Sekai* (World), March, 1990.
Shinozuka, Eiko. *Employment Adjustment in Japan: Labor Market After the Oil Shock* [J]. Tokyo: Toyo Keizai Inc., 1989.
Shinozuka, Eiko. The Necessity of Long Term Vision for Foreign Worker Problem [J]. In: *Weekly Economist*, April 7, 1992.
Shinpo, Seiji. Deindustrialization Arises From the Stagnation of Investment [J]. In: *NM*, August 22, 1994.

Society for the Study of Economic Policy (ed.). *The Social and Economic System of Japan* [J]. Tokyo: Yuhikaku, 1995.

Suzuki, Takashi. *Analysis on Japanese Economy: From the Rapid Economic Growth Period to the 1990s* [J]. Tokyo: Toyo Keizai Inc., 1990.

Suzuki, Yoshio. *Future Image of Japanese Economy* [J]. Tokyo: Toyo Keizai Inc., 1994.

Tachi, Ryuichiro. (tr. Walker, Richard) *The Contemporary Japanese Economy: An Overview*. Tokyo: University of Tokyo Press, 1993.

Tachibanaki, Toshiaki. The Myth of the Equal Income Distribution Has Collapsed [J]. In: *Sekai*, March, 1994.

Tachibanaki, Toshiaki. *Economic Differentials Within Japan: Income and Asset Gaps* [J]. Tokyo: Iwanami Shinsho, 1998.

Tadokoro, Masayuki. "Something is Wrong" in the Japanese Employment System [J]. In: *Weekly Economist*, October 2, 1990.

Takada, Ryoji. *An Analysis on the Structure of Medium and Small-Sized Businesses: Changes in Employment and the New Dual Structure* [J]. Tokyo: Shin Hyoron, 1989.

Takahashi, Makoto. *The Problem of Land and Housing and Fiscal Policy* [J]. Tokyo: Nihon Hyoronsha, 1990.

Takao, Yoshikazu. *The Heisei Financial Depression: An Interim Report of the International Economic Crisis* [J]. Tokyo: Chuko Shinsho, 1994.

Takarabe, Seiichi. Jusen: Its Birth, Bankruptcy and Disposal [J]. In: *Ushio*, special number, March, 1996.

Takashima, Zenya. *Visions of Civil Society* [J]. (His collected treatises ed. by Yamada Hideo) Tokyo: Shinhyoronsha, 1991.

Takayama, Noriyuki. Emerging from the Uniform Image of the Aged [J]. In: *NM*, June 20, 1992.

Takayama, Noriyuki (ed.). *Stock Economy: An Economic Analysis of Assets Formation and Savings/Pensions* [J]. Tokyo: Toyo Keizai Inc., 1992.

Takenaka, Heizou. Reasonable Ground Is Necessary for the Introduction of Official Funds [J], in: NM, December 10, 1995.

Tamura, Keiji. Why was the Nagoya branch manager of Sumitomo Bank shot to kill [J]. In: *Ushio*, March, 1996.

Tanaka, Hiroshi. Overseas Transfer and Deindustrialization Are Not Directly Connected [J]. In: NM, August 9, 1994.

Tanaka, Shoji. *Theories on Civil Society and Today: Issues of the Day and Reconsideration of the Modern Thought* [J]. Tokyo: Ochanomizu Shobo, 1994.

Tateishi, Toru. Nonbanks Have Begun a March to the Death [J]. In: *Weekly Economist*, February 27, 1996.

Teruoka, Shuzo and Seiyama, Takuro (eds). *The Structure of Contemporary Japanese Economy and Policies* [J]. Kyoto: Minerva Shobo, 1989.

The Economic Planning Agency (ed.). *Track of the Postwar Japanese Economy: 50-Year History of the Economic Planning Agency* [J]. Tokyo: Printing Bureau, Ministry of Finance, 1997.

The Society for the Study of Social Policy (ed.). *Annals of the Society for the Study of Social Policy. No. 34. Japanese Enterprises and Foreign Workers* [J]. Tokyo: Ochanomizu Shobo, 1990.

Tominaga, Ken'ichi. *Modernization of Japan and Social Changes* [J]. Tokyo: Kodansha Gakujutsu Bunko, 1990.

Tona, Naoki. *The Structure of the Japanese-Type Flexibility* [J]. Kyoto: Horitsu Bunkasha, 1993.

Tsuda, Masumi. *The Japanese-Style Management* [J]. Tokyo: Toyo Keizai Inc., 1980.

Tsuru, Shigeto. *Japan's Capitalism: Creative Defeat and Beyond*. Cambridge: Cambridge University Press, 1993.

Uchihashi, Katsuto, Okumura, Hiroshi and Sataka, Makoto (eds). *Principles of Japanese Company, Vol. 2: Japanese-Style Management and the International Society* [J]. Tokyo: Iwanami Shoten, 1994.

Uekusa, Kazuhide. *Final Accounts of Japan* [J]. Tokyo: Kodansha, 1999.

Urabe, Kuniyoshi. *The Japanese-Style Management Evolves* [J]. Tokyo: Chuo Keizaisha, 1984.

Urry, John. (tr, Seino, Masayoshi.) *The Anatomy of Capitalist Societies*. Kyoto: Horitsu Bunkasha, 1986.

Uzawa, Hirobumi. *A Criticism on the Contemporary Japanese Economy* [J]. Tokyo: Iwanami Shoten, 1987.

Waltzer, Michael. (tr. Takahashi, Yasuhiro.) The Civil Society Argument. In: *Shisou*. Tokyo: Iwanami Shoten, 1996.

Watanabe, Hisashi, Tezuka Kazuaki, Nakao Hiroshi and Ronald Ruprecht (eds). *Symposium: Auslandische Arbeitnehmer in Japan und Deutschland* [J]. Tokyo: Akashi Shoten, 1991.

Watanabe, Hisashi and Klenner, Wolfgang (eds). *Trial of the Types: Structural Changes and Economies of Japan and Germany* [J]. Tokyo: Shinzansha, 1998.

Watanabe, Osamu. *An Analysis on the Ruling Structure in Contemporary Japan: Center and Periphery* [J]. Tokyo: Kadensha, 1988.

Watanabe, Osamu. *The Structure of an "Affluent Society" Japan* [J]. Tokyo: Rodo Junposha, 1990.

Wolferen, Karel van. *The Enigma of Japanese Power: People and Politics in a Stateless Nation*. New York: Vintage Books, 1990.

Wolferen, Karel van. *The False Realities of a Politicized Society* [J]. Tokyo: Mainichi Shinbunsha, 1994.

Wolferen, Karel van. *Why Can't the Japanese Love Japan*? [J]. Tokyo: Mainichi Shinbunsha, 1998.

Yamada, Toshio and Boyer, Robert (eds). *Postwar Japanese Capitalism: An Analysis of Regulation and Crisis* [J]. Tokyo: Fujiwara Shoten, 1999.

Yamashita, Takayuki. *The Development of the "Japanese-Style Management"* [J]. Kyoto: Horitsu Bunkasha, 1991.

Yamazaki, Hiroaki and Kikkawa, Takeo (eds). *Japanese Business History, Vol. 4: Continuity and Discontinuity of the "Japanese-Style" Management* [J]. Tokyo: Iwanami Shoten, 1995.

Yamazaki, Ryuzo (ed.). *The Modern Economic History of Japan* [J]. Tokyo: Yuhikaku Books, 1985.

Yanbe, Yukio. *False Crisis and Real Crisis* [J]. Tokyo: Toyo Keizai Inc., 1997.

Yoshida, Kazuo. *Strengths and Weaknesses of the Japanese-Style Management System* [J]. Tokyo: Toyo Keizai Inc., 1993.

Yoshida, Kazuo. *The Decade of the Heisei Depression* [J]. Tokyo: PHP Shinsho, 1998.

Yoshii, Atsuko. *Legislation Responsible for the Collapse of Financial Institutions* [J]. Tokyo: Taga Shuppan, 1999.

Yoshikawa, Hiroshi. *The Japanese Economy at a Turning Point* [J]. Tokyo: Iwanami Shoten, 1999.
Yoshino, Yotaro. (tr, Uchida, Yukio.) *Japan's Managerial System: Tradition and Innovation*. Cambridge, MA: MIT Press, 1968.
Yoshitomi, Masaru. *The Contemporary Japanese Economy: Transformation of the World Economy and Japan* [J]. Tokyo: Toyo Keizai Inc., 1977.
Yoshitomi, Masaru. *The Truth about the Japanese Economy* [J]. Tokyo: Toyo Keizai Inc., 1998.

3. Selected Internet Homepages

3.1 Government Agencies

Prime Minister's Official Residence	http://www.kantei.go.jp/
Statistics Bureau and Statistics Center	http://www.stat.go.jp/
Economic Planning Agency	http://www.epa.go.jp/
Ministry of Foreign Affairs	http://www.mofa.go.jp/
Ministry of Finance	http://www.mof.go.jp/
Financial Services Agency	http://www.fsa.go.jp/
Ministry of International Trade and Industry	http://www.miti.go.jp/

The reorganization of Japanese ministries and agencies in January 2001 has meant changes to web-site addresses. The listings shown here were correct, however, as of, November 2000.

Cabinet Office	http://www.cao.go.jp/
Ministry of Public Management, Home Affairs, Post and Telecommunications	http://www.soumu.go.jp/
Ministry of Education, Culture, Sports, Science and Technology	http://www.mext.go.jp/
Ministry of Health, Labour and Welfare	http://www.mhlw.go.jp/
Ministry of Agriculture, Forestry and Fisheries	http://www.maff.go.jp/
Ministry of Economy, Trade and Industry	http://www.meti.go.jp/
Ministry of Land, Infrastructure and Transport	http://www.mlit.go.jp/
Ministry of Environment	http://www.env.go.jp/
Japanese Patent Office	http://www.jpo.go.jp/

3.2 Government-Related Institutions

Asian Development Bank	http://www.asiandevbank.org/
The Overseas Economic Corporation Fund, Japan	http://www.oecf.go.jp/
Japan External Trade Organization	http://www.jetro.go.jp/
Institute of Developing Economies–JETRO	http://www.ide.go.jp/

National Diet Library	http://www.ndl.go.jp/
National Institute of Population and Social Security Research	http://www.ipss.go.jp/
Bank of Japan	http://www.boj.or.jp/
Development Bank of Japan	http://www.jdb.go.jp/
Japan Bank for International Cooperation	http://www.jbic.go.jp/
National Life Finance Corporation	http://www.kokukin.go.jp/
The Japan Institute of Labour	http://db.jil.go.jp/
The Government Housing Loan Corporation	http://www.jyukou.go.jp/
Japan Finance Corporation for Small Business	http://www.jfs.go.jp/
National Center for Science Information Systems	http://www.nacsis.ac.jp/

3.3 *Private Research Institutions*

Japan Center for Economic Research	http://www.jcer.or.jp/
Research Institute on the National Economy	http://www.kkri.org/
The Japan Research Institute	http://www.jri.co.jp/
Nomura Research Institute	http://www.nri.co.jp/
Mitsubishi Research Institute	http://www.mri.co.jp/
Daiwa Institute of Research	http://www.dir.co.jp/
Nikko Research Center	http://www.nikko.co.jp/NRC/index.jp.html
Asahi Bank Research Institute	http://www.asahibank-soken.co.jp/
Sakura Institute of Research	http://www.sakura.co.jp/sir/
The Sanwa Research Institute and Consulting	http://www.sric.co.jp/
Daiichi Kangyo Bank	http://www.dkb.co.jp/
Daiwa Bank	http://www.daiwabank.co.jp/
Fuji Research Institute	http://www.fuji-ric.co.jp/
Bank of Tokyo–Mitsubishi	http://www.btm.co.jp/
NLI Research Institute	http://www.nli-research.co.jp/
Mitsui Marine and Fire Insurance	http://www.mituimarine.co.jp/
Yasuda Research Institute	http://www.yasuda-ri.co.jp/
Meiji Life Insurance	http://www.meiji-life.co.jp/
Mitsui Knowledge Industry	http://research.mki.co.jp/
Japan Real Estate Institute	http://www.reinet.or.jp/
Marketing Intelligence	http://www.mictokyo.co.jp/mic/
Dentsu Institute for Human Studies	http://www.dihs.co.jp/
Hakuhodo Institute of Life and Living	http://www.hakuhodo.co.jp/
Tokyo Shoko Research	http://www.tsr-net.co.jp/
Teikoku Data Bank	http://www.tdb.co.jp/

3.4 Others

Nihon Keizai Shinbunsha	http://www.nikkei.co.jp/
Asahi Shinbunsha	http://www.asahi.com/
Yomiuri Shinbunsha	http://www.yomiuri.co.jp/
Mainichi Shinbunsha	http://www.mainichi.co.jp/
Toyo Keizai Inc.	http://www.toyokeizai.co.jp/
Japan Times	http://www.japantimes.co.jp/
Kyodo News	http://www.kyodo.co.jp/
The Japan Chamber of Commerce and Industry	http://www.jcci.or.jp/
Tokyo Chamber of Commerce and Industry	http://www.tokyo-cci.or.jp/
Japan Federation of Economic Organizations	http://www.keidanren.or.jp/
The Japanese Trade Union Confederation	http://www.jtuc-rengo.or.jp/
Tokyo Stock Exchange	http://www.tse.or.jp/
Japan Agricultural Cooperatives	http://www.rim.or.jp/ci/ja/
Japan Securities Dealers Association	http://www.jsda.or.jp/
Japan Consumer Information Center	http://www.kokusen.go.jp/
Japan Department Stores Association	http://www.depart.or.jp/
Japan Automobile Dealers Association	http://www.jada.or.jp/
Accounting Data on Companies in Japan	http://port.nikkei.co.jp/
Government Books	http://www.gov-book.or.jp/

Matsuba Masafumi

1948	Born in Osaka
1972	Bachelor of Arts degree, Osaka University of Foreign Studies
1975	Master of Business Administration degree, Osaka City University
1980	Associate Professor (Modern Economics), Faculty of Social Sciences, Ritsumeikan University, Kyoto
1989	Doctor of Economics degree, Kyoto University
1991	Professor, Ritsumeikan University